Toxic Terror

RENEWALS 458-4574.

DATE DUE

GAYLORD			PRINTED IN U.S.A.

BCSIA Studies in International Security
Published by The MIT Press

Sean M. Lynn-Jones and Steven E. Miller, series editors
Karen Motley, executive editor
Belfer Center for Science and International Affairs (BCSIA)
John F. Kennedy School of Government, Harvard University

Allison, Graham T., Owen R. Coté, Jr., Richard A. Falkenrath, and Steven E. Miller, *Avoiding Nuclear Anarchy: Containing the Threat of Loose Russian Nuclear Weapons and Fissile Material* (1996)

Allison, Graham T., and Kalypso Nicolaïdis, eds., *The Greek Paradox: Promise vs. Performance* (1996)

Arbatov, Alexei, Abram Chayes, Antonia Handler Chayes, and Lara Olson, eds., *Managing Conflict in the Former Soviet Union: Russian and American Perspectives* (1997)

Bennett, Andrew, *Condemned to Repetition? The Rise, Fall, and Reprise of Soviet-Russian Military Interventionism, 1973–1996* (1999)

Blackwill, Robert D., and Michael Stürmer, eds., *Allies Divided: Transatlantic Policies for the Greater Middle East* (1997)

Brom, Shlomo, and Yiftah Shapir, eds., *The Middle East Military Balance 1999–2000* (1999)

Brown, Michael E., ed., *The International Dimensions of Internal Conflict* (1996)

Brown, Michael E., and Šumit Ganguly, eds., *Government Policies and Ethnic Relations in Asia and the Pacific* (1997)

Elman, Miriam Fendius, ed., *Paths to Peace: Is Democracy the Answer?* (1997)

Falkenrath, Richard A., *Shaping Europe's Military Order: The Origins and Consequences of the CFE Treaty* (1994)

Falkenrath, Richard A., Robert D. Newman, and Bradley A. Thayer, *America's Achilles' Heel: Nuclear, Biological, and Chemical Terrorism and Covert Attack* (1998)

Feldman, Shai, *Nuclear Weapons and Arms Control in the Middle East* (1996)

Forsberg, Randall, ed., *The Arms Production Dilemma: Contraction and Restraint in the World Combat Aircraft Industry* (1994)

Hagerty, Devin T., *The Consequences of Nuclear Proliferation: Lessons from South Asia* (1998)

Heymann, Philip B., *Terrorism and America: A Commonsense Strategy for a Democratic Society* (1998)

Kokoshin, Andrei A., *Soviet Strategic Thought, 1917–91* (1998)

Lederberg, Joshua, *Biological Weapons: Limiting the Threat* (1999)

Shields, John M., and William C. Potter, eds., *Dismantling the Cold War: U.S. and NIS Perspectives on the Nunn-Lugar Cooperative Threat Reduction Program* (1997)

Tucker, Jonathan B., ed., *Toxic Terror: Assessing Terrorist Use of Chemical and Biological Weapons* (2000)

Utgoff, Victor A., ed., *The Coming Crisis: Nuclear Proliferation, U.S. Interests, and World Order* (2000)

Toxic Terror

Assessing Terrorist Use of Chemical and Biological Weapons

Editor
Jonathan B. Tucker

BCSIA Studies in International Security

MIT Press
Cambridge, Massachusetts
London, England

Fourth printing, 2001

© 2000 by the Belfer Center for Science and International Affairs
John F. Kennedy School of Government, Harvard University
Cambridge, Massachusetts 02138
(617) 495-1400

Library of Congress Cataloging-in-Publication Data

Toxic terror : assessing the terrorist use of chemical and biological weapons /
[edited by] Jonathan B. Tucker.
p. cm.—(BCSIA studies in international security)
Includes bibliographical references and index.
ISBN 0-262-20128-3 (hc. : alk. paper)—ISBN 0-262-70071-9 (pbk. : alk. paper)
1. Terrorism—Case studies. 2. Terrorists—Case studies. 3. Chemical warfare—
Case studies. 4. Biological warfare—Case studies.
I. Tucker, Jonathan B. II. Series.
HV6431 .T68   2000
363.3'2'0973—dc21   99-048256
                                                                CIP

Cover photo: A Japanese policeman in a protective suit uses a caged canary as a
primitive nerve-gas detector during a search of Aum Shinrikyo headquarters in the
Mt. Fuji foothills in late March 1995. © Asahi Shimbun Photo-Service

Contents

Acknowledgments

The editor is grateful to the following outside analysts who provided valuable comments on the case studies: Javed Ali, Research Planning, Inc.; Cornelius G. McWright, The George Washington University; Roger Medd, Science Applications International Corporation; Michael Moodie, Chemical and Biological Arms Control Institute; Joseph Pilat, Los Alamos National Laboratory; and Brad Roberts, Institute for Defense Analyses.

Professor William Potter, director of the Center for Nonproliferation Studies (CNS) at the Monterey Institute of International Studies, deserves credit for his strong and consistent support of the project. John Parachini and Melinda Lamont-Havers ably organized the authors' conference held at the Monterey Institute office in Washington, D.C., on June 22–23, 1998. Special thanks are also due to Jason Pate of CNS for superb editorial assistance, to Sean Lynn-Jones and Karen Motley at the Belfer Center for Science and International Affairs at the John F. Kennedy School of Government for overseeing the editing and publication process, and to Hope Steele for her meticulous copyediting.

—Jonathan B. Tucker
  Monterey, California
  April 1999

Toxic Terror

Chapter 1

Introduction

Jonathan B. Tucker

On March 20, 1995, the Japanese Aum Shinrikyo doomsday cult carried out a terrorist attack in the Tokyo subway system with the chemical nerve agent sarin, killing a dozen people, injuring more than a thousand, and frightening millions. This incident demonstrated that chemical and biological weapons (CBW) are within the technical reach of sophisticated terrorist organizations. Although the Tokyo subway attack probably inflicted fewer fatalities than a conventional bombing would have, the use of an invisible, lethal poison created a pervasive sense of fear and insecurity.

Since then, senior federal government officials and the news media have expressed alarm about the emerging threat of CBW terrorism, and the U.S. Congress has responded by appropriating billions of dollars for counterterrorism programs. Yet much of the discussion to date has focused on the *vulnerability* of large cities to terrorist attacks, while neglecting a careful assessment of the *threat*. Since the vulnerability of modern urban society to CBW attacks is potentially unlimited, such assessments do not provide a sound basis for policy decisions about the level and type of investment warranted to meet the emerging terrorist challenge.

In order to understand the actual nature of CBW use by non-state actors, it is essential to look at the historical record, which is more extensive than is generally believed. A 1994 study that defined terrorism broadly to include the deliberate contamination of food, water, and drugs identified more than 244 incidents of CBW terrorism in twenty-six countries since World War I. Of these episodes, 60 percent involved the actual use of chemical or biological agents, 30 percent involved threatened use, and 10 percent acquisition only. Only 25 percent of the surveyed incidents were linked to political motives; the rest were perpetrated by criminals, psychotics, disgruntled employees, and others.[1] A more recent survey focusing on "bioterrorism and biocrimes" identified more than 110 alleged cases in which terrorists, criminals, or covert state operators employed, acquired, threatened to use, or took an interest in biological warfare (BW) agents.[2]

Ever since the Tokyo subway attack, incidents involving CBW have been on the rise. Before the late 1990s, the Federal Bureau of Investigation (FBI) typically encountered about a dozen cases a year involving threats or actual attempts to acquire or use chemical, biological, radiological, or nuclear materials. In 1997, however, the FBI opened 71 investigations of this type, and in 1998, it launched 146.[3] Although about 80 percent of cases of alleged CBW terrorism have been hoaxes, some incidents have involved unsuccessful attempts to disperse toxic or infectious agents.[4]

Robert Blitzer, formerly the FBI's chief of domestic terrorism and counterterrorism planning, testified at a congressional hearing in 1998 that the perpetrators of domestic CBW incidents generally fall into two categories: "lone offenders" who are mentally unstable, seeking revenge for personal grievances, or pursuing vendettas against other citizens; and "extremist elements of right-wing groups" who believe in the violent overthrow of the federal government. Blitzer divided the major threats from foreign sources into three groups: state-sponsored terrorists, terrorist organizations, and loosely affiliated extremists, who pose the most urgent threat.[5]

The number of hoaxes involving chemical or biological agents also has risen sharply in recent years. The FBI recorded more than 150 hoaxes involving anthrax in 1998, compared to a single one in 1997.[6] Responding

---

1. Harvey J. McGeorge, "Chemical and Biological Terrorism: Analyzing the Problem," in *The ASA [Applied Science and Analysis] Newsletter*, No. 42 (June 16, 1994), pp. 1, 12–13.

2. W. Seth Carus, *Bioterrorism and Biocrimes: The Illicit Use of Biological Agents in the 20th Century* (Washington, D.C.: Center for Counterproliferation Research, National Defense University, August 1998).

3. Gretchen Schuldt, "Area Law Enforcement Moves to Head Off Terrorism Threat," *Milwaukee Journal Sentinel*, January 25, 1999, p. 1.

4. Tim Weiner, "Reno Says U.S. May Stockpile Medicine for Terrorist Attacks," *New York Times*, April 23, 1998, p. A12.

5. Donna Abu-Nasr, "FBI: Domestic Terror Threats Grow," Associated Press, October 2, 1998.

6. Associated Press, "Anthrax Hoaxes Are On the Rise: Law Enforcement Officials Say Threats Are Difficult to Combat," *Boston Globe*, January 2, 1999, p. A4; Maria Elena

to such incidents can be disruptive and costly.[7] One possible cause of this phenomenon may be the intense attention focused on the threat of CBW terrorism in the U.S. news media and in Hollywood movies, bestselling novels, and other mainstays of popular culture. This sensational and at times hysterical coverage may have had the unintended effect of popularizing and even glamorizing these weapons in the minds of potential perpetrators.

Characteristics and History of CBW

Many people tend to confuse chemical and biological weapons, which in fact have quite different characteristics. Chemical warfare (CW) agents are man-made, supertoxic chemicals that can be dispersed as a gas, vapor, liquid, aerosol (a suspension of microscopic droplets), or adsorbed onto a fine talcum-like powder to create "dusty" agents. Basic classes of chemical agents include choking agents that damage lung tissue (e.g., chlorine, phosgene), blood agents that interfere with cellular respiration (e.g., hydrogen cyanide), blister agents that cause severe chemical burns to the skin and lungs (e.g., mustard gas, lewisite), and nerve agents that disrupt nerve-impulse transmission in the central and peripheral nervous systems, causing convulsions and death by respiratory paralysis (e.g., sarin, VX). Chemical agents vary greatly in toxicity and persistence. Volatile agents such as sarin disperse rapidly, whereas persistent agents such as VX nerve agent or sulfur mustard remain toxic for days or weeks and require costly decontamination and clean-up.

Chemical weapons were first employed on a massive scale on the battlefields of Europe during World War I. Although all of the major combatants in World War II produced large chemical stockpiles, mutual restraint prevailed in the European theater, and chemical arms were used in significant amounts only by Japan against China. The chemical arms race continued throughout the Cold War, however, with both the United States and the Soviet Union accumulating tens of thousands of tons of blister and nerve agents. Although war between the superpowers fortunately never materialized, chemical weapons were employed in several

---

Fernandez, "Anthrax Hoaxes Are Sent in Mail," *Washington Post*, February 5, 1999, p. B8; Presentation by Special Agent Dave Baker, WMD Coordinator, FBI Regional Office in Los Angeles, for the Criminal Justice Course on "Terrorism" at the California Specialized Training Institute, San Luis Obispo, California, February 4, 1999.

7. Rene Sanchez, "Calif. Anthrax Threats Spawn Costly Wave of Fear," *Washington Post*, January 11, 1999, p. 2; Don Terry, "Treating Anthrax Hoaxes with Costly Rubber Gloves," *New York Times*, December 29, 1998, p. A10.

lesser conflicts such as the Yemen civil war (1963–67),[8] the Iran-Iraq War (1980–88),[9] and the war between South Africa and Mozambique (1992).[10] Unproven allegations of chemical warfare include use by the Soviet Union in Afghanistan in 1980–83[11] and by Bosnian Serb forces in Bosnia in 1995.[12]

More than 125 countries, including several states with chemical arsenals such as the United States, Russia, China, India, and Iran, have signed and ratified the 1993 Chemical Weapons Convention (CWC). This global treaty, which entered into force in April 1997, mandates the internationally monitored destruction of all chemical stockpiles within ten years and bans their reacquisition. The United States is currently destroying its entire chemical stockpile with high-temperature incineration and chemical neutralization technologies. Russia has made a similar commitment to eliminate the vast chemical arsenal it inherited from the Soviet Union, although it faces major financial obstacles in doing so. Several countries suspected of retaining clandestine chemical weapons stocks have refused to join the CWC, however, including states that support terrorism such as Iraq, Libya, Syria, and North Korea.

Biological warfare (BW) agents are living microorganisms that cause fatal or incapacitating diseases, as well as toxins—nonliving poisons extracted from living bacteria, plants, and animals, or synthesized in the laboratory. Whereas chemical weapons act within minutes or hours, biological weapons typically have an "incubation period" of two days or more before acute symptoms develop. Microbial pathogens that have been developed in the past for military purposes include bacteria (e.g., the causative agents of anthrax, tularemia, and plague), viruses (Venezuelan equine encephalitis, Marburg hemorrhagic fever, and smallpox), and rickettsiae (Q fever). Early U.S. developers of biological weapons preferred veterinary diseases such as anthrax and tularemia that are not

---

8. W. Andrew Terrill, "The Chemical Warfare Legacy of the Yemen War," *Comparative Strategy*, Vol. 10, No. 2 (1991), pp. 109–119.

9. Lee Waters, "Chemical Weapons in the Iran/Iraq War," *Military Review*, Vol. 70, No. 10 (October 1990), pp. 57–63.

10. Truth and Reconciliation Commission (South Africa), Chapter 6: "Special Investigation into Project Coast, South Africa's Chemical and Biological Warfare Program, 'Mozambican Incident'" *Final Report*, Volume II (Cape Town: Truth and Reconciliation Commission, October 29, 1998).

11. U.S. Department of State, *Chemical Warfare in Southeast Asia and Afghanistan: Report to the Congress from Secretary of State Alexander M. Haig, Jr.*, Special Report No. 98 (Washington, D.C.: U.S. Department of State, March 22, 1982).

12. Human Rights Watch, "Chemical Warfare in Bosnia? The Strange Experiences of Srebrenica Survivors," *Human Rights Watch*, Vol. 10, No. 9 (D) (November 1998).

contagious in humans, making the effects of a BW attack more control-lable. The Soviet Union, in contrast, weaponized highly contagious dis-eases such as pneumonic plague and smallpox for strategic attacks against distant targets, in the belief that the resulting epidemic would not boomerang against the Soviet population.

At least in theory, germ weapons are much more potent on a weight-for-weight basis than even the most lethal chemical weapons. Nerve agents such as sarin can kill in tiny doses if inhaled, but they must be delivered in massive quantities to produce lethal concentrations over large areas. For example, a chemical attack that caused 50 percent casu-alties over a square kilometer would require about a metric ton of sarin. In contrast, microorganisms infect people in minute doses and then mul-tiply within the host to cause disease. For example, a mere 8,000 anthrax bacteria—an amount smaller than a speck of dust—are sufficient to infect a human being. As a result, a biological attack with a few kilograms of anthrax could inflict the same level of casualties over a square kilometer as a metric ton of sarin—provided that the anthrax was efficiently dis-seminated.

Despite the potential lethality of BW agents, their actual use in war has been extremely rare, with the only well-documented case in the twentieth century being Japan's use of plague and other bacterial agents against China during World War II.[13] The United States unilaterally re-nounced its offensive BW program in 1969, and the development, pos-session, and transfer of biological and toxin weapons are banned by the 1972 Biological Weapons Convention (BWC). More than 140 countries are parties to the treaty, but about a dozen states—among them Egypt, Iraq, Iran, Israel, Libya, North Korea, Russia, and Syria—are suspected of possessing or of actively seeking biological weapons. Although Moscow was one of three key sponsors of the BWC, in April 1992 Russian Presi-dent Boris Yeltsin admitted that the Soviet Union and then Russia had retained an offensive BW program for nearly two decades in violation of the convention. Yeltsin issued an edict dismantling the offensive program, but some analysts suspect that it still persists at a lower level. According to a U.S. government report, some former Soviet biological weapons–related facilities, "in addition to being engaged in legitimate activity, may be maintaining the capability to produce BW agents."[14]

13.   John W. Powell, "Japan's Biological Weapons: 1930–1945," *Bulletin of the Atomic Scientists*, Vol. 37, No. 8 (October 1981), pp. 43–51; Sheldon H. Harris, *Factories of Death: Japanese Biological Warfare 1932–45 and the American Cover-Up* (New York: Routledge, 1994).

14.   U.S. Arms Control and Disarmament Agency, *Threat Control Through Arms Control: Annual Report to Congress, 1996* (Washington, D.C.: ACDA, 1997), p. 87.

A dilemma associated with efforts to control the spread of biological weapons is that the equipment needed to produce them is "dual-capable," meaning that it has both civilian and military applications. Indeed, nearly any plant that produces vaccines, antibiotics, feed supplements, or fermented beverages could potentially be diverted to the illicit production of BW agents. The rapid diffusion of commercial biotechnology industries throughout the developing world has therefore created a burgeoning potential for biological weapons development.

Hurdles to Terrorist Acquisition of CBW

Although a terrorist would need only a few dozen liters of nerve agent to inflict significant casualties among unprotected civilians, the production of chemical weapons is not as easy as is often suggested in media accounts. The synthesis of nerve agents such as sarin and VX requires the use of highly reactive and corrosive ingredients that may be difficult to acquire and are dangerous to handle. Terrorists seeking a chemical capability would therefore have to overcome significant technical hurdles and would run major safety risks, particularly in the event of an accidental explosion or leak.

Aum Shinrikyo, whose vast financial resources enabled it to recruit trained organic chemists from Japanese universities and to build a sophisticated three-story chemical-weapons production plant known as "Satian 7," still failed in its attempt to carry out a devastating chemical attack against the population of Tokyo. Aum's release of sarin on the Tokyo subway caused mass disruption but limited fatalities: twelve people died, fewer than would have been killed by an explosive device. One reason was that the delivery system was crude. A diluted solution of sarin was poured into eleven two-ply plastic bags, which were then sealed. Cult members carried these bags, concealed in folded newspapers, on board subway cars. At the appointed time, the terrorists punctured the bags with sharpened umbrella tips, releasing puddles of nerve agent that slowly evaporated and exposed people nearby. Aum's sarin was also of poor quality, having been synthesized hastily the day before and diluted with solvent so that the perpetrators would have time to escape before being overcome by the fumes. Had Aum produced high-grade sarin and dispensed it as an aerosol—a fine, inhalable mist—the Tokyo attack could easily have inflicted thousands of casualties. Nevertheless, the fact that the cult did not succeed in its effort to inflict mass casualties suggests that chemical terrorism is not as easy as some analysts contend.

Development and production of a biological weapon by terrorists would also entail significant technical challenges. First, the terrorists would have to obtain a sufficiently virulent strain of a lethal or incapacitating disease agent. Obtaining highly virulent strains from natural sources is not easy, however. Most of the pathogens developed as biological weapons have been deliberately bred or genetically modified for virulence, stability, ease of production, and other characteristics. The next step, cultivation of the agent, would be relatively easy for individuals trained in microbiology. Since all the necessary equipment is "dual-use," terrorists could use commercially available laboratory glassware or a desktop fermentor and standard nutrient media to brew up a batch of lethal bacteria. Viruses are significantly harder to mass-produce because they cannot multiply outside of living cells, but they can be grown in fertilized eggs. Even so, cultivating infectious pathogens can be hazardous to one's health. Because of sloppy laboratory practices, members of the Aum Shinrikyo cult reportedly became infected with Q-fever, a rickettsial disease they were preparing as a biological weapon. Even cult leader Shoko Asahara is believed to have acquired the debilitating illness.[15]

Dissemination of BW agents poses even greater technical hurdles. Whereas persistent chemical agents such as sulfur mustard and VX nerve gas are readily absorbed through the intact skin, no bacteria and viruses can enter the body by that route unless the skin has already been broken. Thus, BW agents must either be ingested or inhaled to cause infection. To expose large numbers of people through the gastrointestinal tract, possible means of delivery are contamination of food and drinking water, yet neither of these scenarios would be easy to accomplish. Large urban reservoirs are usually unguarded, but unless the terrorists dumped in a massive quantity of BW agent, the dilution effect would be so great that no healthy person drinking the water would receive an infectious dose. Moreover, modern sanitary techniques such as chlorination and filtration are designed to kill pathogens from natural sources and probably would be equally effective against a deliberately released agent.[16] Bacterial contamination of the food supply is also unlikely to inflict mass casualties. Cooking, boiling, pasteurization, and other routine safety precautions are generally sufficient to kill pathogenic bacteria. Moreover, although the only known incident of biological terrorism in the United States involved

---

15.   Sheryl WuDunn, Judith Miller, and William J. Broad, "How Japan Germ Terror Alerted World," *New York Times*, May 27, 1998, p. A10.

16.   Sydney J. Freedberg, Jr. and Marylyn Werber Serafini, "Be Afraid, Be Moderately Afraid," *National Journal*, No. 13 (March 27, 1999), p. 810.

the deliberate contamination of food, the method of delivery was crude and inherently limited: the terrorists sprinkled cultures of *Salmonella* bacteria onto restaurant salad bars (see Chapter 8).

The only potential way to inflict mass casualties with a BW agent is by disseminating it as a respirable aerosol: an invisible cloud of infectious droplets or particles so tiny that they remain suspended in the air for long periods and can be inhaled by large numbers of people. A high-concentration aerosol of anthrax or some other germ weapon, released into the air in a densely populated urban area, could potentially infect thousands of victims simultaneously. After an incubation period of a few days, depending on the type of agent and the inhaled dose, the exposed population would experience an outbreak of an incapacitating or fatal illness.

Although aerosol delivery is potentially the most lethal way of delivering a biological attack, it involves major technical hurdles that most terrorists would be unlikely to overcome. To infect through the lungs, infectious particles must be microscopic in size—between one and five microns (millionths of a meter) in diameter. Terrorists would therefore have to develop or acquire a sophisticated delivery system capable of generating an aerosol cloud with the necessary particle size range and a high enough agent concentration to cover a broad area.

An important trade-off exists between ease of production and effectiveness of dissemination. The easiest way to produce microbial agents is in a liquid form, yet when such a "slurry" is sprayed into the air, it forms heavy droplets that fall to the ground so that only a small percentage of the agent is aerosolized. In contrast, if the bacteria are first dried to a solid cake and then milled into a fine powder, they become far easier to aerosolize, yet the drying and milling process is technically challenging. Some experts believe that only a major state-sponsored BW program could overcome these hurdles; others are less convinced.[17] Conceivably, terrorists might seek to obtain the necessary weaponization know-how by recruiting germ weapons scientists formerly employed by the Soviet Union, South Africa, or some other country that had a technically advanced BW program.

Even if aerosolization is achieved, the effective delivery of biological agents in the open air is highly dependent on atmospheric and wind conditions, creating additional uncertainties. Only under highly stable atmospheric conditions will the aerosol cloud remain close to the ground where it can be inhaled, rather than being rapidly dispersed. Moreover, most microorganisms are sensitive to ultraviolet radiation and cannot

---

17. Ibid., p. 810–811.

survive more than thirty minutes in bright sunlight, limiting their effective military use to nighttime attacks. The one major exception is anthrax bacteria, which can be induced to form spores with tough outer coats that enable them to survive for several hours in sunlight. Terrorists, of course, could stage a biological attack inside an enclosed space such as a building, a subway station, a shopping mall, or a sports arena. Such an attack, if it involved a respirable aerosol, might infect thousands of people, but even here the technical hurdles would be by no means trivial.

Indeed, Aum Shinrikyo failed in ten attempts to conduct BW attacks with either anthrax or botulinum toxin between 1990 and 1995, suggesting that despite the cult's extensive scientific and financial resources, it was unable to overcome some or all of the technical hurdles associated with acquisition of a virulent strain, cultivation of the agent, and efficient delivery. According to Larry Johnson, former deputy director of the State Department's Office of Counter-Terrorism, "Producing these types of weapons requires infrastructure and expertise more sophisticated than a lab coat and a garage. Besides being tough to produce, these weapons also are difficult to use."[18] In sum, only a small subset of terrorist groups or organizations is likely to possess the technical know-how needed to carry out an effective chemical or biological attack.

A "New Breed" of Terrorists?

To pose a real threat of toxic terror, a group must have both the capability and motivation to acquire and use chemical or biological weapons. What can one say about the motivational side of the equation? Terrorism expert Bruce Hoffman has argued that a terrorist act is conceived and executed in a manner that simultaneously reflects the group's particular aims and motivations, fits its resources and capabilities, and takes account of the target audience at which the act is directed. "The tactics and targets of various terrorist movements, as well as the weapons they favor," he writes, "are . . . eluctably shaped by a group's ideology, its internal organizational dynamics and the personalities of its key members, as well as a variety of internal and external stimuli."[19]

To examine terrorist motivations, it is first important to define the

---

18. Testimony by Larry Johnson before the National Security, International Affairs and Criminal Justice Subcommittee of the House Government Reform and Oversight Committee, October 2, 1998, cited in *The CBW Conventions Bulletin*, No. 42 (December 1998), p. 35.

19. Bruce Hoffman, *Inside Terrorism* (New York: Columbia University Press, 1998), p. 157.

term "terrorism." According to the definition adopted by the U.S. Department of State, terrorism is "premeditated, politically motivated violence perpetrated against noncombatant targets by subnational or clandestine agents, usually intended to influence an audience."[20] The case studies in this book suggest that the traditional definition is problematic, however, because apolitical or personal motivations may lead terrorists to acquire and use CBW agents. A better working definition might be as follows: "Terrorism is the instrumental use or threatened use of violence by an organization or individual against innocent civilian targets in furtherance of a political, religious, or ideological objective."

Historically, terrorist organizations with concrete political agendas, such as social-revolutionary or nationalist-separatist groups, have not sought to acquire or use chemical or biological weapons. Likely explanations for this pattern include unfamiliarity with the relevant technologies; the hazards and unpredictability of employing toxic and infectious agents; and moral constraints. The most important consideration, however, is that politically motivated terrorists generally view mass-casualty attacks as counterproductive. Since such groups are trying to extract a political concession of some kind or to gain attention for their cause in the court of public opinion, they must carefully calibrate their use of violence. Indiscriminate attacks could kill supporters as well as enemies, would alienate current or future supporters of the group, and would probably provoke severe government repression that could result in the group's destruction. Finally, the decision to acquire or employ CBW agents may create strong tensions within the group and jeopardize its cohesion if some members object on moral grounds. Such individuals may defect and become informants for law enforcement agencies, putting the survival of the group in jeopardy.

Despite the disincentives to CBW use by politically motivated terrorists, several analysts have argued that a "new breed" of terrorists has appeared on the scene that may be willing to employ mass violence for a variety of motives unrelated to clear political goals.[21] Indeed, the conventional bombings of the World Trade Center in New York in 1993 and the Alfred E. Murrah Federal Building in Oklahoma City in 1995 were clearly intended to inflict indiscriminate civilian casualties, and have raised the specter of a more virulent form of terrorism. Examples of

---

20. U.S. Department of State, *Patterns of Global Terrorism*, Office of the Coordinator for Counter-terrorism (Washington, D.C.: U.S. Department of State, April 1997), p. vi.

21. Jose Vegar, "Terrorism's New Breed," *Bulletin of the Atomic Scientists*, Vol. 54, No. 2 (March/April 1998), pp. 50–55.

apolitical terrorist groups include nationalist-religious terrorists whose hatred and fanaticism are so intense that they are prepared to resort to any weapon to destroy their enemies; millenarian sects and cults that believe that God or some higher power has ordered them to bring about an apocalyptic final battle in which the unbelievers will be vanquished and the righteous will receive their reward; white supremacists lashing out at hated minority groups; and radical ecologists who believe that the human race must be decimated to preserve the natural balance.

Some of the most serious new threats of mass-casualty terrorism come from professional terrorists who have associated themselves with nationalist-religious causes such as pan-Islamic identity. Ramzi Yousef, the mastermind behind the World Trade Center bombing, sought "eye-for-an-eye" retribution for U.S. and Israeli attacks on Arab states that claimed civilian lives. Similarly, Osama bin Laden, believed responsible for the August 1998 terrorist bombings of the U.S. embassies in Kenya and Tanzania, declared in an interview, "We don't consider it a crime if we tried to have nuclear, chemical, biological weapons. Our holy land is occupied by Israeli and American forces. We have the right to defend ourselves and to liberate our holy land."[22] Bin Laden stressed that any American citizen who pays taxes and supports the U.S. government is a legitimate target "because he is helping the American war machine against the Muslim nation."[23]

Ever since the Aum Shinrikyo attack on the Tokyo subway, the frightening potential of CBW use has transformed terrorism from little more than an irritant into a perceived threat to national security. Will the "new breed" of terrorists break the deep-seated moral taboo against the large-scale use of these weapons? Terrorism has traditionally relied on relatively unsophisticated weapons such as guns and bombs, which have been used in a small number of ways to inflict relatively modest damage with limited social and political impact.[24] At the same time, the historical record includes hundreds of cases in which individuals or groups motivated by criminal, economic, political, or religious objectives have employed CBW agents. None of these incidents has involved mass casualties, either because the motivation or the capability to conduct such an

---

22. Jamal Ismail, "I Am Not Afraid of Death" [interview with Osama bin Laden], *Newsweek*, January 11, 1999, p. 37.

23. Ibid, p. 37.

24. Philip B. Heymann, *Terrorism and America: A Commonsense Strategy for a Democratic Society*, BCSIA Studies in International Security (Cambridge, Mass.: The MIT Press, 1998), p. 8.

attack was lacking. Accordingly, it is difficult to extrapolate the probability of such events in the future or to predict their potential impact.[25]

Terrorism expert Walter Laqueur contends that the danger of CBW terrorism has become particularly great because of the confluence of two trends: the growing accessibility of mass-casualty weapons and the emergence of new and more ruthless forms of religious and ideological fanaticism.[26] It is not yet clear, however, whether Laqueur's lines of capability and motivation have actually intersected.

Purpose of this Book

Although the technical hurdles involved in producing and disseminating CBW have been extensively analyzed,[27] the motivational side still re-

25. Whether terrorists will employ CBW has been a topic of heated debate among specialists, with some contending that such attacks are inevitable and others that they are extremely unlikely. Examples of articles and books reflecting different assessments of the threat include: Jonathan B. Tucker, "Chemical/Biological Terrorism: Coping with a New Threat," *Politics and the Life Sciences*, Vol. 15, No. 2 (September 1996), pp. 167–183, with roundtable commentaries on pp. 185–247; Walter Laqueur, "Postmodern Terrorism," *Foreign Affairs*, Vol. 75, No. 5 (September/October 1996), pp. 24–36; John F. Sopko, "The Changing Proliferation Threat," *Foreign Policy*, No. 105 (Winter 1996/97), pp. 3–20; Brad Roberts, ed., *Terrorism with Chemical and Biological Weapons: Calibrating Risks and Responses* (Alexandria, Va.: Chemical and Biological Arms Control Institute, 1997); James K. Campbell, "Excerpts from Research Study 'Weapons of Mass Destruction and Terrorism: Proliferation by Non-State Actors,'" *Terrorism and Political Violence*, Vol. 9, No. 2 (Summer 1997), pp. 24–50; Richard A. Falkenrath, Robert D. Newman, and Bradley A. Thayer, *America's Achilles' Heel: Nuclear, Biological, and Chemical Terrorism and Covert Attack*, BCSIA Studies in International Security (Cambridge, Mass.: The MIT Press, 1998); Ehud Sprinzak, "The Great Superterrorism Scare," *Foreign Policy*, No. 112 (Fall 1998), pp. 110–124; Walter Laqueur, "The New Face of Terrorism," *Washington Quarterly*, Vol. 21, No. 4 (Autumn 1998), pp. 169–178; David C. Rapoport, "Terrorists and Weapons of the Apocalypse," paper prepared for the Nonproliferation Policy Education Center short course titled "Three Nonproliferation Dialogues: Grand Terrorism, Counterproliferation, and Dual Containment," Annual Meeting of the American Political Science Association, Boston, Mass., September 2, 1998; Ashton Carter, John Deutch, and Philip Zelikow, "Catastrophic Terrorism: Tackling the New Danger," *Foreign Affairs*, Vol. 77, No. 6 (November/December 1998), pp. 80–94; Richard A. Falkenrath, "Confronting Nuclear, Biological and Chemical Terrorism," *Survival*, Vol. 40, No. 3 (Autumn 1998), pp. 43–65; comments on the previous article by Karl-Heinz Kamp, Joseph F. Pilat, and Jessica Stern, and a response by Richard A. Falkenrath in "WMD Terrorism: An Exchange," *Survival*, Vol. 40, No. 4 (Winter 1998/99), pp. 168–183; and Jessica Stern, *The Ultimate Terrorists* (Cambridge, Mass.: Harvard University Press, 1999).

26. Laqueur, "The New Face of Terrorism," p. 171.

27. See, for example, U.S. Congress, Office of Technology Assessment, *Technologies Underlying Weapons of Mass Destruction*, OTA-BP-ISC-115 (Washington, D.C.: U.S. Gov-

mains obscure, a gap in current knowledge that this study seeks to address. What types of terrorist groups or individuals are most likely to acquire and use such weapons, and for what purpose? Further, what types of CBW agents are most likely to be produced, and how would they be delivered? Faced with these questions, most analysts have engaged in *a priori* speculation about terrorist motivations without taking the time and effort to examine historical cases in which individuals or groups have actually sought to acquire or use CBW agents. Even more problematic, information on past incidents of CBW terrorism in the academic literature is anecdotal and often factually incorrect.[28] Without a realistic threat assessment based on solid empirical data, government policymakers lack the information they need to design prudent yet cost-effective programs for preventing or mitigating future incidents.

To remedy this situation, the Chemical and Biological Weapons Non-proliferation Project at the Center for Nonproliferation Studies of the Monterey Institute of International Studies commissioned leading scholars in the CBW and terrorism fields to prepare in-depth case studies of twelve groups or individuals who, over the period from 1945 to 1998, sought to acquire or use CBW agents. The cases selected were those most often cited in the academic terrorism literature, including religious cults, right-wing and left-wing terrorist organizations, and "amateur" terrorists. Each case study was researched from primary sources including court documents, declassified government files, and interviews with law enforcement officials, attorneys, judges, and, where possible, the former terrorists themselves.

The case-study method, like every other methodological approach employed in political science, has drawbacks when it comes to assessing a bewilderingly complex reality. Some analysts contend that historical case studies are of limited value for predicting the future threat of CBW terrorism because the nature of terrorism is changing, making it more difficult to extrapolate from past events. In fact, many of the seemingly "new" trends described in the terrorism literature, such as groups or individuals motivated by religious fanaticism, right-wing ideology, or white supremacism, are already well represented in the historical record. Neo-Nazi cells, religious cults, and other unconventional groups have

---

ernment Printing Office, December 1993); and Karl Lowe, "Analyzing Technical Constraints on Bio-Terrorism: Are They Still Important?" in Roberts, ed., *Terrorism with Chemical and Biological Weapons*, pp. 53–64.

28. The contradictory and often erroneous information on incidents of CBW terrorism contained in the secondary literature is amply documented in Ron Purver, *Chemical and Biological Terrorism: The Threat According to the Open Literature* (Ottawa: Canadian Security Intelligence Service, June 1995).

existed for decades, but in the past they were treated as an epiphenom-enon and largely ignored because of the tendency of academic specialists and intelligence analysts to focus narrowly on traditional, politically motivated terrorist organizations. Given this fact, the study of past inci-dents involving apolitical terrorists should provide insights into motiva-tions and behaviors of individuals and groups that have become of much greater concern today because of their potential acquisition and use of CBW agents.

Others may object that the small number of case studies in this volume constitutes far from a comprehensive universe or even a statisti-cally representative sample, and that the historical record itself is flawed and incomplete. Indeed, an unknown number of incidents of CBW ter-rorism may have occurred but remained undetected if they did not produce recognizable casualties or were not covered by the news media— a situation analogous to Bishop Berkeley's proverbial tree falling in the woods with no one around to hear it. Definitional problems also exist in distinguishing incidents of CBW terrorism from strictly criminal acts, such as cases of extortion or murder involving poisons.

Despite these methodological limitations, however, the study of the past can provide important insights for the present and the future. As-sessing the risk of future incidents of CBW terrorism requires identifying which types of terrorist groups have the technical capability to produce, weaponize, and disseminate these agents; the motivation to inflict mass casualties; and the organizational structure needed to evade law enforce-ment penetration and arrest. Case studies are invaluable for this purpose because they help us to think concretely about the problem.

Part I
Historical Case Studies

Chapter 2

Avenging Israel's Blood (1946)

Ehud Sprinzak and Idith Zertal

In April 1946, a small team of Jewish Holocaust survivors poisoned the bread of thousands of Nazi SS storm troopers held at Stalag 13, an American prisoner-of-war camp outside of Nuremberg, Germany. According to the German news agency DANA, 2,283 prisoners become ill and 207 were hospitalized, with fatalities unknown.[1] The Nuremberg team, consisting of seven men and two women, was part of a larger group of about sixty former anti-Nazi partisans known as "DIN"—both the Hebrew word for "judgment" and a Hebrew acronym for "Avenging Israel's Blood" (*Dahm Y'Israel Nokeam*). DIN's actions were motivated by the desire to avenge the murder of six million Jews, including many of the members' immediate relatives, in Nazi-occupied ghettos and concentration camps. In fact, the organization initially planned to kill hundreds of thousands of Germans.

The first account of the Stalag 13 operation appeared in a 1967 book by Israeli writer Michael Bar Zohar that received surprisingly little attention.[2] In recent years, more public and scholarly attention has focused on DIN, including several television documentaries and eyewitness testimonies by some of the individuals involved.[3] Even so, the growing literature

---

1. Michael Bar-Zohar, *The Avengers* (Tel Aviv: Levin-Epstein, 1967, in Hebrew), pp. 40–53. The book was translated into French and English. The English edition is Michael Bar-Zohar, *The Avengers*, trans. Len Ortzen (London: Arthur Barker Publishers, 1968).

2. An early book that also referred to DIN was Michael Elkins, *Forged in Fury* (London: Judy Piatcus Publishers, 1971). A second edition appeared in 1981, and Corgi Books reprinted it in 1982.

3. By far the most extensive account of DIN is Levy Arie Sarid, "The 'Revenge' Organization—Its History, Profile and Deeds," *Moreshet* No. 52 (1992), pp. 35–102 (in Hebrew). See also Tom Segev, *The Seventh Million: The Israelis and the Holocaust* (New

on the use of chemical and biological weapons by radical and terrorist organizations has made little reference to this extraordinary case, which sheds valuable light on the factors that can motivate desperate people to employ such weapons.[4]

From Catastrophe to Vengeance: The Origins and Collective Psychology of DIN

The DIN organization was founded in February 1945 by group of young Jewish ghetto fighters and partisans in Lublin, Poland. World War II was still raging in parts of Europe, and Jews were still being murdered by the Nazi death machine. The Holocaust survivors who gathered in Lublin saw themselves as the last Jews on earth, the remnants of Armageddon. They had seen their families slaughtered before their eyes, their communities destroyed, their ancient culture wiped out. They were phantoms living beyond history, beyond any law or rule they had known in their previous lives.

Indescribable rage, an ultimate sense of humiliation and despair, and suicidal thoughts were common among the Lublin group. "When the Russians crossed the border I escaped from Auschwitz," recalled one of the organization's founders, Yehudah Wasserman. "We were a small and desperate group of friends . . . . While lying on the ground a friend said to me: 'What now? We are at the climax. This is the moment to end our lives.' I had only one goal in going on living—to send to Palestine the story of our group in Krakow and then putting an end to it all."[5] Eliezer Lidovsky, one of the leaders of the Jewish underground in Poland, remembered that on his return to Rovno, he met hundreds of Jewish partisans. "They were immersed in a terrible state of despair, one that I had never witnessed before either in the ghetto or the partisan camps.

York: Hill and Wang, 1993), pp. 140–152. The most significant memoirs include Eliezer Lidovsky, *And the Ember Was Not Extinguished* (Tel Aviv: The Partisans Organization, 1986, in Hebrew) and Joseph Harmatz, *From the Wings* (Sussex, England: The Book Guild, 1998). Documentaries include *Revenge* (New York: Set Productions, 1996), a somewhat different BBC production in 1997, an ABC *Nightline* program that aired in 1996, and an Israeli TV Channel One production titled *The Avengers* that aired on February 9, 1999.

4. A reference to DIN in the context of mass-casualty terrorism appears in Ehud Sprinzak, "The Great Super-Terrorism Scare," in *Foreign Policy*, No. 112 (Fall 1998), p. 114.

5. Yehudah Wasserman in "DIN Veterans' Gathering," series of meetings from February through April 1985 (unpublished mimeographed proceedings), p. 85.

With no will to live . . . [they] all began to ask, 'What for? Why have we survived at all?'"[6]

The idea of revenge was omnipresent in the survivors' minds, their conversations, and their nightmares. According to Zvia Lubetkin, one of the heroes of the Warsaw ghetto uprising, "We knew only one thing. If we would find the people, and if we would have within ourselves the power needed for it, there should be only one thing to do: to take revenge! We were not living with a sense of reconstruction, only with a will to destroy, destroy as much as possible, as much as we could."[7]

A member of DIN told an interviewer more than thirty years later of the psychological and historical background of the group:

I want you to think of a person coming out of the camps or the forests in 1945. All he wishes for is to get out of Europe where everyone he loved is dead, his whole people murdered, and they do not let him go. . . . This individual looks at the world and what does he see? The eyes that were closed to his suffering are closed still; the hands that were not lifted to help him are not lifted now. The Germans who killed the Jews are free. They till their soil, have their jobs and families, are the mayors, the policemen, and the respected ones, and the Jews are a homeless vermin. . . . Every word I say to you now felt like a knife cutting flesh. For what we learned in 1945 was . . . that nobody in the world but the Jew cares about the Jew. In the entire world there is no justice for the Jew except that justice which the Jew can take for himself. That's what we did. We stood at the crossroads then and we turned our backs on Palestine and we started to take our own justice—justice and vengeance![8]

The founders of the revenge organization believed that by dedicating themselves to the killing of Germans, they were assuming a sacred responsibility bestowed upon them by their murdered families and friends. Vengeance was the last will of the victims. They whispered or screamed the word before dying; they wrote it in their blood on synagogue walls and in the death camps; they called upon the remnants of the Jewish people not to rest until their blood had been avenged. A synagogue wall in the town of Kovel bore the inscription: "Dearest Munyek, avenge the blood of your father, brother and sister, fallen at the hands of the murderers. Remember, this should be your mission in

---

6. Eliezer Lidovsky, "Testimony," Oral Documentation Department, The Hebrew University of Jerusalem, tape 600, p. 3.

7. Zvia Lubetkin, *The Last on the Wall* (Tel Aviv: Ha-Kibbutz Ha-Meuchad, 1947, in Hebrew), p. 46. Translated by the authors.

8. Michael Elkins, *Forged in Fury* (London: Corgi Books, 1982), pp. 180–181.

life!"[9] The admired poet Yitzhak Katzenelson, in his *Vittel Diary*, imagined a horrific vengeance of a kind the world had never seen. "For this despicable, tainted nation [Germany] must perish, all its millions will perish . . . their elders and youth, their women and children will perish because of Israel."[10]

Zipora Birman, a brave young Bialystok leader of the *Dror* youth movement who died in the Holocaust, wrote of the survivors' obligation to avenge her and her people's murder:

I address you, friends, wherever you are; you bear a complete obligation to exact our vengeance. Not a single one of you should rest; not a single one of you should sleep his night's sleep. As long as we live under the shadow of death, the light of vengeance for our spilled blood shall direct you. Cursed be the reader of these words who reads them and, with a complacent sigh, returns to his daily life. Cursed be the person who is satisfied with tears and crying for our souls—we call upon you to take revenge with no mercy, no sentiments, no talk about "good" Germans. For the good German—an easy death. He will die last, as they promised to their good Jew, "You will be shot last." This is our demand. . . . Our crushed bones all over Europe will never rest in peace. The ashes scattered over the crematoria will not settle until you take our revenge. Remember and carry out our will and your obligation.[11]

A Charismatic Leader: The Case of Abba Kovner

How did the revenge idea, so powerful in the survivors' minds, take concrete form? What were the circumstances of DIN's birth? Although organization members did not speak for many years about their revenge activities, and despite subtle attempts to silence them lest they damage Israel's image, the story is now widely known. Most of the accounts, however, are forty- to fifty-year-old memoirs of the participants, which casts some doubt on their accuracy.

"There were many discussions [in the forests]," remembered Pasha Reichman (Yitzhak Avidov), about the question of what to do immediately after the war. After several attempts to smuggle Jewish survivors from the Soviet Union to the West, Pasha and a few comrades-in-arms moved to Lublin, where they met other ghetto fighters and partisans,

---

9. Shlomo Perlmutter, *Moreshet*, No. 35 (1982), p. 32, quoted in Sarid, "The 'Revenge' Organization," p. 36.

10. Yitzhak Katzenelsohn, *The Vittel Diary* (Tel Aviv: Ha-Kibbutz Ha-Meuchad, 1947, in Hebrew), p. 172. Translated by the authors.

11. Zipora Birman, in *The Book of Kibbutz Tel Hai in Bialystok*, pp. 359–360.

including Abba Kovner.[12] All of them saw in Kovner's arrival a turning point in the formation of the organization. Eliezer Lidovsky, a former resistance fighter in Baranovitz and later a partisan in the forests, testified that the organization was born out of his "historical deliberation with Kovner" shortly after the latter's arrival in Lublin.[13]

A mythical figure in the Jewish Resistance, a poet, and a partisan, Abba Kovner was indeed the key player in the formation of DIN. Reichman wrote in his personal diary:

I met with Abba Kovner the night of his arrival in Lublin. I see him leaning on the table, testing and asking me, "Well, what will happen?" I told him that I was determined not to leave the place without taking revenge on the Nazi enemy. Abba hugged and kissed me. Trembling with emotion, he said to me: "Pasha, this is what I have been thinking about all the time. I have devoted to this matter endless, endless hours." We all felt that we had here before us a man who could navigate our boat to great distances, a man of intelligence such as we had never seen before.[14]

Another member of the original Lublin group, Bezalel Kek (Michaeli), a former partisan and underground fighter in his hometown of Rokitana, also spoke of Kovner's vital role in the formation of the group. "Much was talked about the issue of vengeance that filled our souls in the woods and in Rovno, but the idea only started to take shape upon the arrival of Abba Kovner, whom I knew before, in Lublin. . . . Abba designed the form of the organization and gave it its substance: not personal, local revenge but a great scope—a national vengeance . . . for which we, in Rovno, did not have the imagination."[15]

Abba Kovner was born on March 14, 1918, in Sevastopol on the shores of the Black Sea, the son of an educated family then traveling from Vilnius to Palestine. When Abba was eight years old, the family returned to Vilnius, known as the "Jerusalem of Lithuania" for its eminent centers of Jewish learning and its cultural and political ferment. As a student at the Tarbut ("culture" in Hebrew) Gymnasium, Kovner joined a radical Zionist movement called *Ha-Shomer Ha-Tzair* ("The Young Watchman").

12. Pasha Reichman (Yitzhak Avidov), "Testimony," Oral Documentation Department, The Hebrew University of Jerusalem, tape 160, p. 4.

13. Sarid, "The 'Revenge' Organization," p. 46.

14. Pasha Reichman, "Life in Extremity" (unpublished pamphlet), p. 43, cited in Sarid, "The 'Revenge' Organization," p. 46.

15. Bezalel Kek (Michaeli) in "DIN Veterans' Gathering," pp. 52–53, quoted in Sarid, "The 'Revenge' Organization."

His responsibilities in the movement became so demanding that he dropped out of school before graduation and only later passed his university entrance exams. In addition to his work for the movement, Abba supported his family by giving private lessons.[16] Prior to the outbreak of World War II, Kovner became the uncontested leader of *Ha-Shomer Ha-Tzair*, the head of its secretariat, and the region's commander.[17] Though physically unimposing and somewhat aloof, Kovner was a charismatic leader who wrote, gave lectures, and directed seminars.

When Vilnius came under the Soviet zone of control, life for the city's Jews remained more or less unchanged. As Kovner described it, Vilnius was a Noah's ark resting on Mount Ararat in the midst of the flood.[18] On June 24, 1941, however, the German Army captured the city and forced its Jewish community of 60,000 into a cramped quarter that became known as the "Vilna ghetto." Kovner and a few friends found refuge in a convent on the town's outskirts, but when the Nazis began killing Jews in collaboration with German and Lithuanian gangs, Kovner returned to the ghetto. There, his group and other youth movements started to plan for Jewish resistance.[19] "In order to fight under any conditions, not to mention ghetto conditions, one needs, first and foremost, an organization," Kovner said in his testimony at the Eichmann trial in 1961. "An organization of fighters can either be established by the decree of a national authority or by an inner force. For European Jewry there was no—could not be—a rule of authority. Such an organization could be constituted only by people of the utmost determination, who usually cannot be found among the desperate, the broken, or the persecuted. This war, called for some reason the war of despair, was waged by believers, people who believed that there was meaning and purpose in dying an hour earlier for something that was greater than life."[20]

Already at the end of 1941, Abba Kovner spoke in the Vilna ghetto about the inevitability of resistance—the vital need for the Jews to fight their oppressors, not because there was any chance of winning but be-

---

16. Shalom Luria, "Abba Kovner and the Realms of his Poetry" in Abba Kovner, *On the Narrow Bridge: Essays* (Tel Aviv: Sifriyat Poalim, 1981, in Hebrew), pp. 227–233. Translated by the authors.

17. Ibid., p. 232.

18. Abba Kovner, "The Place where the Arch Rests . . ." in *De Profundis* (journal), Vilna, January 1940, pp. 11–12.

19. Ruzka Korczak, *Flames in the Ashes* (Tel Aviv: Moreshet and Sifriat Poalim, 1965, in Hebrew), p. 16. Translated by the authors.

20. *The Prosecution v Adolf Eichmann, Testimonies A* (Jerusalem: Yad Vashem, 1962, in Hebrew), p. 344. Translated by the authors.

cause it was the only way to retain their dignity. "The core of the matter," he said, "is how can we *not* fight! In order to take this road we need plenty of heroism, sacrifice, and faith. The act we are about to carry out is not an act of despair. It is not the end of all things. Objectively, it is possible that [death] will be the outcome, but today we are called upon to make the ultimate choice. . . . When the realization that we are the masters of death penetrates the bloody darkness, a great light will touch upon us. Then our life will dawn again."[21] Masters of death, or rather masters of one's own death, was the essence of Jewish resistance in Nazi-occupied Europe: to die an hour earlier, but at a time of one's own choosing and on one's own terms.

Kovner's life and activity in the Vilna ghetto were interwoven with the organization of the general Jewish resistance, the United Partisan Organization (FPO). Kovner was the thinker of the resistance as well as its operational commander, at once a poet and a soldier. Three weeks before the formation of the FPO, Kovner wrote a call for resistance, a seminal document in the annals of Jewish history. "Let's not go like sheep to the slaughter!" he declared. "Hitler plans to kill all the Jews of Europe. The Jews of Vilna are the first in line. . . . We may be weak and defenseless, but the only possible answer to the enemy is resistance."[22] Kovner's manifesto was the first call for resistance in the entire Nazi-occupied zone, and the first time that the mass killing of Jews by Nazi *Einsatzgruppen* was understood as part of a master plan for the destruction of all European Jewry.[23] In July 1945, referring to his and his friends' decision to fight the Nazis in the ghetto and in the forests, Kovner said, "We just wished to die, but to die in a way we would always remain alive in your memory."[24]

Kovner's command of the Vilna ghetto was darkened by two personal tragedies. The first commander of the resistance organization was betrayed to the Nazis, and Kovner, his deputy, took his place. The shadow of this painful affair, which has never been fully resolved, accompanied Kovner all his life. A second tragedy occurred during the final deportation of the Jews from the Vilna ghetto in September 1943, when Kovner directed the resistance organization's escape into the forests. At that critical moment he decided not to take his mother with him, leaving

---

21. Ruzka Korczak, *Flames in the Ashes*, p. 53.

22. Israel Gutman (ed.), *Encyclopedia of the Holocaust*, Vol. 2 (New York: Macmillan, 1990), pp. 822–824.

23. Ibid.

24. Aviva Kempner, *Partisans of Vilna* (documentary film), 1986.

her behind to an almost certain death. This painful moral decision tormented Kovner for years.[25] "We left behind us the mass grave of an entire nation," he wrote. "Wrecked devastation and walls covered with blood, and a resistance battle that lasted two years. Those who descended into the abyss did not think of themselves as survivors."[26]

Many of the ghetto fighters and partisans who gathered in Lublin in 1945 knew of Kovner's tragic ordeal, which added a dark edge to his uncontested leadership. In spite of the small number of people present at the first meetings of the revenge group, those formative days were crucial in establishing the main principles of the organization. Later on in Bucharest, Romania, where DIN was formed, the group developed its ideological infrastructure and first operative plans. DIN was an intimate and cohesive secret organization, composed of individuals forged by common experiences of loss, agony, and armed resistance. The organization was apolitical and stressed high moral values and total commitment. Although communists, bundists (members of a non-Zionist doctrinaire workers' movement), and activists of organizations subject to external authority were excluded, the DIN organization was ready to admit former communists, religious believers, and members of Zionist movements. Recruitment was conducted, however, primarily through personal contacts of the founders and key activists. According to Bezalel Kek, a member of the original Lublin group, "There was a selection, but if someone said he was with Abba at the FPO in Vilna . . . People whom Abba or Pasha knew and personally recommended were usually admitted as organization members."[27]

Although DIN's intimacy, camaraderie, and inner cohesion were essential for the organization's clandestine nature, they were also key to the organization's sense of autonomy and independence. According to Pasha Reichman,

All we did during the war, or afterwards, was done with no authority of this or that organization; in the underground we acted against the mindset of the *Judenrat* [the Jewish Councils appointed by the Germans]. The same happened regarding the escape to the forests, an act they saw as a terrible threat to the existence of the ghetto. After the war, we acted in opposition to the old Zionist leadership. We started smuggling people to Palestine with neither

---

25. Ibid.

26. Abba Kovner, "First Attempt to Tell," *On the Narrow Bridge*, p. 25

27. Bezalel Kek (Michaeli), "DIN Veterans' Gathering," p. 53, quoted in Sarid, "The 'Revenge' Organization," p. 54.

guidelines nor permission of the national institutions. Why? Because we saw ourselves as emissaries of the Jewish fate. . . . Our conscience was our only compass.[28]

A dark streak of pessimism also marked the organization's ethos. Kovner himself repeatedly stressed his death wish, suicidal thoughts, and recurrent depressions. This state of mind is recorded in the four-point document he scribbled in the spring of 1945:

1. The danger of extermination of the Jewish people is not yet over with the military defeat of Hitlerism;
2. Many people contributed to the murder of the six million. A number of them are ready to go on with it. It is inconceivable that the notion that Israel's blood is indefensible will remain in the mind of humanity;
3. Not only did the free world not answer and compensate for the devastation, but the attempt to make peace with the murderers has become a norm. This means the nurturing of a new generation of murderers;
4. That is why we assume the mission of preventing oblivion, committing an indispensable act that will be more than revenge: this will be the law of the murdered Jewish people. Our name will, therefore, be DIN ["Judgment"]. Many generations will therefore know that there is judgment in this ruthless world.[29]

A Window of Opportunity for Revenge

The first slogan of the DIN organization read: "For us the war has not come to an end; we keep on our war against the Germans."[30] Fully aware of the short time available for meaningful revenge—the period of chaos before a stable government was formed in Germany—Kovner sought to find the entire German nation guilty for the Jewish catastrophe and then execute the sentence: "an act that would forever burn the German memory with the realization that after Auschwitz one cannot wash one's hands." The questions were those of feasibility: How could such a massive attack be carried out? At this time, the idea of resorting to unconventional weapons emerged. "If we shall not hesitate to use unconventional means, the completion of our goal will be possible," said Kovner to his associates, trying to convince himself as well. "Six million for six

---

28. Pasha Reichman, "Testimony," Oral Documentation Department, tape 160, p. 4.

29. Kovner, in "DIN Veterans' Gathering," pp. 6–7, quoted in Sarid, "The 'Revenge' Organization," p. 49.

30. Avidov's testimony to Sarid, May 11, 1983, quoted in Sarid, "The 'Revenge' Organization," p. 47.

million. . . . The unconventional weapon, ferocious, cruel, must be comparable with the ruthlessness and inhumanity of the acts the Germans carried out against the Jews. Not one of us, by virtue of our upbringing and education, could have imagined beforehand that such a lethal weapon would become so central in our thoughts."[31]

Poison was the "unconventional" weapon DIN members chose to use.[32] The main principles according to which the acts of revenge were to be carried out defined the entire German people—men and women, soldiers and civilians, even children—as legitimate targets. The group rationalized that the Germans had not discriminated among the Jews but had murdered everybody. Consequently, the revenge action had to be equally "indiscriminate" for history to record that justice had been carried out against the German people.[33] As Reichman explained:

The principle of equality had to be realized not only by the quantity but also through the means of killing: they poisoned millions to death, we shall also use poison. Our point of departure was that every nation is responsible for its leaders. Hitler repeatedly declared his intentions concerning the Jews, and the great majority of the Germans accepted these plans either passionately or tacitly. Don't forget whom the Germans murdered! Mostly working Jews: artisans, laborers, hard-working shopkeepers and poor people. Their propaganda regarding well-to-do Jewish "bourgeoisie" was one of their many despicable lies. . . . Didn't they see the true picture with their eyes? As a matter of fact, the Germans expected a great act of vengeance from the Jewish survivors; they were terrified and looked for American and British protection from an avenging Jewish hand.[34]

---

31. Kovner in an interview with Sarid, quoted in Sarid, "The 'Revenge' Organization," p. 48.

32. A preliminary plan to use a bacteriological weapon against Nazi Germany had been developed earlier by David Raziel, the commander of the right-wing Irgun militia in Palestine. After a January 30, 1939, speech by Adolf Hitler that advocated the destruction of the entire Jewish nation, Raziel took the threat seriously and instructed Irgun members in Europe to start looking for a bacteriological agent with the thought of disseminating it covertly over Nazi Germany in case of need. Irgun scientists were not able to develop a workable formula, however, nor did they have an airplane and pilot with which to carry out the operation. This anecdote appears in a biography of Raziel by Arye Naor titled *David Raziel: The Life and Times of the Commander-in-Chief of the "Irgun" Underground in Palestine* (Tel Aviv: Israel Ministry of Defense, 1990, in Hebrew), pp. 153–154, 180. Naor's source was Dr. Reuven Hecht, an Austrian Jew whom Raziel asked to study the possibility of a bacteriological attack on Germany.

33. Harmatz's testimony in "DIN Veterans' Gathering," p. 48, quoted in Sarid, "The 'Revenge' Organization," p. 48.

34. Reichman's "Testimony," Oral Documentation Department, tape 160, p. 51.

Still, there were many unanswered operational questions. What kind of poison should be used? Where could the organization obtain enough toxic material for such a massive operation? How would the poisonings be carried out? Assuming these technical problems could be solved, DIN members concentrated on "Plan A," the lethal contamination of the water supplies of a number of large German cities. According to this scheme, the operation had to be carried out immediately after the liberation in order to target the German population without harming the occupation forces.

Preparing to Implement Plan A

Concrete preparations for implementing Plan A began in Tarvisio, Italy, a safe-haven reached by the sixty members of the newly created DIN organization in the summer of 1945.[35] Beginning in mid-July, members of DIN met with soldiers of the Jewish Brigade, a unit of Zionist volunteers from Palestine serving in the British army. During their passionate but painful meetings in Tarvisio, the anti-Nazi partisans and the Zionist volunteers found that they shared, at least in part, the idea of revenge. DIN members were thrilled to discover that some members of the Jewish Brigade did not need encouragement to start hunting down Nazi criminals. Soon after their arrival in Italy, groups of Brigade soldiers began executing Nazi officials without trial in raids carried out at night under heavy secrecy.[36] Brigade members also gave the DIN plotters official British uniforms, soldiers' paybooks, and vehicles so that they could move freely around Europe disguised as British soldiers.

In addition to Plan A, Kovner devised a smaller fallback operation called Plan B, which was directed specifically at Nazi war criminals. The idea came from Jeshajahu Weinberg, a soldier in the Jewish Brigade and the head of the team clandestinely established to coordinate the Brigade's

35. DIN members arrived in Italy as leading activists in the Brigade of Jewish Survivors from Eastern Europe, which sought to help Holocaust survivors to leave war-ravaged Europe and sail to Palestine. Unlike other activists in the Brigade, DIN members were determined to remain in Germany until the completion of their revenge mission. Bar Zohar, *The Avengers*, pp. 43–45; authors' interview with Weinberg, Tel Aviv, September 14, 1998.

36. The number of Nazis or alleged Nazis executed is uncertain, with figures ranging from 50 to 300. On the revenge teams of the Jewish Brigade, see Mordechai Naor, *Laskov* (Jerusalem: Israel Defense Ministry and Keter, 1988, in Hebrew), chap. 11; Bar Zohar, *The Avengers*, pp. 22–39; Sarid, "The 'Revenge' Organization," footnote 11, p. 103; and authors' interview with Weinberg, Tel Aviv, September 18, 1998.

anti-Nazi revenge. Weinberg proposed to Kovner that the group should target several large prisoner-of-war camps holding former SS and Gestapo soldiers, as well as Nazi underground organizations that had survived the German defeat.[37]

Weinberg later testified that Kovner had told him about another, "rather fantastic, bizarre" poisoning plan the group had developed. The plan consisted of rendering a large number of Germans sexually impotent by means of poisonous envelopes mass-mailed throughout Germany. This action was to constitute revenge for the mass castration and sterilization of Jews by Nazi doctors in the concentration camps as part of their "medical experiments."[38] The chemist expected to produce the unique toxin died mysteriously, however, leaving the plan on the shelf.

While determined to preserve their independence, DIN leaders were aware of the need for logistical assistance, intelligence, and communications. Members of the Jewish Brigade provided informal support but had no official authority to support Plan A.[39] It was therefore decided that Kovner would travel to Palestine to sell the revenge idea to the *Yishuv* (the Zionist political leadership) and the *Haganah* (the major Jewish militia in Palestine), obtain material support, and bring back enough poison to kill hundreds of thousands, perhaps millions, of Germans. In mid-August 1945, Eliyahu Cohen, a member of the Jewish Brigade and a senior commander in the *Haganah*, was assigned to escort Kovner to Palestine.[40]

Meanwhile, DIN members decided to use the time until Kovner's return to identify several major German cities as revenge targets and to begin preparations for poisoning their water systems. The organization's headquarters was established in Paris and a system of couriers set up to ensure the control and coordination of field operations in Germany. Reichman temporarily replaced Kovner as DIN's commander and Bezalel

---

37. Weinberg, "On Anti-Nazi Revenge Activities"; authors' interviews with Weinberg, Tel Aviv, September 14 and 18, 1998.

38. Jeshajahu Weinberg, "On Anti-Nazi Revenge Activities of the Jewish Brigade after World War II" (unpublished mimeograph, 1989); authors' interview with Weinberg, Tel Aviv, September 9, 1998. Although the witness is known to the authors as a reliable person and his testimony is written with great modesty, it is important to note that this particular story has not been corroborated by any other source.

39. Zionist political circles were skeptical about all revenge operations. According to Ambassador Gideon Raphael, who served as the coordinating officer between the Jewish Agency and the British Army, David Ben Gurion was vehemently opposed to the revenge plan. Authors' telephone interview with Raphael, September 28, 1998.

40. Sarid, "The 'Revenge' Organization," pp. 55–57.

Kek was named deputy commander. Two women, Vitka Kempner and Dorka Reichman (Pasha's wife), became the organization's couriers. Using fake documents, they traveled between Paris and Germany and within Germany.[41]

In addition to coordinating the revenge operations, DIN's Paris headquarters had to raise money for the operational teams and to maintain contact with supporting organizations and individuals, including the Jewish Brigade, individual Jews serving in the Allied forces, former members of the French Resistance, former anti-Nazi partisans, and envoys of Zionist organizations active in Europe. Although DIN leaders were eager to gain official approval for their operations, they were determined to rely on government aid as little as possible. Aware that the political thinking of *Yishuv* leaders in Palestine left little room for emotional issues such as revenge, DIN was especially wary of financial dependence on the Zionist establishment.

In addition to the operational units in Germany, a number of DIN activists remained in Italy and at the group's Paris headquarters. Most of them were involved in the *Bricha*, a rescue operation that involved transporting Jewish refugees from displaced-person camps in Europe to Palestine.[42] Maintaining close contacts with DIN headquarters in Paris, they helped to generate funds for the operational teams in Germany. Several of them moved across Europe, selling and buying money on the black market. The large gap between the value of the British and American currencies in several countries enabled them to practice arbitrage successfully.[43] One organizational principle was strictly adhered to: DIN members involved in financing the organization were not allowed to participate in the risky revenge operations.[44]

According to Plan A, the operational teams were to infiltrate group members as local workers, poison urban water supplies, and escape.[45] Detailed execution of the plan would require ingenuity, courage, and persistence. The members of each team had to disguise themselves as displaced war refugees on their way to the United States or Canada, establish nonsuspicious identities, and remain as unnoticed as possible. Four German cities were selected as targets—Munich, Hamburg, Frank-

---

41. Ibid., p. 75.

42. On the *Bricha*, see Yehuda Bauer, *Flight and Rescue* (New York: Atheneum, 1970).

43. Authors' interview with Joseph (Yulek) Harmatz, Washington, D.C., June 21, 1998.

44. Sarid, "The 'Revenge' Organization," pp. 75–77.

45. Ibid., pp. 50–52; Harmatz, *From the Wings*, pp. 130–132.

furt, and Nuremberg—along with SS and Gestapo prisoner-of-war (POW) camps near Dachau and Buchenwald.

The deployment of DIN operational teams in Germany began in September 1945. During Kovner's months in Palestine, the teams settled in their assigned German cities and carefully studied the water-supply systems. The Munich group included five men and one woman, all experienced partisans who had fought the Nazis in Vilnius, Rodniki, Vohlin, and Krakow. Their task was to manage logistics and transportation for all other units in Germany. After the arrival of the poison, they would deliver it to the various operational locations. In Hamburg, where a major action was to take place, a team of five members was stationed under the command of Hasia Warshawchic, a female partisan from the Rodniki forest. A team of three DIN members went to Berlin to prepare for a potential operation there, but after failing to identify accessible targets they moved to Frankfurt to prepare a strike on that city. Three DIN members were sent to Dachau, where 30,000 former SS soldiers were imprisoned, including a "privileged" unit of some 100 former Wehrmacht generals. Another small DIN team planned a strike on an SS prison camp in Buchenwald.

The Nuremberg team, numbering eight fighters, was particularly large because DIN strategists considered the city, one of the birthplaces of the Nazi Party, to be of high operational value. The team arrived in Nuremberg in the fall of 1945 and settled in the nearby town of Furth. Posing as Polish refugees on their way to the United States and Canada, they were soon free to concentrate on their operation. A Germanic-looking Jew named Willeck who had an engineering degree and spoke perfect German managed to get a position at the city's water-filtration center. Within a few weeks, he obtained detailed information about the water-supply system, including the gauges of various pipes, the connections and alternative supply systems, and precisely how the water supply to the American residential areas could be cut off to avoid inflicting casualties among non-Germans.[46]

By December 1945, all of the teams were ready to strike. Living a miserable life in their hated target cities, often without adequate food or housing, DIN members dreamed of revenge. Ironically, the Nuremberg team was preparing the poisoning scheme at the time that senior Nazi officials were being tried before the War Crimes Tribunal. DIN's response to the Nuremberg trials was highly negative. According to Yulek Harmatz, the team leader, the group failed to understand why dealing with

---

46. Harmatz, *From the Wings*, pp. 131–132.

arch-Nazis required complicated legal procedures. There was only one solution—to execute them all immediately. During the long months of waiting for Kovner's return from Palestine, the Nuremberg team became so frustrated with the Nazi trials that they considered breaking into the courtroom and shooting the defendants in the dock at point-blank range. This operation was not carried out because Jewish officers serving in the U.S. Army, approached about the plan, refused to cooperate.[47]

The Transition to Plan B

A highpoint of Kovner's mission in Palestine was his meeting with Chaim Weizmann, the President of the World Zionist Organization, a chemist of high repute, and the director of the Ziv Institute—later renamed the Weizmann Institute of Science in his honor. Kovner chose not to share Plan A with the aging leader but presented his idea for poisoning a large number of Nazi war criminals (Plan B). In contrast to the strongly negative attitude toward revenge actions expressed by most of the *Yishuv* leaders and by David Ben Gurion, then the leading Jewish political figure in Palestine, Weizmann was highly receptive. He instructed the Ziv Institute's director, Professor Ernst David Bergman, to provide Kovner with the desired poison. The young scientist instructed by Bergman to prepare the poison was Ephraim Katchalsky (later Katzir), who in 1972 became the fourth President of Israel. Katchalsky obtained 50 kilos (110 pounds) of arsenic, which were packed in canisters used to store powdered milk.[48] Weizmann's support was further expressed in a personal letter he sent to Ernst Mohler, a leading Jewish industrialist in Haifa, asking him to make a major financial contribution to DIN.[49]

---

47. Authors' interview with Harmatz, Washington, D.C., June 21, 1998.

48. Israel Television Channel One documentary, *The Avengers*, broadcast on February 9, 1999.

49. The first description of the Weizmann-Kovner meeting, which has been questioned by a number of historians, appeared in 1973 in Elkins, *Forged in Fury*, pp. 218–220. It was later repeated by Segev, *The Seventh Million*, p. 143. The most documented version is by Sarid, "The 'Revenge' Organization," pp. 60–61. Nevertheless, the Weizmann story was never confirmed by anyone other than Kovner. Living DIN members report that some of them heard it from Kovner as early as 1946 but kept it secret for many years. Given Weizmann's international prominence (he served as president of Israel during 1948–1952), his support for Plan B is puzzling. Still, one can assume that Kovner, a powerful speaker and poet, told Weizmann in chilling detail about his horrific experiences in the Vilna ghetto. According to Kovner, the aging

Several months later, Kovner sailed back to France aboard a British ship, disguised as a British soldier on his way from Palestine to his unit in Europe. He was escorted by several soldiers in the Jewish Brigade who were actually returning to their units in Europe. Thanks to Weizmann's efforts, he had in his possession a large sum of money in gold coins and the canisters of arsenic, which he carried with him on board ship in a large knapsack.[50]

In mid-December 1945, shortly before the ship arrived in Toulon in southern France, the British suddenly arrested Kovner. He had time to warn his escorts about the knapsack hidden in his cabin, which they dumped overboard. Following his arrest, Kovner was taken to Alexandria, Egypt, for additional questioning. This ordeal was followed by months of imprisonment, first in Egypt and later in Jerusalem.[51]

Because of Kovner's arrest and the loss of the arsenic he had obtained in Palestine, DIN members were told that it would be necessary to switch from Plan A to Plan B, which involved poisoning the food of Nazi inmates in POW camps. Long before his arrest, however, Kovner had already

---

leader became emotional and told Kovner that if he were a young man, he would join DIN. Among Jewish leaders, however, Weizmann was the exception. The involvement of Katchalsky (who later changed his name to Katzir) was first exposed by the Israel radio program *The Avengers* on February 9, 1999. Katzir refused to be interviewed but told the reporters, "it was agreed never to talk about this." On February 25, in a short telephone interview with Sprinzak, Katzir confirmed the story, as well as his involvement.

50. Some analysts have speculated that Bergman supplied Kovner with a biological rather than a chemical agent. But according to Professor Emeritus Alex Keinan, who was involved in Israel's early research on biological weapons and knew Professor Bergman well, Bergman was an organic chemist who in 1946 had no interest in or access to biological agents. Indeed, no Jew in Palestine at that time had any knowledge of or interest in biological weapons. Although Keinan is skeptical about the entire Weizmann story, he is certain that if it *is* true, the substance in question could only have been a chemical poison. Sprinzak interview with Keinan, Jerusalem, January 25, 1999.

51. Sarid, "The 'Revenge' Organization," pp. 62–64. The British did not ask Kovner about DIN nor did they ever give him the reason for his arrest. Members of DIN suspected for years that the *Haganah*, worried about damaging political fallout from the execution of Plan A, had betrayed him to the British. Today, however, it is clear that the reason for Kovner's arrest had nothing to do either with DIN's revenge plans in Germany or the *Haganah*'s fear of the possible consequences. Instead, Kovner was detained because the British suspected that he was a member of *Lehi*, a right-wing anti-British underground movement, and was on his way to Europe to conduct terrorist operations against British installations. This explanation was confirmed to Sprinzak in a conversation with Professor Yoav Gelber, Military Historian of the *Haganah*, on September 10, 1998.

begun leaning toward Plan B.[52] The reservations expressed by several political and military leaders in Palestine about indiscriminate attacks on the German population had caused him to reconsider.[53] As early as August 28, 1945, Kovner had reported to Reichman in Paris about the serious problems with Plan A.[54]

DIN activists greeted the decision to abandon Plan A with consternation. Haunted by their Holocaust memories and their survival guilt, they felt that they had to carry out a large-scale revenge action against the German people before they could return to normalcy. As a result, the adoption of Plan B threatened to destroy the organization from within. The only factor that kept DIN from collapsing was the leaders' solemn commitment to return to Plan A in the foreseeable future. To prepare for eventual implementation of the plan, a number of deactivated DIN fighters agreed to move to displaced-person camps in Europe and wait for the order to strike. Only two action teams remained operational, those assigned to Nuremberg and Dachau, since both cities had large American POW camps nearby.[55]

DIN's next operational challenge was to find a supply of poison in Europe. The group made contacts with former Jewish partisans, black marketeers, and even underworld criminals, but the fear of being discovered prematurely deterred Reichman from consummating any potential deal. Because DIN members had learned during the war to trust only each other, they sought a Jewish source who would never betray the cause. Yitzhak Ratner, a chemical engineer, fitted this description. A former partisan in the Vilna ghetto and a close acquaintance of Kovner, he was then working in Italy for the *Bricha*.

Though not an official DIN member, Ratner immediately agreed to help. Without informing his superiors, who were suspicious of the revenge plans, he moved to Paris and set up a makeshift laboratory at DIN headquarters to select and prepare the poison. DIN needed an odorless, tasteless poison with delayed effects that would give the perpetrators sufficient time to escape. After testing and rejecting several toxic compounds, Ratner selected an arsenic mixture that met the requirements. Friends in the leather industry who worked with arsenic provided him

---

52. Sarid, "The 'Revenge' Organization," pp. 62–63, 77–81.

53. Weinberg was, according to his own testimony, the person who persuaded Kovner to abandon Plan A in favor of Plan B, poisoning inmates of Nazi prisoner-of-war camps. Interviews with Weinberg on September 14 and September 18, 1998.

54. Sarid, "The 'Revenge' Organization," p. 59.

55. Ibid., p. 78.

with more than 18 kilos (40 pounds) of the deadly substance in ten packages.[56] The poison was then smuggled into Germany.[57]

After weeks of surveillance and deliberation, the Nuremberg team decided to target an American POW camp called Stalag 13, where 15,000 former SS storm troopers were imprisoned. Since the team members wanted to ensure that no non-Germans would be killed in the attack, they decided to poison the black rye bread consumed almost exclusively by the German inmates. The American guards received a special delivery of white bread.

The operational challenges facing the Nuremberg team were to penetrate the camp bakery, smuggle a large amount of poison into the camp, and apply it to thousands of loaves of black bread without being detected. Two team members managed to get hired by Stalag 13, one as a driver and one as a storehouse worker; others found work as clerks in the compound, and one woman was employed in the camp's communication center.[58] Leibke Distal, a young man from Vilnius who had miraculously survived several Nazi death camps in Estonia and Germany, was the team's point man inside the camp bakery. For nearly five months he studied its operations and befriended the bakery's storeroom manager. In exchange for a few bottles of wine, he gained unlimited access to the storeroom.[59]

Meanwhile, the three-member DIN team targeting the large American POW camp at Dachau was also making preparations for an attack, including penetration of the camp bakery. On April 11, 1946, however, just two days before the date of the planned strike, the Dachau team was ordered to abort its operation and evacuate the area immediately. DIN courier Lena Zatz-Hamel transmitted the bad news without further explanation. Pasha Reichman, who ordered the evacuation, later explained that an American Jewish officer in charge of Dachau's intelligence unit had warned of the impending arrest of two members of the team. In response, Reichman decided to terminate the Dachau operation, fearing that exposure of the plot would result in heightened security measures at all POW camps across Germany. He was determined to make sure that at least one successful poisoning, at the Nuremberg camp, would finally take place.[60]

---

56. Ibid., pp. 81–82.

57. Ibid., p. 81.

58. Harmatz, *From the Wings,* pp. 138–141.

59. Sarid, "The 'Revenge' Organization," pp. 83–84.

60. Ibid., pp. 86–87.

The Attack on Stalag 13

Although the Nuremberg team's initial plan had been to inject the poison into the bread loaves at Stalag 13, testing revealed that the poison did not spread evenly and the plotters feared that large amounts would be wasted. Accordingly, they decided to smear the poison on the bottom of the loaves by preparing a mixture of arsenic, glue, and additional ingredients. Team members would apply the poison with special brushes and wear protective glasses and gloves.[61]

Six members of the Nuremberg team had access to the bakery storeroom at Stalag 13. Because food thefts were common, the U.S. Army maintained tight security around the camp bakery, including bright lights, guards, and watchdogs. Over a period of days, team members smuggled into the storeroom several bottles filled with the arsenic-containing mixture, which they concealed under the floorboards. In the event of discovery of the team by the German police, the plotters were prepared to escape or to carry out a shoot-to-kill rescue operation.

The poisoning operation at Stalag 13 took place late in the night of Saturday, April 13, 1946, although unexpected obstacles caused it to be scaled down. A bakers' strike led to an early shutdown of the camp bakery, preventing the entire DIN team from entering the storeroom on time. Only three members who had been smuggled inside earlier were left to carry out the mission. As a result, they had time to poison only between 2,500 and 3,000 loaves, rather than the 14,000 originally planned.[62] Immediately after the operation, the members of the Nuremberg team fled to Czechoslovakia and then proceeded through Italy to southern France. Joining other DIN members, they boarded a ship to Palestine, where they settled and joined the struggle for an independent Jewish homeland.

The numbers of dead and injured caused by the poisonings at Stalag 13 are difficult to establish.[63] Although the U.S. Occupation Forces in Germany investigated the incident, American officials refused to provide specific details because of concern about inciting panic in an unstable and

---

61. Harmatz, *From the Wings,* pp. 139–140.

62. Ibid. This information is also based on the authors' interview with Harmatz, Washington, D.C., June 21, 1998.

63. A search of the U.S. National Archives in College Park, Maryland, for information on the Stalag 13 incident yielded few results. Also unsuccessful were attempts at the U.S. Military Archives in Harrisburg, Pennsylvania, to find records from the Nuremberg hospitals that treated the poisoning victims, or from Colonel Samuel T. Williams, the commanding officer of the 26th Infantry Regiment responsible for Stalag 13. Although two brief references to the Stalag 13 poisoning were found, there was no

volatile situation. Press accounts of the incident appeared in slightly different versions in German and French newspapers and in two short news items published in *The New York Times* on April 20 and 23, 1946, with no follow-up. On April 24, the Munich newspaper *Süddeutsche Zeitung* reported that "tests taken immediately following the event showed that the bread contained the poison arsenic. Four bottles filled with poison and two empty ones were found in the bakery. Out of 15 thousand inmates, 2,283 fell ill from the poisoning, with 207 hospitalized. According to the hospital's records, there were no fatalities."[64]

Other than press reports, the only sources of casualty information are accounts by DIN members recorded forty or more years after the event. Bar Zohar writes, for example, "Members of the group believe that about 4,300 inmates became sick as a result of the poisoning. Out of the 1,000 hospitalized in the following days and weeks, 700 to 800 were paralyzed or died."[65] Had the Nuremberg team been able to verify the numbers of sick and dead, these accounts might have a measure of credibility, but DIN members left the area immediately after the attack, never to return. What they learned came from rumors in Prague as well as German and Czech newspaper stories. They may also have inflated the numbers of dead and injured for their own gratification.

The Breakup of DIN

Although the Nuremberg team was elated by the news of casualties at Stalag 13 and decided to emigrate to Palestine, most other DIN activists were not satisfied with this outcome. The decision to abandon the organization's solemn commitment to take large-scale revenge frustrated and troubled them. This second group, including Pasha Reichman and Bezalel Kek, moved from Germany to France and finally reached Toulouse. After reading press accounts of the Stalag 13 poisonings, they decided to remain in Toulouse for a few more weeks before moving on to Marseilles, the departure port for Palestine. In Marseilles, they received a long letter from Kovner describing his ordeal in prison and his profound depression on learning of DIN's failure to implement large-scale revenge, which he called "the act that was supposed to build the bridge for a new day and

---

discussion of casualties. It therefore appears that the relevant records have been lost. Memo, H. TUSA, Gen & Spect Staff Rpts, Headquarters, Third U.S. Army, APO 403; April 27, 1946; G-2 Section; National Archives, Box 12 8/79/28/1, No. 833533.

64. Sarid, "The 'Revenge' Organization," pp. 84–86.

65. Bar Zohar, *The Avengers*, p. 51.

life. My faith betrayed me: instead of a bridge—a dark void outside and inside. . . ."[66]

At first, Kovner wrote, he had intended to commit suicide. But out of the depths of his depression had come a new sense of meaning and defiance. "The well-fed and content can afford to sink into history, to despair," he wrote. "We cannot. . . . Our utmost obligation is to be strong. Those who went to the grave knew that one must be strong even to die, and one certainly has to be strong to begin a new life." To his friends, whose agony Kovner fully understood, he wrote that the significance of their revenge could not be measured solely by the number of Germans killed. "It is neither the numbers nor the consequences that determine the meaning of the operation, but the mental readiness to accomplish one's dream and idea."[67]

Kovner's letter concluded with a practical suggestion. DIN members should emigrate to Palestine, "breathe the air of the land [of Israel] and plant the first seeds in its soil," regroup and recuperate. Kovner understood that most members of the organization would not be satisfied until they achieved their full revenge, but he suggested a temporary hiatus. He also recommended that, at least in the beginning, they should collectively join kibbutzim and act in concert.[68]

Kovner's letter to his comrades confirming the indefinite postponement of Plan A did not put an end to their emotional turmoil. A number of DIN members were furious with their leader and seriously considered a split, but the group's poor living conditions in France and Reichman's persuasive powers prevented a breakup at that time. On June 24, 1946, all members of DIN boarded the ship *Biriya* bound for Palestine. After a number of adventures at sea and a short detention by the British, the entire group reached Kibbutz Ein Hahoresh, Kovner's new home in Palestine. DIN members were allocated a special quarter in the kibbutz. They received a warm welcome from members of the *Haganah* and leading officials of the Labor movement, and they traveled throughout the country. For the first time in their lives, they lived within a Jewish majority and could experience the struggle to establish a Jewish state from a position of strength.[69]

The quest for vengeance refused to disappear, however. Six months after their arrival in Palestine, with no indication of a concrete plan to

---

66. Sarid, "The 'Revenge' Organization," pp. 89–92.

67. Ibid.

68. Ibid.

69. Ibid., p. 88.

return to Europe to complete DIN's sacred mission, several members of the group under Bolek Gwirtzman demanded a decision. "Do we continue or not? And if not, why not disband and let everybody go his own way?" These questions led to long nighttime discussion sessions filled with bitter debate and self-criticism. Kovner, the target of most of the hard questions, was vague. While hinting that something might be done in the future, he had no concrete answers. He did make clear, however, that Plan A was out because the situation on the ground had changed. Now that large numbers of foreign soldiers and officials had settled in German cities, acts of large-scale revenge that could have been carried out immediately after the war were no longer possible. Kovner's answer implied a transition to hunting down individual Nazi war criminals, but dissenting members of DIN who sought to punish the entire German people challenged this view.[70]

Between February and March 1947, nine months after their arrival in Palestine, a group of nine DIN members defied Kovner by leaving the kibbutz, determined to revive Plan A in Germany. They moved to Haifa, where Abba Hushi, a local Labor Party leader, helped them to settle and organize, and then returned to Europe at the beginning of 1948. Other DIN members did not officially break away from the group but left Kibbutz Ein Hahoresh and settled in various parts of Palestine.

The DIN members who returned to Europe were unsuccessful. Not only did they fail to carry out Plan A, but they faced serious financial and logistical problems. After the founding of the West German state on May 23, 1949, it became much more difficult to operate without organizational support, and the group's actions against individual Nazis were largely ineffective. In order to sustain themselves, DIN members became involved in risky criminal activities and many were arrested. Increasingly, their major challenge was to escape from German jails with the help of former members of the French Resistance.[71]

Between 1950 and 1952, most DIN members who had gone to Europe returned to Israel individually or in small groups. Their leader, Bolek Gwirtzman, explained in an interview, "If I had not done it, I could never have faced myself in the mirror. But I will not be specific because we failed. Our great natural revenge was not consummated and to this very day I am at pains about it."[72] In retrospect, the window of opportunity

---

70. Ibid., p. 92.

71. Ibid:, pp. 93–94.

72. Ibid., p. 94.

for large-scale revenge had closed, and any renewed operation was doomed to failure.

Conclusion

A retrospective examination of DIN suggests that between the winter of 1945 and the summer of 1946, all members of the organization were determined to disregard political considerations and to carry out a massive and indiscriminate act of catastrophic terrorism against the German population. It goes almost without saying, however, that DIN does not fit any known model of a terrorist organization. Sensitive, moral, and devoid of a political or religious agenda, DIN members acted against the background of the Holocaust—an unprecedented disaster for the Jewish people and perhaps a unique event in world history. Yet DIN should not be looked upon as an accident or an historical aberration. Instead, the organization exemplifies a special category of candidates for catastrophic terrorism: small radical organizations representing "heavily brutalized communities," or populations devastated by genocide, ethnic cleansing, or massive destruction. Such organizations may allow their sense of profound desperation, anger, humiliation, guilt, and burning sense of revenge to overwhelm their survival instinct and moral inhibitions, motivating them to carry out a "super-terrorist" attack.[73]

DIN members believed that the entire German people bore collective guilt for the Holocaust by having allowed Hitler to come to power and by remaining silent in the face of Nazi atrocities. This conviction made it possible for them to be concerned about sparing the lives of the occupation troops while being totally blind to German civilians as human beings. Such dehumanization appears essential for the conduct of terrorist acts. Even so, the group's decision to employ poison weapons in an act of catastrophic terrorism was not taken lightly. It involved lengthy deliberations and was taken against the better judgment and pressure of the *Haganah* and the majority of *Yishuv* leaders.

Most DIN members believed that their lives were meaningless without taking revenge and were ready to die in the course of its execution. The reluctance of many members to abandon Plan A, and the determination of Bolek Gwirtzman's group to return to Europe in 1948 even after

---

73. The authors define "super-terrorism" or "catastrophic terrorism" as the use of weapons of mass destruction (WMD) to bring about a major disaster with a death toll reaching tens to hundreds of thousands or more. Super-terrorism must be conceptually distinguished from the small-scale, tactical use of WMD to enhance conventional attacks.

a realistic possibility of executing the plan had passed, provide important clues to the collective psychology of organizations acting on behalf of heavily brutalized communities. In addition to an extreme hatred of the ruthless enemy, such individuals are haunted by a powerful sense of guilt and shame for having survived an inferno that consumed family, friends, and a large number of other victims.

To some extent, the mentality of DIN members resembles that of messianic and millenarian cultists who believe the world is so evil that it deserves to suffer a redeeming catastrophe of vast proportions. Nevertheless, a major difference between millenarian cults and groups representing heavily brutalized communities is the absence in the latter case of any hope for a glorious future. Whereas millenarian organizations have in mind an afterlife filled with perfection and bliss, heavily brutalized groups function in the context of the real world. In an extraordinary act of vengeance that presupposes their own certain death, they wish to send a message to the community of nations that never again will their people be exterminated without a response in kind.[74]

The major reason that most known terror organizations are unlikely to consider indiscriminate attacks is that they view terrorism as an instrument for accomplishing political goals. They wish to live on after the act of terrorism and to benefit from its execution. In contrast, most insurgent organizations that plan a catastrophic act of terror understand that this will be their last operation and that the authorities will respond with a harshness that will almost certainly destroy them. For these reasons, organizations acting on behalf of heavily brutalized communities—particularly those with little hope of recovery—are among the very few candidates likely to consider catastrophic terrorism. Facing inevitable destruction or believing that life has lost all meaning, they may convince themselves that their sole possibility for self-assertion is to strike back massively against their executioners.

Remarkably, despite their devastating experiences, DIN members were not devoid of hope or plans for the future. The group's first action after the German defeat in Poland was not to seek revenge against the Nazis but to help Jewish survivors emigrate from Europe to Palestine. DIN members also tried to form a unified political front representing survivors and Jews who had fought against the Nazis. Out of the ashes of the Holocaust, they aspired to forge a new type of political organiza-

---

74. The model of heavily brutalized communities is an abstraction that does not exist in a pure form. Thus, one should expect that actual brutalized communities will deviate from the model in certain ways and will have idiosyncratic features.

tion that was universalistic, non-sectarian, and ethical.[75] One can only speculate about what would have happened if DIN had been utterly devoid of hope for a political and personal future, and if this sense of hopelessness had been shared by a larger number of surviving Jews. In that case, the search for catastrophic revenge would not have ended with the poisonings at Stalag 13. The regret expressed by DIN members—even forty or fifty years later—over their failure to carry out Plan A suggests that they would probably have attempted a series of additional large-scale terrorist attacks.[76]

Although DIN failed to implement its scheme for mass killing, the group provides a useful prototype of "super-terrorist" thinking and planning. Organizations representing heavily brutalized communities do not exist under ordinary conditions but are ad hoc entities that emerge only after colossal human disasters. Given humanity's repeated experience with genocide, ethnic cleansing, and large-scale massacres, however, the possibility that another DIN may arise is not unrealistic.

---

75. Authors' interview with Harmatz, Washington, D.C., June 21, 1998.

76. According to Harmatz, Abba Kovner and most DIN members never regretted the Stalag 13 operation nor changed their minds about the desirability of Plan A. Although they admittedly did not have the inner strength to pursue it, they repeatedly said they would have loved to see it happen after the war. Authors' interview with Harmatz, Washington, D.C., June 21, 1998.

Chapter 3

The Weather Underground (1970)

John V. Parachini

For more than twenty years, academic papers on the terrorist use of chemical and biological weapons have referred to an attempt by the Weather Underground, a radical leftist Vietnam War–era group, to acquire incapacitating agents from the U.S. Army's biological warfare and defense research center at Fort Detrick, Maryland.[1] Scholars generally refer back to a single article written by *Washington Post* columnist Jack Anderson that appeared on November 20, 1970.[2] The following day, articles on the Anderson story written by the Associated Press (AP) and United Press International (UPI) ran in a number of papers around the country, as did a four-paragraph, unsigned column in *The Washington Evening Star.*[3] An analysis of these sources suggests that, contrary to the conventional wisdom, the Weather Underground probably did not seek to acquire or employ biological or chemical weapons.

---

1. Scholarly articles citing the case of the Weather Underground include Robert W. Mengel, "Terrorism and New Technologies of Destruction: An Overview of the Potential Risk," from "Disorders and Terrorism: Report of the Task Force on Disorders and Terrorism," 1976, reprinted in R. Augustus Norton and Martin H. Greenberg, eds., *Studies in Nuclear Terrorism* (Boston: G.K. Hall, 1979), p. 203; and Robert K. Mullen, "Mass Destruction and Terrorism," *Journal of International Affairs,* Vol. 32, No. 1 (1978), p. 88. For a comprehensive list of secondary sources that cite the alleged incident, see Ron Purver, *Chemical and Biological Terrorism: The Threat According to the Open Literature* (Ottawa: Canadian Security Intelligence Service, June 1995), p. 35.

2. Jack Anderson, "Weatherman Seeking BW Germs," *Washington Post,* November 20, 1970, p. D15.

3. Associated Press story reprinted in the *New York Times,* "Army Tells of Plot to Steal Bacteria From Ft. Detrick," November 21, 1970, p. 34; United Press International story reprinted in the *Los Angeles Times,* "Army Told of Plot to Poison Water Supply," November 21, 1970, p. 8; and "Germ Theft Plot Told to Army," *Washington Evening Star,* November 21, 1970, p. A20.

The Organization

During the late 1960s and 1970s, the Weather Underground established itself as the most notorious domestic terrorist organization in the United States by conducting a series of conventional bombings around the country. The group was a radical offshoot of Students for a Democratic Society (SDS), a national student movement mobilized by opposition to the Vietnam War. During the fractious SDS national convention in June 1969, the organization's militant "Action" faction issued a statement in which it declared its independence and charted a new and more radical course as the "Weathermen," whose leadership was called the "Weather Bureau."[4] The militants' statement concluded with the slogan "You Don't Need a Weatherman to Know Which Way the Wind Blows," conveying their view that the political situation in the United States required a new organization to wage a truly revolutionary struggle.[5]

During a "war council" held in Flint, Michigan, in December 1969, the Weathermen decided to close the national SDS office in Chicago and to continue their revolutionary struggle by means of cells that operated "underground, rather than as a protest movement demonstrating in the streets and debating in convention halls."[6] From October 8 to 12, 1970, members of the Weather Bureau held a series of violent anti-war actions in Chicago known as the "Days of Rage." In a December 1970 communiqué titled "New Morning," the leaders of the group renamed themselves the "Weather Underground."

The group viewed its struggle within the United States as complementing the international struggle against U.S. imperialism by helping to create a revolutionary consciousness. According to one of the Weather Underground's communiqués, "Winning state power in the U.S. will occur as a result of the military forces of the U.S. overextending themselves around the world and being defeated piecemeal; struggles within the U.S. will be a vital part of this process, but when the revolution triumphs in the U.S., it will have been made by the people of the whole

---

4. Reprinted in Federal Bureau of Investigation, *Foreign Influence—Weather Underground Organization*, CG 100–40903, Chicago, Illinois, August 20, 1976, pp. 7–15.

5. For a chronology of the Weather Underground, see Ron Jacobs, *The Way the Wind Blew: A History of the Weather Underground* (London: Verso, 1997). For Weather Underground statements, see *Outlaws of Amerika: Communiqués from the Weather Underground* (New York: The Liberated Guardian Collective, 1971).

6. "The Weather Underground," Report of the Subcommittee to Investigate the Administration of the Internal Security Act and Other Internal Security Laws, Committee of the Judiciary, U.S. Senate, January 1975, p. 23.

world."[7] Emulating rebel leader Che Guevara and guerilla warfare organizations such as the Tupamaros, Weather Underground members styled themselves as "urban guerillas" waging war in a modern industrialized society. They also established contact with international terrorist groups such as the Provisional Irish Republican Army, the Palestinian Al-Fatah, and the Puerto Rican FALN (Fuerzas Armadas de Liberación), and traveled to Vietnam and Cuba, arousing the ire of U.S. government authorities.

A profile of the Weather Underground prepared by the Federal Bureau of Investigation (FBI) summarized the group's ideology (based largely on its leaders' rhetoric) as consisting of two fundamental beliefs: "one, an unremitting commitment to armed struggle as the ultimate necessity to seize state power, and two, an unshakable faith that imperialism will only be defeated through a worldwide linking up of revolutionary process."[8] The FBI profile exaggerated the importance of doctrinaire Marxism-Leninism, which did not influence the organization's ideology as much as opposition to the Vietnam War and a general alienation from authority. The burgeoning counterculture, the backdrop of the Vietnam War, and the civil-rights movement factored significantly in the group's activities. Weather Underground members lived in a communal arrangement, pooling funds, sharing sex partners, praising the drug culture, and often breaking their family ties. The string of bombings carried out by the group was chiefly a symbolic response to dramatic political developments, including the escalation of the war in Vietnam, the U.S. invasion of Cambodia in April 1970, and the shooting of four Kent State University students by National Guardsmen on May 4, 1970.

Bombing Targets

Throughout the history of the Weather Underground's bombings, its targets tended to be symbols of the establishment power structure such as banks, courthouses, and federal buildings. An FBI informant stated in congressional hearings that the group sought to wage "strategic sabotage against the symbols of authority with the United States."[9] Decisions on bombing operations and targets were made through what one former

---

7. Federal Bureau of Investigation, *Foreign Influence*, p. 8.

8. Ibid., p. i.

9. U.S. Senate, Committee of the Judiciary, Subcommittee to Investigate the Administration of the Internal Security Act and Other Internal Security Laws, Hearings on "Terroristic Activity," September 23, 1974, p. 107.

Weather Underground leader described as "democratic centralism."[10] When a particular cell proposed a date and target for an attack, this suggestion would be passed to the central cell composed primarily of the organization's founders, who would evaluate the suggestion and assign various roles for other cells to perform. With each bombing, the organization gained valuable experience and became more effective at constructing explosive devices and delivering them undetected.

An FBI chronology of Weather Underground bombings and attempted bombings lists thirty-five incidents between October 1969 and September 1975.[11] The symbolic importance of the group's targets escalated over time. The first bombing occurred in October 1969, destroying a police statue in Chicago. In December of that year, the Weather Underground bombed police squad cars in revenge for the killings of Black Panther Party leaders Mark Clark and Fred Hampton. In February and March 1970, the group bombed several police stations around the country.

On March 6, 1970, three founders of the Weather Underground were killed in New York City when a bomb they were assembling in a Greenwich Village townhouse exploded accidentally. This bomb had been slated for use at a U.S. Army dance at Fort Dix, New Jersey, and would probably have claimed the first casualties of the bombing campaign. Ironically, the bombers themselves were the only victims. Their deaths were a serious setback to the group and demoralized the surviving members. According to former Weather Underground leaders, this event changed their thinking about killing people as an inevitable component of revolutionary activity and crystallized their disinclination to use violence to seize control of the state or to assassinate people within the state structure.[12]

In the aftermath of the townhouse explosion, the Weather Underground continued to call for radical political change, but their bombings became more an expression of radical solidarity than a means to overthrow the system. Moreover, all of the targets were symbolic and the timing of the blasts was deliberately chosen to avoid inflicting casualties. In late May 1970, the group attacked the National Guard Association building in Washington, D.C., and in mid-June 1970 they bombed the Hall of Justice in San Francisco, the headquarters of the New York City Police Department, and a Manhattan branch of the Bank of America. During a fall 1970 offensive, the Weather Underground bombed courthouses, Na-

---

10. Jacobs, *The Way the Wind Blew,* pp. 129–130.

11. Ibid., pp. 176–185.

12. Jeremy Peter Varon, "Shadowboxing the Apocalypse: New Left Violence in the United States and Germany," Ph.D. dissertation, Cornell University, 1998, pp. 179–184.

tional Guard facilities, and criminal detention centers. In March 1971, the group bombed the U.S. Capitol building and a year later the Pentagon, with a score of other attacks in between.[13] The Weather Underground disbanded as an organization in 1976, ending their impressive string of bombings.

The Alleged CBW Conspiracy

The Jack Anderson column published in November 1970 alleged that the Weather Underground had attempted to acquire biological and chemical weapons from Fort Detrick, Maryland, the headquarters of the U.S. Army's offensive and defensive biological warfare program.[14] This story was based on copies of three confidential reports by a U.S. Customs Bureau informant, who claimed to have met with a "drug pusher" purportedly making inquiries on behalf of "SDS Weathermen."[15] The confidential Customs Bureau reports were dated November 3, 11, and 13, 1970.

According to Anderson, the November 3 report stated that a drug pusher had approached the informant seeking "information on what kind of bacteria would be effective and would bypass the filtering system of a city and would incapacitate a population by infection for seven to ten days."[16] The informant also said that the drug pusher "was merely engaged in a discussion with some SDS Weathermen as to the possibility of this."[17] The drug pusher asked the informant to contact a homosexual Army officer the pusher knew at Fort Detrick and suggested the use of blackmail to force the officer in question to cooperate.[18] Anderson quoted what appeared to be instructions from the informant's Customs Bureau

---

13. Federal Bureau of Investigation, *Foreign Influence*, pp. 154–156.

14. Although President Richard Nixon formally renounced the U.S. offensive biological-weapons program in November 1969 and extended the ban to toxins in February 1970, the total destruction of antipersonnel BW agent stocks was not accomplished until between May 1971 and May 1972. Thus, during 1970, Fort Detrick retained seed stocks of several BW agents, including incapacitating agents such as Venezuelan equine encephalitis and Staphylococcal enterotoxin B. See William C. Patrick III, "A History of Biological and Toxin Warfare," in Kathleen C. Bailey, ed., *Director's Series on Proliferation*, No. 4 (Livermore, Calif.: Lawrence Livermore National Laboratory, UCRL-LR-114070-4, May 23, 1994), p. 19.

15. Anderson, "Weatherman Seeking BW Germs."

16. Ibid.

17. Ibid.

18. Ibid.

handler stating that "it is necessary that this information be passed to G-2, military intelligence of the Department of the Army, as even the thought of such attempted theft from Detrick is staggering to imagine."[19]

Drawing on the second Customs Bureau report, dated November 11, Anderson quoted the informant's claim that the pusher had approached him and "suggested that [the informant] obtain pictures and records that could be used to blackmail this [homosexual] officer into furnishing information as to the nature and character of a BW weapon that (1) is capable of felling by infection, but not fatal infection, the entire population of a large city for seven-to-ten days, and (2) would pass through the water filtering plant of a large city and go directly into the homes of the population."[20] The second report provided more detail on the blackmail plan and reiterated the intent of the attack to "incapacitate" a population for a limited period of time.

In the third Customs Bureau report quoted by Anderson, dated November 13, the pusher made a new request. According to the informant, the pusher "stated that in addition to the germ cultures previously described, that he also wanted a quantity of nerve gas similar to Mace"—but more powerful—"that will absolutely put out of consciousness a large number of people at one time, but one that will not be fatal."[21] Anderson concluded that the pusher was seeking, on behalf of the Weather Underground, nonlethal incapacitants of both a biological and chemical nature.

Three follow-up articles published on November 21, 1970, the day after the Anderson column appeared, reported the U.S. Army response to the column but gave no new details on the alleged Weather Underground conspiracy. The Army's response does, however, provide some insights into the nature and credibility of the threat.

The AP story reported that according to a U.S. Army spokesman, the Army had "been informed of an alleged plot by a group of revolutionaries to steal bacteriological weapons from Ft. Detrick, Md."[22] The spokesman added, however, that the Army "was unaware of anyone being approached at the installation by persons wanting to steal biological weapons."[23] In addition, the Army had "got its information from the U.S.

---

19. Ibid.

20. Ibid.

21. Ibid.

22. Associated Press, "Plot to Steal Germs Told," reprinted in the *Chicago Tribune*, November 21, 1970, p. 11.

23. Ibid.

Customs Bureau, which had been tipped off by an unnamed inform-ant."[24] The Customs Bureau, for its part, refused to comment on the veracity of the story.[25]

The UPI story reported that Army officials had denied "there was any homosexual officer at the fort who had access to biological cultures" and that "personnel whose duties require access to biological toxic mate-rials are subject to strict security investigations, and these investigations are periodically reviewed to make certain that no personnel are vulner-able to blackmail."[26] Army officials quoted in the article also stated that "materials at Fort Detrick, the Army's biological research center, would be insufficient to carry out such a plan."[27] In particular, they noted that "the fort has no stockpile of antipersonnel biological material capable of achieving the effects described" and that "there are only test-tube quan-tities of antipersonnel biological materials used in defense research."[28]

Is the Case Credible?

Several aspects of the Weather Underground case raise doubts about its validity as a genuine terrorist attempt to acquire biological and chemical weapons. The first weakness of the story stems from the source of the allegation. A drug pusher "engaged in a discussion with some SDS Weathermen" and reporting to a Customs Bureau informant hardly con-stitutes a direct link to the organization known in November 1970 as the Weather Underground. Bill Ayers, a founding member, noted that at the height of the organization's notoriety in the early 1970s, groups of young people all around the country identified themselves as members of the Weather Underground without necessarily having a connection to it.[29] Without more information about the identity of the drug pusher and the people with whom he claimed to have spoken, it is hard to know if the organization involved was in fact the Weather Underground, a cell out-side the direction of the group's main leaders, or merely a few individuals falsely claiming membership.

---

24. Ibid.

25. Ibid.

26. Ibid.

27. Ibid.

28. Ibid.

29. Author's telephone interview with William "Bill" Ayers, founding member and former National Educational Secretary of the Weather Underground Organization, June 17, 1997.

A second factor raising doubt about the accuracy of the Customs Bureau report is the fact that the informant used the name "SDS Weathermen" to identify the Weather Underground. As mentioned above, the acronym "SDS" stands for Students for a Democratic Society, which collapsed after its fractious national convention in June 1969. An FBI informant testified that the Weather Bureau went completely underground in February 1970.[30] Thus, by the fall of 1970, someone actually affiliated with the Weather Underground would probably not have referred to himself as a member of the "SDS Weathermen." Moreover, the reported request for a nonlethal chemical agent was a clear indication that the "drug pusher" and the alleged Weather Underground member did not understand that Fort Detrick was strictly a biological warfare and defense facility and had nothing to do with chemical weapons.

Third, a thwarted terrorist plot involving dangerous biological materials would presumably have been a memorable event. Yet William C. Patrick, the chief of product development at Fort Detrick at the time, said in an interview that he was unaware of any clandestine attempt to obtain biological materials.[31] Furthermore, the public affairs office at the U.S. Army Medical Research Institute of Infectious Diseases (USAMRIID) claimed to have never heard of the case.[32] The USAMRIID historian, who arrived at Fort Detrick in the mid-1970s, stated that he did not have any information on the case nor did he think "there might be something of value either here or at another location."[33] He added that he suspected that "such [information] is contained in top secret intelligence files—where, I don't know."[34] Cornelius G. McWright, a former FBI official who handled domestic terrorism cases at the time, indicated that he had never heard of the alleged plot, even though his duties at the Bureau covered precisely these types of cases.[35]

---

30. U.S. Senate, Committee on the Judiciary, Hearings on "Terroristic Activity," p. 99.

31. Author's telephone interview with William C. Patrick III, former senior scientist at Fort Detrick, June 9, 1998.

32. Author's telephone interview with Caree van der Linden, Public Affairs Officer, Fort Detrick, June 2, 1998.

33. Norm Covert, Command Historian, USAMRIID, personal communication with the author, April 22, 1998.

34. Ibid.

35. Comment made at the Monterey Institute of International Studies case study workshop, Washington, D.C., June 22, 1998.

Weather Underground Attitudes Toward Violence

Also raising doubts about the allegation are the Weather Underground's consistent pattern of confining their attacks to symbolic targets and their statements opposing nuclear arms. Although the group's violent activities escalated over time and their rhetorical targets occasionally included human "enemies," the self-inflicted casualties in the Greenwich Village townhouse accident appear to have halted any progression toward indiscriminate attacks. Indeed, many members of the group were proud that during the period of active operations, 1969 to 1976, none of their bombings had resulted in any deaths.[36] According to former Weather Underground leader David Gilbert,

It's not accidental that [in] over twenty or thirty [actions] no one got hurt. . . . There are some situations of revolutionary struggle where people do get hurt, but the point is that revolutionary morality has a very high standard. You don't want innocent bystanders hurt. You try to minimize casualties. It's not like reactionary violence, ruling class violence, that's napalm on villages. . . . It is against a population in general. It does use torture as a common instrument. It is fairly random. Revolutionary violence should be the opposite [and be] as strategic as possible in removing the oppressor.[37]

The Weather Underground was also strongly opposed to nuclear weapons. In an action plan included in *Prairie Fire,* a book-length treatise published in 1974, the Weather Underground emphasized the importance of opposing "nuclear war and [the] U.S. threat of nuclear war."[38] This consistent pattern of behavior raises serious doubts about the allegation that the group sought to acquire a biological or chemical weapon that could have harmed large numbers of people, if only temporarily.

One might counter that the Weather Underground's abhorrence of inflicting indiscriminate fatalities does not necessarily rule out the possibility that they sought a nonlethal incapacitant that would put large numbers of people to sleep long enough to create havoc, perhaps as a means to demonstrate their continued political salience after the Greenwich Village accident. The problem with this interpretation is that any attack that inflicted mass casualties—even nonfatal ones—was clearly inimical to the group's objective of inciting a revolution that would

---

36. Varon, "Shadowboxing the Apocalypse," p. 191.

37. Ibid., pp. 199.

38. Weather Underground, *Prairie Fire: The Politics of Revolutionary Anti-Imperialism* (Communications Co., 1974), p. 141.

benefit the oppressed peoples of the world. Such an indiscriminate attack would have been comparable to the "reactionary" violence against the Vietnamese people for which they castigated the U.S. government.

Finally, despite the Weather Underground's ability to produce and deliver conventional bombs against highly symbolic targets, there is no evidence that the group had any technical know-how relevant to chemical or biological weapons. Indeed, the townhouse explosion demonstrated that their skills in handling conventional explosives were less than perfect.

In an interview, Ayers claimed never to have heard of the Jack Anderson article or the Weather Underground's alleged attempt to acquire a biological weapon, and he was highly skeptical of the story.[39] Using a biological weapon against people, he insisted, would have been "completely counter to anything we'd ever do."[40] He speculated that the Anderson article could have been "some weird disinformation bit from somewhere to discredit us. . . . Who knows?"[41]

Ayers did acknowledge that like many other anti-war and revolutionary youth organizations of the time, the Weather Underground made many outrageous statements that were not intended to be taken literally. For example, an FBI informant reported that Bernardine Dohrn, a founding member, suggested that young people should emulate Charles Manson and "bring the war home, off your parents."[42] In response to questions about the alleged acquisition of a biological weapon, Ayers (who later married Dohrn) said that "someone may have said something like that," although no one ever seriously contemplated carrying it out.[43] With so much outrageous talk in the air, perhaps the drug pusher had passed on to the Customs Bureau informant some wild statement he had overheard.

Some Loose Ends

Despite the serious questions about the validity of the Weather Underground allegation, a few loose ends remain. A declassified, formerly top-secret FBI chronology of Weather Underground bombings and at-

---

39. Author's telephone interview with Ayers, June 17, 1997.

40. Ibid.

41. Ayers, personal communication with the author, May 28, 1998.

42. U.S. Senate, Committee on the Judiciary, Hearings on "Terroristic Activity," p. 131.

43. Author's telephone interview with Ayers.

tempted bombings raises some new questions about the case.[44] Of the thirty-one dates in the chronology from October 1969 until September 1975, the entry for November 21, 1970, is the only date for which the FBI redacted (blacked out) all of the entries to protect information that remains classified. Yet no source on the Weather Underground reports any organizational activity of note on that date. November 21, 1970, was the day news stories appeared reporting the Army's reaction to the Jack Anderson column. If the alleged attempt to acquire biological and chemical agents from Fort Detrick were true, however, one would expect that the incident would have been mentioned in the FBI chronology prior to that date. Moreover, several Freedom of Information Act requests filed with the Department of the Army, the U.S. Customs Service, and the Department of Justice failed to turn up any documents pertaining to the original allegations reported by Jack Anderson.

Conclusion

The inconsistencies in the Jack Anderson story, the dubious credibility of the source, the statements of former Weather Underground leaders, and the fact that the organization's conventional bombing campaign was limited to symbolic targets all call into question the allegation that the Weather Underground sought to acquire biological or chemical weapons. The few references that remain classified, and the possibility of some people falsely claiming to be group members as the actual source of the report, prevent one from drawing a definitive conclusion. Unless new evidence emerges, however, terrorism scholars should drop the case of the Weather Underground as an early example of terrorist groups seeking weapons of mass destruction.

---

44. Federal Bureau of Investigation, *Foreign Influence*, p. iii.

Chapter 4

R.I.S.E. (1972)

W. Seth Carus

On January 17, 1972, the Chicago Police arrested two college students, Allen Charles Schwandner, 19, and Stephen J. Pera, 18. According to city officials, they belonged to a terrorist organization called R.I.S.E. and were on the verge of releasing typhoid bacteria into the Chicago water supply system as part of a plot to commit mass murder.[1] This account is the first effort to tell the story of R.I.S.E. from primary sources.[2] Despite significant

The views expressed in this chapter are those of the author and do not necessarily reflect the official policy or position of the Department of Defense or the U.S. government. The study was supported by the Center for Counterproliferation Research of the National Defense University and the Monterey Institute of International Studies. In addition, the author would like to acknowledge the Office of Richard A. Devine, State's Attorney of Cook County, Illinois. Without the assistance of Gerald E. Nora and Alan Goldenberg it would have been impossible to research this case properly, and the author is grateful for their hospitality and assistance.

1. The story received extensive newspaper coverage at the time. See Ronald Koziol, "Tighten Water Plant Guard After Poison Scare Arrests," *Chicago Tribune*, January 19, 1972, p. 1; Gene Bludeau, "Two in Chicago Accused of Plot to Poison Water," *Washington Post*, January 19, 1972, p. A3; and Andrew H. Malcolm, "2 Youths Charged With Plot to Poison Water of Chicago," *New York Times*, January 19, 1972, p. 18. The incident is often mentioned in the academic literature on biological terrorism. A review of such accounts, however, indicates that many are inaccurate and none appears to have been based on original research. Some analysts claim incorrectly that a group known as the "Order of the Rising Sun" was responsible for the plot and that those responsible held neo-Nazi views. Although most accounts accurately note that the organization had cultures of typhoid bacteria, none reports that the group possessed at least three additional agents. Finally, none of the existing accounts accurately describe the alternative dissemination means that the perpetrators intended to employ. A summary of previously published accounts appears in Ron Purver, *Chemical and Biological Terrorism: The Threat According to the Open Literature* (Ottawa: Canadian Security Intelligence Service, June 1995), p. 37.

2. The most important single source for this case study was the transcript of the preliminary hearing held in early February 1972 before the Circuit Court of Cook

gaps in the available information, it is possible to piece together a rough chronology of Schwandner and Pera's actions in the months leading up to their arrest.[3]

Origins of R.I.S.E.

Born in late 1952, Allen Schwandner was an adopted child who apparently never got along well with his adoptive parents. As a youth, he spent time in a psychiatric hospital and was sentenced to reform schools. He was paroled on April 8, 1971, and moved into a basement apartment at 6501 North Fairfield Street in Chicago that would later become the focal point of R.I.S.E. activities.[4] Schwandner, known to his friends as "Lonnie," often spelled his name without the second "n" (Schwander). He wore long hair and dressed in hippie-style clothing, was extremely suspicious of "straights," and apparently used marijuana and possibly amphetamines.[5]

Stephen Pera lived at his parents' house in Evanston, Illinois, where his father was a school principal. Pera was considered a genius by many who came into contact with him.[6] (Schwandner once claimed that Pera

---

County to justify the request for an indictment against the two defendants. That material was supplemented by additional records obtained from the Cook County State's Attorney's Office and the Cook County Court Clerk. Unless otherwise noted, all documents cited in this account came from the files of the Office of Richard A. Devine, State's Attorney of Cook County, Illinois. The most important single document is the transcript of the preliminary hearing held in early February 1972. During that hearing, four people recruited by Schwandner testified about R.I.S.E. In addition, the author interviewed Bankruptcy Judge Jack Schmetterer, who was First Assistant State's Attorney in 1972; Thomas Burnham, an Assistant State's Attorney at the time; and Joseph G. DiLeonardi, currently U.S. Marshall for the Northern District of Illinois, who was the lead Chicago Police investigator on the case. This account also draws on reports in the Chicago press at the time of the incident and on recent interviews with some of those responsible for investigating and prosecuting the case.

3. At the time of their arrest, Schwandner and Pera denied the allegations against them and investigators were unable to learn about aspects of the case known only to the two key perpetrators. Some of those details might be available from alternative sources, but the author did not interview any of the surviving participants. In addition, no effort was made to obtain material concerning the case that might be in the files of the Federal Bureau of Investigation, the U.S. Centers for Disease Control and Prevention, or the Illinois Department of Public Health.

4. This background information on Schwandner comes from the Chicago Police Department, Background Report, January 21, 1972.

5. Robert Unger, "Poison Plot Story Stuns Friends of Two Suspects," *Chicago Tribune*, January 19, 1972.

6. Ibid.

had an IQ of 193.) Since Pera provided all the scientific expertise available to R.I.S.E., his activities are critical to an understanding of the group's potential for using biological agents. Pera had only limited formal education in microbiology and was largely self-taught. He took at least one biology course at Mayfair College, a community college in Chicago, during the spring 1971 semester but never finished the class, apparently because he found it insufficiently challenging.[7] Still, he had sufficient promise to be selected in July 1971 for a work-study program in microbiology sponsored by the International Foundation for Microbiology. This program gave students an opportunity to earn money during the summer while taking college-preparatory courses in chemistry, biology, and other sciences. Pera reportedly did not get along with the other students, however, and was asked to leave.[8]

Later that summer, Pera met with Dr. Charles Kallick, the Section Chief for Ambulatory Pediatrics at Presbyterian-St. Luke's Hospital in Chicago, and offered to work without pay on a research project in order to learn more about microbiology. Kallick agreed to Pera's request, and in August, Pera began working with a team that was exploring the possible involvement of a specific microorganism in the cause of the autoimmune disease lupus erythematosus.[9] Pera was responsible for making smears of blood taken from patients suffering from lupus, staining the slides, and examining them under a microscope to look for the microorganism in question.[10] Although the laboratory technicians at Presbyterian-St. Luke's Hospital thought Pera was extremely gifted, he was still a novice at microbiological techniques.[11]

The available evidence suggests that Schwandner and Pera met in September 1971 after Schwandner enrolled at Mayfair College.[12] At that

---

7. Edmund J. Rooney and Dennis Sodomka, "2 Arrested in Threat to Water Here," *Daily News* (Chicago), January 19, 1972 (red flash edition), p. 16. This article claims that Pera took two biology courses in the spring 1971 semester at Mayfair College.

8. Memorandum to Chief, Criminal Division, [Cook County] State's Attorney's Office, from investigators Andrew Grace and James O'Connor, [Cook County] State's Attorney's Office, January 24, 1972.

9. Testimony of Charles Arthur Kallick, Preliminary Hearing, February 4, 1972, pp. 94–95, and testimony of Jacqueline Mary Klansek, Preliminary Hearing, February 4, 1972, p. 8. The research was published in C.A. Kallick, S. Levin, K.T. Reddi, and W.L. Landau, *Nature New Biology*, Vol. 236 (April 5, 1972), pp. 145–146.

10. Testimony of William Landau, Preliminary Hearing, February 4, 1972, p. 24.

11. The cultures examined by the state health laboratory contained multiple organisms, suggesting that Pera lacked the skill to prevent contamination of his cultures.

12. Mayfair College was renamed Truman College in 1976 and is now one of the colleges that comprise the City College of Chicago. The school was founded in 1956,

time, Schwandner was already talking about the need to create a new society.[13] He signed up for fall semester courses in modern Russian history, psychology, literature, humanities, and physical education, but he only attended three sessions of the Russian history course and none of the others. Pera took what appears to have been an intermediate level biology course, Biology 201 (Independent Projects), but the available records do not indicate the nature of his activities.[14]

Schwandner's Manifesto

R.I.S.E. was apparently founded in mid-November 1971.[15] The precise meaning of the group's name is unknown, but one police informant indicated that the "R" stood for Reconstruction, the "S" for Society, and the "E" for Extermination (the source could not recall the meaning of "I").[16] Schwandner articulated the group's ideology in a six-page "manifesto" that he kept in a binder in his apartment. Although this document appears not to have survived, testimony from the preliminary court hearing provides some indication of its contents.[17]

The manifesto started with an assertion that mankind was destroying itself and the planet, and that the only way to preserve the environment was for the human race to be wiped out except for a select group of people who would live in harmony with nature. According to the document, the world would be a better place if it were inhabited only by a small group of like-minded people who agreed on how to address its problems.[18] With the ultimate aim of repopulating the planet, Schwand-

---

and at the time of the events discussed here probably had about 4,000 students. For a short history of the college, see http://www.ccc.edu/truman/history.htm. Some accounts refer to Mayfair College as Mayfair City College or Mayfair Community College.

13. Interview of John Regan by Sergeant Joseph DiLeonardi, no date (probably around January 19, 1972).

14. Testimony of Richard Kampwirth, Preliminary Hearing, February 8, 1972, p. 473.

15. The earliest date associated with R.I.S.E. was given by Kimberly Konarski, Schwandner's fiancée, who claims to have first heard about R.I.S.E. about a week after meeting Pera in mid-November. She had known Schwandner since May 1971. See Testimony of Kimberly Konarski, Preliminary Hearing, February 8, 1972, p. 398.

16. Testimony of Wendy Tempkins, Preliminary Hearing, February 8, 1972, p. 312; interview of Tempkins by Sergeant Joseph DiLeonardi, January 20, 1972.

17. The document is mentioned by several sources. See the testimony of Wendy Tempkins, Preliminary Hearing, February 8, 1972, p. 303; and the testimony of Steven Gajewski, Preliminary Hearing, February 8, 1972, pp. 404–405.

18. Testimony of Steven Gajewski, Preliminary Hearing, February 8, 1972, pp. 400–404.

ner planned to recruit people into the group who would select a mate of the opposite sex. He reportedly envisioned that R.I.S.E. would ultimately include sixteen people, comprising eight male-female pairs.[19]

To the extent that R.I.S.E. had an ideology, it clearly had a "green" orientation. Schwandner's manifesto was an extreme environmentalist tract, suggesting that R.I.S.E. is best described as an "ecoterrorist" group.[20] No evidence supports the frequent assertions in the scholarly literature that Schwandner and Pera were neo-Nazis or had racist tendencies.[21] Schwandner's views were based on a simplistic understanding of the revolutionary rhetoric then permeating certain parts of American society, but his rejection of the status quo probably had more to do with his inability to adjust to the existing social system than it did with any deeply considered political philosophy.

To accomplish the objective outlined in his manifesto, Schwandner began to recruit people into the R.I.S.E. organization. His first and most important recruit was Pera, the only member with any scientific expertise. The exterminationist ideology that Schwandner had developed led him to search for a weapon capable of killing literally billions of people. Schwandner and Pera decided that infectious disease agents would accomplish this objective by creating a worldwide epidemic that would eliminate all of humanity except for the small number of R.I.S.E. members who had been immunized against the pathogens being disseminated. In addition to the need for a weapon that could inflict death on a global scale, Schwandner's choice of biological agents was constrained by Pera's knowledge of microbiology.

Schwandner's plan was to disseminate the agents as an aerosol spray over major cities and rely on air currents to disperse them around the world.[22] He told one person recruited into the group that R.I.S.E. intended to employ "botulism, meningitis, typhoid, bubonic plague." Another recruit recalled "typhoid, meningitis, botulism, anthrax, and diphtheria."[23] The plotters apparently believed that the simultaneous appearance of so many diseases would confuse any investigation into the outbreak

---

19. The need for around sixteen people is mentioned by all of the people whom Schwandner attempted to recruit into the organization.

20. Relatively little has been written on the topic of ecological terrorism. See Sean P. Egan, "From Spikes to Bombs: The Rise of Eco-Terrorism," *Studies in Conflict and Terrorism*, Vol. 18 (1996), pp. 1–19.

21. Author's interview with Joseph G. DiLeonardi, March 19, 1998.

22. Testimony of Steven Gajewski, Preliminary Hearing, February 8, 1972, p. 407.

23. Testimony of Edward Dunst, Preliminary Hearing, February 7, 1972, p. 202; Testimony of Wendy Tempkins, February 8, 1972, p. 291.

and delay the identification of the cause until it was too late. In addition, the plotters discussed using aircraft to disseminate biological agents in the atmosphere along the borders of inaccessible countries such as China and the Soviet Union. Schwandner did not want totalitarian states to take over the world in the power vacuum left by the destruction of the Western countries.[24]

On December 13 or 14, Schwandner recruited Wendy Tempkins, and on December 18 or 19, he recruited Edward Dunst. Other identified members of R.I.S.E. included Kimberly Konarski (Schwandner's girl-friend), Steven Gajewski, and John Regan. The available evidence suggests that eight to ten people were directly associated with the group, although only Schwandner and Pera took an active role in any of its activities.[25] Access to the R.I.S.E. manifesto was limited to members or those being recruited for membership. Since Schwandner sought to destroy the existing social system rather than change it, he apparently saw no need to publicize his views, although he did openly discuss his ideas with people he encountered in social situations.

At some point after Schwandner and Pera began working together, Schwandner put together a "War Room" in a bedroom of his apartment that had previously stored unused furniture. He posted a banner bearing the group's name, along with maps of the places where the group planned to spread biological agents. A map of the world showed air currents, apparently reflecting Schwandner's understanding of the likely atmospheric transport patterns for the pathogens that R.I.S.E. intended to disseminate. In addition, a map of the states around Chicago was marked with the locations where biological agents were to be released.

Acquisition of Information and Biological Agents

Pera collected information on biological warfare from a variety of sources. He exploited his position at Presbyterian-St. Luke's Hospital to gain access to relevant books and scientific articles, which appear to have been his primary source of information on technical issues related to biological warfare. These publications included military manuals, reports prepared

---

24. Testimony of Edward Dunst, Preliminary Hearing, February 7, 1972, p. 214.

25. Regan told police that he thought R.I.S.E. had ten to twelve members. See Report from Investigator William McCoy to Commander Keating, Homicide Division, [Chicago Police Department], Subject: Overdose Investigation (Conspiracy to destroy the world), January 13, 1972.

by government-funded research institutes, and foreign publications translated by the U.S. government.[26] The FBI discovered additional books and scientific articles when Pera's parents allowed them to search their son's room.[27] Among the books in his possession were *Viruses and the Nature of Life; Introduction to Bacteria; Tomorrow's Weapons* (a popular treatise on biological warfare); and *Symposia on Quantitative Biology, Volume XXXV.* He also had copies of several scientific articles, one of which was on anaerobic bacteria.[28]

Pera showed an interest in eight different microbial pathogens, although the list may have changed over time.[29] Little is known about his efforts to acquire these agents. Sometime during the fall of 1971, Pera approached the Chief of the Microbiology Department at the University of Illinois Hospital and requested cultures of *Vibrio cholerae* (cholera), *Yersinia pestis* (plague), *Neisseria meningitidis* (bacterial meningitis), and

---

26.   The list of government publications in Pera's possession was obtained from the files of the Office of the Cook County State's Attorney's Office. The list includes U.S. Department of Army, *Military Biology and Biological Warfare Agents* (apparently a 1956 manual issued jointly by the Departments of the Army and the Air Force); U.S. Army Medical Service, *Medical Defense Against Biological Warfare* (probably a 19-page pamphlet issued in 1953 by the Graduate School of the U.S. Army Medical Service Corps); Boris Vladimirovich Kokosov, *Antiatomic, Antichemical, Antibacteriological Protection of the Soldier in Combat* (an English translation published by the U.S. Joint Publications Research Service in 1958); U.S. Chemical Corps, *Bibliography on Biological Warfare, and Supplement* (compiled by the U.S. Army Chemical Corps, Biological Weapons Laboratory, at Camp Detrick, Maryland, in 1953 and 1957); Midwest Research Institute, *Fundamental Laboratory Research Investigation for the Development of Submicron Dry BW* and *Stabilization of BW Aerosols* (two technical research reports prepared by Midwest Research Institute in Kansas City, Missouri, under contract to the U.S. Army Chemical Corps' Biological Weapons Laboratory); and U.S. Office of Naval Research, *Biological Warfare Operations* (probably a journal produced by the Office of Naval Research starting in 1960).

27.   Memorandum from Sergeant J. DiLeonardi to Chief, Criminal Investigation Division, Chicago Police Department, January 21, 1972.

28.   Ibid. One of the scientific articles seized in the War Room was titled "Isolation of Anaerobic Bacteria from the Clinical Material." This article appeared in the *Indian Journal of Pathological Bacteriology*, April 1970, pp. 55–61.

29.   Information about the biological agents of interest to R.I.S.E. comes from three sources. First, Schwandner talked about specific agents with some of the people whom he tried to recruit into the group. Second, Pera mentioned several agents to people from whom he was attempting to acquire agents or to obtain technical advice. Finally, the Chicago Laboratory of the Illinois Department of Public Health conducted tests on the material seized by the Chicago Police from the laboratory at Mayfair College and from Schwandner's apartment. These tests identified *Shigella* (dysentery), typhoid strains, diphtheria strains, and a *Clostridium* organism.

Salmonella typhi (typhoid fever).[30] He was given seed cultures of the last two microorganisms.[31] Pera was not satisfied, however, and continued to search for additional agents. On December 17, he wrote a letter to the "National Center for Disease Control," an apparent reference to the U.S. Center for Disease Control (CDC) in Atlanta, Georgia, requesting a catalogue of all the microorganisms obtainable from the center.[32] The CDC responded on December 30 with a letter informing him that it did not sell cultures.

Of the five biological agents that Pera possessed, a source has been identified only for the typhoid fever and bacterial meningitis cultures he obtained from the University of Illinois Hospital. It is not known whether Pera tried to obtain *Bacillus anthracis* (anthrax) and it is possible that he relied on samples from the natural environment for *Clostridium botulinum* (botulism).[33] The source of the *Corynebacterium diphtheriae* (diphtheria) and *Shigella sonnei* (dysentery) cultures that the authorities found in his possession is unknown (see Table 4.1).

In late November or early December 1971, Pera began taking steps to cultivate biological agents using the facilities at Presbyterian-St. Luke's Hospital.[34] Initially, the lupus research project had worked in the spaces

---

30. *Neisseria meningitidis* is a leading cause of bacterial meningitis, a disease characterized by fevers, nausea and vomiting, headaches, and rashes. The case fatality rate is 50 percent, but modern medical treatment can reduce the rate to between 5 and 15 percent. The agent can be transmitted by aerosol particles but rarely results in systemic disease. Abram S. Benenson, ed., *Control of Communicable Diseases Manual*, 16th edition (Washington, D.C.: American Public Health Association, 1995), pp. 303–304. *Salmonella typhi* causes typhoid fever, an enteric disease characterized by a severe fever and acute headaches. The case fatality rate is typically about 10 percent, but proper treatment can reduce the fatality rate to less than 1 percent. Typhoid fever is normally transmitted through food or water contaminated by feces and urine from infected people. Benenson, *Control of Communicable Diseases Manual*, pp. 502–503.

31. Memorandum to Chief, Criminal Division, [Cook County] State's Attorney's Office, January 24, 1972.

32. The CDC has since changed its name to the Centers for Disease Control and Prevention.

33. *Clostridium botulinum* produces a toxin that is among the most potent poisons known to science. Foodborne botulism causes nerve impairment and paralysis. The case fatality rate is 5 percent, but recovery can take months. The toxin is destroyed by boiling. Benenson, *Control of Communicable Diseases Manual*, pp. 66–69.

34. This statement is based on the recollection of William Landau. In late November or early December 1971, Pera asked Landau for advice on how to grow certain biological agents, suggesting that he was having problems with the cultures. It was after that conversation that Landau observed Pera working on cultures in the laboratory. Testimony of William Landau, Preliminary Hearing, February 4, 1972, pp. 31, 38–39.

Table 4.1. R.I.S.E. Biological Agents.

Biological Agent	Number of sources reporting interest	Known effort to acquire agent?	Possession of agent confirmed?
Bacillus anthracis	1		
Clostridium botulinum	2		Possible
Corynebacterium diphtheriae	1		Yes
Neisseria meningitidis	2	Yes	Yes
Salmonella typhi	2	Yes	Yes
Shigella sonnei	0		Yes
Vibrio cholerae	0	Yes	
Yersinia pestis	1	Yes	

SOURCES: Various reports in the files of the Cook County State's Attorney's Office, Chicago, Illinois.

of the hospital's Microbiology Department and Pera had become friendly with the laboratory technicians there. Even after the lupus project moved to another building within the hospital complex, Pera retained access to the microbiology laboratory. Although he had no formal authorization to work in the lab, he exploited his personal relationships with the staff and his activities were not considered a problem.

Pera also used his position at Presbyterian-St. Luke's to seek advice from technicians and physicians with expertise in infectious diseases. In late November or early December, he approached Dr. William Landau, a bacteriologist in the hospital's Microbiology Department, and asked him about procedures for growing *Clostridium botulinum*, *Neisseria meningitidis*, and *Salmonella typhi*. Landau told Pera that all the information he needed was in textbooks and that there were no particular difficulties in working with those organisms.[35] When Pera was having difficulty culturing *Clostridium botulinum*, one of the laboratory technicians at the hospital obtained a new anaerobe jar and helped him with catalysts that eliminated oxygen from the jar to create an anaerobic growth environment.[36]

Sometime in December 1971, the technicians became aware that Pera was growing bacteria inside an incubator in the laboratory. The incubator contained a number of petri dishes, some marked with a "T" (possibly for *Salmonella typhi*) and others with an "M" (possibly for *Neisseria men-*

---

35. Ibid., pp. 30–31.

36. Testimony of Jacqueline Mary Klansek, Preliminary Hearing, February 4, 1972, pp. 9–10.

ingitidis). In addition, the incubator contained at least one anaerobic jar for growing *Clostridium botulinum*.[37] Pera explained that the cultures were for a school project and that he needed to use the hospital's equipment because the incubator in his college laboratory was not working.[38]

Methods for Agent Dissemination

Schwandner and Pera mentioned three techniques for disseminating biological agents: aerosolization, contamination of water supplies, and contamination of food.[39] Although press accounts focused heavily on the plan to contaminate the Chicago water system, the testimony of people involved in R.I.S.E. strongly suggests that aerosolization was to be the primary method of dissemination. One of Schwandner's recruits described a sprayer intended for this purpose: "It was around seven inches long and it had a glass container the same length and it was connected with a metal attachment. The bacteria would be kept in this glass container and it would be sprayed."[40]

The plan called for using the aerosol device to disperse biological agents in supermarkets and large buildings.[41] Schwandner also discussed the use of aircraft to disseminate biological agents. He claimed that a former girlfriend owned or had access to a jet aircraft, which he imagined could be operated like a crop duster to spread biological agents around the world, greatly increasing the affected area.[42] R.I.S.E. also developed plans to contaminate water systems. It is unclear, however, whether the group ever developed a specific plan for disseminating biological agents in food.

Confiscation of Pera's Cultures

In late December 1971, just before the Christmas holiday, Pera undermined his position at Presbyterian-St. Luke's Hospital by attempting to

---

37. Testimony of William Landau, Preliminary Hearing, February 4, 1972, pp. 43–45.

38. Testimony of Jacqueline Mary Klansek, Preliminary Hearing, February 4, 1972, p. 8.

39. Testimony of Edward Dunst, Preliminary Hearing, February 7, 1972, p. 207.

40. Ibid., pp. 230–231.

41. Testimony of Steven Gajewski, Preliminary Hearing, February 8, 1972, p. 407.

42. Testimony of Kimberly Konarski, Preliminary Hearing, February 8, 1972, pp. 371–372. According to the testimony of Edward Dunst (Preliminary Hearing, February 7, 1972, pp. 234), Schwandner claimed that his one-time girlfriend was aware of the plot.

acquire illicit drugs. He allegedly submitted a form to the hospital pharmacy requesting quantities of two barbiturates (secobarbital and amobarbital) and one amphetamine (dexedrine). The form had Dr. Kallick's signature on it, but Kallick later denied any knowledge of the request. Concerned by what appeared to be an attempt to gain access to controlled substances, Kallick tried to get in contact with Pera to determine what had happened, but Pera avoided him. After the two met by accident in a hospital hallway, Pera agreed to set up an appointment to discuss the issue but then failed to show up. As a result of this episode, Pera's status at the hospital was in jeopardy.[43]

On January 3, 1972, Schwandner and Pera visited Fort Sheridan, the headquarters of the Fifth Army outside of Chicago. The two young men were given a tour of the base and obtained information on its water-supply system. Some witnesses later saw a map of the Fort Sheridan water system in the War Room in Schwandner's apartment. The map was marked to show where the group intended to inject typhoid fever organisms.[44]

On the morning of January 7, Dr. Kallick met with Dr. Landau, the bacteriologist who worked in the Microbiology Department at Presbyterian-St. Luke's Hospital. Landau told Kallick about the cultures that Pera was growing and mentioned that they included *Salmonella typhi*, meningococcus, and some other organism. Alarmed by this revelation, Kallick decided to ban Pera from the hospital and ordered the confiscation of his cultures. That afternoon, Kallick sent Pera a certified letter informing him that he would not be allowed into the hospital above the first floor.[45] On January 10, all of Pera's cultures were destroyed at the direction of hospital security.[46]

Pera and Schwandner made several attempts to recover the cultures. On the afternoon of either January 10 or 11, Schwandner went to the hospital dressed in a white laboratory coat and acted as though he were a hospital employee. He went up to the Microbiology Department and entered Landau's laboratory. Seeing Landau, Schwandner said, "Isn't it too bad about Steve?" Landau responded, "Well, that depends on what you are referring to." Schwandner reportedly replied, "Steve was just

---

43. Testimony of Charles Arthur Kallick, Preliminary Hearing, February 4, 1972, pp. 98–100.

44. Testimony of Edward Dunst, Preliminary Hearing, February 8, 1972, pp. 210, 225–226.

45. Testimony of Charles Arthur Kallick, Preliminary Hearing, February 4, 1972, pp. 100–101.

46. Testimony of William Landau, Preliminary Hearing, February 4, 1972, pp. 54–55.

fired by Dr. Kallick, and he had been doing good work on the research project." Landau asked where Pera was, and Schwandner told him that he was meeting with Kallick. Schwandner then went to the laboratory next to Landau's and looked inside the incubator, apparently searching for something on the bottom shelf. When Schwandner admitted that he was looking for Pera's cultures, Landau told him that they had been confiscated. He refused to explain why the action had been taken but told Schwandner that Kallick would certainly tell Pera during their meeting.[47]

The failure to recover the cultures had a major impact on Schwandner and Pera. Although their original concept had called for a global release of biological agents, they abruptly altered their dissemination plans. According to one member of R.I.S.E., Schwandner told him early on January 11 that "security leaks" had forced a cancellation of the plan to destroy the entire world. A new plan was devised, focusing on the destruction of five Midwestern states by disseminating biological agents into the water and the air.[48] On January 11, two members of R.I.S.E. were immunized against typhoid fever.

Pera quickly took steps to replace the lost cultures. He returned to his source at the University of Illinois Hospital and requested an additional culture of *Neisseria meningitidis*, claiming that he had lost the previous sample. On January 12, Pera and Schwandner went to the laboratory at Mayfair College and began to set up efforts to grow an unspecified anaerobic organism, presumably *Clostridium botulinum*. When Pera discovered that the college lacked the appropriate growth media, he ordered three different anaerobic media.[49] Later that day, he prepared two cultures and had them placed in the lab's incubator.

Pera obtained a culture of *Neisseria meningitidis* from the University of Illinois Hospital on January 13.[50] That same day, Schwandner recruited a new member of R.I.S.E. named Steven Gajewski. On Friday, January 14, Pera called Landau and asked if he could send someone over to get his cultures. Landau agreed to a meeting at 3:00 P.M. and promptly called hospital security. A few minutes before the appointed time, an uniden-

---

47. Ibid., pp. 46–55.

48. Testimony of Edward Dunst, Preliminary Hearing, February 7, 1972, pp. 228–230.

49. Testimony of Jean Burton, Preliminary Hearing, February 9, 1972, pp. 443–449. According to Burton's testimony, Pera ordered thioglycollate and a meat-based growth medium from a laboratory supply company, but she could not remember what the third medium was.

50. Memorandum to Chief, Criminal Division, [Cook County] State's Attorney's Office, January 24, 1972.

tified woman came to the hospital and asked for the cultures. She was told that they could not be found. About 4:30 P.M., Pera again called Landau and asked if it would be possible to stop by and pick up the cultures the following Monday.[51] Pera was then told that he had been denied access to the hospital.

That same Friday, Pera and Schwandner returned to the Mayfair College biology laboratory and began to culture some unknown organisms. According to a laboratory technician who observed them, Pera transferred cultures from the tubes that had been in the incubator to two flasks containing growth media. At the time, these were the only cultures in the incubator.[52]

The End of R.I.S.E.

R.I.S.E. began to fall apart in January 1972. The difficulties began almost as soon as Schwandner began recruiting additional members for the group. On January 12, John Regan, a newly recruited member, arrived at a hospital emergency room reporting that he had been injected with an unknown substance by a group called R.I.S.E. that planned to destroy the world with biological weapons. The Chicago Police Department interviewed Regan and launched an investigation.

On January 15, three other people recruited by Schwandner contacted the Chicago office of the Federal Bureau of Investigation (FBI) with concerns about R.I.S.E. Police reports indicate that Dunst, Gajewski, and Tempkins went to the FBI when they came to believe that Schwandner and Pera actually intended to disseminate biological agents. Although the FBI did not take the informants' initial reports seriously, the Bureau agreed to support an investigation by city authorities. Based on information provided by Regan, Chicago Police officials alerted the Office of the Cook County State's Attorney. Jack Schmetterer, the Assistant State's Attorney, organized an intensive investigation into the activities of Schwandner and Pera. The probe was led by the Chicago Police Department, supported by agents from the State's Attorney's Office and the FBI.

On January 16, Dunst and Tempkins agreed to operate as informants and allowed themselves to be wired so that the Chicago Police could record their conversations with Schwandner and Pera. Statements indicating that R.I.S.E. was within days of disseminating a biological agent led to a decision to arrest the two main perpetrators on January 17. Chicago Police also raided the biology laboratory at Mayfair College,

---

51. Testimony of William Landau, Preliminary Hearing, February 4, 1972, pp. 46–55.

52. Testimony of Jean Burton, Preliminary Hearing, February 9, 1972, pp. 454–460.

where they seized six petri dishes, three test tubes, and six culture tubes suspected of containing biological pathogens.[53] It is unlikely, however, that this small number of cultures could have provided more than a limited quantity of biological agent.

According to the Illinois Public Health Department, the culture material seized by the Chicago Police Department contained the following organisms: *Salmonella typhi* (typhoid fever), *Shigella sonnei* (dysentery), *Corynebacterium diphtheriae* (diphtheria), and a species of *Clostridium*.[54] This list of agents was not necessarily complete, however, because Pera's cultures at Presbyterian-St. Luke's Hospital had been destroyed before they could be analyzed.[55] It was also known that Pera had acquired at least one additional agent, *Neisseria meningitidis* (bacterial meningitis), which he either destroyed before it could be seized or managed to hide from the Chicago Police.[56]

Based on the surviving evidence, it is impossible to determine how much agent R.I.S.E. actually possessed. The only published estimate states that the group produced 30 to 40 kilograms of typhoid culture, but a review of the existing evidence casts doubt on the accuracy of this figure.[57] Certainly, there is no indication that the Chicago Police ever seized that quantity of agent. The Illinois Public Health Department's Chicago Laboratory, which analyzed the material seized by the Chicago Police Department, provided no quantitative estimates. Moreover, the fact that Presbyterian-St. Luke's Hospital destroyed Pera's cultures made it impossible to estimate the quantity of agent he had produced.

A preliminary hearing was held in early February 1972 before the

---

53. Report from the Director, Criminalistics Division [Chicago Police Department], to First Deputy Superintendent, Chicago Police Department, Subject: State Toxicological Laboratory, January 21, 1972.

54. At the time, the laboratory was unable to determine whether the *Clostridium* species was the toxigenic *Clostridium botulinum* or the nontoxigenic *Clostridium sporogenes*.

55. The samples were provided to the CDC for further analysis, but the results of those tests are unknown. In addition, the state laboratory lost one of the cultures, so that its contents were never identified. Letter from Richard A. Morrissey, Chief Public Health Microbiologist, Division of Laboratories, State of Illinois Department of Public Health, to Commander Francis Flanagan, Chief, Chicago Crime Laboratory, Chicago Police Department, January 24, 1972; and letter from Richard A. Morrissey, Chief Public Health Microbiologist, Division of Laboratories, State of Illinois Department of Public Health, to Akbert Balows, Chief, Bacteriology Section, Laboratory Division, Center for Disease Control, January 24, 1972.

56. Testimony of William Landau, Preliminary Hearing, February 4, 1972, pp. 54–55.

57. Purver, *Chemical and Biological Terrorism: The Threat According to the Open Literature*, p. 37.

Circuit Court of Cook County to justify the request for an indictment against the two defendants. Lawyers representing Pera and Schwandner attempted to call into question the seriousness of their defendants' actions. They argued that it was scientifically impossible for the defendants to cause harm in the manner discussed by the witnesses. To buttress their argument, the defense attorneys claimed that the amount of biological agent that the defendants possessed was not significant and that obtaining large quantities of biological agent was beyond their resources.[58] In addition, the attorneys argued that it was impossible to disseminate the agents in the manner alleged "because you can't take them and put them in squirt bottles and squirt them in the bus station, all this kind of nonsense."[59] Finally, the defense suggested that the case was politically motivated by claiming that the prosecutors were trying to gain publicity for a possible bid at elective office.[60]

The prosecutors responsible for the case were unsure about the seriousness of the plot but believed that it warranted attention. Accordingly, they prosecuted the case more vigorously than some law enforcement officials thought was necessary. Given the intent of the perpetrators and the dangerous character of the microorganisms they were culturing, however, this vigilance was justified.

Pera and Schwandner were given bail of $250,000, which was reduced on appeal to $50,000. After being released from prison, they jumped bail and fled to Jamaica. On March 21, 1972, they hired a sightseeing aircraft in Jamaica and highjacked it to Cuba, apparently believing that they would be welcome there. In fact, the Cuban authorities had little sympathy for the two would-be revolutionaries. According to a Cuban death certificate, Schwandner died on November 7, 1974.[61] As Pera was in poor health, the Cuban government allowed him to leave the country on January 27, 1975. He returned to the United States and surrendered to authorities. Pera eventually pleaded guilty and was sentenced to five years' probation.[62]

---

58. See, for example, the exchange in the Preliminary Hearing, February 8, 1972, p. 430, in which one of the defense attorneys claims that it would cost $5 million to produce a bottle of botulinum toxin.

59. Preliminary Hearing, February 9, 1972, p. 466.

60. Ibid., p. 430.

61. A copy of Schwandner's autopsy certificate from the Institute of Legal Medicine was provided to the United States Interests Section in Havana on November 9, 1974. The FBI gave a copy to the Cook County State's Attorney on June 10, 1975.

62. A transcript of Pera's sentencing hearing is in the records of the Cook County Court.

Bioterrorism or Biofantasy?

How dangerous was the R.I.S.E. plot? The seriousness of the crime as seen from the perspective of the criminal justice system is probably accurately reflected in the five years' probation that Pera ultimately received, although he might have gotten a stiffer sentence if he had not voluntarily returned for trial. In retrospect, it is clear that R.I.S.E. could never have accomplished its more grandiose ambitions. The master plan to spread diseases globally was preposterous given the group's limited resources. Even the scaled-down plan to disseminate biological agents in the Chicago area probably was beyond their capabilities. The only person associated with the plot who had any scientific background was Pera, and his expertise and experience were limited.

Schwandner claimed that R.I.S.E. was within days of staging a biological attack, which might suggest that he thought the group already possessed or would soon obtain sufficient quantities for its purposes. Yet Pera's hurried efforts to culture agents at Mayfair College in the days before his arrest implies that he was still trying to produce enough agent for the planned attacks. The agents selected were probably not well suited for aerosol dissemination, and the plots to contaminate water supplies were totally impractical. Pera had no idea of the infective dose needed to have an effect, and he appears to have had no understanding of the complexities associated with agent dissemination. In sum, although R.I.S.E. appears to have been motivated to conduct a mass-casualty attack with biological weapons, it lacked the scientific and technical expertise to carry it out.

Chapter 5

The Alphabet Bomber (1974)

Jeffrey D. Simon

One of the most fascinating cases of chemical terrorism is that of Muharem Kurbegovic, also known as the "Alphabet Bomber." Kurbegovic committed his criminal acts in the United States in the 1970s and can be considered a terrorist ahead of his time. He was one of the first to threaten to release nerve agents in populated areas, to acquire sodium cyanide, and to use the media in a systematic way to communicate his message and to spread fear among the public.

Kurbegovic did not need the logistical or financial support of an organized group. He built his own terror network through the use of conventional explosives and threats communicated through the media and the U.S. mail. His actions received attention at the highest levels of government. In addition to targeting innocent civilians, he planned to assassinate the President of the United States, members of Congress, and all nine justices of the Supreme Court.

The Alphabet Bomber represents the type of individual who will always be a candidate for using chemical and biological warfare (CBW) agents: a mentally unstable yet highly intelligent and technologically sophisticated person who is driven by anger and revenge. Understanding the Alphabet Bomber's motivations, strategies, and tactics can shed light on the mindset of those individuals and groups who might escalate their violence to weapons of mass destruction.

The Making of a Terrorist

There are many different roads to becoming a terrorist. Some terrorists are born from ethnic-nationalist and religious conflicts, where hatreds and desires for revenge are handed down from one generation to the next. Terrorists also evolve from allegiances to various political and social causes in which violence is seen as an instrument for achieving the group's objectives. Drug cartels are additional breeding grounds for terrorists, as members of the cartel engage in ruthless killings of judges, journalists, policymakers, and anyone else who interferes with their operations.

Another road to becoming a terrorist is based on personal motives. This path involves individuals who are not part of an organized group yet who utilize terrorist tactics, sometimes in the name of a fictitious group, to obtain money, revenge, or publicity. Individual criminals have been among the most tactically innovative, introducing new forms of violence that more established terrorist groups eventually imitate. The first midair bombings of aircraft, hijackings of planes, and product contamination cases in the United States were the work of criminals. At times, criminal terrorists can evoke public and government reactions that match or even exceed those elicited by political or religious terrorists.[1]

Muharem Kurbegovic took the personal road to becoming a terrorist. He was born in Sarajevo, Yugoslavia, in 1943, and studied engineering at universities in Europe before emigrating to the United States via Canada in 1967. He claimed that he had an undergraduate degree in mechanical engineering and a master's degree in hydraulic engineering. He also claimed that he fled Yugoslavia for Germany to escape political persecution. In taped messages that he left with the media during his campaign of violence in Los Angeles, he expressed strong anti-communist beliefs. He described himself to a friend as a liberal socialist. His mother, who may have been mentally ill, remained in Yugoslavia, and Kurbegovic regularly sent her money once he started working as an engineer.[2]

Kurbegovic was a legal alien in the United States and worked at various engineering jobs in Los Angeles between 1967 and 1974. He was a quick learner who was well liked by his coworkers and supervisors. He changed jobs frequently in the late 1960s and early 1970s because of the cyclical nature of the aerospace industry. One of his jobs was with a firm that was involved in the Apollo space program, and it is believed that some of Kurbegovic's engineering designs and drawings became part of that program.[3]

Kurbegovic was able to acquire a good reputation at work even

---

1. Jeffrey D. Simon, *The Terrorist Trap: America's Experience with Terrorism* (Bloomington: Indiana University Press, 1994), pp. 333–337.

2. Narda Z. Trout and Mike Goodman, "Suspect's Double Life: Chatty to Landlady, a Mute at Work," *Los Angeles Times*, August 22, 1974, Part I, p. 34; *People v Kurbegovic*, Book No. 138, California Appellate Reports, Third Series (138 Cal.App.3d.), pp. 738–739.

3. *People v Kurbegovic*, 138 Cal.App.3d., pp. 739, 747.

though he never talked and communicated only by writing notes. He explained to people that his muteness was the result of a traumatic incident he had witnessed as a child involving his mother and the Yugoslav secret police. The real reason he pretended to be mute, however, was so that he could avoid being drafted into the U.S. Army during the Vietnam War. When he found out that aliens such as himself were subject to the draft, he visited a physician to inquire about obtaining a 4-F Selective Service classification exempting him from military service on the basis of a physical disability. Pretending that he was mute was one way to avoid the draft. He never once slipped up at work, even accidentally burning himself without uttering a sound.[4]

Kurbegovic did, however, occasionally chat with his elderly neighbors in the apartment building where he lived just west of downtown Los Angeles. A reclusive man, he had a one-room apartment and drove a battered old Volkswagen. There were no women in his life except for those he would meet at the "taxi dance halls" he frequented: clubs in downtown Los Angeles where customers paid money to dance with hired women for a specified period of time. Kurbegovic wanted to open one of these dance halls himself, telling friends that it would be a way for him to become rich.[5]

An incident at one of these dance halls triggered a sequence of events that put Kurbegovic on his path of violence. In March 1971, he was arrested for lewd conduct—masturbating in a dance hall restroom. "His masturbation arrest . . . became the be-all and the end-all of his life," recalled Gerald Chaleff, his public defender after his arrest for violent activity in 1974.[6] Kurbegovic represented himself during the lewd conduct trial and was acquitted by a jury. The judge, Allan G. Campbell, was irritated with Kurbegovic's antics during the trial and chastised him after the verdict was read: "In my opinion you have purposefully, consistently taken advantage of every possible opportunity to turn this trial into a vehicle of your play-acting and pantomiming and for your taking advantage of every possible trick in the book."[7]

---

4. Author's interview with Dinko Bozanich, Deputy District Attorney, Los Angeles County (prosecutor in Muharem Kurbegovic's 1980 trial), Norwalk, California, December 23, 1997; author's telephone interview with Robert T. Altman, Judge of the Superior Court, Los Angeles County (prosecutor in Muharem Kurbegovic's 1970s competency hearings), March 19, 1998; *People v Kurbegovic*, 138 Cal.App.3d., pp. 746, 753–754.

5. *People v Kurbegovic*, 138 Cal.App.3d., p. 739.

6. Author's interview with Gerald L. Chaleff, Attorney at Law (public defender for Muharem Kurbegovic from 1974 to 1977), Los Angeles, California, February 10, 1998.

7. *People v Kurbegovic*, 138 Cal.App.3d., p. 736. Campbell would later become one of

In May 1972, Kurbegovic appeared before the Los Angeles Police Commission to apply for a permit to open a taxi dance hall. He told the commission that it would be an establishment where a patron "could pay a fee and get anything you want [from a woman.]" That comment, along with his prior arrest, led to the denial of the permit. One member of the commission, Emmet McGaughey, made a motion to deny the permit while another member, Marguerite Justice, seconded the motion.[8]

Kurbegovic began taking his revenge in the early morning hours of November 9, 1973. He set fires at the homes of commission members McGaughey and Justice and Judge Campbell. Since it was possible to drive to all three houses in only nineteen minutes, police speculated that the fires could be the work of one person, but no one suspected that Kurbegovic was the arsonist. Seven months later, Kurbegovic placed an incendiary device in the gas tank of McGaughey's car. He also telephoned McGaughey, posing as a member of the Symbionese Liberation Army—a terrorist group active in Los Angeles at the time that became famous for kidnapping and coopting heiress Patty Hearst—and threatened that McGaughey would be executed within thirty days.[9]

Until this point, Kurbegovic's campaign of terror had focused on the three individuals whom he felt had done him wrong. But the Yugoslav immigrant was about to embark upon a much more violent campaign, with potentially catastrophic results. Kurbegovic frequently asked Stephen Smith, who was both his supervisor and friend at RPM Industries, questions about how to build bombs, always by writing notes since he continued to pretend that he was mute. Smith, who never thought that Kurbegovic would actually use explosives to harm anyone, told him that all he had to do was purchase the necessary chemicals from a supply house. Kurbegovic began buying chemicals from the Erb and Gray Company in Culver City, posing as a representative of Hughes Aircraft. He expressed to Smith his surprise at how easy it was to obtain chemicals. Erb and Gray finally became suspicious of his numerous purchases and refused to sell him any more. Soon thereafter, an explosion occurred at

---

the targets of Kurbegovic's campaign of violence and would testify in Kurbegovic's criminal trial. By then the judge's demeanor had changed significantly since the time that he had chastised Kurbegovic. "If I ever saw a scared witness, Judge Campbell was it," recalled Nancy Watson, the judge who presided during Kurbegovic's 1980 criminal trial. "He was really nervous. He didn't want to be in the same courtroom as Kurbegovic." Author's interview with Nancy B. Watson, Judge of the Superior Court, Los Angeles County, retired, Rancho Mirage, California, April 2, 1998.

8. *People v Kurbegovic*, 138 Cal.App.3d., p. 736.

9. Ibid.

the supply house. Although Kurbegovic was never charged in the incident, investigators believed that he was responsible for the explosion.[10]

A Summer of Terror

The nation's attention was focused during the summer of 1974 on the unfolding Watergate scandal, which culminated in August with the resignation of President Richard Nixon. But law enforcement officials in Washington, D.C., and Los Angeles had their own crisis to deal with.

On July 5, a security guard at *The Los Angeles Times* found a tape cassette in a planter box in the lobby that contained a chilling message from a man who identified himself as Isaiak Rasim, "Chief Military Officer of Aliens of America." The tape began: "We, the Aliens of America, have developed four nerve gases, designated AA1, AA2, AA3, and AA4S nerve gas. The AA4S nerve gas is an organo mercuric [*sic*], organo phosperous [*sic*] compound with quantitive [*sic*] killing capacity exceeding that of sarin by the order of 10 to the fifth power." Rasim claimed that his group had tested the AA4S nerve gas on over 1,000 animals and six human beings and was convinced that they had "a military weapon which not only liberates us from audacity and terror of United States Government, but places the burden on our shoulder to liberate entire humankind."[11]

Although Kurbegovic purported to be the "Chief Military Officer" of Aliens of America and in one tape stated that the group had an active membership of eleven people,[12] he acted alone. (It is not known why he chose the pseudonym "Isaiak Rasim.") Kurbegovic most likely got the idea of pretending to be part of a group from Smith, who once described his experience in trying to influence a school board on a particular issue. Smith said that although he was not able to accomplish much as an individual, once he began writing letters claiming to be from a "taxpay-

---

10. George Lardner, "Terrorist Reportedly Sent a Justice Toxic Chemicals," *Washington Post*, December 20, 1983, p. A3; Trout and Goodman, "Suspect's Double Life," p. 34; *People v Kurbegovic*, 138 Cal.App.3d., p. 739; author's interview with Bozanich.

11. Transcript of tape recovered on July 5, 1974, at the Los Angeles Times (Los Angeles Police Department Item No. 1339, Files, Los Angeles Country District Attorney's Office); *People v Kurbegovic*, 138 Cal.App.3d., p. 736.

12. Transcript of tape recovered by the FBI on August 12, 1974, from Glen Evans after initial recovery by Evans in late July–early August 1974 in the vicinity of radio station KPFK (Los Angeles Police Department Item No. 1341, Files, Los Angeles County District Attorney's Office).

ers' concerned group," he received widespread media attention.[13] This observation appears to have impressed Kurbegovic.

Rasim asserted on tape that his group had already used nerve agents to attack all the justices of the Supreme Court, whom Kurbegovic blamed for the existence of the immigration, naturalization, and sex laws that he wanted abolished. "On June 15, 1974," he stated, "we have sent nine postcards to the United States Supreme Court Justices. Each postcard shows the Palm Springs home of entertainer Bob Hope and reads as follows: 'It is justices of your greatness that made this nation so great. Respectfully, Bob Hope.' Underneath the 11 cents postage stamp on each postcard there is a disc of lead containing approximately .01 milligram of AA4S nerve gas together with approximately 1 milligram of camouflaging compounds and volatility inhibitors."[14]

Rasim also claimed that time-release devices containing AA4S nerve gas had been placed in several cities, including New York, Denver, Miami Beach, Ottawa, London, Paris, Moscow, Tokyo, and Hong Kong. "We . . . possess the ability to deliver an exterminating, selective, and precisely timed blow to mass population centers throughout the world." Rasim issued an "ultimatum to surrender" to governments around the world and called for an "end to all Nationalism, Religionism [sic], Fascism, Racism, and Communism." He expressed particular hatred for the U.S. Supreme Court, stating that "we have chosen United States Supreme Court justices as historical monuments of crime, a criminal who has repeatedly ruled that an alien is not a human being and that consequently the constitutional provisions relating to [the] term 'people' do not apply [to aliens]."[15]

A similar tape was received by the Washington, D.C., bureau of United Press International. Although Aliens of America was an unknown group and Rasim's claims about placing nerve gas in cities around the world were far-fetched, his threats could not be dismissed outright because he had partially followed through with at least one of them. On June 16, 1974, nine postcards addressed to each of the Supreme Court justices were intercepted at the Palm Springs Post Office. Just as Rasim had described, the front of the postcard had a picture of Bob Hope's Palm Springs home and the back of the card had the greeting to the justices. "We received these postcards in the pickup from the city mail," post office foreman Arthur Smith told a grand jury later that year, "and they were run through the canceling machine. . . . [T]he cancelers that we have kind

---

13. *People v Kurbegovic*, 138 Cal.App.3d., p. 748.

14. Transcript of tape recovered on July 5, 1974.

15. Ibid.

of ripped them up, at least, tore up their stamps because . . . there was something underneath the stamps." Smith thought at first it was toy caps, but on further inspection "you could see that they were metal vials of something." He testified that when each vial went through the canceler, "whatever was in it discolored the stamps."[16]

Robert Altman, who was a deputy district attorney in Los Angeles at the time and questioned Smith at the Grand Jury hearing, recalled the postcard incident as being a hoax.[17] In a tape made later in the summer of 1974, Kurbegovic confirmed that there was no nerve gas under the stamps: "The postcard hoax itself was thought out by our theoreticians who claim that a reasonable man will pause to think if someone points a gun at him, whether the gun is loaded or empty. We were pointing an empty gun, but we were not pointing it at a reasonable man. This is why it was inescapably necessary to load our gun with one bullet, to fire it, and to see what would happen. We hope that we will never have to fire another bullet."[18]

The one "bullet" that Rasim referred to was a bomb that exploded on August 6 in a locker at the overseas passenger terminal lobby of Pan American World Airways at Los Angeles International Airport. The 11-pound bomb created a 10-by-15-foot hole in a wall and devastated a 100-foot area in the lobby, sending bodies, metal, glass, and debris flying through the air. The blast killed three people—two who died at the scene and one later in a hospital—and injured thirty-five others, including one man who had to have his leg amputated. It was one of the deadliest incidents of random violence in Los Angeles history. Late that night, a man telephoned Conrad Casler, the city editor of the *Los Angeles Herald-Examiner,* and claimed credit for the bombing. He correctly gave the publicly undisclosed locker number, T-225, where the bomb had exploded. He said that his name was Rasim and that the bombing had been committed by Aliens of America.[19]

---

16. Transcript of the Grand Jury testimony of Arthur J. Smith, Los Angeles, September 1974 (Files, Los Angeles County District Attorney's Office).

17. Author's telephone interview with Altman.

18. Transcript of tape recovered on August 16, 1974, at 11th and Los Angeles Streets (Los Angeles Police Department Item No. 1345, Files, Los Angeles County District Attorney's Office). Rasim's statement that it was necessary to "load our gun with one bullet," and then "fire it" in order to have his message taken seriously was similar to the following passage that appeared years later in Unabomber Theodore Kaczynski's manifesto: "In order to get our message before the public with some chance of making a lasting impression, we've had to kill people." ("The Unabomber Manifesto," quoted in Joan Didion, "Varieties of Madness," *New York Review of Books,* April 23, 1998, p. 18.)

19. *People v Kurbegovic,* 138 Cal.App.3d., p. 737.

Three days later, Rasim telephoned the CBS television station in Los Angeles and told them that a tape cassette about the bombing could be found in a trash bin outside a local bank. When police recovered the tape, they found with it the key to the airport locker where the bomb had exploded. "This first bomb was marked with the letter A, which stands for Airport," Rasim said on the tape. "The second bomb will be associated with the letter L, the third with the letter I, etc., until our name has been written on the face of this nation in blood."[20] Kurbegovic had indeed stamped the words "Aliens of America" on the lip of the canister of the airport bomb.[21]

Rasim thus became known in the media as the "Alphabet Bomber." Although anti-American terrorist incidents were common overseas, few major terrorist incidents had occurred within U.S. borders. Now one of America's largest cities was the target of a mysterious bombing campaign by a person who was toying with the authorities through his messages to the media. In one tape he warned that the letter "O" in the name Aliens of America would be associated with an attack on an oil refinery.[22] The public was frightened because no one knew when, or where, the Alphabet Bomber would strike next. "He had credibility," recalled Dinko Bozanich, who would later prosecute Kurbegovic during his criminal trial. "He had the city of L.A. in fear."[23]

In the first tape claiming credit for the airport bombing, Rasim displayed a logic that had to be chilling to investigators. He acknowledged that since he would likely face the death penalty for the bombing, he now had nothing to lose by escalating his violence. He demanded that all immigration, naturalization, and sex laws be declared unconstitutional. "We have earned death penalty many times over and we intend to go as far as is necessary, or as far as we can, to not only eliminate such [immigration, naturalization, and sex] laws, but to punish those who tolerate its [sic] existence. We deeply believe that somewhere in U.S. Government, there will be one man who will have a [sic] strength to save this nation. We indeed possess material ability and emotional capacity to destroy it."[24]

In using the media to publicize his cause, Rasim was following the

---

20. Transcript of tape recovered on August 9, 1974, in Maywood, California, following call to CBS (Los Angeles Police Department Item No. 1340, Files, Los Angeles County District Attorney's Office).

21. Author's interview with Bozanich.

22. Transcript of tape recovered on August 16, 1974.

23. Author's interview with Bozanich.

24. Transcript of tape recovered on August 9, 1974.

example of the Symbionese Liberation Army, which began to drop off tape recordings after they kidnapped Patty Hearst. "He learned a lot from them," said Bozanich. "Just how to go about this, as well as how law enforcement reacts to this stuff."[25] The Alphabet Bomber also gained the attention of Senator Alan Cranston, a Democrat from California, who issued a public appeal to Rasim to end his violence and to confer with him about what could be done to improve the treatment of aliens.[26] In one of the tape recordings that Rasim had made before the airport bombing, he called on Cranston, whom he described as "an informed man" and a person who did not "appeal to emotions, but [rather to] reason," to "get down to business of saving this nation from its two most acute ills, sex laws and immigration and naturalization laws." Rasim concluded that tape with the following warning: "I hope, Mr. Cranston, you will not underestimate our strength and our determination to be treated with dignity and respect in accordance to our contribution to the greatness of this nation. I deeply believe you will succeed."[27]

Cranston, however, did not receive the tape until several weeks after Rasim had placed it in the vicinity of a local radio station. A passerby found the cassette in the street and took it home but did not play the tape for several days. After finally listening to its contents, he turned the tape over to the FBI.[28] The lack of a response from Cranston was one of the reasons Rasim cited for the need to set off the airport bomb. In a tape made after the bombing, he said "the bomb is our temporary response to the reaction that Senator Alan Cranston displayed to the taped message we have delivered to KPFK radio station few weeks earlier."[29] Rasim also referred to Cranston when he phoned the *Herald-Examiner* to claim credit for the bombing. He told the newspaper that "Sen. Alan Cranston knows about it."[30]

When Cranston finally heard the tape, he tried to explain to Rasim why there had been no reply. "It's only just been found and given to me," Cranston appealed to Rasim through the media on August 16. "That's why I haven't responded until now." He urged the bomber to "call me

25. Author's interview with Bozanich.

26. Conrad Casler, "Bomb at Bus Station, Another One Planted, Tape Warns," *Los Angeles Herald-Examiner,* August 17, 1974, p. A1.

27. Transcript of tape recovered by the FBI on August 12, 1974.

28. Joan Sweeney, "Man Who Claims He Bombed Airport Makes New Threat," *Los Angeles Times,* August 17, 1974, Part II, p. 5.

29. Transcript of tape recovered on August 9, 1974.

30. "Airport Takes 3 Steps to Boost Security," *Los Angeles Herald-Examiner,* August 8, 1974, p. A3.

right now before you do anything else."[31] The *Herald Examiner* even printed Cranston's local office address and phone number on its front page, informing Rasim that there will be "office personnel manning the phone today and all next week awaiting a call from members of Aliens of America."[32]

Rasim never called Cranston's office. He did, however, call the *Herald Examiner* a few days before Cranston's appeal to warn that he had planted another bomb. On Tuesday, August 13, city desk editor Casler received a call from Rasim. "We have placed another one which will go off this Sunday in a crowded area," Rasim said. Casler asked him if the bombing would be at the airport. "No, sir," replied Rasim. "We will not say where it will be, but the bomb is 25 pounds and we will tell you where it is if the charges for murder have been brought against former Los Angeles Police Commissioner Emmet C. McGaughey." Rasim also wanted murder charges brought against a retired police captain, George Milemore. He claimed that both men had murdered two Mexican nationals in a skid row apartment and then covered up the killings as a mistaken shooting.[33]

Although there had been a mistaken killing by police of two Mexican nationals in Los Angeles in 1970, neither McGaughey nor Milemore had been involved in the incident. The mention of Milemore's name, however, gave investigators one more clue in their frantic search for Rasim's true identity. Milemore was the former head of investigations for the police commission that had denied Kurbegovic's application for a permit to open a taxi dance hall in 1972. In a tape recovered a day earlier by the FBI, Rasim admitted that it was Aliens of America that had set fires at the homes of Commissioners McGaughey and Justice and had placed an incendiary plastic bottle in the gas tank of McGaughey's car. In that tape he also mentioned the name of Judge Campbell, criticizing him for sentencing "innocent aliens."[34]

Investigators now had the names of four people against whom the Alphabet Bomber might have some type of grudge: McGaughey, Justice, Campbell, and Milemore. Although the police had investigated the 1973 fires at the homes of McGaughey, Justice, and Campbell, they had never identified Kurbegovic as a possible suspect. They had been looking for

---

31. Sweeney, "Man Who Claims He Bombed Airport Makes New Threat," p. 5.

32. Conrad Casler, "A Reprieve from 3rd Alphabet Bomb?" *Los Angeles Herald-Examiner*, August 18, 1974, p. A1.

33. Transcript of August 13, 1974, telephone call to Conrad Casler of the *Los Angeles Herald-Examiner* (Los Angeles Police Department Item No. 1342, Files, Los Angeles County District Attorney's Office).

34. Transcript of tape recovered by the FBI on August 12, 1974.

someone who had a possible revenge motive against all three victims. Since Kurbegovic had been acquitted in his lewd-conduct trial in Campbell's court, his name did not appear on the list of suspects who might want to take violent action against the judge. But now Rasim was mentioning Campbell as somebody who had sentenced innocent aliens. Despite the implication that an alien had actually been "sentenced," the investigators decided to look again through all of Campbell's records, searching even for the names of aliens who had been acquitted of their charges. Since these were the days before most criminal records were computerized, the investigators had to check and cross-reference thousands of cases by hand. That would take time, which was not on their side. Rasim had already issued a new threat to set off another bomb in a crowded area in a few days, and his claims about experimentation with nerve gas had investigators and the public on edge.

On August 15, the following headline appeared in the *Herald-Examiner*: L.A. BOMBER PLEDGES GAS ATTACK. The newspaper article was accompanied by the transcript of a tape recovered by the *Herald-Examiner* the night before. Rasim warned that a nerve gas attack would take place during the next few months. Claiming that the United States was "no longer an alternative to Communism or religionism [*sic*]," Rasim issued the following threat: "We, the Aliens of America, indeed intend to make this nation an alternative to life elsewhere, and the only way we can do that is by fighting. We, however, do not intend to fight a long, agonizing battle. . . . Our goal is three months from now as we shall have at latest within three months from now, two tons of sarin nerve gas which we shall deliver in one-quarter ton shells to the Capitol Hill by the use of eight single-shot cannon barrels. With it we shall destroy the entire personnel of Capitol Hill."[35]

The threat of nerve gas attacks was prominent in several of Rasim's tape recordings. As noted earlier, he stated that he had developed a nerve agent, "AA4S," that was more potent than sarin. He also made repeated threats to use sarin in attacks against the U.S. government. "Imagine what will happen if we are lucky and the wind blows from Supreme Court to Capitol Hill to White House to Pentagon," Rasim said.[36] In the same tape, he indicated that he was researching different ways to disperse chemical warfare (CW) agents so as to kill as many people as possible. "We just

35. Conrad Casler, "L.A. Bomber Pledges Gas Attack," *Los Angeles Herald-Examiner*, August 15, 1974, p. 1; Transcript of tape recovered on August 14, 1974, at 1355 South Olive Street (Los Angeles Police Department Item No. 1343, Files, Los Angeles County District Attorney's Office).

36. Transcript of tape recovered by FBI on August 12, 1974.

acquired the plans of thirty major skyscrapers' air conditioning systems," he warned. "We visit the building, see where its air inlet is . . . and take a walk. Maybe watch a Dodgers' game and enjoy ourselves."[37]

The prospect of CW agents being fed into the air-conditioning systems of Los Angeles skyscrapers alarmed prosecutor Bozanich. "How many high-rise buildings are there in just downtown Los Angeles, in a very small confined area?" he asked. "How many people are in one of these high-rise buildings? And if you do put something into the ventilation system [it] could cripple or kill hundreds, thousands [of people]. And yet this guy, he clearly had the brains to be able to read and understand [how to do it]."[38]

Rasim claimed that one of the "soldiers" of Aliens of America had gone to the Supreme Court on four different occasions during the spring of 1974 with the intent to kill all of the Supreme Court justices. "But even though we deeply believed that he will have emotional strength to jump over the Supreme Court bench, and then behind such bench draw his two carefully concealed Smith and W [Wesson] 59s, each filled with fifteen mercury bullets, and thus make an example of what happens when supercrimes such as immigration and naturalization law lingers on; but he failed, his hands froze four times. God knows and we know he tried his best."[39]

That failure, Rasim said, convinced his group to try different tactics. "Since our defeat of being emotionally unable to deport U.S. Supreme Court justices to heaven, where they belong, we intensified the development of our military strength, and immediately focused on two [of] our most potent war weapons, fire and nerve gas. So far, we have demonstrated we can use the fire; we hope to use nerve gas not more than once, and turn the entire Capitol Hill into a mortuary. Presently, we have only laboratory quantities of sarin, but we are sure we will have two tons of it within the next four months. We believe two tons will do the job."[40]

---

37. Ibid.

38. Author's interview with Bozanich.

39. Transcript of tape recovered by the FBI on August 12, 1974. Rasim's lament about how the soldier "froze" and did not have the "emotional strength" to kill the Supreme Court justices is similar to Unabomber Theodore Kaczynski's expression of regret about not being able to carry out a planned murder. Kaczynski wrote the following in his journal in December 1972: "About a year and a half ago, I planned to murder a scientist—as a means of revenge against organized society in general and the technological establishment in particular. . . . Unfortunately, I chickened out. I couldn't work up the nerve to do it." (David Johnston, "In Unabomber's Own Words, A Chilling Account of Murder," *New York Times*, April 29, 1998, p. A16.)

40. Transcript of tape recovered by the FBI on August 12, 1974.

Investigation and Arrest

The effort to catch Rasim involved the U.S. Secret Service and other federal law enforcement agencies. During his campaign of violence in 1974 and his subsequent years in prison, Kurbegovic threatened the life of every U.S. president.[41] A special office in the basement of the White House was set up to aid in his capture. The CIA provided sophisticated audio equipment to analyze the cassette tapes, and linguists worked to identify Rasim's accent. "They not only figured out that he was Yugoslavian, but where he came from [within Yugoslavia]," recalled Nancy B. Watson, the judge in Kurbegovic's criminal trial.[42] This information, combined with Rasim's having mentioned the names McGaughey, Justice, Campbell, and Milemore on one of his tapes, eventually led investigators to identify Kurbegovic as the Alphabet Bomber. The investigators "went through every criminal case [in Judge Campbell's records]," recalled prosecutor Bozanich. "Even though [he was] found not guilty, Kurbegovic's name pops up."[43]

The identification would not occur until August 20. In the meantime, police were desperately trying to locate the site of the second bomb that Rasim had pledged would go off in a crowded area. But there were just too many potential targets that could be associated with the letter "L" to be able to predict where the bomb might be. Rewards totaling $100,000 were posted for information leading to Rasim's arrest and conviction. On August 16, Rasim placed another call to the *Herald-Examiner* stating that there was a tape to be picked up at a gas station that would describe "much, much bigger things" that would happen.[44] On the tape, he disclosed the location of the "L" bomb. "The letter 'L' in our name stands for 'locker' and it also stands for 'life,'" Rasim said. "We have planted an extremely sensitive, delinquent, and unpredictable bomb in a locker number 625 at L.A. Greyhound Bus Depot downtown. We believe that whoever would have attempted to remove that bomb would cause it to explode. The bomb contains no evidence whatsoever that could lead to us and consequently we can disclose its location before it blows up on its

41. Author's interview with Watson.

42. Joseph D. Douglass, Jr. and Neil C. Livingstone, *America the Vulnerable: The Threat of Chemical and Biological Warfare* (Lexington, Mass.: Lexington Books, 1987), pp. 30–31; author's interview with Watson.

43. Author's interview with Bozanich.

44. Transcript of August 16, 1974, telephone call to Frederick Lanceley, FBI agent stationed at the *Los Angeles Herald-Examiner* (Los Angeles Police Department Item No. 1344, Files, Los Angeles County District Attorney's Office).

own. . . . Thus, we have decided because our cause is getting publicity that it is momentarily not necessary to continue to horrify the population of this land, and we can afford the luxury of revealing the location of such a bomb and let it stand for the word 'life'! Nothing could make us happier than if we could conclude that we can reveal the location of bomb 'I' which is already planted."[45]

Police rushed to the Greyhound Bus station and evacuated approximately 1,000 people who were there on a busy Friday night. The bomb was found in the locker where Rasim had said it would be. Using a 30-foot rope, the bomb squad removed the explosive device from the station and into the street, where they placed it in a specially constructed bomb-carrier on a trailer behind a police panel truck. They intended to remove the bomb to the desert and detonate it. But as the trailer was being pulled through downtown Los Angeles with a motorcycle police escort, smoke started coming out of the bomb-carrier. On seeing this, all of the motorcycle officers quickly moved away from the trailer. Moments later, the detonator exploded but did not set off the main explosive charge. The 25-pound bomb, packed in a briefcase, was at that time one of the largest bombs in the history of Los Angeles. Had it gone off at the station, approximately 100 people would have been killed.[46]

Rasim telephoned the *Herald-Examiner* the next day to inform them that he had decided to postpone his next bombing, which he had earlier warned would be associated with the letter I. "Nothing will happen on Sunday," he said.[47] Nevertheless, more than 1,000 extra police were deployed throughout Los Angeles to find a possible bomb, searching movie theaters, churches, parks, and any other place where crowds gather. "We're going to look everywhere and won't disregard a place just because it begins with an 'M' and not an 'I,'" a police spokesman told reporters. "We learned from the Greyhound experience that we don't have his alphabet formula down yet. Who would think of the Greyhound site as an 'L' place? It was a throw-off."[48] People stayed at home that weekend,

---

45. Transcript of tape recovered on August 16, 1974.

46. *People v Kurbegovic*, 138 Cal.App.3d., p. 738; Casler, "Bomb at Bus Station," p. A1. Author's interview with Bozanich; author's interview with Watson.

47. Transcript of August 17, 1974, telephone call to Leo Batt of the *Los Angeles Herald-Examiner* (Los Angeles Police Department Item No. 1346, Files, Los Angeles County District Attorney's Office).

48. Al Martinez and Bill Hazlett, "Threat of Bombing Called Off but Police Aren't Taking Any Chances," *Los Angeles Times*, August 18, 1974, Part I, p. 28.

fearful that the Alphabet Bomber would strike again. A Watts Summer Festival concert at the Los Angeles Coliseum that was expected to attract 70,000 people drew only 3,500.[49]

The police did not find a bomb that Sunday, but by August 20 the exhaustive local and federal investigation had finally identified Kurbegovic as the prime suspect. He was put under surveillance in the hope that he would lead the authorities to possible accomplices. A special unit of the Los Angeles Police Department followed him as he drove along Wilshire Boulevard to Santa Monica beach where, sitting in his car, he made another tape recording. He then returned home and that evening drove to Hollywood wearing a red wig, glasses, and a green coat. He parked his car and walked to a Carl's Jr. restaurant where he placed a tape cassette in the restroom. After he left the restaurant the police removed the tape and listened to its contents in their car, verifying that it was similar to the tapes that Rasim had made during the previous two weeks.

Kurbegovic, for unknown reasons, returned to the restaurant moments later and reentered the restroom. Since the tape had already been removed, the police realized that he would now know he was being followed. A police officer went into the restroom and arrested him without a struggle.[50] Kurbegovic's need to communicate ultimately led to his arrest. "What really did him in," recalled Judge Watson, who presided during Kurbegovic's criminal trial, "was [that] he couldn't resist being heard."[51]

The Home-Made Explosives Factory

When police searched Kurbegovic's apartment after his arrest, they were astonished at what they found. Among the items recovered were live pipe bombs, explosive materials, fuses, timing devices, two gas masks stamped "U.S. Army," a box of ten gas-mask filters and a nose piece, catalogues for purchasing chemicals and laboratory equipment, and several books and articles on explosives, unconventional warfare, law enforcement operations and strategies, and chemical and biological weapons.[52]

---

49. "Bomber Ties Self to Blast Downtown," *Los Angeles Herald Examiner*, August 19, 1974, p. A2.

50. Author's interview with Bozanich; *People v Kurbegovic*, 138 Cal.App.3d., pp. 740–741.

51. Author's interview with Watson.

52. *People v Muharem Kurbegovic*, Case No. A-311331, Receipt No. 611198, *Central Criminal Microfilm*, Roll 352, A-311218 through A-311435.

Police also found maps of Washington, D.C., and London's Heathrow Airport and discovered that he had visited a travel agency at least twice in the weeks prior to his arrest to inquire about travel to Europe.[53]

Among the books in Kurbegovic's possession were *Guide to Germ Warfare*, *Guide to Chemical and Gas Warfare*, *The Book of Poison*, *Poisons as Weapons of War*, *Improvised Munitions Handbook*, *Grenades and Pyrotechnics*, *Military Explosives*, *Explosives and Demolitions*, *Unconventional Warfare Devices and Techniques*, *Criminal Investigation*, *Defense Tactics for Law Enforcement*, and *Law Enforcement Equipment*.[54] Some of the books were recently declassified military documents. "It was like a little library that he had," recalled prosecutor Bozanich, "and if you could read and understand all of this you had access to what had been highly classified material only a couple of years before in the United States military."[55] Judge Watson was not surprised that he had acquired these books. "Kurbegovic would have the talent to find out about things that had been classified and then become declassified and how to get them," she said. "I mean that's the way his mind worked."[56]

Stephen Smith said that Kurbegovic had borrowed several books from him on chemicals and described his friend as being "like a kid with a new toy" when he fooled around with explosives and wrote notes to him about it.[57] Arleigh McCree, one of the police officers who searched Kurbegovic's apartment and who would later head the Los Angeles Police Department's bomb squad, told a reporter in 1983 that Kurbegovic had acquired all but one ingredient needed to build a rudimentary nerve gas bomb and was about to pick up the last item, an organophosphate chemical, at the time of his arrest.[58]

It is likely that the nerve gas McCree was referring to was sarin, since

---

53. Author's interview with Bozanich; Jack Jones, "Bombing Suspect Trapped Himself," *Los Angeles Times*, August 22, 1974, p. 33.

54. Ibid.

55. Author's interview with Bozanich.

56. Author's interview with Watson.

57. Trout and Goodman, "Suspect's Double Life," p. 34.

58. Lardner, "Terrorist Reportedly Sent a Justice Toxic Chemicals," p. A3. McCree, along with another police officer, was killed in 1986 while defusing a bomb. McCree was a nationally recognized expert on explosives who impressed both Bozanich and Watson. "McCree was so familiar with [explosives] that when we were going through [the books found in Kurbegovic's apartment]," Bozanich recalled, "[he would] take a piece of evidence and . . . say what [it] did, . . . where [it] fit in. . . . Then he would immediately reach over for not only the book, but get to the actual page number that he would then show you. So he could immediately cross-reference. . . . I was flabbergasted that he knew the books that well." (Author's interview with Bozanich).

Kurbegovic had threatened to use sarin in many of his tapes and claimed that he was already conducting experiments with it. Nerve agents such as sarin, soman, tabun, and VX interfere with the transmission of nerve impulses, causing convulsions and death by respiratory paralysis.[59] According to Bozanich, the extent of Kurbegovic's involvement with nerve gas may never be known.[60]

Kurbegovic may also have been experimenting with other chemical warfare agents in addition to sarin. In November 1976, more than two years after his arrest, he stated in court that his former apartment still contained over 100 pounds of explosives and other items. When police searched the apartment again, they found hidden behind a medicine cabinet mounted on a false wall a large stash of chemicals, among them a blue metal drum labeled "twenty-five pounds sodium cyanide," a plastic bottle labeled "nitric acid," and a bottle labeled "carbon tetrachloride." Police also found several other chemicals including phosphoric acid, sodium chlorite, ammonium nitrate, and chloroform, as well as smokeless powder, silencers, and guns.[61]

The amount of sodium cyanide in Kurbegovic's apartment was startling. He may have been planning future threats and actions involving the nerve agent tabun, of which sodium cyanide is a chemical precursor, or the use of sodium cyanide to release lethal hydrogen cyanide gas.[62] Since Kurbegovic stated that he had acquired plans for the air-conditioning systems of thirty major skyscrapers, he may have been thinking about using sodium cyanide in a future attack on such a target. The finding of nitric acid, carbon tetrachloride, and chloroform in Kurbegovic's apartment also suggests that he may have been experimenting with the choking agent phosgene, since these chemicals, among others, are used in its manufacture.[63] Of course, the availability of chemicals from supply houses may have been a key factor in his choosing them.

"[McCree] was superb," Watson said. "Absolutely outstanding. Possibly the best expert witness I ever had in a courtroom." (Author's interview with Watson.)

59. U.S. Congress, Office of Technology Assessment, *Technologies Underlying Weapons of Mass Destruction*, OTA-BP-ISC-115 (Washington, D.C.: U.S. Government Printing Office, December 1993), p. 18.

60. Author's interview with Bozanich.

61. Ibid.

62. U.S. Congress, Office of Technology Assessment, *Technologies Underlying Weapons of Mass Destruction*, p. 24.

63. *Global Proliferation of Weapons of Mass Destruction, Hearings*, Part 1, p. 613; "Lab Chemical Safety Summaries (LCSS): Carbon Tetrachloride" (http://www.hhmi.org/science/labsafe); "LCSS: Chloroform" (http://www.hhmi.org/science/labsafe).

Understanding Kurbegovic's Motivations

Since Kurbegovic acted alone in his campaign of violence and was mentally unstable, any analysis of the decision-making process involved in
his threatened use of chemical weapons would require trying to understand the psyche of a very troubled individual. Based on what he said in
his numerous tapes, however, it is likely that Kurbegovic believed that
conventional weapons were not sufficient to achieve his goal of forcing
the U.S. government to abolish all immigration, naturalization, and sex
laws. Although he used conventional weapons in his terrorist activity in
Los Angeles, he believed that only by threatening to release nerve gas
over Washington, D.C., would he gain the attention he desired from the
U.S. government.[64] In addition, Kurbegovic had applied for U.S. citizen-
ship but had not yet taken the test, apparently fearing rejection because
of his arrest record.[65] An understanding of his motivations can be seen
in the following excerpt from one of his tapes:

Those who are rightfully or wrongfully arrested for any reason never become
citizens and, ah, [sic] great number of them are deported to the countries they
sometimes never knew. We believe that immigration and naturalization laws
of this country are great insult to the dignity of this nation, and we believe
them to constitute treason. In the past we have approached several political
leaders and appealed to their moral, religious, and patriotic conscience, but
have always been totally ignored. We have discovered this land and built it
into an economic giant. As a reward for our work we were awarded with
immigration and naturalization laws which are in relative historical space
more vicious than Gestapo laws regarding Jews. What our children and
grandchildren have failed to realize, however, is that whoever had the
strength and ingenuity to build this nation, he also must have equal ability
to destroy it once he realizes that it has become his worst enemy.[66]

There are also references in several of the tapes to the need to
eliminate all laws relating to sexual conduct. For example, in one tape
Kurbegovic states that "all sex laws must disappear and Congress must
more specifically separate church and state, as well as prohibit itself from
ever passing any law relating to human sexual behavior."[67] In another
tape, he complains that "a man is prohibited to exercise his God-given

---

64. Transcript of tape recovered by the FBI on August 12, 1974.

65. Trout and Goodman, "Suspect's Double Life," p. 34.

66. Transcript of tape recovered by the FBI on August 12, 1974.

67. Transcript of tape recovered on August 9, 1974.

nature in the matter of sex, thus again losing his most fundamental freedom."[68]

Anti-clerical and anti-communist themes were prevalent in many of Kurbegovic's communiqués. He chose the *Los Angeles Herald-Examiner* as the recipient of most of his tape recordings and telephone calls because of his "deepest admiration" for the newspaper's "heroic and historic battle against Communism."[69] In one of his tapes, he stated:

We, the Aliens of America, are not willing to live a life where Bible is shoved down our throat by force. Our desire to live a free life from anybody's religious terror, especially religious terror crystallized into legalities such as sex laws of this country, is as strong as our desire to live free of Communism. And we shall fight to the last drop of our blood to see this nation free of religionism [sic], Communism, and all other pornographies of human mind. Freedom to us does not mean that Billy Graham is free to become a millionaire in the name of the Lord. Freedom to us means that John Doe has a right to open a hot dog stand and survive.[70]

In the same tape, Kurbegovic also criticized U.S. policy toward the Soviet Union and Israel:

Recently, due to the absence of foreign-born people in United States Government, this nation has engaged in signing meaningless pieces of paper with Communists, living in an insane illusion that Communists will honor their signature. The only reason Communists negotiate is to find the soft and weak points of his adversary so that he can more successfully kill him when the right time comes. Instead of letting Soviet Communism collapse to its natural decay, the inexperienced leadership of this nation is intending to give it the free man's technology so that it can use it to enslave more people. On the other front, this nation is supporting the insanity of Zionism and insisting that 200 million Jews have a right to immigrate to Israel. Israel is a very small country. Just where are all those people going to go? Or are they going to spill over into Arab land?[71]

Kurbegovic's tapes also had a global revolutionary theme. As noted above, he issued an ultimatum to all governments of the world to surrender to Aliens of America and stated that his objective was to bring

---

68. Transcript of tape recovered on August 20, 1974.

69. Transcript of tape recovered on August 14, 1974.

70. Transcript of tape recovered on August 16, 1974.

71. Ibid.

about a society free of nationalism, religion, fascism, racism, and communism.[72]

Finally, Kurbegovic may have been motivated by the possibility of extortion. "I think it was mercenary," said prosecutor Bozanich about Kurbegovic's objectives. "He is killing two birds with one stone. He is also getting off his chest a lot of things he doesn't like. But he is going to make some money out of the deal."[73] Kurbegovic once asked Smith how a person would be able to carry out a scheme to demand $10 million after setting off one bomb, in exchange for not setting off a second.[74] He did not, however, make any monetary demands in his tapes or telephone calls to the media.

Technical Know-How

Although Kurbegovic acquired books on both chemical and biological warfare, he sought only chemical agents, probably because he had learned in one of his jobs how to purchase explosive chemicals. As noted above, he claimed to have developed a new nerve agent, "AA4S," which he boasted was more potent than sarin. In most of his chemical threats, however, he talked of using sarin.

Kurbegovic obtained the scientific know-how to produce nerve agents by reading books and articles on the subject and by asking questions at work about chemicals and explosives. "FBI cannot catch us," he boasted in one tape, "because we studied the same books as FBI did, and we studied the same books as U.S. Army did."[75] Although he did not receive external assistance from other individuals, companies, foreign governments, or terrorist organizations, he did have numerous conversations about chemicals and explosives with his friend Stephen Smith, who never suspected that he had criminal intentions. As noted above, Kurbegovic purchased the necessary chemicals and equipment for experimenting with nerve agents from commercial supply houses.

Since Kurbegovic was trained as an engineer, he had sufficient technical and scientific expertise to understand how to synthesize homemade nerve agents once he began reading about them. His mental illness, which was diagnosed as paranoid schizophrenia, gave him "the ability to concentrate in a way that most normal people don't because he doesn't get

---

72. Transcript of tape recovered on July 5, 1974.

73. Author's interview with Bozanich.

74. *People v Kurbegovic*, 138 Cal.App.3d., p. 739.

75. Transcript of tape recovered by the FBI on August 12, 1974.

distracted by anything," said Gerald Chaleff, Kurbegovic's public defender during the competency trials. "And so he would focus on something and he could accomplish it. He could be incredibly intelligent when he focused on anything."[76]

The fact that Kurbegovic had so many different and dangerous chemicals in his apartment leads one to wonder what his future intentions would have been had he not been caught. Since he enjoyed experimenting with chemicals, it may have only been a matter of time before he produced a one-man chemical arsenal. According to Prosecutor Bozanich, "He seemed to become fascinated in this area relatively shortly before he was apprehended. He showed enough canny ability to process information in the stuff that he would read about, discuss maybe with co-employees . . . [and] then turn around and build something and do something. There is only so much that can be done within a six-month period of time, for example. You can't become a bomb expert, a fire expert, and do all this thinking and accomplish it all within six months. So maybe what happened was that [nerve agents] was next on his agenda and he didn't get around to following up on that, but [he] had done enough reading where he could bluff it."[77]

Public Defender Chaleff also wondered about his client's future activities had he not been arrested. "I think the interesting thing is how he escalated," Chaleff recalled. "He started with burning logs in front of people's houses and then he went to [putting incendiary devices] in gas tanks, and then he escalated to actually setting off a bomb."[78]

The Criminal Trial

Kurbegovic's criminal trial did not begin until February 1980. The delay of more than five and a half years from the time of his arrest resulted from legal questions concerning his mental competency to stand trial.[79] Kurbegovic, who by this time was no longer pretending to be a mute,

---

76. Author's interview with Chaleff.

77. Author's interview with Bozanich.

78. Author's interview with Chaleff.

79. Under California law, a person cannot be tried if he has a mental disorder that makes him incapable of understanding the nature of the charges against him and of assisting his lawyer in a rational manner. William Keene, a Los Angeles County Superior Court judge, found Kurbegovic incompetent to stand trial in 1974. The prosecution demanded a jury trial on the competency issue, and in 1975 a jury found Kurbegovic competent. Notwithstanding this verdict, Keene found Kurbegovic mentally incompetent. Kurbegovic was sent to Atascadero State Hospital, and as required by law he was brought back to court eighteen months later for a review of his mental

acted as his own attorney during the trial. He often wore a colorful Yugoslav costume made by a female spectator in the courtroom who had become infatuated with him. At one point in the proceedings he asked Judge Watson to declare him the Messiah, which she refused to do. At another point, when he was cross-examining a pastor who had lost his leg in the airport bombing, Kurbegovic shocked the courtroom by asking the victim, "So where was your God when this bomb went off?" Judge Watson told the pastor not to answer the question and admonished the defendant for his cross-examination. Kurbegovic's outrageous behavior in the courtroom took its toll on the judge. "I really felt beaten down after a while," she recalled. "I remember saying one morning . . . to my husband, 'You know, I've so enjoyed sitting on the bench but I'd rather take a beating then go to court today.' I mean it was just unending with him. Just unending."[80]

The trial lasted eight months, with the jury finding Kurbegovic guilty of twenty-five counts of murder, arson, attempted murder, possession of explosive material, and exploding a bomb. He did not face the death penalty because California's death-penalty law, which had been in effect at the time of the 1974 airport bombing, was declared unconstitutional by the California Supreme Court while Kurbegovic was in custody. Although the death penalty was reinstated by the time the criminal trial began, it was not retroactive and hence could not be applied to his case. Kurbegovic also did not face a sentence of life in prison without the possibility of parole, since that sentence had been included in the same statute that was declared unconstitutional.[81]

Judge Watson sentenced Kurbegovic to life in prison. Complaining that a life sentence was too vague, he asked the judge to change it to 1,000 years "so I can have something to look forward to." During the sentenc-

---

status. In the meantime, the Court of Appeals had reversed Keene's judgment of incompetency, finding that while he had the power to enter that judgment, he had acted improperly in doing so because there was substantial evidence to support the jury's verdict that Kurbegovic was competent to stand trial. Yet once again Keene found Kurbegovic incompetent to stand trial, and the prosecution again demanded a jury trial. In October 1976, a jury returned a verdict that Kurbegovic was incompetent and he was sent back to Atascadero. In November 1978, he was returned to court and criminal proceedings reinstated. But Keene again declared a doubt concerning Kurbegovic's competency to stand trial, so a third competency hearing was begun in early 1979. This time, with a new judge presiding, Leslie Light, a jury found Kurbegovic competent to stand trial. *People v Kurbegovic*, 138 Cal.App.3d., pp. 741–742; Charles Maher, "Long Trial Delay Stirs Controversy," *Los Angeles Times*, April 28, 1980, Part 1, p. 3.

80. Author's interview with Watson.

81. Author's interview with Watson; author's interview with Bozanich.

ing, Watson told Kurbegovic that she considered him to be "the most dangerous person in custody that I know of." She said that Kurbegovic had an "enormous capacity for feelings of vengeance and anti-social acts," and that he had intended to "kill as many people as he could" with his bombs. As he was led from the courtroom, Kurbegovic held up a sign that read, "I shall return!"[82]

California prison officials have had their hands full in dealing with Kurbegovic. He tried to escape from the Criminal Courts Building in Los Angeles during one of his competency trials and punched one of his public defenders during another competency trial. He is currently serving his sentence at Pelican Bay, the most secure prison facility in California, situated just south of the Oregon border near the coastal community of Crescent City. While in different prisons, he has set fires, tried to kill other inmates, and continued to harass his prosecutor—for example, by sending a letter under Bozanich's name to Campbell's, the company that makes alphabet soup, complaining of food poisoning.[83] Kurbegovic's threats to the lives of U.S. presidents have repeatedly brought Secret Service agents to his parole hearings to argue against his release. "I've been told," Judge Watson said, "that I need not worry about his getting out."[84] Prosecutor Bozanich has stated that state parole officers would have blood on their hands if they ever released Kurbegovic.[85]

Conclusion

The Alphabet Bomber demonstrated that a highly intelligent, angry person with a technical background can effectively use the threat of a chemical attack to spread fear among the public and concern in the government. That he was able to acquire so much knowledge about chemical warfare agents from open sources in a relatively short period of time was remarkable. It would be even easier today. The information that it took Kurbegovic a few months to acquire in the 1970s by checking out books from the library and obtaining declassified government documents would probably take a person today only a few hours by searching the Internet. Moreover, some of the chemicals and other equipment that

---

82. Robert Welkos, "Life Term Given in Alphabet Bomber Case," *Los Angeles Times*, November 25, 1980, Part II, pp. 1, 6.

83. Author's interview with Bozanich.

84. Author's interview with Watson.

85. Frank Candida, "Alphabet Bomber Gets Life Sentence in LAX Deaths," *Los Angeles Herald-Examiner*, November 25, 1980, p. A3.

Kurbegovic purchased in person from a supply house could now be bought online with a credit card.

There is no evidence that Kurbegovic actually followed through on any of his several threats to use nerve gas. He did, however, give a lot of thought to different ways of carrying out a nerve gas attack, including placing time-release devices containing nerve agents in major cities around the world, putting nerve agents in metal discs under postage stamps and sending postcards to the intended victims, distributing toxic agents through the air-conditioning systems of skyscrapers, and firing sarin-filled shells at the U.S. Capitol.

Had Kurbegovic not been caught when he was, it is likely that he would have eventually committed a terrorist act with a chemical agent. He had escalated his threats during the summer of 1974, was accumulating a stockpile of chemicals, and was continuing to learn more about synthesizing nerve agents. He had proven that he could build powerful bombs and place them in crowded public places with deadly results. He was determined to prove that he could do the same with homemade chemical weapons. Whether he would have traveled to Washington, D.C., to carry out his threat to release sarin gas over Capitol Hill, or used the large amount of sodium cyanide in his possession to perpetrate a different type of chemical attack, cannot be determined. But when a person is experimenting with chemical agents and states that he will not stop until he achieves his goals, and when those goals are as irrational as Kurbegovic's were, it is probably only a matter of time before the threats turn into actual incidents.

A quarter of a century ago, a troubled and vengeful man living in Los Angeles foreshadowed one of the future trends in terrorism. No longer is it shocking to learn that terrorists and criminals are thinking about ways to unleash chemical or biological weapons on civilian populations. The Alphabet Bomber was among the first to do so. Unfortunately, he will not be the last.

Chapter 6

The Baader-Meinhof Gang (1975)

David Claridge

Several secondary sources and academic papers discussing the terrorist use of chemical and biological weapons report that in April or May 1975, members of the West German left-wing Baader-Meinhof Gang stole fifty-three steel canisters containing mustard gas from a U.S. ammunition bunker in West Germany and threatened to use them against Stuttgart and possibly other German cities.[1] Investigation of this alleged incident suggests, however, that it probably did not take place.

The Organization

The Baader-Meinhof Gang was born out of the New Left and Extra-Parliamentary Opposition student movements, which had large-scale support among German students in the 1950s and 1960s, particularly in opposition to the U.S. war in Vietnam. These movements did not themselves espouse violent action against the state but preached passive resistance. Nevertheless, a relatively small violent faction evolved from the larger movements.

In 1967, a visit of the Shah of Iran to West Germany provoked massive student demonstrations and new police tactics to counteract them. Dur-

---

1. Articles in the terrorism literature that reference the Baader-Meinhof incident include the following: Brian Jenkins and Alfred P. Rubin, "New Vulnerabilities and the Acquisition of New Weapons by Nongovernment Groups," in Alona E. Evans and John F. Murphy, eds., *Legal Aspects of International Terrorism* (Lexington, Mass.: Lexington Books, 1978), pp. 221–276; Wayman C. Mullins, "An Overview and Analysis of Nuclear, Biological, and Chemical Terrorism: The Weapons, Strategies and Solutions to a Growing Problem," *American Journal of Criminal Justice*, Vol. 16 (Summer 1992), pp. 95–119; Robert H. Kupperman and Jeff Kamen, *Final Warning: Averting Disaster in the New Age of Terrorism* (New York: Doubleday, 1992); and Paul Wilkinson, *Terrorism and the Liberal State*, 2nd ed. (London: Macmillan, 1986), p. 149.

ing a demonstration on June 2, the police shot a university student named Benno Ohnesorg in the head at point-blank range. The apparently cold-blooded nature of this killing shocked and galvanized some of the demonstrators. A left-wing student group known as Kommune I jokingly suggested, on learning of a department store fire in Brussels, Belgium, that arson of such stores would be a good way to bring home the Marxist revolution. The pranksters were arrested for incitement to arson.

The Ohnesorg murder, together with the trial of the Kommune I pranksters, appear to have motivated the rise of a new terrorist group led by Andreas Baader. The basic premise of the Baader group was that the German state needed to be overthrown because it was part of a corrupt international system under the capitalist, imperialist domination of the United States.[2] Baader sought to foment a Marxist-Leninist revolution in West Germany by committing violent acts that would force the state into a repressive response. It was assumed that this reaction would rouse the proletariat from their apathy and into a direct confrontation with the state.[3]

The first actions of the Baader group were attacks on symbols of the capitalist system. In April 1968, eleven days after the Kommune I members were acquitted for incitement to arson, Baader and three colleagues, including his girlfriend Gudrun Ensslin, placed fire-bombs in two department stores in Frankfurt am Main. Both Baader and Ensslin were arrested and imprisoned for their involvement in these attacks, but they were released in 1969. Around this time, a leftist lawyer named Horst Mahler proposed the creation of a true German urban guerrilla movement, based on the model of the Tupamaros in Uruguay and employing a level of violence much greater than simple arson.[4] A fledgling terrorist group was formed with Baader, Ensslin, and Mahler at its core.

In April 1970, soon after the group's formation, Baader was arrested for a second time. He and another member of the group, Astrid Poll, were stopped by traffic police—tipped off by a government informant—after they attempted to obtain guns from a buried weapons store. Ensslin, desperate to get her partner released, asked anti-establishment journalist Ulrike Meinhof for assistance. A rescue operation was mounted in which Meinhof obtained permission from the authorities to interview Baader in

---

2. Ulrike Meinhof, *The Concept Urban Guerrilla* (excerpt), 1971 (http://www.baader-meinhof.com/forstudents/resources/communique/engconcept.html).

3. Yonah Alexander and Denis Pluchinsky, *Europe's Red Terrorists: The Fighting Communist Organizations* (London: Frank Cass, 1992).

4. Richard Huffman, "This Is Baader-Meinhof: 1969" (http://www.baader-meinhof.com/timeline/1969.html).

a reading room outside his prison cell, after which the two fled together through a window. During the escape, an elderly man was shot and wounded, causing Meinhof to go underground to evade arrest. Despite the involvement of several other individuals, Meinhof's sensational role in Baader's escape led the West German press to label the group "the Baader-Meinhof Gang."

During the latter part of 1970 and into 1971, the group—which called itself the *Rote Armee Faktion* (Red Army Faction, or RAF)—expanded its coffers by conducting several successful bank robberies. By 1972 it was ready to launch a full-scale terrorist campaign.[5] Given the roots of the RAF in the movement against the Vietnam War and the major U.S. military presence in West Germany, American interests were an obvious target. The group also attacked representatives of the West German government, particularly those in direct pursuit of the group.

Throughout the month of May 1972, the RAF conducted several spectacular acts of terrorism. On May 11, two pipe bombs exploded at the I.G. Farben Building in Frankfurt, the headquarters of the U.S. Army in West Germany, killing one U.S. officer and injuring thirteen others. An RAF communiqué claimed that the attack was in retaliation for the U.S. mining of North Vietnamese harbors. The following day the police headquarters in Augsburg was destroyed by a bomb, and the State Criminal Investigation Office in Munich was the target of a car bomb. On May 15, the car of a Karlsruhe judge, who had signed most of the warrants for the arrest of the RAF suspects, exploded when his wife turned the ignition key; she survived but was badly wounded. On May 19, several bombs exploded at the Springer Press building in Hamburg, injuring seventeen employees; and on May 24, two car bombs smuggled into the U.S. Army Supreme European Command in Heidelberg killed three Americans and injured five others. Again, the RAF claimed responsibility for the attack as retaliation for U.S. activities in Vietnam. All six attacks took place in a span of less than two weeks. The group's violent spree was finally brought to a halt on June 1, 1972, when the police arrested Baader, Jan-Carl Raspe, and Holger Meins in Frankfurt. Within two weeks, Ensslin, Meinhof, and other key members were also arrested. For the next three years, the RAF terrorists were held in German prisons

---

5. This chronology was constructed from the following sources: Huffman, "This Is Baader-Meinhof"; Jillian Becker, *Hitler's Children: The Story of the Baader-Meinhof Gang*, (London: Michael Joseph, 1977); Jeremy A. Builta, *Extremist Groups: An International Compilation of Terrorist Organizations, Violent Political Movements and Issue-Oriented Militant Movements* (Chicago: Office of International Criminal Justice, 1996), pp. 360–367; and the RAND Database of International Terrorism, RAND Corporation, Santa Monica, California.

awaiting trial. The arrest of its senior leadership left the group reeling, and from June 1972 until November 1974, it conducted no terrorist activity.

Emergence of the June 2 Movement

The death in jail of RAF activist Holger Meins on November 9, 1974, following a hunger strike to protest prison conditions, prompted an almost immediate response. On November 10, the day after Meins's death, the president of the West German Supreme Court, Günter von Drenkmann (who had no connection to the forthcoming Baader-Meinhof trials) was assassinated at his home. The June 2 Movement, a group sympathetic to the RAF cause and with close associations to it, claimed responsibility for the murder.[6]

Over the following months, the June 2 Movement became a significant player in West German terrorism. The origins of this group are somewhat obscure. During the formative period of the RAF in the late 1960s and early 1970s, a number of small anti-establishment cells existed throughout West Germany. Various disaffected individuals passed through these groups; some fell under the sphere of influence of the RAF while others remained on the periphery. The June 2 Movement was more proletarian in nature than the overwhelmingly bourgeois RAF, and some members of the June 2 Movement were probably expelled from the RAF for being anarchists rather than communists.[7] Other members of the June 2 Movement were drawn from Kommune I and the defunct West Berlin Tupamaros.[8]

The June 2 Movement began its campaign of violence in early 1972. Its targeting preferences were similar to those of the RAF and included symbolic targets such as banks, foreign military bases, and whatever else would provide leverage to stall investigations and get their members out of jail. The group's tactics also resembled those of the RAF: a mixture of assassinations, small bombings, and kidnappings. Although the June 2 Movement could be deadly when necessary, they were also whimsical and conscious of their public image. During one bank robbery, for example, the terrorists distributed candies and cakes to bank customers.

In February 1972, the June 2 Movement placed a bomb in a boathouse frequented by British Army officers, killing a German employee. The

---

6. Becker, *Hitler's Children*, p. 260.

7. Ibid., p. 258.

8. Huffman, "This Is Baader-Meinhof: 1971" (http://www.baader-meinhof.com/timeline/1971.html).

terrorists claimed responsibility for the attack in support of the Provisional Irish Republican Army. In May of the same year, the June 2 Movement placed a bomb at the Turkish consulate in Berlin to protest the killing of student activists in Turkey. When this bomb failed to explode, the group decided to bomb the Turkish embassy in Bonn but were arrested as they slept on the side of the road on their way to the capital. Like the RAF, the June 2 Movement seemed to be suffering from a terminal case of amateurism.

On February 27, 1975, however, the June 2 Movement kidnapped Peter Lorenz, a Christian Democratic Union (CDU) politician, from his car in West Berlin. In exchange for Lorenz's release, the group demanded that six of their comrades be freed from prison. None of the RAF prisoners were on their list, and the June 2 Movement detainees had been imprisoned for relatively minor offenses. On March 4, determined to ensure that Lorenz was released unharmed, the West German government capitulated and flew most of the detainees to South Yemen, where they were given asylum. Lorenz was released unharmed within hours of the granting of safe passage. Although the Lorenz kidnapping showed the hallmarks of a more professional terrorist operation, coupled with a surprising level of compliance by the West German government, the June 2 Movement remained rooted in the student political scene. After the Lorenz kidnapping, the group's next action was to steal thousands of tickets for the public transport system and distribute them to houses during the night for free use by citizens of West Berlin.

Since the West German authorities had capitulated to the June 2 Movement on the Lorenz kidnapping, the RAF concluded that the government would give in to terrorist threats against other prominent targets. On April 24, 1975, a six-member RAF team occupied the West German embassy in Stockholm. To force the Swedish police to withdraw from the lower portion of the building, the terrorists threatened the life of the military attaché. When the police refused to disperse, the terrorists shot the attaché three times and he later died in the hospital.

At the beginning of the operation, the RAF assailants had planted an explosive charge inside the embassy building, which they threatened to detonate in the event of a police raid. They then demanded that all twenty-six jailed RAF members (including Baader, Meinhof, Ensslin, and Raspe) be freed. When the West German authorities refused to grant the RAF the same concessions they had given the less significant June 2 Movement, the terrorists threatened to shoot one hostage for every hour their demands were not met. They started by killing the embassy's economic attaché, leaving his body hanging from an open window.

After the West German government's refusal to negotiate with the RAF, the Swedish police prepared to storm the building. Before the operation could be mounted, however, a short-circuit in the fuse system of the TNT bomb caused a massive explosion. One RAF terrorist was killed outright and two others were badly wounded, one of whom later died in the hospital. Shaken by the blast, the remaining terrorists surrendered without resistance, allowing the surviving hostages to walk away unharmed.[9]

On May 23, 1975, the trial against RAF leaders Baader, Meinhof, Ensslin, and Raspe began at Stammheim Prison in Stuttgart. They were formally charged with four counts of murder, fifty-four counts of attempted murder, and one count of forming a criminal organization.[10] Although the Bonn government had adopted a policy of no concessions to terrorist demands, the RAF refused to acknowledge this change and conducted a series of high-profile actions with the intention of freeing the imprisoned leaders of the original group.

The most dramatic RAF action was the kidnapping in October 1977 of Dr. Hanns-Martin Schleyer, the President of the Employers Association and the Federation of German Industry. In a supporting operation, the Popular Front for the Liberation of Palestine (PFLP) hijacked a Lufthansa aircraft to Mogadishu, Somalia. The aircraft was subsequently stormed by German counterterrorism commandos at the Mogadishu airport, freeing the hostages. Schleyer was found shot in the back of the head forty-three days after his capture. Devastated by the multiple failed attempts to free them, Baader, Raspe, and Ensslin committed suicide in their cells. Meinhof had committed suicide in May 1976.

The Alleged Chemical Weapons Incident

This chronology provides the historical background for the allegations, reported in May 1975 by the West German tabloid *Bild Zeitung* and the *Times* of London, that members of the Baader-Meinhof Gang had stolen some chemical munitions and were threatening to use them against German cities. The alleged threat came at a time of intense terrorist activity because of the approaching trial of RAF leaders Meinhof, Ensslin, Baader, and Raspe, which was scheduled to begin at Stammheim Prison in late May. Ron Purver of the Canadian Security and Intelligence Service,

---

9. For a full account of the incident see Becker, *Hitler's Children*, p. 274–279.

10. Huffman, "This Is Baader-Meinhof: 1975" (http://www.baader-meinhof.com/timeline/1975.html).

in his survey of unclassified literature on chemical and biological terrorism, reviews several secondary accounts of the alleged incident:

[A]ccording to Jenkins and Rubin: "West German authorities received threats that unless the government granted immunity to all political prisoners, the gas would be used against the population of Stuttgart, where the leaders of the Baader-Meinhof gang were about to go on trial." In referring to this incident, Kupperman and Kamen maintain that "terrorists successfully stole canisters of this agent from U.S. stocks in West Germany." Mullins also implies that the terrorists were responsible for the theft and had thereby actually acquired the agent in question when he writes that "fortunately, German police arrested the terrorists before the chemical could be released." However, Jenkins and Rubin state that "it is not known whether this threat was authored by the same people who took the gas," adding: "some but not all of the canisters were later found." That the threats may have been made on more than one occasion and against a number of different targets is suggested by Kupperman and Trent, who report simply that "in 1975 and 1976 the Baader-Meinhof Gang in West Germany threatened to use chemical agents against German cities."[11]

There were two stages to the story. First, a quantity of mustard gas was reported missing, after which a German terrorist group—presumed to be the RAF but possibly the June 2 Movement—threatened to use it. Clearly, the terrorists did not have to possess the toxic agent to issue the threat but simply needed to have heard of the reported theft.

Despite the initial stories in the German and British press, there were no follow-up articles in the English-language news media, which would have been expected if the reports had been substantiated.[12] Another problem with the alleged incident is that the details in the secondary literature regarding the origins of the stolen materials are incorrect. The chemical weapons that went missing were not American but rather British canisters of mustard gas that had been stored since World War I by the British Army of the Rhine, and had been handed over to the German military for disposal at the chemical weapons destruction plant in Munster, Lower Saxony.[13] The British stocks consisted of ninety-nine steel

11. Ron Purver, *Chemical and Biological Terrorism: The Threat According to the Open Literature* (Ottawa: Canadian Security Intelligence Service, June 1995), pp. 84–85.

12. A search of thousands of English-language publications was conducted using the LEXIS-NEXIS online service. No articles referring to the incident were published after 1975.

13. For further information on the German chemical weapons destruction program, see Bernd Staginnus and Hermann Martens, "The Federal Armed Forces Scientific Institute for Protection Technologies-NBC Protection, Munster, Germany," *ASA Newsletter* (Applied Science and Analysis, Inc.), No. 58, February 7, 1997, pp. 3–4.

one-liter bottles of mustard agent in liquid form. Allegedly, fifty-three of the canisters had been stolen from a concrete bunker in Munster approximately two weeks before the May 13, 1975, report in the London *Times*.[14] It was also reported that the Munster police were "convinced" that the stolen canisters were in the hands of terrorists.

Despite the evidence of British ownership of the mustard canisters, it was possible that the U.S. military could have been involved in guarding the material. Investigation revealed, however, that the U.S. military had little or no involvement with the Munster plant.[15] A Central Intelligence Agency (CIA) assessment obtained under the Freedom of Information Act gives perhaps the most plausible explanation of the incident that sparked media interest, although it provides no hard evidence of an actual theft. According to the CIA report:

On 27 April guards discovered that an opening had been cut at the Test Center no. 53 in Lower Saxony. The facility contains mustard gas and other weapons awaiting eventual destruction. An examination of the area and an inventory revealed that two metal containers were broken open and that two one-liter canisters of mustard gas were unaccounted for. A complicating factor is that the gas, made in the UK during World War I, is old and some of the containers have deteriorated to the point where unauthorized opening could occur without visible signs of tampering. Also, no physical count was made when the gas containers were sent to the FRG [Federal Republic of Germany] by the British. There is no absolute proof, therefore, that the gas was actually stolen during the break-in, although FRG authorities assume that such a theft did occur.[16]

It is notable that the CIA report describes only two canisters as having been stolen, not fifty-three as was reported elsewhere. The larger

---

14. Dan van der Vat, "Bonn Issues New Security Measures Before Trial," *The Times* (London), May 13, 1975, p. 7.

15. In the United States, the author submitted Freedom of Information Act (FOIA) requests to the U.S. Army European Command in Stuttgart, the Defense Intelligence Agency, the Central Intelligence Agency, and the National Archives and Records Administration. Discussions were also conducted by the author with the U.S. Army Archives, the U.S. European Command's official historian, and various former U.S. bomb-disposal and chemical weapons experts. In England, attempts to investigate the incident through the British Army Records Society and the Army Historical Branch at the UK Ministry of Defence proved fruitless because the "thirty-year rule" restricting public access to government documents remains in effect.

16. "Possible Theft of Mustard Gas by Terrorists in West Germany," *Weekly Situation Report on International Terrorism*, June 10, 1975, p. 1. (Declassified U.S. government document obtained from the Central Intelligence Agency under FOIA, Reference: F-1997-02667).

figure probably was the result of a misreporting of the Test Center facility number (no. 53) as the number of stolen canisters. In response to a written inquiry, however, the Anti-Terrorist Branch of the Federal German Police Agency (*Bundeskriminalamt*, or BKA) issued a statement that the alleged theft had never occurred and that it was not the modus operandi of the Baader-Meinhof Gang/RAF to attempt to acquire or use chemical or biological weapons. Requests to discuss the matter with the State Criminal Police Agency of Lower Saxony (*Landeskriminalamt Niedersachsen*) in Munster were denied because of restrictions under German privacy law.

A Ph.D. dissertation written at the University of St. Andrews in Scotland provides further evidence that the alleged theft of chemical weapons did not actually take place.[17] The author, Bruce Scharlau, refers to a work by Sebastian Cobler referencing German news reports (initially from *Bild Zeitung*) that describe the loss of the fifty-three canisters. *Bild Zeitung* quoted a German secret service officer as saying, "The B-M gang made plans years ago to rob the depot."[18] Cobler also cites a news report claiming that the intended target of the planned mustard gas attack was the West German Parliament. It was subsequently revealed, however, that less than two liters of mustard gas were missing, a discrepancy that could have been the result of an accounting error. Indeed, a few months later, an article titled "Missing Poison Gas Canisters Found" appeared in the German press.[19] Cobler's conclusions broadly match those reported by the CIA.

Given the information provided by the BKA, the CIA, and by Scharlau and Cobler, it is reasonable to conclude that the "missing" canisters of mustard gas were never actually stolen but were improperly inventoried. This finding does not preclude the possibility that the Baader-Meinhof Gang, or a related group, attempted to bluff the authorities into freeing the RAF prisoners by claiming they possessed the purportedly missing canisters.

A contemporary report in *The Economist* claims that an unnamed terrorist group had sent a letter (postmarked Hamburg) to a newspaper in Stockholm threatening that if the "political prisoners" in Germany—including the RAF prisoners—were not freed, the group would commit

---

17. Bruce Scharlau, "Left-Wing Terrorism in the Federal Republic of Germany" (Ph.D. dissertation, St. Andrews University, Scotland, 1992), p. 219.

18. *Bild Zeitung*, quoted in Sebastian Cobler, *Law, Order and Politics in West Germany* (London: Penguin, 1978), p. 46.

19. Ibid.

various acts of terrorism, including the assassination of Princess Christina of Sweden, her husband, and a member of the Swedish government.[20] Reportedly, the letter also threatened the use of SAM-7 missiles, bombs, and mustard gas against the city of Stuttgart. The level of detail reported to be contained in the letter, and the fact that it was received outside of Germany, provide reasonably convincing circumstantial evidence that the letter did exist. To date, however, attempts to locate the letter in the files of Swedish newspapers have been unsuccessful.

After detailed examination of the communiqués issued by the Baader-Meinhof Gang/RAF and the June 2 Movement, Scharlau could not recall having seen any threat to use mustard gas during 1975. Since the letter to the Swedish newspaper appears to be missing, however, it is possible that the communiqué in question was not among those examined by Scharlau. Given the context of the RAF siege of the West German embassy in Stockholm in April 1975, it would not be implausible for that organization to have been in contact with the Swedish media. Yet since the news reports did not specifically link the letter to the RAF but rather to an unnamed "terrorist group," it is possible that a more obscure organization was responsible, such as the June 2 Movement or an ad hoc group of RAF sympathizers.[21]

Conclusion

Except for the dramatic terrorist campaign of May 1972, the Baader-Meinhof Gang/RAF was not particularly effective. Within a year of the group's formation, fourteen of its members had been arrested or killed.[22] Thus, although the RAF was professional enough to construct bombs and deliver them fairly effectively, they were distinctly amateur when it came to evading capture.

The RAF and the June 2 Movement were ideologically similar and felt a close affinity for one another. Thus, a key objective for both groups was to secure the freedom of the original RAF leaders. Since the June 2 Movement had succeeded in obtaining the release of some of its own members by kidnapping a prominent politician, it was reasonable for the RAF to conclude that the West German state would eventually capitulate if the right buttons were pushed. They believed that seizing the West German embassy in Stockholm would provide a sufficient source of

---

20. "Germany: Fortress Trial," *The Economist,* May 17, 1975, p. 50.

21. For a further example of a contemporary report, see "Terrorist Use of Gas Feared," *Washington Post,* May 13, 1975, p. A17.

22. Becker, *Hitler's Children,* p. 204.

leverage, but they underestimated the Bonn government's desire to see Baader, Ensslin, Meinhof, Raspe, and the other RAF terrorists convicted. Even the disastrous failure of the Stockholm action, however, did little to dissuade the RAF that sufficient pressure would eventually succeed in liberating their leaders.

Within this context, the news of the suspected theft of mustard gas hit the headlines. At the time the reports seemed quite plausible, although historical investigation has since cast serious doubt on their veracity. What almost certainly happened is that members of a left-wing terrorist organization learned that canisters of mustard gas had been reported missing from the Munster plant and seized this opportunity to increase the pressure on the West German government over the impending RAF trial by claiming to be in possession of the "missing" chemical weapons. Members of the June 2 Movement are the most likely suspects. Indeed, some evidence suggests that the group threatened to poison West German water supplies in support of the RAF defendants in May 1975, although this allegation has been impossible to confirm.[23] On the other hand, the RAF had a closer association with Stockholm, where the threat was allegedly received in the form of a letter to a local newspaper. Thus, either terrorist group could have been involved in making the threat, and they may even have been working together.

In any event, the assessment by the German BKA that neither group would have sought to escalate to the use of chemical or biological weapons is almost certainly correct. Given the ideology, tactics, and targeting preference of both groups, an indiscriminate, mass-casualty weapon was not an attractive choice and was probably regarded as abhorrent. In a few cases, as in the May 15, 1972 car bombing in Karlsruhe, RAF members employed indiscriminate tactics for assassination, apparently giving little thought to possible loss of civilian life. Usually, however, the group focused its attacks on symbolic buildings or visible representatives of the state.

On a cost-benefit basis, both groups had already suffered badly at the hands of the police, who surely would have left no stone unturned in hunting for terrorists who had used mustard gas against a civilian population. There was nothing to be achieved by seeking to obtain, or using, mustard gas or any other chemical or biological agent. At the same time, the somewhat whimsical nature of both groups would probably have led them to consider the idea of making *threats* about the use of chemical weapons as a means of ensuring the release of the RAF leadership.

---

23. See the RAND Database of Incidents Involving Chemical or Biological Weapons, RAND Corporation, Santa Monica, California.

During the hysteria preceding the RAF trial, the claim of a threatened terrorist attack with chemical weapons was seized on by the media. Various anonymous sources then built up the story by claiming that the stolen-material hypothesis was correct. Once the story was in the public domain, it became further distorted by journalistic sensationalism. Finally, although the alleged incident had been debunked in the specialist literature on left-wing terrorism in Germany, none of the U.S. terrorism experts who repeatedly cited it took the time to confirm its veracity. Once one author accepted the rumor as fact, others simply followed suit, a case of "incestuous inter-quote." In conclusion, if one were to categorize this case in the history of terrorism, it would be better placed under the heading "terrorism and the media" than "terrorism and chemical and biological weapons."

Chapter 7

The Red Army Faction (1980)

Terence Taylor and Tim Trevan

The allegation that the Red Army Faction (RAF), a left-wing terrorist group based in West Germany, sought to acquire biological weapons in the early 1980s has been frequently cited in the scholarly literature about terrorism. According to reports in the French newspaper *Le Figaro* and the German magazine *Neue Illustrierte Revue,* French police raided an RAF safe house in Paris on October 14, 1980, and found a basic biological laboratory and vials containing *Clostridium botulinum.* This bacterium produces botulinum toxin—one of the most lethal poisons known to science.

When asked about the alleged incident, officials of the Public Prosecutor's Office in Karlsruhe, the German government agency responsible for prosecuting the RAF terrorists, declined to be interviewed but indicated that the journalistic accounts were false. There are two possible explanations for this response: the German authorities are covering up evidence of a real incident for unknown reasons; or the incident never occurred. On balance, the authors of this chapter are inclined to believe the latter.

The Organization

The RAF is widely described as having passed through three successive generations. The first generation was the Baader-Meinhof Gang, which founded the RAF (see Chapter 6). The second generation included members of the German Sozialistische Patientenkollektiv (Socialist Patients' Collective) who joined the RAF when most of its founders were imprisoned or forced to flee Germany in the early 1970s. The third generation arose mainly to free the imprisoned members of the first two generations and was active in the run-up to the trials of Baader, Meinhof, and others in 1975. This third generation included several younger siblings or "significant others" of the earlier generations.

Given the prominence of the RAF in the 1970s and 1980s, its structure, ideology and activities are well documented.[1] At trials, in interviews, and in press releases, members explained the group's ideology to outsiders in various ways, but all these statements expressed strong and violent anti-establishment views and prescriptions. RAF leader Horst Mahler argued that the organization was engaged in "a war—it will be the last and at the same time the longest and bloodiest war of history, because the exploiters do not hesitate to use the most horrendous actions to retain their dominance. It is not a war among nations but a war of classes, which will sweep all nations, social, cultural, and religious boundaries and barriers forever from the stage of history."[2]

The RAF was loosely organized, consisting of twenty to thirty cadres (hard-core participants in acts of terrorism) and up to 200 supporters who provided refuge and logistical support for operations. Although RAF members all subscribed to left-wing ideology, the group appears never to have developed a rigid or monolithic command structure. On several occasions, individual members or subgroups released statements that contradicted those of others, and several RAF groups split up because of internal conflicts.

Initially, the RAF attacked targets symbolic of capitalism such as banks and the property of large corporations, but later on group members engaged in the kidnapping and assassination of leading German industrialists and U.S. military personnel. At the peak of the RAF's notoriety in 1971, when its actions were aimed exclusively against property, an opinion poll in West Germany indicated that 20 percent of the population under the age of thirty had some sympathy with the group and that 10 percent would be willing to shelter an RAF activist for a night.[3] Once the RAF become involved in kidnappings and assassinations, however, public support rapidly declined.

In the lead-up to and aftermath of the trial of the founding members of the Baader-Meinhof Gang, the RAF's actions were increasingly aimed

---

1. Peter Jamke, *Guerilla and Terrorist Organisations* (Brighton, England: Harvester Press, 1983), pp. 17–20; *Revolutionary and Dissident Movements* (Harlow, England: Longman, 1991), pp. 110–115; Jillian Becker, *Hitler's Children: The Story of the Baader-Meinhof Terrorist Gang*, 3rd ed. (London: Pickwick Books, 1989); and Joanne Wright, *Terrorist Propaganda: The Red Army Faction and the Provisional IRA, 1968–86* (London: MacMillan Academic, 1991), pp. 23–27, 38–52.

2. Wright, *Terrorist Propaganda*, p. 105.

3. Richard Huffman, "This Is Baader-Meinhof/Timeline" (1998), ⟨http://www.baader-meinhof.com/timeline/timeline.html⟩.

at obtaining the release of the jailed activists and less obviously in pursuit of the organization's anti-capitalist ideals. Later generations of the RAF proved capable of meticulous research and planning for deadly attacks against well-defined targets. Nevertheless, the violent actions attributed to the RAF were almost always aimed at specific individuals or property rather than intended to inflict indiscriminate casualties.

The Alleged Botulinum Toxin Incident

A review of reports of biological terrorism in the open literature compiled by Ron Purver of the Canadian Security Intelligence Service cites numerous reports mentioning "the discovery in Paris, variously dated to 1980, the 'mid-'80s,' or 14 October 1984, of a Red Army Faction 'safe house' that included a 'primitive laboratory' (according to one source, a bathtub) containing quantities of botulinal toxin."[4]

America the Vulnerable, a book by Joseph Douglass and Neil Livingstone, provides the most detailed account of the alleged incident:

The sixth-floor apartment contained typed sheets on bacterial pathology. Marginal notes were identified by graphologists as being the handwriting of Silke Maier-Witt, a medical assistant by profession, terrorist by night. Other items included medical publications dealing with the struggle against bacterial infection. . . . In the bathroom, the French authorities found a bathtub filled with flasks containing cultures of *Clostridium botulinum*.[5]

The alleged RAF production of botulinum toxin is also mentioned in a database of biological terrorist incidents maintained by the Pacific Northwest National Laboratory:

In 1980, a safehouse belonging to the German Red Army Faction terrorist organization was uncovered in Paris, France. Inside the safehouse was an improvised laboratory where flasks of botulism toxin (*Clostridium botulinum*) were found. The safehouse also contained publications on bacterial infection and notes from a group activist employed as a laboratory assistant at a medical research facility. Before this discovery, the Red Army Faction had threatened to poison water supplies for several German towns.[6]

---

4. Ron Purver, *Chemical and Biological Terrorism: The Threat According to the Open Literature* (Ottawa: Canadian Security Intelligence Service, June 1995), p. 36.

5. Joseph D. Douglass, Jr., and Neil C. Livingstone, *America the Vulnerable: The Threat of Chemical and Biological Warfare* (Lexington, Mass.: Lexington Books, 1987), p. 29.

6. Pacific Northwest National Laboratories, "Biological Terrorist Incidents" (http://www.pnl.gov/dcbpweb/incidnts.htm).

All of these reports in the secondary literature appear to have been based on an article published in the French newspaper *Le Figaro* in its weekend edition of November 8–9, 1980.[7] The *Figaro* item referred in turn to an article to be published the following Monday, November 10, in the *Neue Illustrierte Revue* of Hamburg. The *Figaro* article reported the *Neue Illustrierte Revue* article as claiming that:

German and French police raided an apartment on the sixth floor of 41A Chaillot Street in Paris . . . and discovered a miniature laboratory intended for the culture of . . . the "Clostridium botulinum" bacterium. . . . Handwritten notes . . . were identified by graphologists of the German police force as being the handwriting of Silke Maier-Witt. . . . Silke Maier-Witt, 30 years of age, is a medical assistant. She therefore possesses knowledge that is indispensable for the "manufacture of microbes." . . . [T]he culture medium was placed in a special anaerobic retort, sheltered from the presence of oxygen. Maier-Witt may not be the only individual involved in this case. . . . [L]ast 25 July, the German police . . . found clues leading to Mrs. Maier-Witt and Dr. Ekkehard von Seckendorf-Gudent [*sic*]. This Hamburg physician, who joined the forces of terrorism in 1977, settled in Paris during 1978. . . . Seckendorf-Gudent disappeared last June. Both he and Mrs. Maier-Witt are now on the most-wanted list of the Baader gang. . . . French and German authorities refuse to take any position on this matter and continue to pass the buck.

The article added the following footnote:

At police headquarters in Paris, it was confirmed that, on 14 October, a police squad had entered the apartment at 41A Chaillot Street upon the request of a tenant who, after a stay abroad, did not find the Belgian student to whom he had sublet his apartment during his absence. The student gave his name as Jan Dekerk. He was rapidly identified to be none other than Ralf Baptiste Fridrich [*sic*], a German terrorist who was wanted by the police. Before disappearing, he had left a suitcase and five cartons in the apartment. In the suitcase, police found documents and equipment for forging documents. The French police immediately alerted their German colleagues. The latter, who employed a rogatory commission, took possession of the suitcase and the cartons that the French police had seized, without however taking a complete inventory. Therefore, the police refuse to confirm or deny the reports emanating from Germany.

Finally, a brief Reuters report on the incident appeared in the *International Herald Tribune* on November 8–9, 1980. According to this article, West German prosecutor Kurt Rebmann told reporters that in October

---

7. Jean-Paul Picaper (trans. anonymous), "Terrorism: The Bacteriological Weapon," *Le Figaro*, November 8–9, 1980, p. 7.

1980, the French police had discovered in a Paris apartment used by members of the RAF a culture of *Clostridium botulinum*, laboratory equipment, and notes on biological agents written in the hand of Silke Maier-Witt. Rebmann stressed, however, that there was no indication the group was planning to launch a biological attack.[8]

Doubts About the Allegation

Several factual errors in the *Figaro* article raise doubts about its credibility. Although the three people mentioned in the article are known to have been associated with the RAF or its offshoots, the statement that Silke Maier-Witt was a medical assistant with a knowledge of microbiology contradicts a better-documented account of her professional background as an assistant in a lawyer's office and an interpreter.[9] The better-documented account also indicates that, prior to going underground in late 1977, Maier-Witt was wanted in connection with an attempted rocket attack on the Public Prosecutor's Office in Karlsruhe in August 1977 and the kidnapping and murder of Hanns-Martin Schleyer, the President of the Employers Association and the Federation of German Industry, in October 1977.

Maier-Witt was reported to have used the alias of Angelika Gerlach and later of Sylvia Beyer while working as a translator in Berlin in 1985.[10] She was arrested with eight other RAF members in June 1990 and handed over to the West German authorities.[11] Ralf Baptist Friedrich was implicated as a member of the Socialist Patients' Collective.[12] Ekkehard von Seckendorff-Gudent was reported to have been displayed on West German wanted posters in January 1990.[13] No record could be found of either man's apprehension.

---

8. Reuters, "W. German Terrorists Said to Test Bacteria," *International Herald Tribune*, November 8–9, 1980, p. 2.

9. Becker, *Hitler's Children*, p. 274.

10. Ibid.

11. *Revolutionary and Dissident Movements*, p.115; "Falsche Pässe und eine Neubauwohnung von der Stasi," *Berliner Morgenpost*, February 1997 (http://archiv.berliner-morgenpost.de).

12. Ruprecht-Karls-Universität Heidelberg, " 'Aus der Krankheit eine Waffe machen!' Wo aus Psychiatrie-Patienten Revolutionäre werden sollten—das Sozialistische Patientenkollektiv SPK," November 1997 (http://mathphys.fsk.uni-heidelberg.de/hopo/rupr1.html);

13. "Bonn wußte von RAF-Terroristen in der DDR—aber wollte nichts wissen," *Berliner Morgenpost*, February 1997 (http://archiv.berliner-morgenpost.de); "Das

Denials by the German Authorities

In February 1998, the authors made contact with Peter von Butler, the former head of the Disarmament Department in the German Foreign Office. He put the authors in contact with the Embassy liaison officers for the *Bundeskriminalamt* (BKA, the German equivalent of the Federal Bureau of Investigation) and the *Bundesnachrichtendienst* (BND, the Federal Intelligence Service). These contacts both indicated that the Anti-Terrorist Branch of the BKA would be the best starting point for research into the alleged incident.

The Anti-Terrorist Branch agreed to investigate the case and claimed to be eager to learn the results. In April 1998, however, they informed the authors that they were not authorized to release data on the subject and that all public inquiries had to be addressed through the press office of the Public Prosecutor's Office in Karlsruhe, which was responsible for prosecuting members of the RAF. A reply from that office, received on April 29, 1998, stated categorically that the account in *Le Figaro* "did not correspond with the facts and drew false conclusions."[14] The Public Prosecutor's Office added that there was "no evidence whatsoever that members of the 'RAF' had planned or prepared an attack using biological agents."[15] The German authorities declined to provide any official documents to support this brief and categorical statement, refused to be interviewed, and did not respond to requests for information on the current whereabouts of Silke Maier-Witt and Ralf Baptist Friedrich.

Conclusion

The acquisition of biological or toxin agents was not mentioned in any known statement by RAF members. Moreover, the acquisition and use of indiscriminate, mass-casualty weapons would not be consistent with the RAF's track record of meticulously researched attacks against property or prominent personalities representative of the West German political and economic establishment.

Fahndungsplakat gibt Rätsel auf," *Berliner Morgenpost,* February 1997 (http://archiv.berliner-morgenpost.de).

14. Original German text of letter from the Public Prosecutor's Office in Karlsruhe: ". . . *entsprachen nicht den Tatsachen und zogen falsche Schlußfolgerungen.*"

15. "*Denn es ergaben sich aus den Aufzeichnungen keinerlei Anhaltspunkte dafür, daß Mitglieder der 'RAF' einen Anschlag mit bakteriologischen Mitteln geplant oder sogar bereits vorarbeitet hatten.*"

Silke Maier-Witt was apprehended in 1990 for her involvement in two terrorist incidents in 1977, including the kidnapping and murder of Hanns-Martin Schleyer. Yet she was not charged with attempting to manufacture biological weapons, presumably because of insufficient evidence. Given the way prosecutors operate in Germany and France, if substantial evidence of botulinum toxin manufacture and planned use had existed, the German government probably would have gone ahead with the case. In June 1995, Maier-Witt was released from prison, having served half her sentence.[16] She subsequently gave testimony at other RAF trials.[17] Today, she is an official of the Green Party in Oldenburg, a city in northern Germany.

These observations, together with the factual errors in the *Figaro* account, suggest that the alleged botulinum-toxin incident probably did not take place.

---

16. *NRW-Verfassungsschutzbericht 1995*—Kapitel 3.2, November 1996.

17. *Prozesserklärung von Monika Haas,* April 1998 (http://www.comlink.de/nadir/aktuell/msg00015.html).

Chapter 8

The Rajneeshees (1984)

W. Seth Carus

Although the U.S. government has expressed growing concern about potential biological terrorist attacks, the Federal Bureau of Investigation (FBI) has documented only *one* successful incident of bioterrorism. In August and September 1984 a religious cult known as the Rajneeshees employed biological agents against the inhabitants of a small town in Oregon, sickening 751 people.[1] Despite the unique nature of this incident, surprisingly little is known about it. The case is often cited in the terrorism literature, but the accounts are usually inaccurate and always incomplete.[2]

The Rajneeshee incident is significant for several reasons. As the only bioterrorist attack known to have caused illness, it offers an opportunity

The views expressed in this chapter are those of the author and do not necessarily reflect the official policy or position of the Department of Defense or the U.S. government.

1. See the testimony of John P. O'Neill, Supervisory Special Agent, Chief, Counterterrorism Section, Federal Bureau of Investigation, in Permanent Subcommittee on Investigations, Committee on Governmental Affairs, United States Senate, *Global Proliferation of Weapons of Mass Destruction* (Washington, D.C.: U.S. Government Printing Office [U.S. GPO], 1996), p. 238.

2. A typical summary appears in Ron Purver, *Chemical and Biological Terrorism: The Threat According to the Open Literature* (Ottawa: Canadian Security Intelligence Service, June 1995), p. 39. Drawing on other accounts, Purver inaccurately reports that the Rajneeshees used the pathogen that causes typhoid fever, *Salmonella typhi*. In fact they used another strain, *Salmonella enterica* serotype Typhimurium, which is a common cause of food poisoning. For a description of the salmonellosis outbreak from the perspective of the federal and state public health officials involved in the investigation, see Thomas J. Török, Robert V. Tauxe, Robert P. Wise, John R. Livergood, Robert Sokolow, Steven Mauvais, Kristin A. Birkness, Michael R. Skeels, John M. Horan, and Laurence R. Foster, "A Large Community Outbreak of Salmonellosis Caused by Intentional Contamination of Restaurant Salad Bars," *Journal of the American Medical Association*, Vol. 278, No. 5 (August 6, 1997), pp. 389–395.

to understand more fully the incentives that might attract terrorists to biological agents. The case also illustrates some of the complexities facing a terrorist group that would employ unconventional weapons.[3]

The Rajneeshees

The Rajneeshees were a cult that originated in India in the 1960s. Formed and guided by the Bhagwan Shree Rajneesh, the cult attracted a considerable following in Europe and the United States in the 1970s. The Bhagwan, known to his followers as an "Enlightened Master," was charismatic, extremely intelligent, and a master at manipulating people. Influenced by the writings of Nietsche, he saw his followers as "supermen." The Rajneeshee cult attracted thousands of adherents from around the world and had access to substantial financial resources. Many cult members were wealthy and the Bhagwan was known as "the rich man's guru." The group also earned a good income from the sale of books and tapes about the Bhagwan's teachings. Cult members severed all ties to the outside world and worked ten to twelve hours a day, six or seven days a week.

Even as the cult gained an international following, it became increasingly notorious in Poona, India, the site of its commune or "ashram." By 1980, the Rajneeshees faced growing hostility from the Indian government. As a result, the Bhagwan was anxious to move the group to a new location. Under the influence of one of his followers, Ma Anand Sheela,

---

3. This account is based on several sources of information. First, it draws on memoirs of former cult members about life among the Rajneeshees, including several excellent personal accounts. These sources provide useful background material about the group and some of its key members. The best scholarly book on the Rajneeshees in Oregon is Lewis F. Carter, *Charisma and Control in Rajneeshpuram: The Role of Shared Values in the Creation of a Community* (New York: Cambridge University Press, 1990). Personal accounts include Satya Bharti Franklin, *The Promise of Paradise: A Woman's Intimate Story of the Perils of Life with Rajneesh* (Barrytown, N.Y.: Station Hill Press, 1992), and Hugh Milne, *Bhagwan: The God That Failed* (New York: St. Martin's Press, 1986). Other accounts are Kirk Braun, *Rajneeshpuram: The Unwelcome Society* (West Linn, Ore.: Scout Creek Press, 1984); James S. Gordon, *The Golden Guru: The Strange Journey of Bhagwan Shree Rajneesh* (New York: Viking Press, 1988); Donna Quick, *The Rajneesh Story: A Place Called Antelope* (Ryderwood, Wash.: August Press, 1995); and Bert Webber, *Rajneeshpuram: Who Were Its People?* (Medford, Ore.: Webb Research Group, 1990). Unfortunately, none of these accounts was written by anyone familiar with the biological contaminations.

Second, the Rajneeshees received considerable press coverage, including some reporting of the disease outbreak, although most of the stories appeared in the regional and local press and not the national media. Particularly important are the stories published by the Portland *Oregonian*. In addition, the author consulted the local Wasco County newspaper, *The Dalles Chronicle*, especially for the period during the outbreak.

he decided in 1981 to emigrate to the United States.[4] The group operated from a New Jersey mansion while efforts were made to find a suitable location for a new ashram.

After a brief but intensive search, Sheela decided to purchase a property in Oregon known as the Big Muddy Ranch. Although the ranch straddled Jefferson and Wasco Counties, the major portion was located in Wasco County, a largely rural area with a population of about 20,000. The county seat is The Dalles, a small town that in 1985 had a population

---

Third, this account draws on extensive interviews conducted in April and October 1997 with government officials involved in investigating and prosecuting the incident at the local, state, and federal levels, as well as people who interacted with the Rajneeshees around 1984. The author is grateful to them all, although much of the information obtained related to the investigation of the outbreak and was not used in the preparation of this chapter. Especially critical was the assistance of Robert Hamilton, who coordinated the State Law Enforcement Task Force created by Oregon to investigate the Rajneeshees and then was co-counsel for the state grand jury investigation and the subsequent prosecutions of the indictments returned by the grand jury. Jeannie Senior, a correspondent for *The Oregonian*, gave generously of her time and extensive knowledge and was kind enough to join me on a trip to visit the former Rajneeshee ranch. Others who took the time to discuss their experiences with the Rajneeshees were Carla Chamberlain, administrator of the Wasco-Sherman County Public Health Department; Lynn Enyart, then an FBI Special Agent; Ed Goodman, The Dalles Police Department; Fred Hawkins, Oregon State Police; Jim Long of *The Oregonian*, Dan Portwood, The Dalles Police Department; Dean Renfrew, Oregon State Police; Dr. Michael Skeels, director of the Oregon State Public Health Laboratory; Barry Sheldahl, Assistant U.S. Attorney; and an attorney involved in the litigation brought by some of the affected restaurants against the Rajneeshees. Lewis F. Carter and Robert Hamilton provided extensive comments on a draft of the chapter.

Fourth, this case study relies on official documents generated by public health and law enforcement officials at the local, state, and federal levels. The documents came from four sources: (1) Records of the Oregon Attorney General's Office relating to the legal proceedings against the cult brought by the state of Oregon are in the Rajneeshpuram case files, 1981–1989, 91A-081, Oregon State Archives (cited as OSA files). (2) The State of Oregon Attorney General's Office provided copies of certain affidavits, sworn statements, and law enforcement records (cited as AG files). (3) Considerable material relating to this case was available in the records of the U.S. District Court, Portland, Oregon (cited as U.S. District Court files). Among the documentation obtained from this source were statements by several members of the group who participated in the biological contaminations. Unfortunately, some key Rajneeshees who participated in the attacks never admitted involvement or gave statements about what they did, so we do not have accounts written from their perspective. (4) Finally, several people, including the administrator of the Wasco-Sherman County Public Health Department, provided additional material.

4. Followers of Bhagwan Shree Rajneesh were known as "sannyassins." Taking "sannyas" involved becoming a follower of the Bhagwan and taking on the "malla," which was a beaded necklace with a picture of the Bhagwan, and putting on the red, pink, or purple garments that the Rajneeshees wore. At that time, the member received a new name. Many Rajneeshees had identical names, which caused considerable

of about 10,000. It is located just over an hour's drive east of Portland on Interstate 84, a major east-west transportation route.

From the beginning, the Rajneeshees intended to build a substantial community in Oregon. Of a total membership of about 10,000 people, about 4,000 lived at the ranch. The commune was to be a self-contained town with its own municipal services, including an airport, transportation system, water and sewage systems, and other amenities. But the Rajneeshees soon found themselves at the center of a series of political and legal disputes, many of their own making. After a few gestures of friendship, cult members began acting contemptuously toward the local inhabitants and attempted to evade zoning and planning requirements that constrained their activities. As a result, relations between the county residents and the Rajneeshees quickly became contentious. To some extent, cult leaders promoted antagonism against the outside world as a means to enhance the internal cohesiveness of the group. A hard core of 150 Rajneeshees were allowed to carry arms to protect the Bhagwan because of concerns that the FBI might try to kidnap him. Guard posts were stationed along the road to the ashram, and the cult built a visitors' center and maintained strict control over access.

In an effort to evade zoning restrictions, the cult decided to take over the nearby small town of Antelope, which they renamed "Rajneesh," and the Antelope School District. By exploiting Oregon's liberal voter-registration laws, it was easy for the Rajneeshees to move enough people into the community to outnumber the existing inhabitants. This act generated a reservoir of hostility toward the group that remained until the Rajneeshee leaders left Oregon in 1986.

The Rajneeshees were also extremely litigious—they sued people for slander at the slightest provocation and drew on the talents of a team of skilled lawyers. The cult tried to use the courts to steamroll opponents, who often lacked the resources to contest their activities. At the same time, the Rajneeshees demonstrated a less than scrupulous concern for adhering to laws that interfered with the operation of the commune. Sham marriages were arranged to ensure that cult members who lacked a U.S. passport could remain. This practice brought the group into conflict with the U.S. Immigration and Naturalization Service and the U.S. Attorney's Office in Portland, Oregon. In addition, despite years of contemptuously condemning organized religions, the Rajneeshees registered themselves as a religion to take advantage of the tax benefits given to religious groups under U.S. law.

---

confusion. The names of the women were prefaced with the honorific "Ma" and those for the men with the honorific "Swami."

The Rajneeshees also violated Oregon state laws. Oregon has extremely restrictive land-use laws that limit what can be built on rural undeveloped land. To gain control over zoning, the Rajneeshees incorporated a town on the ranch, which they called "Rajneeshpuram." The legal status of this community, also known as "Rancho Rajneesh," provided significant advantages. For example, it enabled the cult to field two authorized police forces, one at Rajneeshpuram and the other at Rajneesh, which for a period of time had access to law-enforcement databases. Eventually, however, the town became the focus of a protracted legal dispute when Oregon's elected Attorney General, Dave Frohnmeyer, concluded that there was no separation between church and state in Rajneeshpuram and that the community was therefore unconstitutional.

Decision-Making in Rajneeshpuram

To understand what happened in August and September of 1984, it is important to recognize that all authority within the cult emanated directly from the Bhagwan, although he was not directly involved in the day-to-day operations of the commune. Sheela, nominally the Bhagwan's private secretary, ran Rancho Rajneesh in his name. Much of her power came from meetings she held every evening with the Bhagwan, except when she was traveling or sick. Through most of this period (until September 30, 1984), the Bhagwan held no public meetings, operating under a "vow of silence." Sheela was the only person not in the Bhagwan's immediate household who had daily contact with him. Accordingly, it was widely understood among the Rajneeshees that Sheela represented the Bhagwan, and he confirmed that she spoke in his name when doubts were raised about her authority.

Under Sheela were a large number of supervisors who directed the operations of Rancho Rajneesh. Most of the people on whom Sheela relied were women who came to be called "moms;" the more senior of them were known as "big moms." At least one disaffected Rajneeshee derisively called these people the "Dowager Duchesses."[5] The two most important people who worked for Sheela were Ma Prem Savita, who was in charge of finances, and Ma Yoga Vidya, who was president of the ashram and responsible for personnel matters, including where people lived and worked. A third tier of cult leaders consisted of five women: Padma, Dolma, Homa, Patipada, and Su. Only one of the key senior people was a man, Krishna Diva (generally known as "K.D."), the mayor

---

5. "The Dowager Duchesses," *The Oregonian*, June 30, 1985, p. A10.

of Rajneeshpuram. In addition, several male cult members were involved in Rajneeshee "dirty deeds."[6]

Two groups at Rancho Rajneesh were not aligned with Sheela. First, the Bhagwan's personal household included a handful of people, including his personal physician, Devaraj, who had more access to the Bhagwan than she did. Sheela resented these people and saw them as a potential threat to her authority within the cult. She also believed that Devaraj was an incompetent doctor who was not taking sufficient steps to document the Bhagwan's health, a necessary measure in supporting the case that the cult leader had health reasons for remaining in the United States. The second group, known as the "Hollywood Crowd," consisted of people whose wealth and fame gave them direct access to the Bhagwan. The leader of this group was Ma Prem Hasya, who had once been married to a celebrated Hollywood producer.[7] Alliances were developing between the Bhagwan's household and the Hollywood clique. Significantly, Hasya married Devaraj, which intimately linked the two groups.

Rajneeshpuram's "Dr. Mengele"

The person most responsible for the acquisition and use of biological agents was Ma Anand Puja, a nurse closely tied to Sheela. Born in Manila, the Philippines, on November 13, 1947, she had grown up in California. In 1976 she received a license as a family nurse practitioner and became a registered nurse the next year. She worked in oncology clinics in the Philippines and Indonesia in 1977 and then traveled around Asia. Puja went to Poona in 1979 and joined the cult after learning about the Bhagwan. In April 1980, she became director of the Shree Rajneesh Ashram Health Center.[8]

Puja was part of the inner circle who ran the community, one of Sheela's "big moms." She held a number of important positions in the

---

6. Unless otherwise noted, all the descriptions draw on "Charged," *The Oregonian*, December 30, 1985, p. B2.

7. Sheela's concern about the Hollywood Crowd was quite reasonable: Ma Prem Hasya replaced Sheela after her departure in September 1985. This account of Rajneeshpuram politics draws on the accounts of the cult cited in note 3 above, as well as interviews of the Rajneeshees conducted by law enforcement officials in October 1985 and found in the referenced archival material.

8. "Interviews Revealed Puja's Medical Background," *The Oregonian*, October 4, 1985, p. D2. This account is based on a 1984 interview with Puja and a 1983 letter that she sent to the Immigration and Naturalization Service. She claimed in the letter that for four years she was director of the Kern County Medical Center outpatient clinic.

cult hierarchy and was secretary-treasurer of the Rajneesh Medical Corporation (RMC).[9] Despite her modest title, Puja had absolute authority over all of the medical facilities in Rajneeshpuram, including the Pythagoras Clinic and the Pythagoras Pharmacy. In addition, her power extended beyond the medical realm because of her relationship with Sheela. At one time, she was a vice president of the church that the Bhagwan had founded, Rajneesh Foundation International (RFI). As one of the church's few "Class A" members, she had the power to appoint or remove RFI's trustees and was responsible for the day-to-day operation of the foundation.[10]

Puja was a sinister figure disliked by most of the members of the commune, who came to refer to her as "Dr. Mengele." This reference to the notorious Nazi concentration camp doctor reveals the strength of the animosity that her actions generated. According to Ma Ava, who worked at the RMC's offices from February 1984 to January 1985, "Puja was feared and disliked by personnel at the RMC. Puja behaved as a tyrant."[11] Ma Prem Taru, who served as a clerk for the RMC, told authorities that Puja was a "loner" who socialized only with Sheela. She even ate her meals alone at her house.[12] K.D. recalled that Puja "delighted in death, poisons, and the idea of carrying out various plots."[13] Another member of the cult, who joined in 1972 and was not involved in any illegal activities, recalled her initial reactions to Puja in the following terms:

There was something about Puja that sent shivers of revulsion up and down my spine the moment I met her. There was nothing I could put my finger on beyond her phony, sickeningly sweet smile; it was years before she became widely-known as the Dr. Mengeles [sic] of the sannyas community, the alleged perpetrator of sadistic medical practices that verged on the criminal; my reaction to her seemed irrational. . . . Sheela trusted her implicitly.[14]

---

9. "The Dowager Duchesses," p. A10.

10. "Profiles: The Key Rajneeshees Under Indictment," *The Oregonian*, October 29, 1985, p. D3.

11. Ava Kay Avalos interrogation, transcribed October 22, 1985, AG files, p. 3.

12. Affidavit for Search Warrant, signed by Lieutenant Dean Renfrow, Oregon State Police, October 1, 1985, OSA files. The document was drafted by Steve Peifer, then Oregon Assistant Attorney General and now an Assistant United States Attorney.

13. From Exhibit E attached to David Berry Knapp interrogation, transcribed November 15, 1985, Federal Bureau of Investigation, AG files.

14. Franklin, *The Promise of Paradise*, p. 136.

This negative impression of Puja was shared by outsiders who had dealings with her.[15] Some former members suspect that Puja was involved in nefarious activities, including multiple poisonings, almost from the time she joined the Rajneeshees. She was accused of involvement in the June 1980 death of Chinmaya, Sheela's first husband, who was sick with Hodgkin's disease at the time. In addition, some former Rajneeshees believe that Puja may have poisoned other people.[16] Among the items found in her possession after she fled Rajneeshpuram in 1985 were numerous items reflecting an intense interest in chemical and biological agents, including information on *Salmonella* infection.[17] Law enforcement investigators discovered that she had a medical reference book, *Handbook for Poisoning,* with markings next to a particular fluorocarbon poison that at least one Rajneeshee physician thought might have been used in an unsuccessful attempt on the life of Devaraj, the Bhagwan's personal physician.[18]

The Plot

The plot to use biological agents originated in the conflicts between the Rajneeshees and the government of Wasco County. K.D. told the FBI that as early as 1983 he had tried to find some way to get the Rajneeshees out from under the authority of Wasco County. He met with some leaders from the nearby Warm Springs Indian Reservation in an unsuccessful bid to set up a new county consisting of the reservation and Rancho Rajneesh.[19]

Sometime in early 1984, Sheela and the Bhagwan decided that it was necessary to take control of the Wasco County Court (the name of the

---

15.   Carla Chamberlain, the administrator of the Wasco-Sherman Public Health Department, met with Puja and Sheela in a futile effort to convince the Rajneeshees to notify the health authorities of cases of reportable diseases. Based on her meeting with Puja, she was not surprised at subsequent reports of Puja's involvement in the various poisoning cases. Author's interview with Chamberlain, April 11, 1997.

16.   Franklin, *The Promise of Paradise,* pp. 136–137.

17.   Affidavit for Search Warrant, signed by Lieutenant Dean Renfrow, Oregon State Police, October 1, 1985, OSA files.

18.   Ibid. For a summary of the affidavit, see Leslie L. Zaitz and James Long, "Sheela Hinted at Sullivan Poisoning," *The Oregonian,* October 4, 1984, p. D2.

19.   David Berry Knapp interrogation, transcribed November 13, 1985, Federal Bureau of Investigation, AG files, p. 1.

county commission) in the November 1984 election. Somehow the 4,000 members of the commune, many of whom were not U.S. citizens and could not vote, would take over a county of 20,000 inhabitants that included some 15,000 registered voters. K.D. remembers Sheela telling him, "Voter fraud, voter fraud. You have to find a way to win these elections."[20]

Brainstorming sessions were held to develop plans for accomplishing this objective. The group discussed renting apartments in Wasco County and registering Rajneeshees under multiple names so that they could vote several times during the election. Under this plan, the Rajneeshees would appear at the balloting places in various disguises. Another idea involved renting apartments in The Dalles, having Rajneeshees register under multiple false names, and then having them vote using absentee ballots to avoid discovery. All of these ideas were rejected because it would be too easy for investigators to discover the fraudulent activity.[21]

The plotters then tried to find an alternate candidate for County Commissioner who would be favorable toward the Rajneeshees. This effort failed when they were unable to obtain enough signatures to get their preferred candidate on the ballot. The Rajneeshees even considered having one of their own members, Ma Jagruti, run for office under an assumed name. But this scheme collapsed when Oregon state officials learned that Jagruti had voted fraudulently in a previous election.[22]

Finally, Sheela came up with the idea of making the citizens of Wasco County sick before the election so that they would be unable to vote. According to K.D., after the meeting in which she raised this idea, Sheela and Puja started looking at books that described "bacteria and other methods to make people ill."[23] Furthermore, he claimed that Sheela said "she had talked with Bhagwan about the plot to decrease voter turnout in The Dalles by making people sick. Sheela said that Bhagwan commented that it was best not to hurt people, but if a few died not to worry."[24]

In addition to the use of biological agents, several of the Rajneeshees came up with the idea of importing homeless people who could be registered as voters. This idea, which came to be known as the "Share-

20.   Ibid., pp. 1–2.

21.   Ibid.

22.   Ibid., p. 2.

23.   Ibid., pp. 2–3.

24.   Report of Interview, Swami Krishna Deva [K.D.], AKA David Berry Knapp, November 25, 1985, AG files, p. 76.

A-Home" program, brought thousands of homeless people to Rajneesh-puram, ostensibly to provide them with a place to live.[25]

Participants in the Plot

It appears that only about a dozen senior members of the Rajneeshees took an active part in the various biological contamination plots. Of these individuals, only three are known to have been involved in the laboratory activities, and eight distributed agent on at least one occasion (see Table 8.1.). Others within the group were aware of the operation but had no direct involvement in its planning or execution. There is no way to know to what extent the Bhagwan participated in actual decision making. His followers believed that he was involved in every important decision that Sheela made, but those allegations were never proven.

Rajneeshee Biological Agents

Puja considered several biological agents for the contamination scheme. The main agent she relied on was *Salmonella enterica* serotype Typhimurium, a strain of bacterium that is a common cause of food poisoning. Puja's interest in *Salmonella* apparently originated in the spring of 1984. At that time, she reportedly asked Dr. Indiver, a urologist who worked in the clinic, about poisons that would make people sick without killing them and that would be difficult to detect. This inquiry was made under the guise of identifying poisons that might be used by outsiders against members of the commune. Dr. Indiver reportedly told Puja that he knew nothing about poisons but mentioned *Salmonella* as a possibility.[26]

Puja considered several other biological agents. One of these was *Salmonella typhi*, the organism that causes typhoid fever. Ma Ava recalled hearing from her friend Parambodhi, the laboratory technician at the RMC, that Puja wanted to culture the organism responsible for typhoid.[27] This allegation was confirmed by K.D., whose recollections were written down by Oregon law enforcement investigators:

---

25. According to K.D., it was either Sheela or K.D. who came up with the original idea to bring in homeless people as voters. See David Berry Knapp interrogation, transcribed November 13, 1985, Federal Bureau of Investigation, AG files, p. 5.

26. Mentioned in the Affidavit for Search Warrant, signed by Lieutenant Dean Renfrow, Oregon State Police, October 1, 1985, OSA files.

27. Ava Kay Avalos interrogation, transcribed October 22, 1985, AG files, p. 12.

Table 8.1. Alleged Participants in Salmonella Contamination Activities.

Participants	Planning	Activity Culturing Agent/ Laboratory Activity	Spreading Biological Agent
Anugiten	X	X	X
Ava	X	?	X
Bhagwan Shree Rajneesh	?		
Bodhi			X
Jayanda	?		
Julian	X		X
K.D.	X		X
Parambodhi		X	
Puja	X	X	X
Savita	X		
Sheela	X		X
Su	X		
Vidya	X		
Yogini	X		?

SOURCES: See text. Also, Exhibit B, attached to the David Berry Knapp interrogation, transcribed November 15, 1985, Federal Bureau of Investigation, from the files of the State of Oregon Attorney General's Office.

Sheela and Puja talked about ordering typhoid in the name of the Rajneesh Medical Corporation (RMC) from a lab somewhere in the United States. K.D. objected, pointing out that the typhoid cultures could possibly be traced back to the RMC. K.D. states Sheela told him not to be so paranoid and not to worry about the typhoid cultures being traced back to RMC. Puja favored using typhoid because it would cause a couple of weeks of fever. As far as Knapp [K.D.] knows, this plan was never implemented.[28]

No information exists in the available records about why Puja decided not to use *Salmonella typhi*. It is likely, however, that Sheela and Puja heeded K.D.'s advice and decided that causing a typhoid outbreak was too risky. According to K.D., Puja also expressed an interest in hepatitis.[29] The available records do not indicate whether she tried to culture hepatitis, but if she did, it is highly unlikely that she was success-

28. Report of Interview, Swami Krishna Deva [K.D.], AKA David Berry Knapp, Oregon State, November 25, 1985, AG files, p. 73.

29. David Berry Knapp interrogation, transcribed November 13, 1985, Federal Bureau of Investigation, AG files, p. 7. There are several forms of hepatitis, including types A, B, C, and E. See Abram S. Benenson, ed., *Control of Communicable Diseases Manual*, 16th ed. (Washington, D.C.: American Public Health Association, 1995), pp. 217–233.

ful.[30] K.D. also claimed that Puja had additional schemes for spreading infection:

Other ideas Puja had of making people sick in The Dalles included the putting of dead rodents, especially "beavers," into The Dalles water system. Puja had explained that beavers naturally contained bacteria in their bodies. There was some comment that beavers could not be put into the water tanks in The Dalles because of screens over the tanks. K.D. recalls someone jokingly suggesting that the beavers be put into a blender (and liquefied). Someone suggested rats or mice could be injected with a substance and placed into The Dalles water system. K.D. heard Anugiten talk of trapping mice. K.D. believes some of the traps were set in The Dalles so that the rodents would be indigenous to the area.[31]

The pathogen associated with beavers is *Giardia lamblia*, a protozoan that causes giardiasis, a diarrheal disease.[32] It is commonly called "beaver fever" in the Rocky Mountain region, where most beavers are infected with giardia. As a result, it is considered unsafe to drink unfiltered water, even from freely flowing streams.[33]

According to K.D., "Puja was always very excited about the disease AIDS." He claimed that "Puja talked about culturing the AIDS virus and she was very secretive concerning her work in that area."[34] According to evidence given to law enforcement officials, Puja questioned one of the medical people who worked with her about culturing AIDS. She was told that the Rajneeshees lacked the necessary equipment, which led to the rush purchase of a "quick-freeze dryer" in September 1984.[35] Given the state of medical knowledge at the time, however, it is extremely unlikely that Puja made any headway in her study of AIDS. Her secrecy may have reflected a desire to protect herself from the appearance of failure, which was always a concern in the internecine struggle for prestige and authority within the cult. Nevertheless, there are unconfirmed reports that she

---

30. It was only in 1988 that successful culturing of hepatitis A virus was reported in the medical literature.

31. Report of Interview, Swami Krishna Deva, AKA David Berry Knapp, Oregon State, November 25, 1985, AG files, p. 73.

32. Benenson, ed., *Control of Communicable Diseases Manual*, pp. 202–204.

33. Stuart Warren and Ted Long Ishikawa, *Oregon Handbook*, 3rd edition (Chico, Calif.: Moon Publications, 1995), pp. 51–52.

34. David Berry Knapp interrogation, transcribed November 15, 1985, Federal Bureau of Investigation, AG files, p. 11.

35. Affidavit for Search Warrant, signed by Lieutenant Dean Renfrow, Oregon State Police, October 1, 1985, OSA files.

may have deliberately infected at least one individual with the HIV virus to see if it was possible to transmit the disease.[36]

Acquisition and Production of Salmonella Typhimurium

At some time between October 1, 1983, and February 29, 1984, the RMC purchased a set of what are called "bactrol disks" from VWR Scientific, a medical supply company in Seattle, Washington. Some of the disks contained *Salmonella* Typhimurium of a strain known as ATCC 14028, which is commonly used in medical settings.[37] Puja apparently took samples of the bacteria from this set of bactrol disks, which were employed by the RMC's state-licensed medical laboratory.[38] The RMC had a legitimate need for *Salmonella* Typhimurium because it was one of the control organisms used to meet the requirements for quality assurance expected of licensed clinical laboratories. The RMC laboratory was required to test the proficiency of its technicians by having them identify samples contaminated with known agents, and it maintained stocks of common pathogens for this purpose. The laboratory also employed the control organisms to ensure the quality of the growth media used in diagnostic tests.[39]

Large-scale production of *Salmonella* Typhimurium reportedly took place in a laboratory in the "Chinese laundry," located near a part of Rajneeshpuram known as Jesus Grove. The laboratory was subsequently moved to the Alan Watts complex, which consisted of about two dozen

---

36. Author's interview with Lynn Enyart, FBI Special Agent, October 23, 1997.

37. Government's Statement of Expected Testimony and Evidence, *U.S. v Ma Anand Sheela, et al*, CR. 86–53, June 21, 1986, U.S. District Court files. This statement was the presented by the U.S. Attorney's Office to the judge in the case and summarizes the evidence that the prosecutors intended to present if the case had gone to trial. Tests by the U.S. Centers for Disease Control (CDC) confirmed that ATCC 14028 was the same strain that was involved in the outbreak at The Dalles.

38. When the clinic was searched on October 2, 1985, a culture of *Salmonella* Typhimurium was seized from the clinic. It proved to be of the same strain as provided on the bactrol disks. See Government's Statement of Expected Testimony and Evidence, *U.S. v Ma Anand Sheela, et al*, CR. 86–53, June 21, 1986, U.S. District Court files.

39. To ensure that a given bacterial growth media will grow the right microorganisms, it is tested by inoculating a sample with certain control bacteria. *Salmonella* Typhimirium is one of the organisms considered suitable for use in tests of several agars used as growth media. Elmer W. Koneman et al., *Color Atlas and Textbook of Diagnostic Microbiology*, 4th ed. (Philadelphia: J.B. Lippincott, 1992), pp. 55–58, 118–120. Koneman specifically mentions five different growth media that can be tested using *S.* Typhimurium as a control organism.

buildings in a canyon northeast of the center of Rajneeshpuram.[40] The production site consisted of two A-frame structures joined together by a bathroom.[41] In a description that Ma Ava gave the FBI, the laboratory contained a large freeze dryer with tubes and other equipment and a green incubator the size of a "small apartment-type refrigerator" that contained petri dishes used to cultivate the *Salmonella* bacteria.[42] Rajneeshee officials identified the site as a "germ warfare" laboratory after Sheela's departure from Rajneeshpuram.[43]

The expertise to produce *Salmonella* Typhimurium apparently came from the RMC's laboratory technician, Parambodhi. When Puja first asked Parambodhi to culture the bacterium, he reportedly objected that it was dangerous, but he ultimately agreed to grow quantities of it for Puja. On one occasion, Ava remembered receiving two large jars filled with a liquid containing *Salmonella*.[44]

The first documented use of biological agents by the Rajneeshees took place on August 29, 1984, during a routine fact-finding visit to Rajneeshpuram by the three Wasco County commissioners. The Rajneeshees gave water laced with *Salmonella* Typhimurium to Judge William Hulse and Ray Matthew, the two commissioners who were hostile to the group. Both became sick and one required hospitalization.[45]

Targeting Restaurants

The most significant use of biological agents by the Rajneeshees targeted restaurants in the town of The Dalles in September 1984. Because of its location on the interstate highway, The Dalles has more restaurants than would normally be typical for a town its size. Cult members contaminated salad bars in ten restaurants with *Salmonella* Typhimurium. Two Rajneeshees later told law enforcement officials about their participation in the effort and described the direct involvement of Sheela and Puja.

---

40. Ava Kay Avalos interrogation, transcribed October 22, 1985, AG files, pp. 14–15.

41. James Long and Leslie L. Zaitz, "Lab Reputedly Used in Germ Experiments," *The Oregonian*, September 28, 1985, p. A1.

42. Ava Kay Avalos interrogation, transcribed October 22, 1985, AG files, p. 14.

43. Long and Zaitz, "Lab Reputedly Used in Germ Experiments," p. A1.

44. Notes of Interview, Ava Kay Avalos (Ma Ava), October 7, 1985, Oregon Department of Justice, OSA.

45. More is known about this incident than any of the others because of first-hand accounts by the victims and one of the perpetrators. Author's interview with Judge William Hulse, April 1997; Interview, Ava Avalos, October 22, 1985, AG files, pp. 15–17.

K.D. admitted to participating in one incident. Puja gave him a plastic bag containing a test tube sealed with a cork stopper and filled with a "mostly clear" light brown liquid. She ordered him to spread the contents of the vial at a restaurant in The Dalles. During a trip into town to attend a meeting with another cult member, K.D. went to the Portage Inn. Because they arrived after lunchtime, the salad bar was closed, but he poured the contents of the vial into the salad dressing.[46]

Ma Ava was involved in contaminating three restaurants. At Sheela and Puja's request, she and another cult member, Swami Satyam Bodhidharma (Bodhi), replaced their distinctive Rajneeshee garments with ordinary clothing. They were given five or six vials purportedly containing *Salmonella* and then drove up to The Dalles. According to Ava's recollections, she and Bodhi poured the vials into the coffee creamers at two restaurants, Johnny's Cafe and The Chuck Wagon, and the blue cheese dressing in the salad bar at a third restaurant, Arlo's.[47]

K.D. told law enforcement officials that he heard an account in which Puja, wearing a wig, had contaminated the salad bar at the Recreation Cafe.[48] Sheela congratulated Puja after the attack.[49] Ava recalled that Puja claimed to have put *Salmonella* in "lots of places."[50] On at least one occasion during this period, a cult member saw Puja change into a disguise.[51] Other cult members were also implicated in the restaurant contaminations. Ava believed that Ma Dhayan Yogini may have placed

---

46. K.D. told the story both to the FBI and to the Oregon state investigators. See Report of Interview, Swami Krishna Deva, AKA David Berry Knapp, November 25, 1985, AG files, p. 74; and David Berry Knapp interrogation, transcribed November 13, 1985, Federal Bureau of Investigation, AG files, p. 4. This was the only time K.D. mentioned involvement in a restaurant poisoning. He dated it to sometime in August 1984, after the time that he contaminated the Wasco County Courthouse. However, press accounts suggest that he was seen by an employee of the Portage Inn on September 12 near the salad bar. Federal prosecutors eventually came to date this incident to sometime between August 16 and September 12. See Roberta Ulrich, "Indictment of Sheela, Onang Applauded," *The Oregonian*, March 20, 1985, p. E6.

47. Ulrich, "Indictment of Sheela, Onang Applauded." Later, salmonellosis victims were reported at Arlo's and Johnny's Cafe, but not at The Chuck Wagon.

48. David Berry Knapp interrogation, transcribed November 13, 1985, Federal Bureau of Investigation, AG files, p. 7.

49. Report of interview, Swami Krishna Deva [K.D.], AKA David Berry Knapp, November 25, 1985, AG files, p. 76.

50. Ava Kay Avalos interrogation, transcribed October 22, 1985, AG files, p. 13.

51. Letter, Daniel Hoarfrost, to Criminal Justice Division, Bob Hamilton, November 20, 1985, and attached proffer, OSA files. The attachment quotes the observations of an unnamed Rajneeshee.

some *Salmonella* at the "Tapadaro," presumably a reference to the Tapadera Inn and Restaurant Lounge.[52]

Unfortunately, information on Rajneeshee efforts to contaminate food at restaurants in The Dalles is incomplete. Although people became sick after eating at ten restaurants, eyewitness accounts exist for attacks on only four. Thus, in the absence of more information, there will continue to be gaps in our knowledge of what happened in The Dalles in August and September 1984.

The Outbreak

On September 17, 1984, the Health Department of Wasco-Sherman County learned of an outbreak of food poisoning when it received a telephone call from a person who had become ill after eating at a local restaurant. By September 21, public health officials had recorded approximately twenty-five cases. At that time, the cases appeared to have resulted from exposures during the period from September 12 through 15, and on September 18. Two restaurants were implicated in the outbreak, which now seemed to be waning.[53]

Wasco County was served by a single hospital, the Mid-Columbia Medical Center, which had only 105 beds at the time, and the local health-care providers were overwhelmed by the number of patients.[54] The pathology laboratory at the medical center cultured stool specimens taken from patients and identified *Salmonella* Typhimurium as the culprit.[55] These results were confirmed on September 21 by tests conducted at the Oregon State Public Health Laboratory in Portland.[56] Thus, within four days of the first reported case, it was known for certain which microorganism was responsible.

52. Ava Kay Avalos interrogation, transcribed October 22, 1985, AG files, p. 13.

53. Jeanie Senior, "Salmonella Poisoning Cases Surpass 200," *The Oregonian*, September 28, 1984, p. C1.

54. Author's interview with Dr. Arthur Van Eaton, hospital pathologist in The Dalles, Oregon, April 11, 1997.

55. The symptoms of salmonellosis include diarrhea, headache, nausea, vomiting, abdominal pains, and headache. It is generally accompanied by fever. Infants and older patients can experience dehydration, but the disease is rarely fatal. *Salmonella* Typhimurium can be detected using stool samples, but the organism is not always present. For that reason, doctors are advised to take several samples over a period of several days. See Benenson, ed., *Control of Communicable Diseases Manual*, pp. 410–415.

56. According to the CDC account of the incident, on September 17 the Oregon Public Health Service Laboratory received a specimen from a victim and isolated *S.* Typhimurium. See letter, Thomas J. Török, et. al., Centers for Disease Control, to John A.

By September 21, public health officials were beginning to breathe a sigh of relief, since it appeared that they had weathered the worst salmonellosis outbreak ever experienced in the county. In fact, the worst was yet to come. Three days later, on September 24, there was a flood of new cases. By September 27, an estimated 200 cases had been reported, making it the largest salmonellosis outbreak in Oregon history. At that time, twenty-eight patients were in the hospital.[57]

Cases continued to appear in what appeared to be a never-ending stream. By September 30, health officials had reports of 423 cases, and twenty patients remained hospitalized.[58] On October 1, the total number of people admitted to the hospital during the outbreak reached 45. At least ten restaurants were later implicated (see Table 8.2.).[59] Ultimately, public health officials identified 751 local people who became sick during the salmonellosis outbreak. The actual number of victims was probably much higher because many out-of-state travelers may have been infected as well. Fortunately no one died, although some people became seriously ill.

Targeting the Water System

Law enforcement officials believed that the restaurant contaminations may have been a test run for a planned follow-up attack involving the town's water supply. According to K.D., sometime during July or August 1984, Sheela ordered him to acquire maps of the water system in The Dalles. When he failed to do so, she became impatient and turned to another Rajneeshee, Sagun, who apparently obtained the maps when he accompanied Sheela on a trip to The Dalles. Subsequently, K.D. was present at a meeting with Sheela and other cult members during which they discussed an operation to contaminate the town's water supply.[60]

Googins, State Epidemiologist, Department of Human Resources, Oregon State Health Division, January 18, 1985, as reproduced in *Congressional Record*, February 28, 1985, p. H901ff. It took some time to confirm that all the cases were from one particular strain of *Salmonella* Typhimurium. Given the technology then available, the CDC was not able to send a report to Oregon until early 1986.

57. Ibid.

58. Jeanie Senior, "Health Sleuths Strive to Trace Food Poison," *The Oregonian*, October 1, 1984, p. B1.

59. Jeanie Senior, "Lettuce Suspected as Source of Food Poisoning," *The Oregonian*, October 2, 1984, p. B4.

60. Ava confirmed that K.D. was at the meeting, but said that he "was in and out of the room." Interview with Ava Kay Avalos (Ma Ava), October 7, 1985, Oregon Department of Justice, OSA [no page numbers].

Table 8.2. Restaurant Contaminations Resulting in Illness in The Dalles, Oregon.

	Restaurants
First Wave (September 11–18, 1984)	Arlo's Restaurant Portage Inn
Second Wave (September 19–25, 1984)	Arctic Circle Restaurant Arlo's Restaurant Burgerville USA Kopper Kitchen Pietro's Pizza Restaurant Portage Inn Recreation Cafe Shakey's Pizza Parlor Skipper's Seafood Restaurant Taco Time

SOURCES: The official investigation by the U.S. Centers for Disease Control (CDC) does not name the individual restaurants but identifies them only by number. The CDC data indicate that ten restaurants were implicated. The federal indictment, however, mentions eleven names, including Johnny's Cafe. See Roberta Ulrich, "Indictment of Sheela, Onang Applauded," *The Oregonian*, March 20, 1986, p. E6. Press accounts at the time of the outbreak identified six restaurants: Arlo's, Burgerville, Pietro's, Portage Inn, Shakey's, and Skipper's. See Jeanie Senior, "Lettuce Suspected as Source of Food Poisoning," *The Oregonian*, October 2, 1984, p. B4.

During this meeting, two Rajneeshees, Julian and Anugiten, discussed visiting The Dalles to examine the water system. Julian reportedly told Puja that they would need considerably more "salsa" (an apparent reference to *Salmonella*) to contaminate the water system. Puja replied that she might not be able to produce sufficient material in time for their return visit to The Dalles.[61] Julian was unhappy with his participation in the operation and asked Sheela if more people could lend a hand. Sheela replied that she would not permit any changes in the plan and that he should not ask again.

It is not altogether clear what material Julian and Anugiten used to contaminate the water supply. K.D. believed that it was *Salmonella*, but Ava thought it might have been a mixture of raw sewage from Rajneeshpuram and dead rodents. According to her recollections, Puja contacted Debal, the Resource Manager at Rajneeshpuram, to obtain raw sewage.

---

61. Report of Interview, Swami Krishna Deva [K.D.], AKA David Berry Knapp, November 25, 1985, AG files, p. 74.

Ava also recalled a lot of empty cages in the "Chinese lab" and suspected that Puja might have mixed dead rats in with the sewage.[62]

Julian and Anugiten made two trips to contaminate the water system in The Dalles with "salsa." According to K.D., "Julian described how he and Anugiten climbed up a hill to a water tank that overlooked a nearby school. He recalled something being mentioned about trying to pry open the screen on the water tank and hearing rushing water."[63] K.D. said that Ma Dhayan Yogini drove the two men on one of the trips, but his recollection was unclear and he may have meant Ava.[64] For her part, Ava reported that she inadvertently played a role in one of the trips to contaminate the water supply. She was ordered by Savita to pick up a car being held at the Portland Airport, clean it inside and out to eliminate any fingerprints, and park it at a specified parking spot in downtown Portland. Ava later concluded that this car had been used by Julian and Anugiten for one of their water-contamination operations.[65] During one of the two trips, a police car showed up and "freaked them out." According to Ava, a decision was made not to use Julian on any more operations because he had a tendency to panic.[66]

Targeting the Community

In addition to the restaurant operations, the Rajneeshees tried other means of spreading *Salmonella* Typhimurium cultures.[67] Sometime in late July or August 1984, Puja gave K.D. a small container, which he remembered as an eye dropper, filled with a "brownish clear liquid." He was instructed to put the liquid on doorknobs and urinal handles in the Wasco

62. Ava Kay Avalos interrogation, transcribed October 22, 1985, AG files, p. 15.

63. Report of Interview, Swami Krishna Deva [K.D.], AKA David Berry Knapp, November 25, 1985, AG files, p. 76. Law enforcement officials confirmed that the metal screens appeared cut on one of the water tanks when they examined it in 1985.

64. David Berry Knapp interrogation, transcribed November 13, 1985, Federal Bureau of Investigation, AG files, p. 6.

65. Ibid., pp. 5–6; Ava Kay Avalos interrogation, transcribed October 22, 1985, AG files.

66. David Berry Knapp interrogation, transcribed November 13, 1985, Federal Bureau of Investigation, AG files, p. 7; Ava Kay Avalos interrogation, transcribed October 22, 1985, AG files, p. 15.

67. Unfortunately, it was more than a year after the incidents occurred that these accounts were recorded. As a result, it is likely that the recollections are inaccurate in some respects and that the participants give incorrect dates for a few of the events.

County Courthouse. Puja warned him to wash his hands after spreading the material.

Although Puja never told K.D. what was in the liquid, he believed that it contained *Salmonella* based on Puja's description that it would give people "the shits." For people to get sick, Puja indicated that the victims would have to get the substance into their mouths. K.D. followed orders and spread the liquid as directed. No one got sick from his efforts, however, and he later told law enforcement officials "that Sheela was frustrated and angry that Puja's substance was not working."[68]

On another occasion, also sometime in July or August 1984, a group of Rajneeshees, including Sheela, Anugiten, Puja, Jayananda, Julian, K.D., and possibly one or two others, visited The Dalles to select targets for disruption attacks aimed at the county government. During that trip, the Rajneeshees stopped at an Albertson's supermarket in The Dalles. K.D. gave a graphic description of this episode:

Sheela said to Puja, "Puji, let's have some fun." K.D. says that Puja giggled and replied "oh boy" (or words to that effect). K.D. recalls that Sheela, Puja, himself, Jayananda, and probably the others went into the store. Both K.D. and Jayananda were Sheela's bodyguards. While in the store, K.D. recalls observing Sheela in the produce department sprinkling on the lettuce what he assumed to be a similar substance he had been given by Puja to put on doorknobs in the courthouse, and salad dressing in the restaurant on an earlier date. K.D. said that Sheela had the container with the substance up her sleeve, at the wrist and palm, to conceal what she was doing. Puja commented to K.D. that she was thinking of injecting the substance into the milk cartons. K.D. objected to her doing that saying it would be obvious that the carton had been tampered with because of the holes in the carton. It was unknown to K.D. if Puja injected the substance into the milk cartons. Comments were made by Sheela that the intent of putting the substance onto the lettuce was to give people in The Dalles "the shits." When they returned to their vehicle Puja was giggling and saying that she had a good time.[69]

Another Rajneeshee, Ma Dhyan Yogini, was involved in an attempt to spread *Salmonella* at a nursing home in The Dalles, although her self-described efforts were less than successful. Finding herself under close observation by the nursing home staff, she felt unable to carry out the plot and dumped the solution in the street. Later, she lied to Puja, claiming that she had carried out the attack.[70] In addition to this abortive

---

68. Report of Interview, Swami Krishna Deva [K.D.], AKA David Berry Knapp, November 25, 1985, Federal Bureau of Investigation, AG files, p. 74.

69. Ibid., p. 75.

70. Testimony of Alma Peralta, Grand Jury Testimony, May 21, 1990, attached to

attempt, Yogini participated in one additional operation. At a political meeting in The Dalles, she put some of the *Salmonella*-contaminated liquid on her hands and held hands with an "older gentleman" she sat with.[71]

The End of the Plot

The September 1984 *Salmonella* poisonings ended the cult's use of biological agents. Participants provided two explanations for the decision to terminate the attacks. According to K.D., "as soon as the Share-A-Home project began to get going, the contamination project seemed to be de-emphasized and everyone concentrated on the Share-A-Home project."[72] This account suggests that the leadership of the cult, which was intimately involved in both activities, was stretched thin. The Share-A-Home project was difficult to manage because many of the homeless people were dysfunctional. As it assumed primacy, there was not enough time to continue the contamination effort.

A complementary explanation was provided by Ma Ava: "The *Salmonella* poisoning of The Dalles was simply an experiment through which Sheela and her associates could assess whether or not they could incapacitate the voting population in The Dalles at the time of voting."[73] K.D. shared this view.[74] Thus, Sheela viewed the *Salmonella* contaminations simply as a means to accomplish a particular end. When the Rajneeshees decided that they could not prevail in the local elections, they abandoned both the Share-A-Home and the contamination projects. Still, the fact that some cult members obtained pleasure from inflicting punishment on their enemies suggests that the *Salmonella* contamination was more than just an experiment.

After the restaurant attacks, the Rajneeshees did not abandon terrorism but changed the focus of their activities. They targeted individuals who were viewed as enemies of the cult or who were seen by Sheela as

---

Hagan Motion to Reconsider Motion to Dismiss Indictment, *U.S. v Susan Hogan and Sally Croft*, CR-146-MA #588, U.S. District Court files, p. 24.

71. Ibid. Ava recalled Yogini talking about spreading *Salmonella* by shaking hands with people. See Ava Kay Avalos interrogation, transcribed October 22, 1985, AG files, p. 13.

72. Interview, David Berry Knapp, November 13, 1985, AG files, p. 7.

73. Interview, Ava Kay Avalos, October 22, 1985, AG files, p. 48.

74. Report of Interview, Swami Krishna Deva [K.D.], AKA David Berry Knapp, November 25, 1985, AG files, p. 76.

rivals, real or imagined. A list of potential targets was drawn up and assassination plots were organized.

In some cases, the plots reached fruition. The most important was the effort to kill the U.S. Attorney in Portland, Charles H. Turner, whom the Rajneeshees viewed as one of their major enemies. To accomplish this objective, two cult members traveled to Texas to purchase handguns. When they found that it was difficult to buy weapons in Texas with out-of-state identification, they continued on to New Mexico, where they obtained false identification cards and bought several pistols. They planned to shoot Turner in the garage of the federal office building in Portland, but were foiled by law enforcement.[75] As of mid-1999, arrest warrants remained outstanding for some cult members in connection with this plot.

The Aftermath

Only two cult members, Sheela and Puja, were tried for their participation in the *Salmonella* contamination scheme. The criminal proceedings were divided between the state and federal courts: the Oregon Attorney General's Office was responsible for prosecuting the poisonings of Judge Hulse and Commissioner Matthew, and the U.S. Attorney's Office assumed responsibility for the restaurant contamination cases.

On July 22, 1985, both Sheela and Puja pleaded guilty in state court to charges of first-degree assault and conspiracy/assault for the August 29, 1984, poisoning of Judge Hulse. Each of these charges carried a maximum penalty of twenty years imprisonment and a $100,000 fine. In addition, the two pleaded guilty to charges of second-degree assault and conspiracy/assault for the poisoning of Commissioner Matthew. Each of those charges carried a maximum penalty of ten years imprisonment and a fine of $100,000.

In total, Sheela received three concurrent twenty-year sentences, was fined $400,000, and was ordered to pay Wasco County restitution in the amount of $69,353.31. Puja was sentenced to two concurrent twenty-year sentences and a concurrent seven-and-a-half-year sentence. Further, the state recommended that Sheela and Puja serve their prison time in federal penitentiaries.[76] The state also mounted a civil proceeding against the Rajneeshees.

75. John Painter, Jr., "Death-Plot Facts Come to Light," *The Oregonian,* June 30, 1991, p. C1.

76. Statement of Attorney General Dave Frohnmeyer, July 22, 1986, OSA files.

Conclusion

Several interesting aspects of the Rajneeshee case merit additional comment. Contrary to the conventional wisdom, the cult's use of biological agents did not follow the normal escalatory curve. Instead of moving from conventional weapons to the use of biological agents, the group resorted to bioterrorism fairly early in their campaign of disruption and attempted murder. Unlike the Aum Shinrikyo cult, which employed biological weapons as a means to fulfill an apocalyptic prophecy, the Rajneeshees viewed biological agents as a tool that could help them achieve a particular objective. When the plot to take over Wasco County failed, they appear to have abandoned their biological weapons activity. They never made public reference to their use of biological agents until September 1995, when the Bhagwan himself accused Sheela and others of responsibility for the salmonellosis outbreaks.

No evidence suggests a formal decision by the cult to abandon the use of biological agents. The actual attempts to use biological agents were experiments and harassing attacks. For cult members, the use of *Salmonella* was quite frustrating because the incubation period created a long delay between action and outcome. According to former Rajneeshees, the leadership became preoccupied with the problems created by the Share-A-Home program and reduced the attention given to the contamination effort. When the political scheme fell apart, so did the need for follow-up attacks timed to coincide with the November 1984 election. Since the Bhagwan was unforgiving about failures, Sheela apparently saw the contamination effort as a potential danger to her position within the cult and abandoned it. When the group decided to attempt to murder the U.S. Attorney in Portland, they acquired handguns.

Like many "closed" cults, the Rajneeshees were characterized by a charismatic, all-powerful leader, isolation from the rest of society, and strict internal controls. Cult members, many of whom had Ph.D.'s, viewed themselves as superior to outsiders and exempt from ordinary moral standards. They lacked an external constituency and hence were not subject to the normal restraints that apply to politically motivated groups. They were also under intense pressure from the Baghwan to achieve results, which may have led to poor judgment. Finally, Puja was a confirmed poisoner who may have murdered Sheela's first husband, in the view of some Rajneeshees.

Chapter 9

The Covenant, the Sword, and the Arm of the Lord (1985)

Jessica Eve Stern

In the mid-1980s, a little known survivalist group calling itself The Covenant, the Sword, and the Arm of the Lord (CSA) acquired a large drum of potassium cyanide with the intention of poisoning water supplies in major U.S. cities. The group's objective was to hasten the return of the Messiah by "carrying out God's judgments" against unrepentant sinners.[1] CSA members also participated in a plot to overthrow the U.S. government, which they believed was controlled by descendants of Satan committed to the "establishment of a world order based on humanism, materialism, socialism and communism."[2]

CSA was unusual among terrorist groups in that its sole objective was large-scale murder rather than influencing government policies. Although it failed to achieve its objective, it might eventually have succeeded if law enforcement authorities had not intervened. The danger would be even greater if the group were operating today, when terrorists are more aware of the potential of chemical and biological weapons for inflicting mass casualties.[3] What did CSA hope to accomplish? Why did

The author would like to thank Darcy Bender and Melinda Lamont-Havers for extraordinary research assistance.

1. Author's telephone interview with Kerry Noble, former second-in-command of CSA, March 2, 1998. For other studies of CSA, see James K. Campbell, *Weapons of Mass Destruction Terrorism* (Seminole, Fla.: Interpact Press, 1997); James Coates, *Armed and Dangerous: The Rise of the Survivalist Right* (New York: Hill and Wang, 1987); Brent Smith, *Terrorism in America: Pipe Bombs and Pipe Dreams* (Albany: State University of New York Press, 1994); and Kerry Noble, *Tabernacle of Hate: Why They Bombed Oklahoma City* (Prescott, Ontario: Voyageur Publishing, 1998).

2. *C.S.A. Journal*, No. 7 (1982), p. 11.

3. For example, Kerry Noble claimed that if CSA leader James Ellison met someone who knew something about biological agents, he might consider using them. Author's telephone interview with Noble, March 2, 1998.

it fail? And what does this case suggest about future terrorist attempts to use CBW agents?

The Origins of CSA

In 1971, James Ellison, a fundamentalist preacher from San Antonio, Texas, had a vision that the United States was heading in the wrong direction.[4] God directed him to go to Arkansas, he claims, "to establish a refuge and take people in."[5] In 1976, he bought a 224-acre lot of remote timberland near Bull Shoal Lake in the Ozark Mountains of Arkansas, which he called "Zarephath-Horeb." In the Bible, Zarephath was a place of refuge for the prophet Elijah during his battle with Jezebel's priests, who had turned from God to worship Baal. As the name suggests, Ellison believed that he was creating a place of refuge for those fighting the worshippers of false gods. He invited seekers, drug addicts, and ex-convicts to join him at his camp, which had its own water supply and generated its own electricity.[6] The community of about 100 people later renamed itself The Covenant, the Sword, and the Arm of the Lord (CSA).[7]

Unlike Aum Shinrikyo's Shoko Asahara, Ellison was not an autocratic leader who imposed discipline by threatening to punish or kill defectors. Instead, he appointed "Elders" to help him make decisions for the community (although he allotted himself two votes) and at times delegated real responsibilities. When Ellison left the compound to seek work in the early 1980s, he left CSA under the control of Elder Randall Radar, who later became an informant for the FBI.

Ellison described the group's objective as "simply be free to exercise our rights the way we want to."[8] But it soon became apparent that Ellison and his followers had unusual—and sometimes anti-social—interests.

---

4. Testimony of James Ellison at his sentencing, *United States of America v James D. Ellison*, 85-20006-01, October 4, 1985, U.S. District Court, Western District of Arkansas, Fort Smith Division.

5. Ibid.

6. Smith, *Terrorism in America*, pp. 62–63; Jane Ashley, "Right-Wing Leader Scoffs at Nazi Label: 'Hitler Not My Idol'," *USA Today*, September 9, 1985, p. 6A; Coates, *Armed and Dangerous*, pp. 136–137.

7. Government's Bill of Particulars Regarding Count IV of the Indictment, *United States of America v David Michael McGuire*, 87-20008-14, February 8, 1988, U.S. District Court, Western District of Arkansas, Fort Smith Division.

8. Testimony of James Ellison before the Grand Jury of the United States District Court for the Eastern District of Oklahoma in the Matter of Guns Violation Investigation, 85-20006-01, September 26, 1984, p. 13.

Residents built several factories for manufacturing grenades, silencers, and other firearm accessories, which they sold at gun shows.[9] They published a series of books, including *Witchcraft and the Illuminati; Christian Army Basic Training Manual; The Jews: 100 Facts;* and *Prepare War!* The *C.S.A. Journal* provided instructions for "spiritual and physical survival," including how to use guns and double-edged knives to kill one's enemies.[10] The group also sold racist, anti-Semitic, and survivalist literature as part of its official book list, including *The Protocols of the Learned Elders of Zion; The Negro and the World Crisis; Who's Who in the Zionist Conspiracy; The Talmud Unmasked;* and *A Straight Look at the Third Reich.*[11]

CSA members erected a sophisticated shooting range called "Silhouette City," modeled after the FBI's shooting range in Quantico, Virginia. Whereas the FBI version has mockups of armed criminals surrounded by women and children, the CSA version had mockups of prominent Jews and federal agents.[12] One wooden cutout of a state trooper wore a Star of David in place of a badge.[13] CSA members used Silhouette City for target practice at their Endtime Overcomer Survival Training School, which was established to provide training in "Christian martial arts." Outsiders paid $500 or more to go through the training course.[14]

CSA Ideology

The ideology of CSA was based on the Christian Identity movement, which over the past thirty years has become the dominant doctrine of the racist right in America. The origins of Christian Identity go back to the seventeenth century, when the Puritans in America saw themselves as the

---

9. Coates, *Armed and Dangerous*, p. 137.

10. The *C.S.A. Journal* was a "self-published" monthly newsletter consisting of xerox copies of a typed manuscript. According to Kerry Noble, it began publication in 1981 and was distributed to a mailing list of about 2,000 people. Noble, *Tabernacle of Hate*, p. 101.

11. *C.S.A. Journal*, No. 7, p. 34.

12. Affidavit for Search Warrant, Jack Knox, April 16, 1985, Defendant's Exhibit B, *United States of America v James D. Ellison*, 85-20015, U.S. District Court, Western District of Arkansas, Fort Smith Division; Smith, *Terrorism in America*, p. 64; Coates, *Armed and Dangerous*, p. 138.

13. Direct Examination of Bill Buford, *United States of America v James D. Ellison*, 85-20006-01, U.S. District Court, Western District of Arkansas, Fort Smith Division, p. 46.

14. Coates, *Armed and Dangerous*, p. 137.

"New Israel," destined to realize God's design in confronting the wilderness much like the biblical Israelites in the book of Exodus.[15] The idea that Northern Europeans might be the true Israelites was first promulgated by followers of British Israelism in the mid-nineteenth century. That movement peaked in England in the 1920s, when it boasted some 5,000 members. It later became more popular—and more vicious—in its American incarnation.[16]

Identity Christians believe that there were two creations in the book of Genesis. The first was of white Aryans, who are the children of Adam.[17] The "Aryan" races—those of Scandinavian, Germanic-Teutonic, and British ancestry—are the lost Sheep of Israel for whom "Jesus was sent to Earth."[18] The second creation was of the Jews, who were borne of the serpent's seduction of Eve in the Garden of Eden.[19] (The serpent was actually Satan in disguise.[20]) Christian Identity asserts that "these children of Satan through Cain are a race of vipers, Anti-Christs who have throughout history always been a curse to true Israel . . . because they do the works of their father the Devil."[21]

Followers of Christian Identity find "proof" that the Jews are descended from Satan in the Gospel of St. John, 8:42–47, when Jesus tells the Jews, "Ye are of *your* father the devil, and the lusts of your father ye will do."[22] Blacks and other non-whites are considered "pre-Adamite" peoples, halfway between apes and human beings. They are servant races but are not necessarily evil.[23] One of CSA's goals was to return America to its Christian (Aryan) roots.

Christian Identity is also a millenarian religion. The millenarian idea is that the present age is corrupt and that a new age will dawn after a

---

15. Michael Barkun, *Religion and the Racist Right: The Origins of the Christian Identity Movement* (Chapel Hill: University of North Carolina Press, 1996), p. 5.

16. Ibid, pp. 5–15.

17. Author's telephone interview with Pastor Robert Millar, April 21, 1998.

18. "Who We Are," *C.S.A. Journal*, No. 7 (1982), p. 15.

19. Direct Examination of Randall Rader, explaining Christian Identity teachings as practiced by CSA, *United States of America v James D. Ellison*, 85-20006-01, p. 126.

20. CSA explained in its journal: "The commonly-called Jews of today are not God's chosen people, but are in fact, an antichrist race, whose purpose is to destroy God's people and Christianity." " Who We Are," *C.S.A. Journal*, No. 7, p. 12.

21. Quoted in Anti-Defamation League, *Religion as Bigotry: The Identity Church Movement* (New York: ADL, October 1991).

22. Raphael Ezekiel, *The Racist Mind: Portraits of American Neo-Nazis and Klansmen* (New York: Penguin Books, 1995), p. 20.

23. Author's telephone interview with Pastor Robert Millar, April 21, 1998.

cleansing Apocalypse. Only a lucky few (usually envisaged to be selected on the basis of adherence to a particular doctrine or ritual) will survive the "Endtime" and experience paradise. Thousands of millennial cults have emerged in recent years, according to the Christian Research Institute, partly in anticipation of the year 2000.[24]

The period leading up to the Endtime is known as the "Tribulation," when the Earth will be plagued by war, famine, earthquakes, and disease—signs of the Messiah's imminent appearance, as predicted in the Gospel of St. Matthew. False prophets will arise bearing "great signs and wonders," which some interpret as new technologies. After the period of Tribulation comes Armageddon, the final battle between the forces of good and evil. To Identity Christians, the Armageddon referred to in the Book of Revelation will be a race war.[25] All Jews and non-white "mud peoples" will be destroyed and only Aryans, and possibly only followers of Christian Identity, will survive.

Many Evangelical Christians believe they will escape Armageddon in the "divine rapture"—the simultaneous ascension to Heaven of all Christians. Followers of Christian Identity, in contrast, do not believe in the rapture and expect to be present during the Apocalypse. Indeed, some are convinced that the period of Tribulation has already begun.[26] This belief is potentially dangerous, since some Christian Identity adherents believe they will need to stockpile every available weapon to ensure their survival.

Most believers in the Apocalypse—the precondition for the appearance of the Messiah—assume that God is responsible for determining the date. A variety of Christian and non-Christian sects, however, subscribe to the view that humans can accelerate the process by committing acts of violence and creating social chaos.[27] For their part, CSA members believed that they could hasten the Messiah's return by killing sinners, "mud people," and Jews.

Also potentially dangerous is the Christian Identity belief (shared by many anti-government groups) that an increasingly totalitarian U.S. government is infringing on citizens' fundamental rights. Christian Patriots fault the federal government for ceding its authority to international

---

24. "'Millennial Madness' Said to Drive Fringe Groups," *Washington Times*, March 29, 1997, p. 3.

25. Ibid.

26. Ibid.

27. A violent subset of the Orthodox Jewish settlement movement known as the *Gush Emunim* ("Bloc of the Faithful") believed that if they destroyed the Muslim holy site in Jerusalem, the Dome of the Rock, the Messiah might be persuaded to appear.

institutions such as the United Nations, the World Bank, and the International Monetary Fund, whose goal, they fear, is to create an oppressive world government. Freedom, they believe, can be secured only through resistance to secular law, which contradicts divine law as expressed in the scriptures.

Meaning of the Group's Name

Ellison and his followers changed the group's name from Zarephath-Horeb to "The Covenant, the Sword, and the Arm of the Lord" at a time when they no longer saw themselves as providing refuge to seekers and instead wanted a name that would reflect their new "paramilitary function."[28] The choice of the new name was highly significant. In the Bible, the word "covenant" refers to the special relationship between God and the Jews. The first covenant was with Abraham, to whose children God promised the land of Israel in return for Abraham's obedience to his commandments (Genesis 12:7). The Lord made a similar covenant with Jacob when he spoke to him in a dream (Genesis 28:12–15).[29] God also made a covenant directly with the twelve tribes of Israel, promising them that if they followed his commandments they would become his chosen people (Exodus 19:5–6).[30] Followers of British Israelism contend that these and other prophecies relating to the latter-day descendants of Israel can readily be shown to have been fulfilled by the Anglo-Saxon and Celtic peoples, who are God's true "chosen people."[31] They interpret the word

---

Fortunately, they did not proceed with this plan because they lacked rabbinical authorization. See Ehud Sprinzak, *The Ascendance of Israel's Radical Right* (New York: Oxford University Press, 1991), pp. 94–97. Similarly, Shoko Asahara, the leader of the Japanese Aum Shinrikyo cult, believed that by carrying out mass murder he would help to bring on Armageddon, hastening the day when he would emerge as the leader of the world.

28. Noble, *Tabernacle of Hate*, p. 100.

29. Jacob's part of the Covenant is that, "if God will be with me, and will keep me in this way that I go . . . then shall the Lord be my God." (Genesis 28:20–21).

30. This Covenant is repeated, for example in Deuteronomy: "Thou hast avouched the Lord this day to be thy God, and to walk in his ways, and to keep his statutes, and his commandments, and his judgments, and to hearken unto his voice: And the Lord hath avouched thee this day to be his peculiar people . . . and to make thee high above all nations which he hath made, in praise, and in name, and in honor. . . ." (Deuteronomy 26:17–19).

31. For example, the "west" in God's covenant with Jacob refers to the United States, the "east" to India and Asia, the "north" to Canada, and the "south" to South Africa

"British" to mean "covenant man," since the Hebrew word for "covenant" is *b'rit* and for "man " is *ish*.[32] This linguistic oddity is taken as further proof that Anglo-Saxon and Celtic peoples are the true Israel and that America is the Promised Land.[33]

The "sword" in CSA refers to God's anger against those who do not obey his commandments (Leviticus 26:25). The "arm of the Lord" refers to God's omnipotence (Deuteronomy 7:19). Thus, the Covenant, the Sword, and the Arm of the Lord represents God's promise to reward those who abide by his commandments and to take vengeance against those who worship false Gods or otherwise disobey his law.

Preparing for Armageddon

In late 1978, Ellison had a vision that convinced him that a breakdown of the American economic system was imminent. Cities would soon be in turmoil, the government would collapse, and people would be unable to defend themselves.[34] The compound began stockpiling food, weapons, ammunition, supplies, and explosives to prepare for the Apocalypse.[35] When Pastor Robert Millar, a leading Identity Christian cleric, visited the CSA compound in the early 1980s, he was "shocked" to see Ellison wearing camouflage gear and carrying a gun. But Millar soon realized that Ellison was "a man with tremendous gifts and ability."[36] Millar later consecrated Ellison as "King James of the Ozarks" at a service on the CSA grounds.

---

and Australia, all former parts of the British Empire. Web site on British Israelism [http://trf.org.au/bi.htm].

32. Web site on British Israelism [http://trf.org.au/bi.htm]; author's telephone interview with Pastor Robert Millar, April 21, 1998.

33. Author's telephone interview with Pastor Robert Millar.

34. Statement of J. Michael Fitzhugh, *United States of America v James D. Ellison*, 85-20017-04, U.S. District Court, Western District of Arkansas, Fort Smith Division, p. 14; United States Court of Appeals for the Eighth Circuit, Appeal from the United States District Court of the Western District of Arkansas, *United States of America, Appellee, v James D. Ellison, Appellant*, No. 85-2094 and 85-2095, July 24, 1985; James Ellison Sentencing, *United States of America v James D. Ellison*, 85-20017-01, September 4, 1985.

35. Affidavit for Search Warrant, Jack Knox, *United States of America v James D. Ellison*, 85-20015.

36. Judy Thomas, "We are Not Dangerous, Leader of Separatists Says," *Kansas City Star*, March 17, 1996.

The Covenant's "military" preparations were inspired by the group's "obediance to the Lord concerning watching and being prepared" for the Apocalypse.[37] *The C.S.A. Journal* detailed the "basic layout" of what would occur during the coming Armageddon:

There will be an economic collapse, riots in the cities, famine, and war. People will kill each other for food, weapons, shelter, clothing, anything. It will get so bad that parents will eat their children. Death in the major cities will cause rampant diseases and plagues. Maggot-infested bodies will lie everywhere. Earthquakes, tidal waves, volcanoes, and other natural disasters will grow to gigantic proportions. Russia and possibly China and Japan will attack America, probably with some limited nuclear warfare. Communists will kill white Christians and mutilate them; witches and satanic Jews will offer people up as sacrifices to their gods, openly and proudly; blacks will rape and kill white women, and will torture and kill white men; homosexuals will sodomize whoever they can. Prisoners from Federal and State prisons will be set free to terrorize, while Cuban refugees will do the same. . . . Our new government will be a part of the one-world Zionist Communism government. All but the elect will have the mark of the Beast.[38]

CSA members pledged not to surrender to these forces of evil:

In the event of the collapse of this Great Republic or the consideration of surrender of our sovereignty by our duly elected governmental officials to an internal or external power, we the undersigned, acting in the spirit of our Forefathers and these great documents—the Declaration of Independence and the Constitution of these United States—refuse any and all such treaty pact, or declaration of surrender. We acknowledge that there can exist no compromise between the principle of Freedom under God and the establishment of a world order based on humanism, materialism, socialism and communism. We accept the principle that it is better to stand, and if need be fall for the cause of Christ and Country than to submit to the coming attempt of satanic and socialistic world order. . . .[39]

To prepare to meet the Apocalypse, CSA members began "plundering the Egyptians" by stealing from department stores and committing arson for profit.[40] They also began thinking about "war."[41] Kerry Noble, who

---

37. "Who We Are," *C.S.A. Journal*, No. 7, p. 12.

38. Ibid.

39. Ibid.

40. *United States of America v James D. Ellison*, 85-20006-01, October 4, 1984, p. 295.

41. Direct Examination of [William] Thomas, *United States of America v James D. Ellison*, 85-20006-01, pp. 122–123.

was then Ellison's principal "God-anointed Elder,"[42] explains: "We thought there were signs of Armageddon, and we believed that once those signs were there it was time for us to act, to make judgments against those who were doing wrong or who refused to repent. . . . The original timetable was up to God, but God could use us in creating Armageddon. That if we stepped out things might be hurried along. You get tired of waiting for what you think God is planning."[43]

At a July 1983 meeting of the Aryan Nations Congress, James Ellison, Richard Butler (leader of the Aryan Nations and pastor of the Church of Jesus Christ Christian, an Identity Christian church in Hayden Lake, Idaho), Robert Miles (former grand dragon of the Michigan Knights of the Ku Klux Klan and leader of the Mountain Church in Cohoctah, Michigan), Louis Beam (ambassador-at-large for the Aryan Nations), and other extreme-right leaders developed an elaborate plan to overthrow what they called the Zionist Occupational Government (ZOG) and create a separate Aryan nation within the United States.[44] The conspirators planned to establish a nationwide computer network linking right-wing organizations.[45] They would assassinate federal officials, politicians, and Jews, sabotage gas pipelines and electric power grids, and bomb federal office buildings, including the Alfred E. Murrah Federal Building in Oklahoma City.[46] They would also poison municipal water supplies with cyanide. These terrorist activities were to serve as catalysts of a revolution that would ultimately result in a whites-only state.

The most violent members of the participating organizations were recruited to form a new group called The Order, named after a fictional terrorist cell in William Pierce's far-right novel *The Turner Diaries*. At least five members were recruited from CSA.[47] The Order was in charge of

---

42. "Who We Are," *C.S.A. Journal*, No. 7, p. 12.

43. Author's telephone interview with Noble, March 2, 1998.

44. Response of United States of America to James D. Ellison's Motion for Reduction of Sentence, *United States of America v James D. Ellison*, Criminal Nos. 85-20006-01 and 85-200017-01, May 11, 1988.

45. Rodney Bowers, "White Radical Activities that Led To Indictments Recounted for 1983–85," *Arkansas Gazette*, April 27, 1987, p. A1.

46. Author's interview with Noble, March 2, 1998; Testimony of James Ellison and Kerry Noble, *United States of America v Robert E. Miles et al.*, 87–20008, March 15, 1988, U.S. District Court, Western District of Arkansas, Fort Smith Division, p. 38. Ellison's recollection of the federal building they had considered targeting was "vague," he claimed in his testimony.

47. Government's Pre-trial Memorandum, *United States of America v Robert E. Miles et al.*, 87–20008, p. 9.

raising money to finance paramilitary activities, which it did through counterfeiting and theft. Over an eight-month period, from December 1983 to July 1984, the Order committed a series of lucrative robberies that netted more than $4 million.[48] CSA was to serve as a depot for weapons and military equipment, not only for its own terrorist operations but also for other "Aryan warriors" participating in the revolution.[49] Some of CSA's arms were stolen from a military base by a member who had been discharged from the U.S. Marine Corps.[50]

Soon after the Aryan Nations Congress, CSA escalated its level of violence. In November 1983, CSA members detonated an explosive device along a pipeline that supplied natural gas to several midwestern cities including Chicago, with the aim of causing a major disruption. The pipeline was damaged but natural gas deliveries were not interrupted.[51] Ellison's deputy, Kerry Noble, was asked why the group had targeted that pipeline. "It was winter," he explained. "We thought people would freeze, that they might start riots."[52] Later that month, CSA members bombed an electric transmission line at Fort Smith, Arkansas.[53] CSA published a manifesto explaining its doctrine called ATTACK, an acronym for "Aryan Tactical Treaty for the Advancement of Christ's Kingdom."

Effective immediately, every action of the enemy shall be met with equal and opposite reaction! CSA is not content with being a "nation within a nation." We want the outer nation to fall and give way to a Kingdom ruled by Jesus Christ! . . . We will lay out the ATTACK plan to our people at various Aryan gatherings. The time has come for the Spirit of Slumber to be lifted off our people! Arise, O Israel, and Shine, for the Light is come, and the glory of our Father is risen upon thee! We shall Attack and Advance into enemy territory within the next two years. Be prepared![54]

---

48. Ibid, p. 7.

49. Response of the United States of America to James D. Ellison's Motion for Reduction of Sentence, 85-20006-01 and 85-200017-01.

50. Ibid., Direct Testimony of [William] Thomas, p. 179.

51. FBI Special Agent Knox claimed that "substantial damage was done to the natural gas pipeline." *United States of America v Steve Scott*, 85-20014-01, U.S. District Court, Western District of Arkansas, Fort Smith Division.

52. Author's telephone interview with Noble, March 2, 1998.

53. Bowers, "White Radical Activities that Led To Indictments Recounted for 1983–85," p. A1.

54. CSA, Zarephath-Horeb Church, "A Christ-Kingdom Society" (newsletter), November/December 1984, p. 2.

The FBI and the Federal Bureau of Alcohol, Tobacco, and Firearms (ATF) began intensifying their investigation of CSA. One of their informants was Randall Rader, who had served as Ellison's deputy prior to joining The Order.[55] The informants told the FBI that James Rolston, a CSA member, had murdered a woman with a 12-inch knife and left her body on a highway. Police had found the woman's body in March 1985 but apparently had not yet identified a suspect. The informants also said that the group was stockpiling hand grenades, automatic weapons, anti-tank weapons, and plastic explosives; fabricating silencers and grenades; converting semi-automatic weapons to automatic ones; conducting para-military training; and burying landmines around the perimeter of the compound. CSA residents had been assigned sniper positions in the event of an FBI raid. CSA members stole cars whenever Ellison felt they were "needed in furtherance of the Lord's work," and then altered or disguised them.[56] The informants also said that Ellison had taken two wives.[57]

During this period, Robert Miles, the Michigan Klansman and pastor of the Mountain Church who had attended the Aryan Nations Congress, wrote a letter to Ellison sympathizing with him about the difficulty of being investigated by federal officials:

We know what you are all going through. We heard of the subpoenas and the interrogations. We know what federal heat is like. Yet it doesn't deter; it purifies and strengthens. It removes doubt. It removes sympathy. It removes compromise. . . . The federal heat only removes the bridges which we each have crossed. There is no turning back. There is no road but the one on which each of us, in his own way, has set his feet.[58]

That road, Miles later explained, was "to a racial nation, to peace."[59]

On April 15, 1985, a Missouri state trooper patrolling a stretch of highway near the Arkansas state line stopped a brown van driven by David Tate. Unbeknownst to the state trooper, Tate was a member of The Order. The trooper was making routine traffic checks as part of a campaign to crack down on drunk driving, unregistered vehicles, and traffic

---

55. Affidavit for Search Warrant, [FBI Special Agent] Jack Knox; Report of BATF, FBI, and Arkansas State Police interview with Kerry Noble, April 22, 1985, 85-20017-04.

56. Affidavit for Search Warrant, Jack Knox, p. 6.

57. Direct Examination of Jack Knox, *United States of America v James D. Ellison*, 85-20006-01.

58. Trial Testimony of Robert E. Miles, *United States of America v Robert E. Miles et al.*, 87–20008-01–14, October 14, 1988, p. 48.

59. Ibid.

violations. He radioed in the false name on Tate's license and discovered that the driver was a neo-Nazi wanted on federal firearms charges. When the trooper approached the van, Tate rolled out of the driver's seat, shot the policeman dead with a submachine gun, and fled the scene.

Missouri and Arkansas state police and FBI SWAT teams carried out a massive manhunt for Tate, employing Cobra gunship helicopters, bloodhounds, and an FBI spy plane equipped with infrared sensors. In the course of the six-day search, they discovered that Tate had been en route to the CSA compound. They also found that other members of The Order had been seeking refuge there and that some residents of the CSA compound had also lived in Elohim City, Pastor Millar's armed compound in eastern Oklahoma.[60] Soon afterwards, the FBI was issued a warrant to search the CSA compound for fugitives, stolen cars, illegal firearms, and equipment for converting semiautomatic weapons to automatic and for manufacturing firearms paraphernalia. An arrest warrant was also issued for Ellison on firearms charges.[61]

The six-day manhunt attracted the attention of reporters, who requested interviews with CSA members. Kerry Noble appeared for interviews wearing jungle fatigues and carrying a rifle, a knife, and a pistol. He pledged that CSA members would resist violently if federal authorities raided the camp. Ellison also appeared briefly during the interview, wearing fatigues and a beret with a gas mask strapped to his leg. He was carrying a rifle with a banana clip.[62]

On April 20, 1985, federal authorities raided the CSA compound. After a three-day standoff between hundreds of law-enforcement officers and the CSA "Home Guard," the residents of the camp surrendered. When law enforcement officers searched the compound, which had been booby-trapped with homemade mines, they found a large stockpile of illegal weapons and ammunition, including fifteen automatic rifles, twenty-three grenades, and an Army light antitank weapon.[63] An armored car was under construction. The officers also found thirty gallons of potassium cyanide, which Ellison initially said was for poisoning

60. Coates, *Armed and Dangerous*, pp. 140–141.

61. *United States of America v James Ellison*, 85-20017-03.

62. Michael Haddigan, "Survivalists Prepared, But Raid Never Comes," *Arkansas Gazette*, April 19, 1985, p. 1.

63. Direct Examination of Jack Knox; Michael Haddigan, "Ellison, 5 Other CSA Leaders Change Their Plea to Guilty," *Arkansas Gazette*, August 13, 1985, p. 3A; Lamar James, "Bond Denied CSA Head Despite Plea by Wife," *Arkansas Gazette*, May 1, 1985, p. 1.

pests.[64] "I'm not into a Jim Jones thing. . . . All I ever used it for was poisoning coyotes," Ellison is reported to have said.[65] Later, Ellison claimed that Miles had given him the cyanide and that Beam, Butler, and Miles had discussed using it to poison water supplies in New York, Chicago, and Washington.[66] Miles denied giving Ellison the cyanide or plotting to poison city water supplies.[67]

When Noble was asked why CSA was stockpiling cyanide, he replied, "We wanted to poison water systems, but we had no particular city in mind." Asked whether CSA members felt any moral scruples about using an indiscriminate weapon that would have killed Aryans as well as Jews and "mud people" (non-whites), he explained, "We felt that God would take care of this [and] that those who were meant to die would be poisoned." When reminded that thirty gallons of cyanide poured into a large reservoir would have so diluted that it would not have killed anyone, Noble replied that the group believed that "God would . . . make sure the poison got to the town."[68]

In 1985, the U.S. government charged CSA members with the August 1983 arson of the Metropolitan Community Church in Springfield, Missouri, whose congregation includes homosexuals; the arson that same month of a Jewish Community Center in Bloomington, Indiana; and the November 1983 bombing of a natural gas pipeline near Fulton, Arkansas. In the course of the trial, it was revealed that CSA members had also plotted to blow up the Murrah Federal Building in Oklahoma City with a rocket launcher but had not followed through.[69]

In a separate case in 1988, the U.S. government charged fourteen people who had participated in the secret July 1983 Aryan Nations Congress, including some members of CSA, with sedition. As defined in Title 18, Section 2384 of the United States Code, sedition involves a conspiracy by two or more persons to "overthrow, put down, or destroy by force the

---

64. Ashley, "Right-wing Leader Scoffs at Nazi Label," p. 6A.

65. Ibid. The reference to "a Jim Jones thing" is to cult leader Jim Jones and the members of the Peoples Temple, more than 900 of whom committed mass suicide in Guyana in November 1978 by drinking poison-laced Kool-Aid.

66. Response of the United States of America to James D. Ellison's Motion for Reduction of Sentence.

67. Trial Testimony of Robert E. Miles, *United States of America v Robert E. Miles et al.*, 87–20008-01–14, October 14, 1988, p. 48.

68. Author's telephone interview with Kerry Noble, March 2, 1998.

69. Ibid.; Testimony of James Ellison and Kerry Noble, *United States of America v Robert E. Miles et al.*, p. 38.

Government of the United States, or to oppose by force the authority thereof, or by force to prevent, hinder, or delay the execution of any law of the United States, or by force seize, take or possess any property of the United States contrary to the authority thereof."[70]

Government prosecutors argued that after the Aryan Nations Congress, "James Ellison returned to Arkansas committed to wage war against this government. For the next year Ellison and his followers at CSA would plot violent strikes against public order. As part of this pattern of violence, CSA 'soldiers' firebombed a synagogue in Bloomington, Indiana; bombed utility pipelines and electrical transmission lines in Arkansas; and plotted robberies directed against 'Jewish' targets."[71]

A year after his conviction in 1985, Ellison began to cooperate with federal law enforcement agencies by providing details about his associates' activities, including the conspiracy to overthrow the U.S. government and to murder two government officials.[72] But Ellison's cooperation with the federal authorities appears to have troubled the jury in the sedition trial. Although most of the jurors refused to talk with the press, one told the *Arkansas Gazette* that "we just didn't believe the government's witness." Ellison and other witnesses who backed him "stood to gain with reduced sentences by testifying for the government."[73] The government lost the case.

In February 1987, Ellison petitioned for a reduction in his twenty-year sentence from the 1985 trial. The government granted his motion in May 1988, in part because it believed that without Ellison's cooperation, the plot to assassinate the two federal officials would not have been uncovered.[74] Ellison's sentence was reduced to five years. He completed his probation three days before the April 1995 bombing of the Murrah Federal Building in Oklahoma City—the same building that he had wanted to attack a decade earlier. This time, however, the plot was carried out and 168 people died. Ellison moved to Elohim City, Pastor Millar's armed compound, and later married Millar's granddaughter.[75] Elohim

---

70. Quoted in *United States of America v Robert E. Miles et al.*, February 9, 1988, p. 11.

71. Ibid., p. 4.

72. Response of the United States of America to James D. Ellison's Motion for Reduction of Sentence, *United States of America v James D. Ellison*.

73. Lamar James, "Jurors Finish 'Hard' Task; Most Decline Comment," *Arkansas Gazette*, April 8, 1988.

74. Response of the United States of America to James D. Ellison's Motion for Reduction of Sentence, *United States of America v James D. Ellison*.

75. Victoria Loe Hicks, "About Face From Hate," *Dallas Morning News*, May 16, 1998.

City came to national attention when the FBI revealed that Timothy McVeigh had phoned the compound while plotting the Oklahoma City bombing.

In a separate trial, Richard Snell, who had been Ellison's chief accomplice in the CSA plot to blow up the Murrah Federal Building, was sentenced to death.[76] In 1983 he had murdered a pawnbroker in Texarkana, Arkansas, whom he mistook for a Jew; and in 1984 he had killed an Arkansas state trooper. Snell reportedly talked a lot about bombs and retribution while in prison. "He repeatedly predicted that there would be a bombing or an explosion on the day of his death," Alan Ables, a prison official, told the *Denver Post*.[77] At 9:10 P.M. on April 19, 1995, twelve hours after the Oklahoma City bombing, which he was not informed about, Snell was executed by lethal injection. Asked whether he had anything to say before he died, Snell said ominously, "[Arkansas] Governor [Jim Guy] Tucker, look over your shoulder, justice is on the way."[78]

Pastor Millar visited Snell just before his death. He denies that Snell's last words referred to the bombing of the Murrah Federal Building. What Snell meant, Millar insists, was that the Lord's victory is imminent.[79] After his death, Snell's remains were buried at Elohim City.

Why Did CSA Fail to Poison Water Supplies?

To carry out a chemical attack, terrorists must overcome three main obstacles: they must acquire the agent; they must disseminate it effectively; and they must avoid detection by law enforcement authorities prior to the planned attack.

CSA overcame the first obstacle. Like most groups that have attempted to use poisons in the past, CSA chose an industrial poison—potassium cyanide—rather than a chemical-warfare agent such as sarin. Although industrial chemicals are easier to obtain than nerve agents, they are also significantly less toxic, making transport and dissemination problematic. Cyanide is present in rat and pest poisons, silver and metal

---

76. Response of the United States of America to James D. Ellison's Motion for Reduction of Sentence, *United States of America v James D. Ellison.*

77. Howard Pankratz, "Blast Blamed on Revenge Attack Linked to Militant's Execution," *Denver Post*, May 12, 1996.

78. Thomas, "We Are Not Dangerous, Leader of Separatists Says"; Pankratz, "Blast Blamed on Revenge Attack."

79. Thomas, "We Are Not Dangerous, Leader of Separatists Says."

polishes, metal plating and photographic solutions, and fumigating products, and can be purchased easily from chemical-supply stores.[80] It is also found in the seeds of apricots, peaches, cherries, plums, and apples. Cyanide is readily absorbed into the body by ingestion, across the skin, or inhalation (although alkali salts are toxic only when ingested). Less than 100 milligrams of cyanide can be fatal, and death may ensue within minutes after absorption of a lethal dose.[81]

With respect to delivery, CSA's plan to use thirty gallons of cyanide to poison a municipal water supply was doomed to failure. Several studies have shown that contaminating a large reservoir would be both costly and futile because dilution would render the poison ineffective.[82] According to a United Nations study, the amount of potassium cyanide needed to poison an untreated reservoir is about ten tons.[83] In the United States, moreover, water in large reservoirs is routinely treated and tested.[84] Nevertheless, CSA members might have found a more effective means of delivering cyanide if they had not been stopped by the FBI. For example, food and pharmaceuticals are considerably more vulnerable than water supplies. CSA would probably have figured this out over time, even without recruiting specialists.

The third obstacle was to plan and carry out the attack without attracting the attention of law enforcement authorities. CSA operated as an open compound rather than as a cult and hence was easily penetrated by law enforcement. The group did not hide its opposition to the U.S. government and, indeed, disseminated its views broadly. Kerry Noble wrote letters to the editor of the *Baxter Bulletin* urging Christians to follow

---

80. Hydrogen cyanide is a gas at room temperature, making it more likely that CSA would acquire sodium or potassium cyanide.

81. Mary O. Amdur, John Doull, and Curtis D. Klaassen, *Casarett and Doull's Toxicology: The Basic Science of Poisons*, 5th ed. (New York: McGraw-Hill, 1996), p. 976.

82. B.J. Berkowitz, M. Frost, E.J. Hajic, and H. Redisch, *Superviolence: The Civil Threat of Mass Destruction Weapons* (Washington, D.C.: Advanced Concept Research, September 29, 1972), pp. 1–15.

83. United Nations General Assembly, *Report of the Secretary General on Chemical and Bacteriological (Biological) Weapons and the Effects of Their Possible Use*, UN Document A/7575, July 1, 1969. These figures assume that a person drank 100 milliliters of untreated, contaminated water.

84. Raymond A. Zilinskas, in *Superviolence*. Zilinskas claims that only 20 percent of potable water in the United States comes from reservoirs. A similar conclusion was reached by J.C. Cotterhill in NATO Document AC/23-D/680, who found that "an attack on large storage reservoirs would be impractical owing to the logistics problems involved." However, service reservoirs, water already in the mains, boreholes, and wells might be feasible targets for terrorists, he claimed.

Biblical teachings rather than obey secular laws.[85] CSA also published detailed instructions for the use of fully automatic guns and other weapons that attracted the attention of law enforcement.[86] Terrorist groups that are closed off from society and led by charismatic leaders who impose tight internal discipline are more likely to succeed in acquiring and using mass-casualty weapons.

Conclusion

Few terrorist groups have used chemical and biological agents, even if they had the technical capacity to do so. But CSA planned to employ a potent chemical poison to carry out mass-casualty attacks. What is it about CSA that freed members from the moral and political constraints that have held most terrorists back? Four broad factors probably played a role.

First, the group was persuaded that Armageddon was imminent. They felt morally obligated to carry out God's judgments, to "pour out the seven bowls of the anger of God upon the earth" and to inflict wounds upon the sinners who are marked by the Beast and worship his image.[87] CSA members had an exaggerated sense of their own importance and their ability to inspire mass disturbances. They had delusions of grandeur and centrality (the belief that they and their actions were of intense interest to everyone, especially their enemies), profound suspicion of the government, and premonitions of doom. Ellison believed that God was guiding him personally. He told his followers about dreams in which God appeared and directed him to change his residence or to prepare for Armageddon. The belief that he was carrying out a divinely inspired plan appears to have given Ellison the ability to commit violence without experiencing pangs of conscience.

Second, CSA members were not particularly fearful of a government crackdown. They flouted the government's authority by acquiring military weapons, selling hate literature at gun shows, and writing anti-government articles in the local paper.

Third, CSA did not care about offending a group of secular sympathizers, since its true constituency consisted of God and fellow anti-government extremists. Ellison believed that if CSA and other anti-gov-

---

85. Two letters to the editor are reprinted in CSA, Zarephath-Horeb Church, "A Christ-Kingdom Society" (newsletter), January 1985, pp. 3–4.

86. *The CSA Survival Manual*, Spring 1982.

87. Revelation 16:1.

ernment groups succeeded in making life sufficiently uncomfortable for the American people, they would eventually realize that the government was powerless. He claimed to be trying to shock the people into becoming "a tool that we could use."[88]

Fourth, CSA members suffered from paranoid fantasies about supernatural as well as political events. They believed that the Tribulation predicted in the Book of Revelation had already begun and were also persuaded that foreign governments were about to strike the United States, triggering an apocalyptic conflict.[89] This pervasive sense of paranoia, combined with the psychological pressure Ellison imposed on his followers and the external pressure from the FBI, could have led members to commit extremely violent acts. Noble believes that CSA members would have been psychologically capable of carrying out mass-casualty attacks. "There were certain people who would have done it [poisoned whole cities], could have done it with no problems. It could very easily have happened," he claims.[90]

Fortunately, Ellison was arrested before he and his followers had a chance to poison an urban water supply, but even if CSA members had managed to carry out their plot, it would have failed for technical and organizational reasons. The group did not know how to disseminate the poison effectively, and they were too vulnerable to FBI surveillance to mount a large-scale attack. Several former CSA members became informants, often because they hoped to get their sentences reduced for unrelated crimes.

In recent years, however, Christian Patriots have become more aware of the danger of penetration by law enforcement authorities and have devised a new way of organizing themselves called "leaderless resistance." Small activist cells are encouraged to act on their own, receiving their marching orders from Internet web sites and avoiding communication with the leadership of the movement. Indeed, Timothy McVeigh operated according to this model. If future terrorists with chemical or biological agents act on their own or in small, secretive groups, the FBI may have difficulty catching them. Communication over the Internet facilitates leaderless resistance by allowing leaders of the movement to convey information to sympathizers worldwide without having to meet them face-to-face.

CSA members did not consider the use of biological weapons because

---

88. Direct testimony of James Ellison, *United States of America v Robert E. Miles et al.*, February 16, 1988 (court reporter's recording, tape 2B, first side).

89. *C.S.A. Journal*, No. 7, p. 6.

90. Author's telephone interview with Noble, March 2, 1998.

no one in the group knew anything about them.[91] After Aum Shinrikiyo's series of attempted attacks with anthrax and botulinum toxin and the press attention they engendered, however, future terrorists will be more knowledgeable about such agents.[92] The next time the U.S. government—and the American people—may not be so lucky.

---

91. Ibid.

92. CSA and The Order may already have inspired other right-wing groups. At a federal court hearing in St. Louis, Missouri, on March 6, 1998, an FBI agent testified that an Illinois white supremacist group called The New Order (presumably after The Order) had been caught plotting a series of attacks, including bombing public buildings, assassinating several individuals, and poisoning water supplies with cyanide. Charles Bosworth, Jr., "2 Plead Guilty of Weapons Charges Involving Extremist Group," *St. Louis Post-Dispatch*, May 15, 1998, p. B3; "Fifth Man Arrested in Supremacists' Plot," *State Journal-Register* (Springfield, Ill.), March 18, 1998, p. 10.

Chapter 10

The Minnesota Patriots Council (1991)

Jonathan B. Tucker and Jason Pate

In 1994 and 1995, four anti-government activists in Minnesota were the first people to be convicted and sentenced to prison terms under the 1989 Biological Weapons Anti-Terrorism Act. The four had acquired ricin, a deadly protein toxin derived from castor beans, by ordering materials and instructions through the mail from a right-wing publication. Members of a tax-resistance group called the Minnesota Patriots Council, they allegedly conspired to assassinate local and federal law enforcement officials. Their story demonstrates that it is relatively easy to acquire certain biological toxins and that some terrorists are motivated to do so.

The "Patriot" Movement

The past two decades have seen the emergence in the United States of a wide variety of anti-government groups under the banner of the "Patriot" movement.[1] Only some of these groups are overtly racist or anti-Semitic, but all subscribe to elaborate conspiracy theories and the belief that the government is increasingly tyrannical. Armed militias, the militant fringe of the Patriot movement, stockpile weapons and munitions to prepare for armed confrontation with the federal government or a feared "New World Order" imposed by foreign troops under United Nations command. Often led by former military or law enforcement personnel, militia cells are acquiring lethal expertise at an alarming rate.

Initially, far-right militias focused on stockpiling automatic weapons, grenades, and other "mainstream" armaments. In recent years, however, an increasing number of groups have turned to more exotic devices such as pipe bombs, booby-trap systems, and, most disturbingly, chemical and

---

1. For a comprehensive discussion of the rise of militias in the United States, see Morris Dees, *Gathering Storm: America's Militia Threat* (New York: HarperCollins, 1996).

biological agents. Right-wing publications routinely advertise books and pamphlets describing how to produce CBW agents in a home laboratory. In particular, cloak-and-dagger accounts of KGB and CIA use of biological toxins for assassination purposes, and the (mistaken) belief that protein-based toxins such as ricin are untraceable in the victim's body, have focused the militia world's attention on these outlawed and taboo weapons.

The Minnesota Patriots Council

The Minnesota Patriots Council was an anti-government group founded in 1970 by Frank Nelson, a retired Air Force colonel from Minneapolis. It had many cells, or local "chapters," throughout Minnesota.[2] Adherents believed that the U.S. government, its laws, and its taxation policies were illegitimate and corrupt. One of the group's cells consisted of about fifty people who met occasionally from 1990 to 1995 in various towns in the central and west-central parts of the state, including Alexandria, Minnesota, a town with a population of about 8,500 approximately 100 miles northwest of Minneapolis-St. Paul.[3]

---

2. Telephone interview with Tom O'Connell, Associate Professor, Metropolitan State University, January 27, 1998; interview with O'Connell in Minneapolis, Minnesota, March 20, 1998; interview with Ken Meter, Minneapolis, March 22, 1998; interview with Douglas County Sheriff Bill Ingebrigtsen and Deputy Sheriff Virgil Kielmeyer, Alexandria, Minnesota, November 10, 1997. There are some indications that the Minnesota Patriots Council evolved from a series of grassroots anti-corporate and anti-government movements in the 1970s and 1980s. In one case, a power company ran a power line by eminent domain across several farms, eliciting a violent response from local landowners in what became known as the "Powerline Incident." This incident was followed by the emergence of a right-wing populist movement known as "Groundswell." It is unclear, however, whether these earlier grassroots movements were linked directly to the formation of the Patriots Council. Another likely progenitor of the Patriots Council was the Posse Comitatus, a national anti-government movement active in the late 1970s and 1980s; the fact that the two groups have the same initials may be significant. According to a description of the Posse Comitatus, "This born-again blend of Identity faith, Survivalism and reactionary politics . . . takes its name from the Latin for 'power of the county.' . . . [M]odern-day Posse adherents, a group of ultra-right-wingers distinguished by their curious zeal for amateur lawyering and Survivalism, treat as a matter of religious faith that the Posse Comitatus principle means that no citizen is bound to obey any authority higher than that of the county sheriff. . . . [R]ecruited largely by word of mouth, the Posse typically exists of cells made up of seven white males along with their families in a given area who operate independent of any national leadership." James Coates, *Armed and Dangerous: The Rise of the Survivalist Right* (New York: Hill and Wang, 1987), pp. 104, 106, 111.

3. Authors' interview with Dennis Dalman, staff writer, and Al Edenloff, editor, *Echo Press*, Alexandria, Minnesota, November 10, 1997.

The Patriots Council believed that the government was taxing them unfairly and keeping them in poverty while supporting minorities and social undesirables.[4] Adherents recognized the authority of the local county sheriffs as legitimate, while repudiating the state and federal governments.[5] People drawn to the Patriots Council were generally disaffected and were often unemployed and embroiled in marital problems and custody battles.[6] Many felt blue-collar frustration at not being able to improve their social status and transferred their anger to the government.[7]

What made the Patriots Council particularly compelling to some people was that its anti-government ideology, focused on tax resistance, was built around a grain of truth. Farmers and other rural residents in Minnesota had suffered terribly during the farm crisis of the 1980s, when thousands of small farmers lost their land, and they had legitimate complaints about the arrogant and callous behavior of the Internal Revenue Service, the Federal Reserve Bank, and the Farm Home Administration. This resentment provided fertile ground for elaborate conspiracy theories.[8] One popular belief was that the Federal Reserve Bank, conspiring with a cabal of international Jewish bankers, was deliberately driving innocent farmers out of business so as to buy up their land and seize control of the country. According to LeRoy Wheeler, a former member of the Patriots Council, "In these theories and philosophies, there's a 10 percent kernel of truth, then they heap 90 percent rumor on it. People need a quick fix. . . . It's a way for people to fill a void. The secret society aspect, being on the threshold of history, is appealing."[9]

Beyond the basic paranoid theme, the ideology of the Patriots Council was a potpourri of ideas borrowed from the far right of the political spectrum and a variety of other sources, including the U.S. Constitution, the Magna Carta, and the Uniform Commercial Code.[10] Various members attended right-wing meetings in the western states, including Idaho, where they learned about conspiracy theories popular with national

---

4. Authors' interview with FBI Special Agent Daniel Lund, FBI Field Office, St. Cloud, Minnesota, November 12, 1997.

5. Authors' interview with Ingebrigtsen and Kielmeyer, November 10, 1997.

6. Authors' interview with Dalman, November 10, 1997.

7. Ibid.

8. For a sampling of right-wing conspiracy theories, see Jim Keith, *Black Helicopters II: The Endgame Strategy* (Lilburn, Ga.: IllumiNet Press, 1997).

9. Authors' interview with LeRoy Wheeler, Alexandria, Minnesota, November 12, 1997.

10. Authors' interview with Lund, November 12, 1997.

extremist groups such as the Posse Comitatus.[11] Some members quoted chapter and verse from the Constitution and the Bible and had obsessive discussions about Armageddon, abortion, and gun control. A few adhered to Christian Identity beliefs, which are white-supremacist, anti-Semitic, and racist, but most members of the group did not subscribe to such extremist views.

Key Members of the Group

Within the larger membership of the Patriots Council was a smaller group of about eight more militant men who gathered separately to discuss violent methods for combating the federal government, including plans to blow up federal buildings. They often met at the home of LeRoy Charles Wheeler, fifty-five, in Alexandria. Wheeler did odd jobs for a living, including construction, painting, carpet cleaning, and carving duck decoys and fish lures.[12] His wife Judy worked at the local supermarket, and they had three children.

Wheeler had been a quiet, reclusive man until his nineteen-year-old daughter Lisa Lynn was killed in an early-morning car crash involving alcohol in 1986.[13] In an interview some months later with the local paper, Wheeler said that he was "very angry" that the sixteen-year-old driver who caused the accident had been intoxicated and had just left a party at which adults were present. Wheeler planned to press charges against the hosts.[14] Eight months after the accident, however, he was informed by a lawyer that under Minnesota civil law, adults who hosted parties at which alcohol was served could not be sued, even if the intoxicated guests were minors and injury or death resulted.[15] Determined to get the law changed, Wheeler and his wife Judy became activists for the Douglas County chapter of Mothers Against Drunk Driving (MADD). LeRoy staffed a MADD booth at the local county fairs and testified twice before the state legislature.[16] After four arduous years of lobbying, a watered-

11. Authors' interview with Ingebrigtsen and Kielmeyer, November 10, 1997; authors' interview with Lund, November 12, 1997.

12. Authors' interview with Wheeler, November 12, 1997.

13. "Early Morning Fatal Crash Under Investigation," *Lake Region Echo,* October 15, 1986, pp. 1, 2A.

14. Dennis Dalman, "Wheelers Feel Change in Law Leaves No Justice," *Lake Region Press,* August 12, 1987, pp. 1, 3A.

15. Ibid.

16. Authors' interview with local resident Paulette Barthelemy, Alexandria, Minnesota, November 11, 1997.

down version of the bill finally passed. By this time, Wheeler had soured on the political process. Shortly after their victory, he and his wife dropped out of MADD, apparently because of jealousies and conflicts within the organization.

Wheeler subsequently became involved in the Patriots Council, probably after he went into the carpet-cleaning business with Bert Henderson in 1990. His wife Judy attributed his decision to become an anti-government activist to the fact that he had never grieved properly for his daughter.[17] But Wheeler claimed to sympathize with Patriot ideology and to enjoy the social aspect of belonging to the group.[18]

Dennis Brett "Bert" Henderson, thirty-seven, was the second of four children and had lived most of his life in the Alexandria area.[19] Henderson graduated from high school in the late 1970s and then studied for a while at Alexandria Technical College. In January 1976 he enlisted in the U.S. Marine Corps. During his four years of service, he was rated as an expert marksman. In April 1978, however, he was charged with having alcohol aboard ship and was fined, restricted, and ordered to do extra duty. In August 1978, he was found with a dangerous weapon (brass knuckles) and ordered to forfeit pay, reduced in rank, and imprisoned for twenty-five days for the infraction.[20]

Henderson married a woman from Alexandria in 1982 and later had a son. The couple divorced in 1990, and the wife retained custody of the child and later remarried. During the marriage Henderson occasionally beat his wife, and he obtained treatment for alcoholism following an episode of domestic violence. His criminal record also reflects a history of alcohol abuse, including two previous convictions for driving under the influence.[21] From 1990 through 1991, Henderson worked as a carpet cleaner at Wheeler's business, known as Carpet Tech. Between 1991 and 1995, he was a janitor at a community center in Vergus, Minnesota. At the time of his arrest, he was doing general cleaning at the Viking Plaza shopping center near Alexandria.[22]

---

17. Authors' interview with Wheeler, November 12, 1997.

18. Authors' interview with Lund, November 12, 1997.

19. Authors' interview with Anne Esterberg, researcher with the Douglas County Historical Society, Alexandria, Minnesota, November 11, 1997.

20. Pamela J. McNulty, "Presentence Investigation," Prepared for Chief U.S. District Judge Paul A. Magnuson, United States District Court for the District of Minnesota, *United States of America v Dennis Bret Henderson*, Docket No. 3:95CR00085-001 [District Court files], pp. 5–6.

21. Ibid., p. 7.

22. Ibid., p. 8.

According to Wheeler, Henderson liked "playing army," often drank heavily, and would "get hold of something and go with it like a pit bull." He had a temper that could turn violent, and he routinely carried a handgun, so that the local people feared and avoided provoking him. He stockpiled dried beans and guns, and often talked loudly in bars about the "final battle" against the federal government.[23] Henderson was a racist who disliked Jews and blacks, whom he referred to as "mud people," and he often quoted Gordon Kahl, a militant leader of the Posse Comitatus who had died in a shoot-out with police.[24] According to Douglas County Sheriff Bill Ingebrigtsen, "Henderson was a loose cannon—not sophisticated. He would have been the one to actually do something with the poison. He was a big-time follower . . . I think he would have been capable of it. On his own, no, but if someone was pushing his buttons, he would have done it."[25]

Richard John Oelrich, fifty-five, of Alexandria, was the "brains" behind the militant subgroup within the Patriots Council.[26] He sold pots and pans for a living but was highly intelligent. A former corporal in the U.S. Marine Corps, he had been honorably discharged and had no criminal convictions. Nevertheless, Oelrich was a right-wing ideologue and determined tax resister who fought a protracted paperwork battle with the Internal Revenue Service (IRS), culminating in the repossession of his home by armed IRS agents and U.S. deputy marshals in the spring of 1994.[27] Although he had no formal training as an attorney, Oelrich studied law books in a local library and sold his "legal services" at meetings of the Patriots Council. According to Wheeler, "Oelrich is a real believer. He's been in this a long time. He's been involved in other groups. He's been at trials in federal court where people were dragged out by marshals."[28]

According to a neighbor, Oelrich kept to himself and was secretive and quiet, only seen at the post office.[29] He suffered from a heart condition and had a defillibrator surgically implanted in his heart. Although

---

23. Authors' interview with Wheeler, November 12, 1997. According to FBI Special Agent Daniel Lund, Henderson built an underground survival bunker on his property, but cows walked across its roof and it collapsed. (Authors' interview with Lund, November 12, 1997.)

24. Authors' interview with Dalman, November 10, 1997.

25. Authors' interview with Ingebrigtsen and Kielmeyer, November 10, 1997.

26. Authors' interview with Dalman, November 10, 1997.

27. Authors' interview with Wheeler, November 12, 1997.

28. Ibid.

29. Authors' interview with Esterberg, November 11, 1997.

Oelrich usually appeared calm and reserved, he could explode into an uncontrollable rage over small matters such as parking tickets. He spent his spare time filing nuisance lawsuits and liens against local and federal officials for millions of dollars, billing them for huge sums in interest if they did not respond.[30] Such tactics for harassing the government through its own courts and legal system had been developed during the 1980s by the Posse Comitatus and other far-right groups.[31]

Douglas Allen Baker, thirty, lived in a mobile home with Colette, his wife of ten years, in Sedan in rural Pope County, about twenty miles from Alexandria.[32] He and his wife heated their mobile home with firewood. Baker did carpentry, wood-gathering, and organic farming during the summer and worked for a Brooten equipment manufacturer in the winter. Friends and family described him as a hard-working, family-oriented man who had always lent a helping hand to the less fortunate.[33] According to Sheriff Bill Ingebrigtsen, however, Baker had become "brainwashed and obsessed" with the anti-government movement and often quoted Common Law.[34]

Baker became involved with the Patriots movement through his activist father, Duane John Baker.[35] The elder Baker was a farmer, minister, and anti-government leader. He had a minor criminal background,

---

30. Authors' interview with Ingebrigtsen and Kielmeyer, November 10, 1997.

31. According to Coates, "Posse members are entranced by legal questions, pore over lawbooks and dream up myriad ways to tackle the system they hate. . . . The IRS report on the tax protesters described how a favorite Posse tactic has become to file 'lien cases against the personal property of judges, Court Commissioners, District Attorneys, Assistant Attorneys General, Clerks of Courts, and newspaper publishers in an effort to clog the court system and to embarrass, impede, and obstruct the trial courts in the administration of justice.'" Coates, *Armed and Dangerous*, pp. 118–119.

32. Transcript of *United States of America v Douglas Allen Baker and LeRoy Charles Wheeler*, United States District Court for the District of Minnesota, Fourth Division (St. Paul, Minnesota), February 24, 1995, pp. 434, 439–440.

33. Dennis Dalman, "Wheeler, Baker Convicted of 'Biological Terrorism,'" *Echo Press*, March 3, 1995, pp. 1A, 5A.

34. Authors' interview with Ingebrigtsen and Kielmeyer, November 10, 1997. According to one source, "Today's common-law court system is an exaggerated version of the Posse Comitatus system created in the 1970s–1980s. . . . The Posse based its common-law philosophy on a combination of old English common law, the Magna Carta, and the belief that people are born with certain God-given rights. . . . Common-law practitioners claim that once their courts grant sovereign status to someone, that person can legally stop paying taxes." Joel Dyer, *Harvest of Rage: Why Oklahoma City Is Only the Beginning* (Boulder, Colo.: Westview Press, 1997), pp. 172–173.

35. Telephone interview with Federal Public Defender Scott Tilsen, February 11, 1998, and interview in Minneapolis on March 17, 1998.

was a reformed alcoholic, and may have developed his right-wing philosophy to fill the void left by not drinking. Poorly educated but intelligent and well spoken, he was self-educated in the law, having taken short-term classes in legal issues.[36] Duane Baker frequently "fought the system" in court. He argued, for example, that no one need obtain a driver's license because "you have a right to travel, and you can't take a right and turn it into a privilege."[37] He also claimed that criminal courts have no authority to levy fines because those are civil penalties.[38] Baker often referred to Oelrich as his "legal advisor" even though Oelrich was not an attorney.

Scott Loverink, thirty-nine, lived in Garfield, Minnesota, and was a former Marine who had never made it out of basic training.[39] In 1982, an Indiana court convicted him of assault with a deadly weapon (a knife) and sentenced him to two years in prison; he was released on parole in 1984.[40] Loverink had been close friends with Wheeler and Henderson since the late 1970s.[41] Henderson introduced him to Oelrich in 1991 and tried to get him involved in the Patriots Council.[42] Shortly thereafter, Loverink allowed Henderson and Oelrich to practice marksmanship on his rifle range.[43] Wheeler later described Loverink as "a loony tune, a would-be marine, a psychopath, and a liar."[44]

The militant subgroup of the Patriots Council met every Sunday, under the guise of religious services, at Fluid Concepts International, Duane Baker's plastic pipe supply company in Brooten. Although the

36. Interview of Duane Baker by Rick Strawcutter in "Terror Scam," a video documentary, undated, probably 1996, distributed by *Proclaim Liberty Ministries* in Adrian, Michigan.

37. Conrad deFiebre, "Pope County Man Sentenced for Possessing Toxin," [Minneapolis] *Star Tribune*, May 19, 1995, p. 3B.

38. Ibid.

39. Transcript of *United States of America v Douglas Allen Baker and LeRoy Charles Wheeler*, February 24, 1995, p. 305.

40. Transcript of *United States of America v Douglas Allen Baker and LeRoy Charles Wheeler*, February 23, 1995, pp. 271–272.

41. Authors' interview with Wheeler, November 12, 1997.

42. Transcript of *United States of America v Douglas Allen Baker and LeRoy Charles Wheeler*, February 23, 1995, p. 275; Transcript of *United States of America v Dennis B. Henderson and Richard J. Oelrich*, United States District Court for the District of Minnesota, Fourth Division (St. Paul, Minnesota), October 23, 1995, p. 28.

43. Transcript of *United States of America v Douglas Allen Baker and LeRoy Charles Wheeler*, February 24, 1995, p. 298.

44. Authors' interview with Wheeler, November 12, 1997.

meetings were shrouded in secrecy, they reportedly involved discussion of conspiracy theories and racist themes, such as the migration of "mud people" into Minnesota.[45] Patriots Council members also listened to tapes by prominent right-wing leaders.[46] Henderson had great ambitions for the group and often said that he wanted the Douglas County chapter of the Patriots Council to be "number one in the state."[47]

Procuring the "Maynard"

Oelrich subscribed to the *CBA Bulletin*, a right-wing publication based in Medford, Oregon.[48] The March 1991 issue carried an advertisement for an inexpensive assassination kit based on ricin, a potent biological toxin. The kit, called "Silent Tool of Justice," was available by mail order from Maynard's Avenging Angel Supply in Ashland, Oregon, a small outlet operated by far-right extremist Maynard Campbell.[49]

Ricin, a protein toxin present in the seeds of the castor bean plant, *Ricinus communis*, is about 200 times more potent than cyanide and has

---

45. In a telephone interview on March 17, 1998, Duane Baker claimed that when the New World Order arrives, the people of the United States will experience the horrors that the people of Bosnia, Somalia, and Iraq have experienced. The attack and occupation will occur when the U.S. government invites the United Nations to establish a police state. Baker said that vast amounts of Soviet equipment is currently stockpiled in secret UN installations throughout the United States, including national parks, and that the timeline for United Nations takeover has been set, albeit with a certain degree of flexibility. By the year 2000, all of the necessary arrangements will be in place. UN troops have maps of the entire United States and directions have been stenciled in code on the backs of road signs to show them the invasion routes.

46. The tapes included speeches by Peter J. Peters, the Christian Identity pastor of the Church of Christ in Laporte, Colorado, and Jack McLamb, a former police officer from Arizona and Patriot movement advocate. According to the Southern Poverty Law Center (http://www.splcenter.org), Peters organized a 1992 summit of Patriot groups in Estes Park, a town north of Denver, Colorado, and has close ties to many Patriot leaders including Bo Gritz, Louis Beam, and Richard Butler. His ministry, "Scriptures for America," disseminates extremist materials through newsletters, radio and television shows, and the ministry's website. McLamb wrote *Vampire Killer 2000*, a book that encourages law enforcement officers to join the Patriot movement.

47. Authors' interview with Wheeler, November 12, 1997.

48. Transcript of *United States of America v Douglas Allen Baker and LeRoy Charles Wheeler*, February 22–23, 1995, pp. 21, 164. "CBA" stands for "Citizens' Bar Association," referring to the common-law doctrine advocated by a number of right-wing groups in the United States.

49. Maynard Campbell, of Ashland, Oregon, was a tax protester, a white-supremacist Christian, and a member of the Posse Comitatus. He wrote *Kingdoms at War*, a guerilla manual for Patriot extremists that advocated autonomous terrorist cells and assassination as a necessary tactic in a war against the federal government. In 1992, Campbell

no antidote. Symptoms of ricin poisoning include vomiting, high fever, malaise, and weakness; death results after several days from systemic failure, similar to shock. In 1978, the Bulgarian secret service used ricin— delivered in a tiny pellet fired from an air-gun concealed in an umbrella— to assassinate Bulgarian dissident Georgi Markov in London.[50]

Maynard Campbell's advertisement read: "Silent Tool of Justice, including instructions for extracting the deadly poison ricin from castor beans. Agent of choice for CIA, KGB, etc. A single bean will kill an evildoer. Interesting suggestions for preparation and delivery, etc." For $12.00, Campbell would supply ten castor beans and an instruction booklet explaining how to extract ricin from the beans in a home laboratory.[51] A second ad, which appeared in the April 1991 issue of the *CBA Bulletin*, incorporated the prior advertisement and added the statement, "This catalogue translates into silent death for those who hate God, freedom and this republic. Author disclaims any responsibility for the misuse [*sic*]." This time the mailing address was in Medford, Oregon.[52]

In April 1991, Oelrich and Henderson were at Wheeler's residence in Alexandria perusing the ricin advertisement in the *CBA Bulletin*.[53] Both admirers of Maynard Campbell, they discussed the advantages of ricin over other deadly poisons, namely that it breaks down in the system after death, making it impossible to detect or trace in the victim's body.[54] After

---

was in an armed standoff with Oregon police for twelve hours, and in 1994 he received a ten-year federal prison sentence. He was murdered in prison in 1997. Southern Poverty Law Center web site (http://www.splcenter.org).

50. David Wise, "Was Oswald a Spy, and Other Cold War Mysteries," *New York Times Magazine*, December 6, 1992, p. 44.

51. On February 19, 1993, FBI Supervisory Special Agent Dr. Thomas Lynch, a chemist at FBI Headquarters who analyzed the ricin powder acquired by the Minnesota Patriots Council, sent a letter and money to "Maynard's Avenging Angel Supply" in an attempt to buy castor beans and the recipe for processing them into ricin. The original letter was returned with a handwritten response on it stating, "Sir—the book and the beans are no longer available. Thank you for your interest. Try your local nursery." Daniel E. Lund, "Application and Affidavit for Search Warrant," files of the United States District Court for the District of Minnesota, p. 1.

52. Transcript of *United States of America v Douglas Allen Baker and LeRoy Charles Wheeler*, February 23, 1995, p. 164.

53. Ibid.

54. Transcript of *United States of America v Douglas Allen Baker and LeRoy Charles Wheeler*, February 24, 1995, pp. 384–385. In fact, the body rapidly forms antibodies to

some discussion, Oelrich and Henderson decided to order the castor beans and the instructions by mail. A few weeks later, in early May 1991, the package was delivered to Wheeler's house in Alexandria.[55] Oelrich and Henderson were both at Wheeler's residence when the package arrived and seemed to be expecting it.[56]

The ricin "kit" from Maynard Campbell consisted of about a dozen castor beans and several photocopied pages of instructions for extracting ricin from the beans. There was also information on how to mix the solvent dimethylsulfoxide (DMSO) with aloe vera hand lotion to create an effective delivery system. When ricin was combined with the DMSO/aloe vera mixture and then applied to an object the victim was likely to touch, the DMSO would transport the toxin across the victim's skin, while the aloe vera gel would keep the solvent from evaporating.[57]

Henderson read the instructions and said there were several steps involved in processing the beans into ricin. Since he had some rudimentary knowledge of chemistry from his work in the carpet-cleaning business, he took charge of extracting the toxin with solvents.[58] Henderson did the extraction in the shed behind the house where Wheeler carved and painted his fish lures. While Henderson was out in the shed, Oelrich indicated that they needed a code word for the ricin and suggested calling it "Maynard" after Maynard Campbell.[59]

The extraction process resulted in a flaky white powder, which Henderson put into a small baby food jar. He then put the jar into an empty red coffee can and placed it on a shelf over the window in Wheeler's shed where no one would notice it.[60] The coffee can remained in the shed for a few months and then disappeared.[61] Wheeler assumed that Henderson had taken it.[62]

---

ricin, which are potentially detectable in the bloodstream of a victim who does not die immediately.

55.   Ibid., p. 390.

56.   Authors' interview with Lund, November 12, 1997.

57.   Transcript of *United States of America v Douglas Allen Baker and LeRoy Charles Wheeler*, February 23, 1995, p. 162.

58.   Authors' interview with Lund, November 12, 1997.

59.   McNulty, "Presentence Investigation," p. 4.

60.   Transcript of *United States of America v Douglas Allen Baker and LeRoy Charles Wheeler*, February 23, 1995, pp. 167–168.

61.   Transcript of *United States of America v Douglas Allen Baker and LeRoy Charles Wheeler*, February 24, 1995, pp. 382–384.

62.   Affidavit by LeRoy Charles Wheeler, August 4, 1994, witnessed by Daniel E.

From spring through summer 1991, Loverink had several conversations with Henderson about the ricin that lasted from fifteen minutes to hours. Sometimes Oelrich was present at those meetings, which took place at Loverink's loft.[63] Oelrich and Henderson refused to talk about ricin in front of other Patriots Council members they apparently did not trust.[64] The conversations dealt with using the "Maynard" to kill various government employees, including IRS officials, U.S. Marshals, and Douglas County law enforcement officials.[65] Oelrich said that the victims would develop a "severe case of bureaucratic flu," including vomiting, diarrhea, dizziness, coma, and death.[66] When Loverink asked Henderson about the effects of ricin, he replied, "As I understand it, they shit themselves to death."[67] Although Oelrich never mentioned any potential target by name, Henderson talked about using ricin to kill Douglas County Deputy Sheriff Dave Ahlquist, against whom he held a grudge because of a run-in they had had some years earlier during the Fourth of July fireworks show.[68]

Henderson told Loverink that the ricin/DMSO/aloe vera mixture could be delivered by smearing it on a doorknob or inside the victim's shoes.[69] He also talked about putting dried ricin powder in a syringe and injecting it into Ahlquist's car through the weather-stripping between the windows. Henderson said it could be done in the winter, when the toxic dust would be blown around by the car fan and then inhaled by the

---

Lund, files of the United States District Court for the District of Minnesota, Fourth Division (St. Paul, Minnesota).

63. Transcript of *United States of America v Douglas Allen Baker and LeRoy Charles Wheeler*, February 23, 1995, p. 256.

64. Transcript of *United States of America v Douglas Allen Baker and LeRoy Charles Wheeler*, February 24, 1995, pp. 297–298.

65. Transcript of *United States of America v Douglas Allen Baker and LeRoy Charles Wheeler*, February 23, 1995, p. 168.

66. Ibid., p. 257.

67. Transcript of *United States of America v Dennis B. Henderson and Richard J. Oelrich*, October 23, 1995, p. 37.

68. Ibid., p. 29; and authors' interview with Wheeler, November 12, 1997. According to Wheeler, Henderson and some of his friends were parked at a local business in the back of a pickup truck drinking beer. Ahlquist came by and asked them why they were there. Words were exchanged, and Ahlquist reportedly said, "Bert, why don't you run and see if my dog can catch you." Bert took that as a death threat from the Sheriff's Office and probably felt humiliated.

69. Transcript of *United States of America v Douglas Allen Baker and LeRoy Charles Wheeler*, February 23, 1995, p. 262.

victim.[70] Although the DMSO delivery method would not have worked, the injected dust would probably have been lethally effective: when ricin is inhaled as an aerosol, it produces a severe diffuse breakdown of lung tissue resulting in hemorrhagic pneumonia and death.[71]

Later, investigators found a map of Alexandria that had been attached to a cardboard backing by a Patriots Council member whose code name was "Conan."[72] On this map, the homes of Douglas County law enforcement officials had been marked with pushpins.[73] It appears that some members of the group may have planned to use the ricin for intimidation purposes.[74] According to Sheriff Ingebrigtsen, "My biggest fear was that if they were going to put this stuff on my car, maybe my wife was going to drive my car, or my daughter. That angered me very much. We've been in this business a long time, and if we make someone angry, they should come for us, not our family."[75]

In late summer 1993, Henderson, Loverink, and one other Patriots Council member rubbed the mixture of DMSO and aloe vera gel on their wrists and tasted the gel five minutes later, demonstrating the solvent's ability to penetrate the skin rapidly.[76] Duane Baker also claims that the group tested the ricin on mice, with no effect.[77] Despite such activities, Wheeler later claimed that he and others in the group considered Henderson's threat to use the poison to be an idle boast. "I decided it was baloney," Wheeler said. "He's a big talker . . . kind of rattling his saber, you know. I didn't think anybody intended to do anything."[78]

---

70. McNulty, "Presentence Investigation," p. 4; authors' interview with Ingebrigtsen and Kielmeyer, November 10, 1997.

71. R.W. Wannemacher, D.A. Creasia, H.B. Hines, W.L. Thompson, and R.E. Dinterman, "Toxicity, Stability, and Inactivation of Ricin," *Toxicologist,* Vol. 10 (1990), p. 166.

72. Telephone interview with former Douglas County Deputy Sheriff Jerry Werner, February 18, 1998.

73. Authors' interview with Ingebrigtsen and Kielmeyer, November 10, 1997. The map was left at Loverink's house and Deputy Sheriff Werner took photographs of it. The purpose of the map was unclear. Sheriff Ingebrigtsen speculated that it was a threat, a way for the Patriots Council to say "we know where you live."

74. Authors' interview with Ingebrigtsen and Kielmeyer, November 10, 1997.

75. Ibid.

76. Transcript of *United States of America v Dennis B. Henderson and Richard J. Oelrich,* October 23, 1995, p. 48.

77. Telephone interview with Duane Baker, March 17, 1998.

78. James Walsh, "Pair Made Lethal Poison, Hatched Plots of Murder, Indictment Says," *Star Tribune,* February 16, 1995, p. 1A.

The Informant

Loverink became alarmed when some members of the Patriots Council began to talk seriously about resorting to violence, and he decided to inform the authorities. In spring 1991, he told his father about his concerns. His father notified the Minnesota Bureau of Criminal Apprehension, which in turn called the Douglas County Sheriff's Department. Sheriff Bill Ingebritsen sent his deputies Jerry Werner and Virgil Kielmeyer to interview Loverink.[79]

On May 1, 1991, Special Agent Albert L. Catallo at the FBI regional office in St. Cloud, Minnesota, received a call from the Douglas County Sheriff's Department. Deputy Sheriff Werner told him that a local man named Scott Loverink had revealed that three of his long-term friends (Oelrich, Henderson, and Wheeler) were members of an anti-government organization called the "Patriots Council" and had been heard discussing plans to blow up a federal building, procure assault rifles, and kill a sheriff's deputy.[80] Loverink's report, however, did not constitute sufficient evidence for the FBI to open a file on the case.[81] Catallo told Werner to stay in contact with the informant and use his best judgment until further developments provided sufficient "probable cause" to launch a federal investigation. In late fall 1991, Loverink began providing information to Werner on a regular basis.[82]

A breakthrough in the local investigation came in early 1992. Henderson, a casual acquaintance of Doug Baker, needed a place to live, and Doug and his wife Colette took him into their home with the understanding that he would cut firewood and help with other domestic chores. About a month later, however, they asked Henderson to leave because he sat around and did nothing except bother Colette while Doug was at work. When he moved out in February or March 1992, Henderson left behind a garbage bag, some old clothes, cans of food, some other possessions, and the red coffee can containing the ricin and the mixture of DMSO and aloe vera gel. At that time, he left a note to Doug Baker warning him to handle the ricin powder with care:

---

79. Transcript of *United States of America v Douglas Allen Baker and LeRoy Charles Wheeler*, February 23, 1995, p. 251.

80. Lund, "Application and Affidavit for Search Warrant," p. 1.

81. According to the Attorney General guidelines, the FBI may only launch an investigation when there is: (1) an allegation of specific criminal activity; (2) knowledge of who is involved; and (3) specific intent to commit a crime. Authors' interview with Lund, November 12, 1997.

82. Transcript of *United States of America v Douglas Allen Baker and LeRoy Charles Wheeler*, February 23, 1995, p. 241.

DOUG, Be extremely careful! After you mix the powder with the gel, the slightest contact will kill you! If you breath [sic] the powder or get it in your eyes, your [sic] a dead man. Dispose all instruments used. Always wear rubber gloves and then destroy them also. Good Hunting!! [Smiley face] P.S. Destroy this note!!

Doug put the red coffee can on the top shelf of a closet, where he kept some of his hunting rifles. About three months later, Colette and Doug had a serious argument in which he threatened her with a shotgun. Terrified, she moved to her mother's house for a few weeks, taking with her the weapons in Doug's closet and the red coffee can. On May 20, 1992, at the urging of her mother, Colette Baker went to the Pope County Sheriff's Department in Glenwood, where she met with Deputy Sheriff Tom Larson.[83] She told him that she planned to leave her husband because he had threatened to kill her, and she feared for her safety and that of her parents. Mrs. Baker said that her husband possessed a large quantity of weapons, ammunition, and some explosive devices in their trailer house in Sedan. She had also found the poison called "Maynard," which Doug had told her could kill a person on contact. She did not want to run the risk that he would put the poison on her parents' door handle or car door.[84]

The next day, Colette Baker arrived at the Pope County Sheriff's Department carrying the coffee can; she appeared pale and nervous and her hands were shaking. Because it was shortly after noon and the sheriff and his deputies were not in the office, Mrs. Baker met with the receptionist, in whose presence she took several items out of the coffee can, exhibited them, and put them back in the can. The items included a baby food jar containing a white powder, a fingernail-polish bottle containing a greenish gel, a pair of white rubber gloves, and the handwritten note from Henderson to Doug Baker warning him to handle the poison with extreme care. Colette read the note out loud and then left the coffee can and its contents with the Pope County Sheriff's Department.

Colette's parents also turned over Doug Baker's stockpile of guns and ammunition to the sheriff. The items included several firearms and two pipe bombs wrapped with large nails and a one-inch fuse. The pipe bombs, along with a 16-ounce can of black gun powder, were stored in an ammunition box with the word "BOOM" printed on the outside.[85] After examining the jar of white powder called "Maynard," the Pope

83. Transcript of *United States of America v Dennis B. Henderson and Richard J. Oelrich,* October 23, 1995, pp. 8, 17.

84. Lund, "Application and Affidavit for Search Warrant," p. 5.

85. United States District Court, District of Minnesota, Fourth Division, Criminal No.

County Sheriff's Department contacted the Minnesota Bureau of Criminal Apprehension, which in turn called the FBI because they did not have a lab capable of determining what the material was. The coffee can and its contents were turned over to the FBI field office in St. Cloud, which forwarded it for analysis to the FBI laboratory at the Bureau's headquarters in Washington, D.C.

Supervisory Special Agent Thomas P. Lynch, a veteran chemist in the FBI's Chemistry/Toxicology Unit, performed a laboratory analysis of the contents of the coffee can. He determined that the baby food jar contained the hull of a castor bean and 0.7 gram of a powder containing ricin.[86] Analysis of the greenish gel in the fingernail-polish bottle revealed a mixture of DMSO and aloe vera. Also at the FBI laboratory, veteran fingerprint specialist Michael Smith found two of LeRoy Wheeler's fingerprints on the inside of one of the rubber gloves and one of his fingerprints on the bottom of the coffee can.[87] The FBI lab then sent the ricin powder to the U.S. Army Medical Research Institute of Infectious Diseases at Fort Detrick, Maryland, where tests determined that the toxin was 5 percent strength, enough (theoretically) to kill 129 people.[88]

Colette Baker had provided the hard evidence that the FBI needed. The fact that corroborating information about the Patriots Council had come from two separate sources—the Sheriff's Departments in Douglas and Pope Counties—meant that there was now "probable cause" to open a federal investigation. In August 1992, FBI Special Agent Al Catallo met with Loverink to enlist him as a paid informant.[89]

The FBI's strategy was first to gather evidence against Wheeler and Baker and then to use their testimony to build a strong case against the apparent ringleaders, Oelrich and Henderson. To this end, the FBI and the U.S. Marshal's Office in Minnesota obtained court-ordered records

---

4-94-92(01), "United States of America, Plaintiff, v Douglas Allen Baker, Defendant, Government's Sentencing Memorandum," May 16, 1995, p. 3.

86. Transcript of *United States of America v Douglas Allen Baker and LeRoy Charles Wheeler*, February 24, 1995, pp. 325, 327–328.

87. Transcript of *United States of America v Douglas Allen Baker and LeRoy Charles Wheeler*, February 23, 1995, pp. 205, 209.

88. Transcript of *United States of America v Douglas Allen Baker and LeRoy Charles Wheeler*, February 24, 1995, pp. 330–332. Lynch testified at trial that one gram of ricin is enough to kill 3,600 people, whereas one gram of sodium cyanide could only kill sixteen people.

89. Transcript of *United States of America v Dennis B. Henderson and Richard J. Oelrich*, October 23, 1995, pp. 39–40. From August 1992 through October 1995, Loverink received $15,400 from the FBI in exchange for his assistance.

from telephones believed to be used by Baker, Wheeler, Oelrich, Henderson, and others.[90] In addition, an informant revealed that a member of the Minnesota Patriots Council had put out a "contract" on the life of Deputy U.S. Marshal William Ott, the official responsible for serving the court papers in the IRS tax-evasion case against Oelrich, and "any other deputy marshal" involved in the seizure of Oelrich's property.[91]

Arrest of Wheeler and Baker

Based on the FBI evidence, a federal grand jury indicted Wheeler and Baker on charges of possessing a lethal poison for use as a weapon in violation of the Biological Weapons Anti-Terrorism Act of 1989 (Title 18, United States Code, Section 175). The pertinent part of this law, which went into effect on May 22, 1990, provides as follows:

Whoever knowingly develops, produces, stockpiles, transfers, acquires, retains, or possesses any biological agent, toxin, or delivery system for use as a weapon, or knowingly assists a foreign state or any organization to do so, shall be fined under this title or imprisoned for life or any term of years, or both.[92]

On August 4, 1994, a team of about twenty heavily armed FBI agents and deputies from the Douglas County Sheriff's Department arrested Wheeler at his mother's farm south of Alexandria.[93] Wheeler had no idea that he had been under FBI surveillance, but Loverink had apparently warned Henderson and Oelrich.[94] The morning of Wheeler's arrest, Henderson told Wheeler that "something big was about to happen" and that he and Oelrich were leaving town.[95] At 8:30 A.M. the same day, an FBI special agent arrested Doug Baker at his place of work in Sedan and then searched his trailer home. Baker made no statement at the time of his

---

90. Michael Reynolds, "Toxic Terror: Use of Chemical and Biological Weapons by Terrorists," *Playboy*, Vol. 43, No. 11 (November 1996), p. 62.

91. Ibid.; "Tax Protesters Charged With Plot to Blow Up Building, Poison Officials," *Grand Forks Herald*, February 17, 1995, p. 6A.

92. The law as written did not provide any sentencing guidelines and had never been applied before, giving the judge in the case enormous latitude.

93. Dennis Dalman, "Local Men Charged with Terrorism," *Echo Press*, February 17, 1995, pp. 1A, 8A.

94. Authors' interview with Wheeler, November 12, 1997.

95. Ibid.

arrest. FBI agents transported him and Wheeler to St. Cloud and then to Minneapolis for booking.

FBI Special Agent Daniel E. Lund interviewed both defendants at the Bureau's field office in Minneapolis.[96] During the interview, Baker admitted possessing a powder called "Maynard" two to three years earlier. He explained that he had intended to use it as an insecticide by sprinkling it on the cabbage plants in his garden, but had not done so.[97] Baker denied receiving the powder from Henderson and claimed that he had been given the coffee can containing the ricin and the greenish gel from a man he did not know.[98] Baker could not recall specific instructions for using "Maynard" except that a person should not breathe or touch it.[99] Lund also interviewed Wheeler and reduced his statement to writing, which Wheeler signed. After five days of questioning, the two men were released on $10,000 bail and were free until the time of their trial.

After the arrest of Baker and Wheeler, the other members of the Patriots Council went underground. "Everyone crawled back in their rat holes after I was arrested," Wheeler said.[100] "They were scared to death that the storm troopers were coming after them next."[101] Local residents reacted with fear, shock, and disbelief that there were potential terrorists in their midst.[102]

The Wheeler/Baker Trial

The indictments against Wheeler and Baker stated that the two were "tax-protest radicals" who planned to use ricin as part of a plot to murder law enforcement agents. Wheeler and Baker both entered not-guilty pleas and denied vehemently that they were part of a conspiracy to murder federal officials. They maintained that the government was persecuting them for holding unpopular views, or what they called "thought crimes." Wheeler told the press, "The government is charging me with this be-

---

96. Transcript of *United States of America v Douglas Allen Baker and LeRoy Charles Wheeler*, February 24, 1995, pp. 374–375, 379.

97. Transcript of *United States of America v Douglas Allen Baker and LeRoy Charles Wheeler*, February 22–24, 1995, pp. 6, 166, 376.

98. Transcript of *United States of America v Douglas Allen Baker and LeRoy Charles Wheeler*, February 23–24, 1995, pp. 166, 376.

99. McNulty, "Presentence Investigation," p. 3.

100. Authors' interview with Wheeler, November 12, 1997.

101. Ibid.

102. Authors' interview with Father Al Ludwig, St. Mary's Church, Alexandria, Minnesota, November 10, 1997; authors' interview with Edenloff, *Echo Press*.

cause they have a need to create criminals."[103] Duane Baker and his wife Mary denied that Doug was involved in any such activity, and that he was being persecuted because he believed in individual rights over the powers of the federal government.[104] Both Doug Baker and Wheeler asked why, if they were in fact so dangerous, the government had taken three years to arrest them and had then released them on bail.[105]

During the trial at the Federal District Court in St. Paul, Minnesota, in February 1995, the prosecution's case centered on testimony given by Loverink. FBI investigators testified that a baby food jar containing ricin had been found inside a coffee can at Baker's Sedan residence and that Wheeler's fingerprints were on the can.[106] Wheeler claimed that his fingerprints were there because he used coffee cans to hold brushes for painting duck decoys.[107]

Federal prosecutor Nate Petterson alleged that the baby food jar contained 0.7 gram of ricin, which was enough to kill "hundreds of people." Although FBI Special Agent Lynch expressed doubts about the ability of DMSO to carry ricin across the skin into the bloodstream because of the protein toxin's high molecular weight, he added that he was certain the defendants were unaware of this problem. Lynch also testified that there could be no other purpose for the particular contents of the coffee can than the intent to use the poison as a weapon.[108] The prosecution did not suggest that Wheeler or Baker had personally planned to kill anyone but that they had knowingly participated in the conspiracy to acquire the poison.

During the three-day trial, the jury heard nothing about Wheeler and Baker's political views. Instead, the judge instructed the jury to determine whether the defendants had intended to use ricin as a weapon, even if the prosecution was unable to pinpoint a precise target for its use.[109] On

---

103. Walsh, "Pair Made Lethal Poison," p. 1A.

104. James Walsh, "2 More Charged in Plot to Make Poison," *Star Tribune*, August 5, 1995, p. 5B.

105. Walsh, "Pair Made Lethal Poison," p. 1A.

106. Transcript of *United States of America v Douglas Allen Baker and LeRoy Charles Wheeler*, February 23, 1995, pp. 196–198.

107. Authors' interview with Wheeler, November 12, 1997.

108. United States District Court, District of Minnesota, Fourth Division, Criminal No. 4-94-92(01), "United States of America, Plaintiff, v Douglas Allen Baker, Defendant, Government's Sentencing Memorandum," May 16, 1995, p. 3.

109. Wayne Wingstad, "2 Minnesota Men First to be Convicted Under Biological Weapons Act," *Saint Paul Pioneer Press*, March 1, 1995, p. B3.

February 28, 1995, the jury found Wheeler and Baker guilty of knowingly possessing a biological toxin for use as a weapon, but not guilty of the more serious charge of conspiracy to use the poison to kill federal officials.[110]

Before his sentencing on May 18, 1995, Baker read a five-page statement full of pseudo-legal language claiming that his constitutional rights had been violated during his arrest and incarceration. "The United States lacked jurisdiction with which to proceed, as the state had never ceded jurisdiction in the alleged case," Baker told Judge Robert G. Renner.[111] "The proceedings herein were fraud, made in bad faith, and in wanton and willful prosecution meant for malice."[112] Baker claimed during his trial that he had already been tried by a "common law court" in Starbuck, Pope County, which had found him not guilty. Thus, his federal trial constituted "double jeopardy" and was unconstitutional. The court rejected this line of argument.[113]

Because Baker and Wheeler were the first to be sentenced under the 1989 Biological Weapons Anti-Terrorism Act, no federal sentencing guidelines existed for their offense. Judge Renner ruled that Baker's crime most closely resembled possession of a poison gas, for which the maximum recommended sentence for someone without a criminal record was two years and nine months.[114] Renner also ordered Baker to spend three years on probation after his release.[115] On June 1, 1995, Wheeler read a statement protesting his arrest, after which he was sentenced to the same term in prison.[116]

---

110. Dalman, "Wheeler, Baker Convicted of 'Biological Terrorism,'" pp. 1A, 5A.

111. Conrad deFiebre, "Pope County Man Sentenced for Possessing Toxin," *Star Tribune,* May 19, 1995, p. 3B.

112. Ibid.

113. Transcript of *United States of America v Douglas Allen Baker and LeRoy Charles Wheeler,* February 22, 1995, p. 50. Baker's common-law trial took place at the Cedar Inn in Starbuck on the evening of February 18, 1995. The organizers invited federal prosecutor Nate Petterson and the members of the grand jury in St. Paul that had indicted Baker and Wheeler to attend the proceedings, but they declined. A crowd of people gathered at the Cedar Inn and appointed a sheriff and judge, after which jurors were selected from among those present. Evidence was presented to the jury in the form of affidavits for and against Baker. After a half-hour of deliberation, the jury foreman pronounced Baker "not guilty" of possessing a biological toxin for use as a weapon. Following the verdict, Baker insisted that the federal case against him was based on "nothing but hearsay and innuendo."

114. deFiebre, "Pope County Man Sentenced for Possessing Toxin," p. 3B.

115. Ibid.

116. Dennis Dalman, "Alex Man Gets 33 Months for Terrorism," *Echo Press,* June 7, 1995, pp. 1A, 2A.

Both Wheeler and Baker appealed. In September 1996, the Eighth U.S. Circuit Court of Appeals reversed Baker's conviction on the grounds that he deserved a separate trial because much of the evidence presented had implicated only Wheeler. The court, however, upheld Wheeler's conviction and sentence.[117] Baker was released on October 21, 1996, from the Federal Medical Center in Rochester, Minnesota, and the community accepted him back.[118]

After Wheeler was released from prison in the summer of 1997, he insisted that he was innocent and that his former friends in the Patriots Council, "godless and full of hate," had lied, betrayed, and given false evidence against him.[119] Ironically, the guards and staff in prison had treated him well and the federal government had kept its word and released him after twenty-eight months.[120] While acknowledging that he had belonged to an informal group that called itself the "Patriots Council," Wheeler denied that there had been any plot to destroy anybody or anything. Noting that three members of the group had been FBI informants, he argued that both his arrest and the Oklahoma City bombing had been orchestrated by the FBI as a pretext for passing draconian counterterrorism legislation.[121]

The Henderson/Oelrich Trial

On July 27, 1995, five months after the conviction of Wheeler and Baker, Henderson was arrested by FBI agents at the home of an acquaintance in Alexandria. A federal warrant for his arrest stated that he was wanted for possessing and distributing biological agents for use as a weapon, conspiracy, and aiding and abetting others to use the poison.[122] Douglas County Sheriff's Department deputies assisted in the arrest, which took place "without incident." On August 3, 1995, FBI agents arrested Oelrich in Becker County, in the Detroit Lakes area, and he was held in federal custody in St. Paul.[123]

117. Associated Press, "Conviction Overturned in Poison Case," *Star Tribune,* September 28, 1996, p. 3B.

118. Authors' interview with Dalman, November 10, 1997.

119. Authors' interview with Wheeler, November 12, 1997.

120. Dennis Dalman, "Relishing Freedom, Wheeler Maintains His Innocence," *Echo Press,* August 29, 1997, pp. A1, A5.

121. Ibid.

122. Dennis Dalman, "Alex Man Arrested for Alleged Tie to Terrorism Plot," *Echo Press,* August 2, 1995, pp. 1A, 3A.

123. Authors' interview with Lund, November 12, 1997.

Henderson and Oelrich were indicted by a federal grand jury in Minneapolis on August 4, 1995, for allegedly possessing ricin for use as a weapon.[124] Assistant U.S. Attorney Petterson would not comment on why Henderson and Oelrich had not been charged months earlier.[125] Both defendants pleaded not guilty, and Petterson prosecuted the case against them.[126] Henderson served as his own attorney and viciously cross-examined Loverink during the trial.[127] Oelrich represented himself but allowed his appointed counsel to assist with evidentiary objections.[128]

The government forced Wheeler to give evidence against Henderson and Oelrich by threatening him with five more years of prison if he did not cooperate.[129] At the trial, Loverink implicated Henderson but testified that he had never seen Oelrich acquire, possess, or transfer the ricin or the DMSO/aloe vera mixture.[130] Colette Baker said that she could not recall much of her previous testimony before a federal Grand Jury, citing memory problems related to the disease lupus. At one point she read a legalistic statement asserting that the court did not have jurisdiction in the case.[131]

On October 10, 1995, Henderson and Oelrich filed "common law affidavits" with the Federal District Court claiming that they were "natural born freemen" who were not residents of the "United States" or the "District of Minnesota" but rather the "country of Minnesota," and hence

124. Dennis Lien, "Minnesota Men Charged with Possession of Deadly Poison to Use as Weapon," *Saint Paul Pioneer Press*, August 5, 1995, p. 2B.

125. Walsh, "2 More Charged in Plot to Make Poison," p. 5B.

126. Dennis Dalman, "'Ricin Plot' Trial Set to Begin Monday," *Echo Press*, October 20, 1995, pp. 1A, 3A.

127. Loverink admitted possessing a sawed-off shotgun and homemade pistol silencer, but he flatly denied Henderson's other accusations, including that Loverink had burned down Douglas County Lumber after being fired from a job there; that he had threatened a local man with a pistol at Wheeler's daughter's wedding reception in the late 1980s; that he planned to fill hollow bullets with mercury for use as an explosive projectile; and that he had filled hollow .30 caliber bullets with rifle primer and tested the explosive projectiles on neighborhood dogs.

128. Transcript of *United States of America v Dennis B. Henderson and Richard J. Oelrich*, October 23, 1995, p. 19.

129. Authors' interview with Wheeler, November 12, 1997.

130. Transcript of *United States of America v Dennis B. Henderson and Richard J. Oelrich*, October 23, 1995, p. 51.

131. Ibid., pp. 5–6. Colette Baker suffered from lupus and claimed that her medication impaired her memory. It is more likely that she was an uncooperative witness and used her illness as an excuse for not answering questions.

that the federal court did not have jurisdiction over them.[132] The court rejected this line of argument.

On October 25, 1995, the jury found Henderson and Oelrich guilty of possessing and distributing a deadly toxin for use as a weapon. They were also found guilty of conspiracy and of aiding and abetting others to use the poison. After the verdict was announced, U.S. Attorney David Lillehaug announced, "We're pleased by the convictions in these two cases of national prominence involving biological weapons. It's lucky that the poison plot was uncovered so that the terrorism apparently planned by the defendants never came to pass."[133] On January 19, 1996, Judge Paul A. Magnuson sentenced Henderson to forty-eight months in prison, followed by three years of supervised release.[134] The following week, Oelrich was sentenced to thirty-seven months in prison and three years of probation.

Conclusion

What lessons can be drawn from this case? First, it is clear that ricin is easily acquired and may become a weapon of choice for right-wing anti-government groups. Ricin is an effective assassination weapon when delivered orally, by injection, or as an inhalable aerosol, but it is not suitable for inflicting mass casualties. Why did these militant members of the Minnesota Patriots Council seek to acquire a biological toxin as opposed to other, more conventional weapons? What about ricin was attractive to them?

---

132. Dennis Henderson, "Common Law Affidavit, Country of Minnesota, Douglas County" [handwritten document], October 10, 1995, files of the United States District Court for the District of Minnesota. Henderson claimed in his affidavit that he had been "kidnapped from the country of Minnesota by foreign agents of the F.B.I. on 27 July 1995. . . . Affiant was taken against his will, over his objection and in chains to a Federal enclave located in Minneapolis Minnesota on 27 July 1995. . . . Affiant was taken by foreign agents of the United States Marshals Service, against his will and in chains to the Anoka County Adult Correctional Facility on 27 July 1995. . . . Affiant has never seen a waiver of extradition executed by your affiant and never will because he has never executed such. Affiant serves the Great Creator, the Holy God of Israel and is a child of same, therefore subject to His Law, i.e. Natural Absolute Law, therefore said sham inferior "District" court has and is committed/committing a trespass upon the Holy Lord God of Israel. Further affiant sayeth not!"

133. Dennis Dalman, "Oelrich, Henderson Found Guilty," *Echo Press*, October 27, 1995, pp. 1A, 2A.

134. "Minnesota Man Sentenced for Possessing Deadly Toxin," *Saint Paul Pioneer Press*, January 20, 1996, p. 2C.

Individually, these men were unemployed or underachievers, suffering from varying levels of low self-esteem and depression. Their lives were plagued with marital disputes, financial problems, and other personal crises and failures. Living in an isolated economic backwater probably contributed to their chronic frustration. Given this lifestyle, coupled with the influence of living in a state with a strong history of grassroots political activism that sometimes included violence, it should come as no surprise that they began to seek people and institutions to blame for their problems. Oelrich was an ideologue committed to the anti-government cause. He probably felt some level of righteous indignation in organizing against the government, although the extent to which he believed in Christian Identity dogma is unclear. He may not have had the will to use ricin to assassinate anyone but almost certainly encouraged others to do so, particularly Henderson.

Henderson had a personal vendetta against at least one law enforcement official and was the type of person who walks around with a chip on his shoulder, ready for a fight. He might be viewed as the Timothy McVeigh of the Patriots Council: an individual with some military training, unattained personal aspirations, and a predisposition to act violently. Wheeler was probably harmless, a "patsy" sitting on the sidelines, feeling that he was part of an exclusive club. Similarly, Doug Baker appeared to have been along for the ride, an ideological sympathizer because of his parents but not a leader or a proactive member of the group.

Understanding these men's individual personalities casts some light on their interaction as a group. Oelrich appears to have been the ringleader, at times reining in Henderson, his henchman, from acting on his violent tendencies. Doug Baker probably did not have much to add to the discussions and was probably in the wrong place at the wrong time. Wheeler had gripes about the government and was therefore sympathetic to the Patriot Council's ideology, but it was probably his previously isolated lifestyle, the psychological trauma of losing his daughter, and his disenchantment with the political system arising from his work with MADD that drew him into the group.

To what extent did ideology drive the Patriot Council's behavior? Anti-government conspiracy theories may have influenced the group to the extent that they were convinced that the U.S. government was illegitimate, hostile, and controlled by foreign interests. This belief that the government was in the hands of evil, subversive forces would allow them cognitively to justify a violent course of action against federal officials. At the same time, members of the group had real personal reasons for hating the government, such as the farm crisis and the IRS foreclosure of Oelrich's home.

The choice of ricin as an assassination weapon was linked to its association with Maynard Campbell, a "hero" of the Patriot movement, as well as its "glamorous" reputation as a covert spy weapon employed by the Soviet KGB. Another apparent motivation on the part of the would-be terrorists was the desire to evade accountability by using a poison that they believed could not be traced. They certainly did not understand the legal implications of acquiring ricin, the possession of which for weapons purposes had only recently been designated a felony under U.S. law.

Chapter 11

The World Trade Center Bombers (1993)

John V. Parachini

The February 1993 bombing of the World Trade Center in New York City marked the beginning of an ugly new phase of terrorism involving the indiscriminate killing of civilians.[1] Like the sarin gas attack on the Tokyo subway in March 1995 and the bombing of the Alfred E. Murrah Federal Building in Oklahoma City in April 1995, the World Trade Center bombing was motivated by the desire to kill as many people as possible.

The target of the bomb plot was the World Trade Center (WTC) complex, a sixteen-acre site in lower Manhattan. Although mostly known for the Twin Towers, which are 110 stories tall and 1,550 feet high, the complex consists of seven buildings, including the Vista Hotel. Although the explosion killed six people and injured more than 1,000, the consequences could have been far worse: on any given day approximately 20,000 people work in the various businesses of the WTC complex and another 80,000 people either visit the complex or travel through it.[2]

On May 24, 1994, during the sentencing of four of the convicted WTC bombers, Judge Kevin T. Duffy asserted that the perpetrators had incorporated sodium cyanide into the bomb with the intent to generate deadly hydrogen cyanide gas that would kill everyone in one of the towers. The Judge stated:

---

1. Jim Dwyer, David Kocieniewski, Deidre Murphy, and Peg Tyre, *Two Seconds Under the World: Terror Comes to America—The Conspiracy Behind the World Trade Center Bombing* (New York: Crown Publishers, 1994), p. 50. See also Laurie Myroie, "The World Trade Center Bomb: Who Is Ramzi Yousef? And Why It Matters," *The National Interest*, No. 42 (Winter 1995/96), pp. 3–15.

2. U.S. Senate, Committee on Judiciary, Subcommittee on Technology, Terrorism, and Government Information, Statement by J. Gilmore Childers, Esq. and Henry J. De-Pippo, Esq., *Foreign Terrorists in America: Five Years After the World Trade Center*, February 24, 1998, http://www.senate.gov/~judiciary/childers.htm.

You had sodium cyanide around, and I'm sure it was in the bomb. Thank God the sodium cyanide burned instead of vaporizing. If the sodium cyanide had vaporized, it is clear what would have happened is the cyanide gas would have been sucked into the north tower and everybody in the north tower would have been killed. That to my mind is exactly what was intended.[3]

Judge Duffy's assertion that the WTC bombers had incorporated cyanide into their bomb went largely unnoticed until it was cited in a Senate staff report submitted for the record during a hearing of the Permanent Subcommittee on Investigations of the Senate Committee on Government Affairs on March 27, 1996. In footnote 2 of the report, Senate staff noted that "the defendants in the World Trade Center case may have tried to use a chemical device but failed in their attempt to create a contemporaneous cyanide gas attack."[4] The annex of the hearings also contained two pages from Judge Duffy's sentencing statement making reference to the possible use of cyanide.[5] Since then, some prominent government officials have referred to the judge's statement as evidence that the WTC bombing marked a new era of terrorism with weapons of mass destruction on U.S. soil.[6] Academic terrorism experts have echoed these concerns.[7]

Since the judge's sentencing statement served as the basis for later statements by policymakers and scholars, it is important to set the record straight about the facts of the case. This chapter largely refutes the claim

---

3. Judge Kevin T. Duffy, Sentencing Statement, *United States of America v Mohammad A. Salameh et al.*, S593CR.180 (KTD), May 24, 1994, p. 36.

4. U.S. Congress, Senate, Committee on Governmental Affairs, Permanent Subcommittee on Investigations, *Hearings on Global Proliferation of Weapons of Mass Destruction*, March 27, 1996, p. 21.

5. Ibid., Appendix, pp. 276–277. Laurie Mylroie, author of the previously cited article in *The National Interest* arguing that Iraq was behind the WTC bombing, claims that she provided the relevant pages from Judge Duffy's sentencing statement to the Senate subcommittee staff. Author's interview with Mylroie, June 19, 1998.

6. For example, in an interview on the PBS Frontline documentary "Plague War," broadcast on October 13, 1998, Secretary of Defense William S. Cohen said that the World Trade Center bombers had "contemplated setting off cyanide" but "failed to ignite [the cyanide] and therefore the great catastrophe did not take place." Cohen's comments were contradictory: either the terrorists merely contemplated using cyanide but did not, or they used cyanide and it failed to ignite.

7. See Chris Seiple, "Consequence Management: Domestic Response to Weapons of Mass Destruction," *Parameters*, Autumn 1997, p. 119; and Richard K. Betts, "The New Threat of Mass Destruction," *Foreign Affairs*, Vol. 77, No. 1 (January/February 1998), p. 29.

that the WTC bombing involved the terrorist use of chemical weapons. Nevertheless, substantial evidence indicates that Ramzi Yousef, the mastermind behind the attack, seriously considered employing chemical agents in the WTC bombing and in subsequent attacks. Examining the motivations and behaviors of terrorists who *would have* used a chemical weapon if it was available, but did not for logistical or financial reasons, may offer important lessons about how to thwart such attacks in the future.

The Perpetrators

The perpetrators of the WTC bombing turned out to be a group of New Jersey men who had been suspected of terrorism for more than two years.[8] Ramzi Yousef remains the central mystery of the case despite his arrest, conviction, and sentence to life imprisonment. A naturalized Pakistani citizen, he entered the United States on September 1, 1992, bearing an Iraqi passport, but he claimed to have been born in Kuwait and to have relatives in Pakistan, Kuwait, Iraq, and Palestine.[9] He used more than twelve different aliases throughout his terrorist career and said in an interview that he considered himself a Palestinian.[10]

Yousef attended a terrorist training camp in Afghanistan, where he honed his skills as an explosives expert. He then traveled around the world working as a professional terrorist in the name of Islamic Jihad, although expressions of religious faith or motivation were notably absent from his statements. Yousef's ability to persuade or "charm" others to join his cause served him well in his terrorist endeavors. After arriving in the United States, Yousef went to live in New Jersey with Musab Yasin, an Iraqi whose brother, Abdul Rahman Yasin, also arrived in New Jersey from Iraq shortly after Yousef.

Whereas Yousef was the leader and mastermind behind the WTC bombing, Mohammad Salameh was a follower and a bumbler. Despite the "evil" terrorist profile that government prosecutors laid out for the jury, Salameh was a pathetic figure. The eldest of a family of eleven, he struggled to achieve mediocrity in life.[11] Salameh attended the Sheikh

---

8. Dwyer et al., *Two Seconds Under the World*, p. 88.

9. Raghidah Dirgham, "Ramzi Yusuf Discusses WTC Bombing, Other Activities," *Al-Hayah*, p. 5; translated in FBIS-NES-95-097 (12 April 1995).

10. Dwyer et al., *Two Seconds Under the World*, p. 162.

11. Ibid., p. 161.

Omar Abdul Rahman Mosque in New Jersey and was a devoted follower of El-Sayid Nosair, the assassin of right-wing rabbi Meir Kahane. When Nosair went to jail, Salameh took up with Mahmud Abouhalima in an effort to free him. Later, he fell in with the cunningly persuasive Ramzi Yousef, whom he met in a New Jersey rooming house. As someone who struggled for acceptance, Salameh made the perfect follower for a manipulator like Yousef.

Abouhalima, an Egyptian native, was a devoted follower of Sheikh Abdul Rahman. A former fighter in the Afghan resistance against the Soviet Union, Abouhalima worked for a car services company in New York, and many of his fares originated across the street from the WTC.[12]

An equally unlikely terrorist was Nidal Ayyad, the most educated member of the group. Born in Kuwait to Palestinian parents, he became a naturalized U.S. citizen, graduated from Rutgers University, and worked as a chemical engineer at Allied Signal.[13] At the time of the bombing, his wife from an arranged marriage was pregnant with their first child.[14] Given his relative career success and new bride, he risked a good life in America by participating in the plot.

The last key player was Ahmad Mohammad Ajaj. Arriving in New York City on the same flight from Pakistan as Ramzi Yousef, the swarthy and bearded Ajaj presented a Swedish passport. The customs agent determined that the passport was suspicious and directed him to the secondary inspection area.[15] During a search of Ajaj's belongings, authorities discovered several other passports, bomb manuals, and bomb-making instructional videos. Ajaj was also suspected of having connections to terrorist factions of Hamas and Al-Fatah.[16] Detained as a danger to the United States, he was charged with passport fraud and sentenced to six months in prison.[17]

---

12. Summation Statement of Henry J. DePippo, Prosecutor, *United States of America v Mohammad A. Salameh et al.*, S593CR.180 (KTD), February 16, 1994, p. 8430.

13. Dwyer et al., *Two Seconds Under the World*, p. 166.

14. Summation Statement of Henry J. DePippo, Prosecutor, *United States of America v Mohammad A. Salameh et al.*, S593CR.180 (KTD), February 16, 1994, p. 8479.

15. U.S. Senate, Committee on Judiciary, Subcommittee on Technology, Terrorism, and Government Information, Statement by Childers and DePippo, *Foreign Terrorists in America.*

16. Dwyer et al., *Two Seconds Under the World*, p. 163.

17. U.S. Senate, Committee on Judiciary, Subcommittee on Technology, Terrorism, and Government Information, Statement by Childers and DePippo, *Foreign Terrorists in America.*

Target Selection

The terrorists apparently selected the World Trade Center as a target not because it was a symbol of Western values or the financial power of the United States, but simply because toppling the twin towers would enable them to inflict a large number of casualties. The only evidence suggesting that the twin towers were selected for their symbolic value comes from a notebook of Rabbi Kahane's assassin, El-Sayid Nosair. In his papers he argued for the need to "demoralize the enemies of Allah . . . by destroying and blowing up the pillars of their civilization and blowing up the tourist attractions they are so proud of and the high buildings they are so proud of."[18] Obviously the WTC comes to mind as one of the "tourist attractions" and "high buildings" in New York City, but the same would apply to the Empire State Building or the Chrysler Building.

Thus, while the symbolism of the World Trade Center cannot be ignored, it does not fully explain its selection over other buildings or places occupied by large numbers of people. Physical attributes and location appear to have been more important. The imposing profile of the twin towers on the New York skyline lay in clear view from New Jersey, where the bombers assembled their weapon. Mahmud Abouhalima also picked up many of the fares for his car service right across the street from the WTC. Finally, the complex had a large underground garage, which is not as common in New York City as one might think. In order to knock down a tall building, the bombers believed they had to get beneath it, and an underground garage made delivery of the bomb much easier.

Building the Bomb

In November 1992, the conspirators started to prepare for an attack on the WTC. It took them more than two months to acquire the chemicals, assemble the sophisticated urea-nitrate bomb, and transport it to the designated target. Ramzi Yousef complemented his talents as an explosives expert with the local talent he found in the orbit of Sheik Omar. Ayyad, a trained chemist, helped to procure and mix the chemicals for the bomb and then acted as the group's spokesman after the attack. Abouhalima, a veteran of the Afghan holy war, had ties with militant

---

18. Quotation in Steven Emerson, "The Other Fundamentalists," *New Republic*, June 12, 1995, reprinted in Frank McGuckin, ed., *Terrorism in the United States* (New York: H.W. Wilson, 1997), p. 44.

Egyptian groups that may have provided funding for the attack.[19] He purchased ingredients for the bomb and often visited the apartment where his co-conspirators prepared their deadly brew.[20] Salameh was ready to do anything the others instructed him to do: get a driver's license, receive shipments of dangerous chemicals, and open bank accounts.

Yousef's explosives training at Camp Caldoun in Afghanistan, and Ayyad's training as a chemical engineer, gave the bombers sufficient expertise to procure and mix at least thirteen different chemicals into a 1,500 pound bomb. Although Yousef claimed that he contributed 90 percent of the know-how and Ayyad only 10 percent, the latter's job as a chemical engineer at Allied Signal gave him a legitimate front for ordering chemical ingredients on company stationery. Some suppliers balked when the order came from outside official channels, when the delivery address was a storage park, or when Yousef tried to pay for the chemicals in cash—but others unfortunately did not.[21]

Despite his prison sentence in upstate New York, Ajaj continued to participate in the plot. He remained in regular contact with the other conspirators throughout the building of the bomb and even requested that the authorities release his belongings (including his terrorist kit) to them. According to Gil Childers, a prosecutor on the case, "Ajaj would call Dallas from prison, and his friend would then either relay messages to Yousef or patch a three-way call through to him, thereby rendering law enforcement efforts to detect contact between Ajaj and Yousef far more difficult."[22]

On February 26, 1993, the terrorists drove a yellow Ford Econoline rental van into the basement of the WTC and set a timer to detonate the 1,500-pound urea-nitrate bomb.[23] The massive blast created a cavernous

---

19. Dwyer et al., *Two Seconds Under the World*, p. 240.

20. U.S. Senate, Committee on Judiciary, Subcommittee on Technology, Terrorism, and Government Information, Statement by Childers and DePippo, *Foreign Terrorists in America*.

21. Summation Statement of Henry J. DePippo, Prosecutor, *United States of America v Mohammad A. Salameh et al.*, S593CR.180 (KTD), February 16, 1994, pp. 8435–8439.

22. U.S. Senate, Committee on Judiciary, Subcommittee on Technology, Terrorism, and Government Information, Statement by Childers and DePippo, *Foreign Terrorists in America*.

23. Dwyer et al., *Two Seconds Under the World*, p. 50.

crater 200 feet by 100 feet wide and seven stories deep in the garage of the World Trade Center, and caused acrid smoke to rise to the 46th floor.[24] The twin towers, built to withstand the impact of a Boeing 707 jet crash, remained in place, but the garage where the bomb detonated crumbled into 6,000 tons of rubble.[25] In all, the explosion killed six people, injured more than 1,000, and caused nearly $300 million in property damage.[26]

The Days After the Bombing

Instead of fleeing after the bombing, Nidal Ayyad served as the undercover spokesman for the group. He called the *New York Daily News* tip line and left a message claiming responsibility for the bombing in the name of the "Liberation Army."[27] He also sent a letter to the *New York Times* from the Liberation Army making various demands, a copy of which the FBI recovered from his computer at Allied Signal.[28] In the letter, the conspirators identified the American people, not a symbolic building, as their target: "The American people are responsible for the actions of their government and they must question all of the crimes that their government is committing against other people. Or they—Americans—will be the targets of our operations. . . ."[29]

Ayyad's letter claiming responsibility for the WTC bombing promised that the "next time it will be very precise and WTC will continue to be one of our targets in the US unless our demands are met."[30] Indeed,

24. Statement of Senator Dianne Feinstein, U.S. Senate, Committee on Judiciary, Subcommittee on Technology, Terrorism, and Government Information, *Foreign Terrorists in America: Five Years After the World Trade Center*, February 24, 1998.

25. Dwyer et al., *Two Seconds Under the World*, pp. 50, 74.

26. U.S. Senate, Committee on Judiciary, Subcommittee on Technology, Terrorism, and Government Information, Statement by Childers and DePippo, *Foreign Terrorists in America*.

27. Ayyad's co-workers at Allied Signal identified his voice during the trial. Summation Statement of Henry J. DePippo, Prosecutor, *United States of America v Mohammad A. Salameh et al.*, S593CR.180 (KTD), February 16, 1994, p. 8480.

28. DNA analysis of the stamp on the envelope sent to the *New York Times* indicated that Ayyad had licked it. *United States of America v Mohammad A. Salameh et al.*, S1293CR.180 (KTD), Government Exhibit 196.

29. Ibid.

30. *United States of America v Mohammad A. Salameh et al.*, S593CR.180 (KTD), Government Exhibit 78-E. See also Summation Statement of Henry J. DePippo, Prosecutor, *United States of America v Mohammad A. Salameh et al.*, S593CR.180 (KTD), February 16, 1994, pp. 8479–8484.

immediately after the blast, Ayyad began calling chemical supply houses seeking to obtain more chemicals, presumably for another bomb.[31] Robert Blitzer, a senior FBI official who worked on the case, suggested that Ayyad may have had more deadly plans in mind.[32] Yousef later indicated that the group had planned another, smaller attack after the WTC bombing with a "more efficient bomb," possibly containing a toxic chemical ingredient.[33]

The first of the conspirators to be arrested was Salameh, who sought to recover the deposit money on the rental van used in the bombing, apparently because he needed the money to get out of the country. The FBI had traced the van's vehicle identification number, which evidence specialists had found on a twisted piece of metal in the debris of the WTC garage. Salameh returned to the rental agency twice, and the second time the FBI was waiting to arrest him.

Three days after the bombing, Abouhalima boarded a plane to Sudan without any possessions, leaving behind his wife and young children. He continued on to Egypt, where the Egyptian authorities arrested him within a few weeks and extradited him to the United States. Imprisoned and awaiting trial, Abouhalima tried without success to negotiate a deal with prosecutors, claiming that Ramzi Yousef had manipulated him and the others to conduct a crime far larger than they had ever imagined.[34]

Yousef escaped to Pakistan on the night of the bombing and traveled around the Middle East and Asia. He and several associates subsequently moved to the Philippines, where in August 1994 he began a conspiracy to blow up twelve United and Delta airliners en route between the United States and Asia within a short time. On December 4, 1994, Yousef and his accomplices bombed the Greenbelt Theater in Manila, and on December 11, he placed a small explosive device on Philippine Airlines Flight 434 en route to Tokyo via Cebu, killing a Japanese businessman. On January 6, 1995, Yousef and two accomplices were mixing chemicals in his Manila apartment when a fire broke out, forcing the conspirators to flee into the street. Concerned that he had left his laptop computer in the apartment,

---

31. Evidence for Ayyad's procurement efforts came from telephone records and witness testimony. Summation Statement of Henry J. DePippo, Prosecutor, *United States of America v Mohammad A. Salameh et al.*, S593CR.180 (KTD), February 16, 1994, p. 8479.

32. Author's telephone interview with Robert Blitzer, Washington, D.C., June 18, 1998.

33. Direct Testimony of Brian Parr, *United States of America v Ramzi Ahmed Yousef and Eyad Ismoil*, S1293CR.180 (KTD), October 22, 1997, p. 4721.

34. Myroie, "The World Trade Center Bomb," p. 10.

Yousef sent one of his associates back to retrieve it. Responding Philippine police arrested the associate and recovered the computer, which contained encrypted files with details of the plot to blow up numerous U.S. airliners in flight.[35] Forced to abort the bombing plot, Yousef traveled to Pakistan where, more than two years after the WTC bombing, neighbors alerted the Pakistani authorities to his location. He was apprehended on February 8, 1995. After being tried and convicted in the Manila bombing case in September 1996, Yousef was extradited to the United States to stand trial in the WTC bombing.[36]

The trials of the four WTC conspirators except Yousef lasted from September 1993 to March 1994 (while Yousef was still a fugitive), followed by Yousef's own trial from August to November 1997. All of the defendants were sentenced to 240-year terms in maximum-security prisons. To prevent them from selling their stories to publishers or movie studios for profit, Judge Duffy imposed fines and restitution fees in the millions of dollars and recommended extremely restrictive visiting privileges.

Who Sponsored the Bombing?

With any major calamity, conspiracy theories tend to emerge when key details of the case appear incomplete. A few analysts suggest that Yousef and Ajaj were either Iraqi agents or freelance terrorists employed by Iraqi intelligence to exploit Islamic militants residing in the United States, as a means of continuing the Persian Gulf War on American soil.[37] A list of unusual coincidences dating back to 1992 forms the basis for suspecting an Iraqi connection to the WTC bombing.[38] Nevertheless, the theory that

35. Statement for the Record of Louis J. Freeh, Director, Federal Bureau of Investigation, before the United States Senate Committee on Appropriations, Subcommittee for the Departments of Commerce, Justice, and State, the Judiciary, and Related Agencies, February 4, 1999.

36. The Yousef chronology was derived from "Work Product (Majority)," Judiciary Subcommittee on Technology, Terrorism, and Government Information (undated).

37. Myroie, "The World Trade Center Bomb," pp. 3–15.

38. The coincidences are as follows: (1) The WTC bombing occurred on February 26, 1993, the second anniversary of the liberation of Kuwait by the U.S.-led coalition against Iraq; (2) in June 1992, shortly after El Sayid Nosair went to jail for charges stemming from the assassination of Rabbi Meir Kahane, Mohamad Salameh made the first of more than forty calls to an uncle in Iraq whom Israeli authorities had imprisoned for terrorist activity before deporting him; (3) Yousef entered the United States on September 1, 1992, carrying an Iraqi passport without a visa and requested asylum; (4) Ahmad Mohammad Ajaj, who flew to New York on the same flight with Yousef, was arrested at the airport with a terrorist kit filled with fake passports and bomb

the Iraqi government sent Yousef on a mission to avenge the Gulf War relies too much on circumstantial evidence to create a compelling case.

Several aspects of the conspiracy also make Iraqi sponsorship unlikely. First, if Yousef really was a state-sponsored terrorist, the co-conspirators he chose for the project were unusual. Abouhalima, Salameh, and Ayyad all had connections to Nosair, Rabbi Kahane's imprisoned assassin, making them likely targets for FBI surveillance. Indeed, the FBI questioned and followed Abouhalima several times prior to the WTC bombing. Furthermore, although Abouhalima may have developed valuable fighting skills as a guerrilla in Afghanistan, Salameh and Ayyad were inexperienced and naive terrorists.

The amateurish mistakes made by the WTC bombers before and immediately after the bombing also suggest that the conspiracy was the work of neophytes, not state-sponsored killers. Six months before the bombing, Salameh tried to get a driver's license in New Jersey but failed the driving test four times and the vision test twice; he finally succeeded in New York.[39] Then, a month before the bombing, Salameh skidded off a wet road, totaling the car. Yousef was injured in the crash and was hospitalized for a week recovering from the accident. Finally, FBI agents apprehended Salameh when he tried to recover his deposit on the rental van that had carried the bomb. Given that Salameh was such a bungler, why would any state sponsor risk including him in such a high-stakes venture? Surely a professional such as Yousef could have selected others who would have made better co-conspirators.

Salameh's difficulties in obtaining enough money to flee the country were not the only financial problem the group faced. The bomb cost the conspirators about $10,000 to make, and they resorted to using discount coupons to rent the van they employed for delivery.[40] As Yousef was being flown from Pakistan to the United States to stand trial, he told Secret Service agent Brian Parr that he would have put sodium cyanide into the WTC bomb if he had had enough money.[41] Yousef also told Parr

---

manuals in his luggage; (5) Yousef lived in New Jersey with Musab Yasin, an Iraqi whose brother, Abdul Rahman Yasin, also arrived from Iraq shortly after Yousef; (6) Salameh lived in the same building and presumably involved his friend and follower of Nosair, Nidal Ayyad, in the conspiracy; and (7) Abdul Rahman Yasin, who showed an FBI agent the apartment where the bomb was made and was considered a "cooperative witness," escaped to Baghdad a day after the FBI released him.

39. Dwyer et al., *Two Seconds Under the World*, p. 171.

40. Summation Statement of Henry J. DePippo, Prosecutor, *United States of America v Mohammad A. Salameh et al.*, S593CR.180 (KTD), February 16, 1994, p. 8443.

41. Direct Examination of Brian Parr, *United States of America v Ramzi Ahmed Yousef and Eyad Ismoil*, S1293CR.180 (KTD), October 22, 1997, pp. 4734–4735.

that the date of the bombing (which coincided with the second anniversary of the liberation of Kuwait by U.S.-led coalition forces during the 1991 Gulf War) had no symbolic significance; instead, the group ran out of money so they used what they had at the time. Presumably if Iraq had sponsored the bombing, money would not have been a problem.

Finally, Yousef's statements about Iraq did not sound like those of an Iraqi agent. A few months after his extradition to the United States, Yousef granted an interview to the Arabic newspaper *Al-Hayah* in which he said that the Iraqi people must not pay for the mistakes made by Saddam Hussein.[42] Similarly, in his statement before Judge Duffy at the time of his sentencing, Yousef chastised the United States for tacitly supporting Iraq during the late 1980s, when Saddam Hussein killed thousands of his own (Kurdish) citizens with chemical weapons.[43] Yousef went on to say that Saddam "is killing them [innocent Iraqi civilians] because he is a dictator."[44] Perhaps Yousef sought to mask the identity of his sponsor by condemning Iraq, but his pattern of rhetoric seems unlikely to come from someone acting on behalf of Saddam or the Iraqi intelligence services.

Instead of state sponsorship, a large body of evidence indicates that the WTC conspirators were "transnational terrorists"—inspired and assisted by several Islamic militant groups operating in the United States and abroad, but not a formal part of any of them. Government prosecutors made a compelling case that Yousef and Ajaj traveled together from Pakistan to the United States to conduct terrorist activities, and that Yousef then recruited local people to help.[45] Salameh and Ayyad, both Palestinians whose families came from Jordan, attended Sheik Omar's mosque but were not part of his inner circle. Abouhalima, Salameh, and Ayyad knew each other from the mosque, but no known evidence suggests a prior link between them and Yousef or Ajaj.[46]

After his arrest in Egypt, Abouhalima's alleged confession made no mention of an Iraqi government connection to the bombing. He reportedly acknowledged his membership in the Egypt-based Gama al-Islamiya fundamentalist organization and explained how he had arranged to collect the funds for the WTC bombing from "Iranian industrialists and

---

42. Dirgham, "Ramzi Yusuf Discusses WTC Bombing," p. 5.

43. Statement of Ramzi Yousef at Sentencing, *United States of America v Ramzi Ahmed Yousef*, S1293CR.180 (KTD), January 8, 1998, p. 10.

44. Ibid.

45. Summation Statement of Henry J. DePippo, Prosecutor, *United States of America v Mohammad A. Salameh et al.*, S593CR.180 (KTD), February 16, 1994, pp. 8509–8523.

46. Dwyer et al., *Two Seconds Under the World*, p. 164.

fundamentalist expatriates living in Europe" with the assistance of the Muslim Brotherhood.[47] While detained in the Metropolitan Correctional Center, Abouhalima reportedly responded to a fellow prisoner's question about how five guys could blow up the WTC by claiming that they did not act alone. He went on to say that "three hundred men across the country . . . would do anything to hurt the United States."[48]

Abouhalima's comments echo a line in the letter sent by Ayyad after the bombing claiming that "more than 150 suicidal soldiers" were ready to stage further attacks if their demands were not met.[49] Yousef also described the "Liberation Army" that took credit for the WTC bombing as "an international movement concerned with affairs of the world's Islamic armed movement."[50] In 1995, investigative journalist Steven Emerson noted that federal investigators had identified links between the WTC bombers and at least five Islamic organizations: the Gama al-Islamiya, Islamic Jihad, Hamas, the Sudanese National Islamic Front, and al-Fuqrah.[51] He observed that these groups work together more closely in diaspora communities outside the Middle East "because they feel they are surrounded by a common enemy: Westerners and their values."[52] Emerson concluded that the WTC bombing was financed by Islamic terrorist groups but not by a state sponsor.[53]

Several historical forces created a fertile climate for a loose collection of individuals to act out their anti-American feelings, even though they were not a part of a formal terrorist organization. The decade-long struggle in Afghanistan against the Soviet Union created a generation of rebel warriors who were fervently anti-Israel and anti-American. Both Ramzi Yousef and Eyad Ismoil, who drove Yousef in the rental van to the WTC garage, claimed to have had relatives killed during the Persian Gulf War or at the hands of the Israelis.[54] Moreover, the political mood throughout

---

47. Ibid., p. 240.

48. Ibid., p. 251.

49. *United States of America v Mohammad A. Salameh et al.,* S1293CR.180 (KTD), Government Exhibit 196.

50. Dirgham, "Ramzi Yusuf Discusses WTC Bombing," p. 5.

51. Emerson, "The Other Fundamentalists," p. 40.

52. Ibid.

53. U.S. Congress, Senate, Committee on Judiciary, Subcommittee on Terrorism, Technology, and Government Information, Testimony by Steven Emerson, *Foreign Terrorists in America: Five Years After the World Trade Center Bombing,* February 24, 1998, p. 41.

54. Dirgham, "Ramzi Yusuf Discusses WTC Bombing," p. 5; Statement of Eyal Ismoil at sentencing, *United States of America v Eyad Ismoil,* S1293CR. 180 (KTD), April 3, 1998, p. 16.

the Middle East immediately after the Gulf War, particularly in the Palestinian community, was strongly anti-American. Iraq's devastating defeat by a coalition of forces under U.S. leadership created a political backlash that led many Arabs to rally to Saddam Hussein's cause.

Yousef and the other WTC conspirators clearly had financial supporters in the Middle East who have never been identified or brought to justice. Abouhalima seemed to have obtained funds from Egyptians in Egypt and Germany, but their identity remains a mystery. Other financial supporters may have been in Afghanistan, Saudi Arabia, Pakistan, and the Philippines. Osama bin Laden, widely believed to have been the mastermind of the August 1998 attacks on the U.S. embassies in Kenya and Tanzania, would seem a natural candidate to support the WTC bombing, but to date none of the government indictments against him indicate a connection to the incident.[55] In sum, although the available evidence does not dispel all doubts, it does suggest that the WTC bombers operated independently of formal state sponsorship.

Evidence Does Not Support CW Use

What evidence, if any, supports Judge Duffy's statement that the WTC terrorists incorporated cyanide into their bomb? During the trial, prosecutors questioned FBI chemist Steven Burmeister about the consequences of mixing sodium cyanide with either nitric or sulfuric acid, both of which were known to be present in the device.

Prosecutor: What happens when you mix sodium cyanide with either nitric or sulfuric acid?
Burmeister: You form hydrogen cyanide, which is a gas, which is extremely toxic.
Prosecutor: . . . When you say hydrogen cyanide is very toxic, could you give us an idea of how toxic that is?
Burmeister: Very toxic, if you breathe it, you're dead. . . .[56]

Despite this chilling testimony, Burmeister never suggested during the trial that his investigation had led him to believe that the bomb actually contained sodium cyanide.

When FBI agents raided a storage shed where the bombers kept

---

55. Indictment, *United States of America v Usama Bin Laden, Muhammad Atef, Wadih El Hage, Fazul Abdullah Mohammed, Mohamed Sadeek Odeh, Mohamed Rashed Daoud Al-'Owhali,* S(2) 98 Cr. 1023 (LBS).

56. Direct Examination of Steven G. Burmeister, *United States of America v Mohammad A. Salameh et al.,* S593CR.180 (KTD), January 24, 1994, p. 6911.

chemicals, they discovered one sealed bottle of aqueous sodium cyanide.[57] This finding does not prove, however, that the conspirators actually incorporated cyanide into the bomb. Aqueous sodium cyanide is used for industrial purposes such as mining and metal finishing, and on a smaller scale for photographic purposes and for flushing fish out of coral reefs. In either aqueous or solid form, sodium cyanide can cost less than three dollars per pound.[58] For industrial use, sodium cyanide is sold in solid form in ton lots or in aqueous form by the tanker truckload. The terrorists' 1,500-pound urea-nitrate bomb would have required such a large quantity of sodium cyanide that a chemical supplier probably would have requested a site visit to ensure that the buyer could handle the shipment safely. Furthermore, a technical analysis of how much sodium cyanide would have been required, and the conditions needed to create hydrogen cyanide, do not support Judge Duffy's assertion.[59]

In an interview, former FBI official Blitzer stated that there was "no forensic evidence indicating the presence of sodium cyanide at the bomb site."[60] In fact, little information about the composition of the bomb could be ascertained from the crime scene because of the enormous amount of physical and liquid debris. The blast tore open the structural bowels of the twin towers, releasing water, sewage, and building materials. Additionally, the cars parked in the WTC garage and their contents were scattered widely. Even chemicals used to melt snow on the sidewalk flowed into the bomb crater. The only catalogue of chemicals that could be made with a high degree of confidence came from purchase orders placed by the terrorists, the contents of the shed where the chemical ingredients were stored, and the apartment where the bomb material was mixed. Investigators worked backwards from these sources to identify the chemicals present at the bomb site.

During his summary statement, Prosecutor Henry DePippo carefully listed all the chemicals the U.S. government believed had been present

---

57. Ibid., p. 6910.

58. A web site sponsored by Brooks Air Force Base described a silver plating process using aqueous sodium cyanide and listed a price of $2.23 per pound of solution (http://xre22.brooks.af.mil/hscxre/97tns/97needs/526.htm). A commercial web site offering prices for solid sodium cyanide indicated a price of approximately 65 cents per pound (http://allchem.com/price.html#S).

59. Richard A. Falkenrath, Robert D. Newman, and Bradley A. Thayer, *America's Achilles' Heel: Nuclear, Biological and Chemical Terrorism and Covert Attack*, BCSIA Studies in International Security (Cambridge, Mass.: The MIT Press, 1998), pp. 32–33.

60. Author's telephone interview with Blitzer, June 18, 1998; author's telephone interview with Steven G. Burmeister, an FBI chemist involved in the WTC investigation, August 6, 1998.

in the bomb. Conspicuous by its absence was any mention of sodium cyanide.[61] The prosecution, in its effort to paint a dark picture of the defendants for the jury, presumably would not have hesitated to add attempted mass killing with a chemical weapon to make the case even more compelling. But if the FBI had not found definitive evidence at the bomb site to prove the presence of sodium cyanide, there was no reason for the prosecution to mention it.

The only other public suggestion from an official source that the WTC bombers attempted to disseminate a chemical agent came from Major General George Friel, the former head of the U.S. Army's Chemical and Biological Defense Command (CBDCOM). A Gannett News Service story carried by the *Detroit News* quoted Friel as stating that the "1993 World Trade Center bombers may have tried to mix a toxic agent—probably arsenic—with the homemade bomb they planted in the skyscraper's garage."[62] A press spokesperson at CBDCOM, which Friel commanded until July 1998, indicated that the general had repeated what he had heard in briefings by the FBI.[63] When asked specifically about Friel's statement, however, an FBI chemist involved in the case stated that he was not aware of any evidence indicating that arsenic was present in the conspirators' collection of chemicals.[64] Most likely, Friel misspoke when he believed he was recounting Judge Duffy's statement.

Explanations for Judge Duffy's Statement

None of the physical evidence presented at the trial appears to support Judge Duffy's assertion in his 1994 sentencing statement that the WTC conspirators had incorporated cyanide into the bomb. Of course, there is a remote possibility that the bomb contained sodium cyanide that was destroyed in the blast without leaving a trace, or that the FBI investigators never found the bombers' secret stash of cyanide. Based on the evidence presented at the trial, there is no way of knowing. In any event, it would have been impossible for the prosecution to charge the defendants with using a chemical weapon if the FBI could find no forensic evidence to support the charge. Some contend that the sealed filings in the court case

61. Summation Statement of Henry J. DePippo, Prosecutor, *United States of America v Mohammad A. Salameh et al.*, S593CR.180 (KTD), February 16, 1994, pp. 8338–8370.

62. John Omicinski, "Terrorists Pursue Bio-Chemical Bombs," *Detroit News*, April 5, 1998.

63. Author's telephone interview with spokesperson for the U.S. Army Chemical and Biological Defense Command, August 6, 1998.

64. Author's telephone interview with Burmeister, August 6, 1998.

may contain a clue to the Judge's assertion.[65] But a key government participant in the trial who is familiar with all the sealed exhibits in the case said in an interview that they do not contain any evidence that the bombers incorporated sodium cyanide in their bomb.[66]

Finally, some indications suggest that Judge Duffy may have changed his mind about the cyanide allegation. At the first trial in May 1994, he made his strong statement about cyanide use when sentencing Salameh, Ayyad, Abouhalima, and Ajaj. At that time, he seems to have drawn his conclusion from the evil intentions of the terrorists and the discovery of a single sealed bottle of sodium cyanide in their storage locker. The trial was highly stressful because the defendants and their attorneys bedeviled the legal process and because death threats were made against Judge Duffy. It is therefore possible that the pressures of the trial may have caused him to overstate an important facet of the case.

At the time of the trial of Ramzi Yousef in January 1998, however, Judge Duffy made no mention of the conspirators' failed attempt to use cyanide or even their intent to employ a chemical weapon, although it would have been logical to do so when sentencing the mastermind of the crime, whom he called "an apostle of evil."[67] It is possible that over time, Judge Duffy came to realize that he had overstated the case for chemical weapon use. Despite several requests by the author, the judge declined to comment on the case.

Yousef's Threats to Use CW

Although proof is lacking for the actual use of cyanide in the WTC bomb, much evidence suggests that the conspirators considered lacing the bomb with poison. During Ramzi Yousef's extradition flight back to the United States, he revealed to Secret Service Agent Parr that he had considered putting sodium cyanide in the WTC bomb but had decided not to because "it was going to be too expensive to implement."[68] Although there might be reasons for Yousef to lie about this matter, his comments fit the

---

65. Author's telephone interview with former Senate staffer John Sopko, January 28, 1998.

66. Author's interview with former U.S. Department of Justice official J. Gilmore Childers, New York, May 20, 1998.

67. Sentencing Statement of Judge Kevin T. Duffy, *United States of America v Ramzi Ahmed Yousef*, S1293CR.180 (TD), January 8, 1998, pp. 21–25.

68. Direct Examination of Brian Parr, *United States of America v Ramzi Ahmed Yousef and Eyad Ismoil*, S1293CR.180 (KTD), October 22, 1997, pp. 4730–4731.

evidence presented by government prosecutors and confirmed by FBI officials.

During the same conversation, Yousef indicated that he had planned to use "hydrogen cyanide in some other form of a bomb, not as large a bomb, but a different type of bomb to disperse that [poison] in the Trade Center."[69] One of the files recovered from Nidal Ayyad's computer at Allied Signal stated that the bombers' "calculations were not very accurate" but promised that the next attack would be "very precise" and that the WTC would remain a target unless their demands were met.[70] Perhaps Yousef's smaller bomb was the one Ayyad referred to as "very precise." Moreover, in the letter that Ayyad sent to the *New York Times* immediately after the WTC bombing, the terrorists warned that if their demands went unmet, other attacks would be conducted, including strikes on "some potential Nuclear [sic] targets."[71]

Once Yousef arrived in the Philippines, he began threatening to use chemical weapons, but this was several months after Judge Duffy's sentencing statement at the first (1994) trial of the WTC bombers.[72] A number of situations arose in which Yousef drafted notes threatening to use chemical weapons if his demands were not met. These threats appeared several times in various letters and statements, and in computer files that he believed he had deleted from his laptop computer. When the Pakistani authorities apprehended Yousef, they recovered two handwritten letters. One letter, signed "The Liberation Army Chief of Staff," threatened to kill the Philippine president and stated that the group could "manufacture different kinds of chemical substances that are deadly and poisonous gases and assemble them from very basic materials that are available to any chemist."[73] Yousef claimed that they would use these weapons "in big cities and big and vital establishments and drinking water sources."[74] In the other letter, Yousef made much the same point:

---

69. Ibid., p. 4734.

70. *United States of America v Muhammad A. Salameh et al.*, S1293CR 180 (KTD), Government Exhibit 78-E.

71. Ibid., Government Exhibit 196.

72. The World Trade Center bombing occurred on February 26, 1993. Judge Duffy issued his sentencing statement for the first trial of the WTC bombers in May 1994. According to the prosecutor in the second trial, Ramzi Yousef arrived in Manila, the Philippines, in January 1995. See Summation Statement of Dietrich Snell, Prosecutor, *United States of America v Ramzi Ahmed Yousef, Abdul Hakim Murad, Wali Khan Amin Shah*, S1293CR.180 (KTD), August 26, 1998, p. 5114.

73. Ibid., Government Exhibit 527.

74. Ibid.

. . . we also have the ability to make and use chemicals and poisonous gas. And these gases and poisons are made from the simplest ingredients which are available in the pharmacies and we could, as well, smuggle them from one country to another if needed. And this is for use against vital institutions and residential populations and drinking water sources and others.[75]

In a press report, a former senior intelligence official indicated that Yousef had "been studying not only chemical but biological weapons."[76] The source of this allegation is unclear. None of the letters confiscated from Yousef at the time of arrest nor the deleted files recovered from his laptop computer and entered into the court record contain any mention of biological weapons. Moreover, a former senior FBI official familiar with all aspects of the WTC bombing case said there was no evidence to support this allegation.[77] Even so, Yousef's terrorist career reflects a clear escalatory pattern, from building conventional explosives, to considering lacing the WTC bomb with deadly chemicals, to threatening attacks on nuclear facilities, to planning for the large-scale use of chemical weapons.

The Bombers' Motivations

Interviews with any of the convicted conspirators are unlikely because of the severe restrictions on visitations imposed by Judge Duffy. Nevertheless, a picture of the terrorists' motives emerges from letters claiming responsibility for the attack, statements to authorities, statements at trials, and letters retrieved from the hard-drives of computers they used. These sources suggest that Yousef was motivated by an inchoate mixture of visceral hatred and personal affirmation, wrapped in a variety of geopolitical rationales.

The primary motivation for the WTC bombing was to kill and injure a large number of Americans. Yousef told Agent Parr that he intended for the explosion to cause one tower to fall into the other, inflicting 250,000 civilian casualties.[78] Yousef also told Parr that he "recalled being disappointed when he heard the initial report that only one person had

---

75. *United States of America v Ramzi Ahmed Yousef, Abdul Hakim Murad, Wali Khan Amin Shah,* S1293CR.180 (KTD), August 26, 1998, Government Exhibit 528-T.

76. William J. Broad and Judith Miller, "The Threat of Germ Weapons Is Rising, Fear Too," *New York Times,* December 27, 1998, Section 4 (Week in Review), p. 1.

77. Author's interview with Blitzer, June 18, 1998.

78. Direct Examination of Brian Parr, *United States of America v Ramzi Ahmed Yousef and Eyad Ismoil,* S1293CR.180 (KTD), October 22, 1997, p. 4721.

been killed."[79] Throughout Yousef's terrorist career in the mid-1990s, he sought to carry out some truly diabolical terrorist acts, all of which he justified by visceral hatred of the United States because of its support for Israel.

Another striking feature of Yousef's motivations is the absence of a religious rationale. The letter Ayyad sent to the *New York Times*, which Yousef claimed to have written, contains no religious references. Similarly, Yousef did not offer any religious rationale for his terrorist activities during his statement at sentencing.[80] In his interview with *Al-Hayah*, Yousef argued that the movement he supported aimed "to pressure the U.S. Administration by carrying out operations against U.S. targets so this administration will stop its aid for Israel." Yousef said that he considered himself "religious," but when asked whether he was a radical fundamentalist, he launched into a diatribe on how "Israel itself was created on a radical fundamentalist principle."[81] Finally, when questioned about whether he was more dedicated to "the cause" than to his children, Yousef stated "we have not chosen this path voluntarily but have been compelled to take it as a result of the killing and the occupation with which we are living."[82] In sum, Yousef's declared motivation was not religious but rather an anti-occupation crusade aimed against Israel and its main supporter, the United States.

In contrast, Ayyad, Abouhalima, and Ajaj all expressed religious sentiments during their statements at sentencing but never admitted any connection to the WTC bombing.[83] Their statements were more affirmations of faith than rationales for a terrorist attack. Given that several of the conspirators were followers of Sheikh Omar, Yousef's lack of religious justification is conspicuous by its absence. He appears to have been a secular terrorist who mobilized others by playing on their religious zeal.

At the root of the WTC bombers' intent to inflict mass casualties was a strong desire to punish, to seek revenge, and to underscore the dignity of Muslims. In the letter claiming responsibility for the bombing, they stated that their "action was done in response for the American political,

---

79. Ibid., p. 4734.

80. Statement of Ramzi Yousef at Sentencing, *United States of America v Ramzi Ahmed Yousef*, S1293CR.180 (KTD), January 8, 1998, pp. 6–18.

81. Dirgham, "Ramzi Yusuf Discusses WTC Bombing," p. 5.

82. Ibid.

83. Statements of Mohammed A. Salameh, Nidal Ayyad, Mahmud Abouhalima, and Amad Mohammad Ajaj at Sentencing, *United States of America v Muhammad A. Salameh et al.*, S1293CR 180 (KTD), May 24, 1994, pp. 26–34, 41–49, 53–65, 65–113.

economical, and military support to Israel, the state of terrorism, and to the rest of the dictator countries in the region."[84] Later, in his statement at his sentencing, Yousef said that he supported "terrorism so long as it was against the United States government and against Israel."[85] Yousef sought to avenge what he perceived as terrorist attacks by Israel against Palestinians by indiscriminately killing Americans because of the U.S. government's support for Israel.

Yousef justified his terrorism as both punishment and revenge. Since the United States never learns, he argued, it must be punished. Yousef equated the U.S. punishment inflicted on Libyan and Iraqi civilians with the punishment he had dispensed: "the United States is applying the system of collective punishment against Iraq and Libya—when either government makes any mistake, the United States punishes the people in their entirety for the government's mistake. We are reciprocating the treatment."[86]

In Yousef's statement at his sentencing, he argued that his terrorist acts were justified because "it is necessary to use the same means against you because this is the only language which you understand."[87] The bombers' letter to the *New York Times* also stated that "the American people must know that their civilians who got killed are not better than those who are getting killed by the American weapons and support."[88] In essence, the terrorists argued that to appreciate the tragedy Palestinians had experienced at the hands of the Israelis, innocent Americans had to die. The implication of Yousef's twisted logic was that as a result of the losses inflicted by terrorism, the American people would come to value Palestinian lives as much as their own and stop supporting Israel.

Yousef also justified terrorism against U.S. civilians as revenge for what he perceived as a long history of moral transgressions by the United States. In his view, the United States had waged terrorism against civilians during the firebombing of Tokyo, the Vietnam War, and the trade embargoes against Cuba and Iraq. Yousef cited the U.S. use of the toxic herbicide Agent Orange in Vietnam and the reluctance of the United States to condemn "Saddam Hussein when he killed thousands of his

84. Ibid.; Government Exhibit 196.

85. Statement of Ramzi Yousef at Sentencing, *United States of America v Ramzi Ahmed Yousef*, S1293CR.180 (KTD), January 8, 1998, p. 18.

86. Dirgham, "Ramzi Yusuf Discusses WTC Bombing," p. 5.

87. Statement of Ramzi Yousef at Sentencing, *United States of America v Ramzi Ahmed Yousef*, S1293CR.180 (KTD), January 8, 1998, pp. 13–14.

88. *United States of America v Muhammad A. Salameh et al.*, S1293CR 180 (KTD), Government Exhibit 196.

people in the 1980s with chemical weapons" as further evidence of the U.S. government's disregard for civilian lives.[89]

Beyond the motives of punishment and historical revenge, Yousef's terrorist acts affirmed who he perceived himself to be. When he was apprehended in Pakistan, he had in his possession a number of newspaper clippings about his terrorist exploits.[90] In the *Al-Hayah* interview Yousef described himself as an "explosives expert" and a "genius." Yousef boldly told the court at his sentencing that he was a terrorist and proud of it.[91]

The dangerous work of a terrorist bomber appears to have fed Yousef's psyche. After suffering the accidental detonation of a bomb in July 1993 that disfigured his hand and damaged one eye, Yousef did not shrink from his trade but went on to build the bombs he used in the Philippines in 1994. Working with deadly materials with the intent to cripple a global superpower by killing its people fed Yousef's view of himself as an expert and a genius. He seemed to get a charge or affirmation as a terrorist bomber with each new attack. The WTC bombing propelled him on to his next terrorist activity. Fortunately, his plan to blow up several American airliners in the sky failed, and he was apprehended before he could make good on his threats to use chemical weapons.

Conclusion

The World Trade Center bombers proved that determined terrorists can obtain large quantities of chemicals, mix them into a potent explosive device, and deliver them to a major target, potentially killing or injuring tens of thousands of people. Although the preponderance of evidence indicates that the WTC bombers did not use a chemical poison in their bomb, they considered that option and, given their expertise in chemistry and explosives, may have been able to accomplish it. Fortunately, the chemical ingredients needed to produce toxic weapons are neither cheap nor simple to acquire. In this case, the terrorists' intent to use a chemical weapon appears to have been thwarted by technical, logistical, and financial obstacles.

Yousef's terrorist crusade appears to have been driven by a

89. Statement of Ramzi Yousef at Sentencing, *United States of America v Ramzi Ahmed Yousef*, S1293CR.180 (KTD), January 8, 1998, p. 12.

90. Bruce Hoffman, *Inside Terrorism* (New York: Columbia University Press, 1998), p. 177.

91. Dirgham, "Ramzi Yusuf Discusses WTC Bombing," p. 5.

confluence of anti-American and anti-Israeli rage and a significant dose of ego rather than religious ideology. He had more in common with the famous Latin American terrorist Carlos the Jackal then he did with the religiously inspired suicide-bombers of Hamas. Although he drew on the diaspora of militant Islamic fundamentalists, his attempt to inflict mass casualties in New York City did not stem from religious conviction. Instead, his twisted belief about how to respond to the plight of the Palestinian people seemed driven by the thrill of being an explosives expert, killing innocent people, and moving on to practice his brand of terrorism another day. His exploits as a transnational terrorist affirmed the high opinion he held of himself. A terrorist who thinks that he is a genius will set the highest goals for practicing his craft. In Yousef's case, that meant attempting to kill as many innocent people as possible.

Chapter 12

Aum Shinrikyo (1995)

David E. Kaplan

In ambition, size, and breadth of activity, Aum Shinrikyo ("Aum Supreme Truth") stands alone among terrorist groups that have sought to use chemical and biological weapons. An apocalyptic religious sect headquartered in Japan, Aum has staged an unprecedented number of attacks with CBW agents, ranging from lone assassinations to attempted mass murder in one of the world's great capitals. A review of official reports from the U.S. and Japanese governments, combined with interviews with law enforcement and intelligence officials, indicates that the cult staged at least twenty attacks between 1990 and 1995, ten with chemical agents and ten with biological ones.[1]

Aum Shinrikyo achieved worldwide notoriety after its March 1995 nerve gas attack on the Tokyo subway system. Prior to that time, the group was a relatively obscure sect with a reputation for insularity, aggressive recruiting, and at times confrontational behavior.[2] Aum was founded in Japan in 1987. The leader of the sect was a charismatic, authoritarian former yoga teacher named Chizuo Matsumoto, who was known within the cult as Shoko Asahara.

Asahara proclaimed himself a uniquely enlightened being with su-

---

1. This account has been drawn from numerous sources. Key published reports are National Police Agency (Japan), *Briefing Paper on Aum*, internal document, 1995; *White Paper on Police 1995 (Excerpt)* (Tokyo: Japan Times, 1996); and *White Paper on Police 1996 (Excerpt)* (Tokyo: Police Association, 1997); U.S. Congress, Senate, Committee on Governmental Affairs, Permanent Subcommittee on Investigations (Minority Staff), *Staff Statement, Hearings on Global Proliferation of Weapons of Mass Destruction: A Case Study on the Aum Shinrikyo*, October 31, 1995. Also sourced are various interviews over a three-year period with intelligence and law enforcement officials in Tokyo and Washington, D.C. See notes below for details.

2. Background on Aum and Asahara is drawn from various sources. See, for example, U.S. Senate, *Staff Statement*, pp. 8–13; and National Police Agency, *White Paper on Police 1996*, pp. 4–5.

pernatural powers who would "walk the same path as Buddha." In his 1992 book, *Declaring Myself the Christ*, he argued that he was also the Christian Messiah. His followers considered him "the only person in Japan, or in the whole world, who has attained supreme enlightenment."[3] Aum theology drew heavily from mystical Tibetan Buddhism but also included influences from other religions, notably Hinduism and Christianity, as well as from sixteenth-century seer-astrologer Nostradamus, the practice of yoga, and a range of pseudoscientific beliefs. Aum doctrine preached that, by following Asahara, members would gain supernatural powers, including the ability to see through walls and to levitate. An important, increasingly dominant doctrine of the cult dealt with the inevitably of Armageddon. Asahara was obsessed with a prophetic vision that a great cataclysm would soon engulf the world, and he spoke with growing frequency about the inevitability of a great apocalyptic war.[4]

The belief in Armageddon appears to have been the primary motivation behind the cult's far-ranging attempts to arm itself with powerful weapons, including biological and chemical agents. Aum leaders believed these weapons were imperative for the cult to survive the coming cataclysm. Aum's actual use of these agents, however, was prompted by a variety of secondary factors, such as attempts to expand the cult's size and influence, to fend off intervention by Japanese authorities, and to destroy its enemies.

The Rise of Aum

Shoko Asahara was born on March 2, 1955, in the southern Japanese town of Yatsushiro. His father eked out a living as a maker of tatami floor mats. Asahara, the fourth son of seven children, suffered from infantile glaucoma and attended schools for the blind. Published reports suggest that he was an ambitious and increasingly frustrated child. His partial sight gave him an advantage at schools for the blind, and his aggressive ways

---

3. The quotes on Asahara as Buddha and his supreme enlightenment are from Shoko Asahara, *The Teachings of the Truth*, Vol. 3 (Shizuoka, Japan: Aum Publishing Co., Ltd., 1992), pp. 69–70 and p. viii, respectively; his vision of himself as Messiah is from Shoko Asahara, *Declaring Myself the Christ* (Shizuoka, Japan: Aum Publishing Co., Ltd., 1992), pp. vii, 15.

4. The dimensions of Aum theology can be seen in the sect's various publications, such as Asahara's *The Teachings of the Truth* and *Tathagata Abhidhamma: The Ever-Winning Law of the True Victors* (Shizuoka, Japan: Aum Publishing Co., Ltd., 1992); and in Asahara's various lectures, reprinted on Aum's web page (www.aum-shinrikyo.com). Also useful were brief descriptions in National Police Agency (Japan), *Briefing Paper on Aum*, internal document, 1995, pp. 3–4; and U.S. Senate, *Staff Statement*, p. 13.

made him a bully. He dreamed of becoming prime minister of Japan and hoped to attend the nation's most prestigious school, Tokyo University, but was refused entrance. Asahara reportedly graduated from a junior college in 1975, began to study acupuncture and yoga, and acquired an interest in extrasensory perception and New Age religion. In 1982, he was arrested for peddling unregulated medicines but apparently escaped with only a fine.

Asahara focused his energies increasingly on religion. In 1984, he set up a profitable yoga school and publishing house, and three years later he transformed the company into the center of a new faith, Aum Shinrikyo, with himself as guru.[5] Fueled by aggressive recruiting and promises of psychic power, the sect grew rapidly. At its peak in 1995, Aum ran twenty facilities across Japan, with a presence in eleven of that nation's forty-seven prefectures. Its major facility was a sprawling compound built at the base of Mt. Fuji, about 100 kilometers from Tokyo. Although founded and headquartered in Japan, the cult sharply expanded its operations overseas, ultimately fielding over thirty branches in at least six countries. Aum ran recruiting and procurement operations in Russia and the United States, a trading company in Taiwan, a tea plantation in Sri Lanka, and a sheep ranch in Australia. Cult members also conducted research in the former Yugoslavia and attempted to expand into Ukraine and Belarus.[6]

Estimates of Aum membership vary, but a generally accepted figure is that by 1995 the sect had 40,000 members worldwide, with 10,000 in Japan, some 30,000 in Russia, and several dozen scattered in the United States, Germany, and elsewhere overseas.[7] Of the 10,000 members in Japan, some 1,400 had renounced the outside world, donated all their assets to the cult, and lived at Aum facilities. These were the cult's hard-core devotees, from whom Asahara's closest aides were drawn. Most of the outside membership, it should be noted, were innocent followers of the cult. Major crimes such as the Tokyo subway attack were committed by a dedicated inner circle around Asahara and a handful of people chosen from the Aum clergy.[8] Beginning in late 1991, the cult grew

---

5. On Asahara's early life, see U.S. Senate, *Staff Statement*, pp. 8–9; and Shoko Egawa, *Kyu Seishu no Yabou* [*Ambitions of a Messiah*] (Tokyo: Kyoiku Shiryo Shuppankai, 1991).

6. U.S. Senate, *Staff Statement*, pp. 10, 29, 59–60; National Police Agency, *White Paper on Police 1996*, pp. 4–5.

7. National Police Agency, *White Paper on Police 1996*, p. 4. Some estimates range as high as 50,000; see U.S. Senate, *Staff Statement*, p. 10.

8. Tokyo District Public Prosecutor, *Opening Statement by the Prosecution in Trial of Masaya Takahashi, Hironobu Hatakeyama, Hiroyuki Okada, and Wakashio Togashi*, October

rapidly in Russia. An investigation by the Russian State Duma's Committee on Security Matters put the number of Russian followers as high as 35,000, with some 5,500 full-time monks and nuns living at Aum facilities. By 1995, Aum maintained at least seven branches within Moscow and eleven in St. Petersburg, Vladivostok, and other cities. The sect produced TV and radio programming, lectured and recruited widely, and built up contacts with influential Russians.[9]

Aum became quite wealthy. Members donated vast amounts of money to the cult, and its leaders managed a growing financial empire aided by volunteer labor and the tax breaks granted to religious organizations. The cult ran a wide variety of businesses, including a chain of computer stores, at least eight restaurants, training centers, a fitness club, a medical clinic, and trading companies.[10] At its peak in 1995, one senior cultist boasted that Aum's assets were worth as much as ¥100 billion. This impressive figure, equal to approximately $1 billion at the time, has been widely cited in reports on the cult. Another indication of the cult's resources comes from a U.S. Senate report that, citing official sources, notes that the cult paid nearly $100 million to electronics companies outside Japan. When Aum was declared bankrupt in 1996, however, the Tokyo District Court reportedly found only ¥2.37 billion in assets. Much of Aum's money may have been hidden or spent by then, or the cult's assets may have been greatly overstated. Even assuming that Aum's resources were close to this smaller figure, however, the cult still had a net worth of more than $20 million—ample resources to plow into its weapon programs.[11]

Arms and Armageddon

Shoko Asahara's statements on the nature and date of the apocalypse vary. As early as 1988, Asahara proclaimed that "the tide of militarism is drawing near to us each day. . . . And the more Aum Shinrikyo grows,

1995, reprinted as "Prosecution Statement Details Aum's Production of Sarin," *Japan Times*, October 21, 1995. See also U.S. Senate, *Staff Statement*, p. 26.

9. National Police Agency, *Briefing Paper on Aum*, pp. 22–25; National Police Agency, *White Paper on Police 1996*, p. 5; U.S. Senate, *Staff Statement*, p. 58.

10. National Police Agency, *Mechanism of Aum Organization* (internal report), 1995, pp. 3–6; see also U.S. Senate, *Staff Statement*, pp. 29–31.

11. The ¥100 billion figure was originally cited by Aum chief scientist Hideo Murai at a Foreign Correspondents Club of Japan press conference, April 7, 1995. The Senate report is *Staff Statement*, p. 30; the smaller figure is noted in "Lower House OKs Bill for AUM Victims to Get More Money," Kyodo News Service, April 9, 1998.

the more conflict will arise."[12] In a 1993 book, he prophesied that the United States would attack Japan with nuclear weapons, turning the nation into a wasteland and wiping out 90 percent of its population. To avert this catastrophe, he warned that 30,000 people must be recruited and enlightened by Aum. At other times, Asahara preached that global war was inevitable, and that Aum would arise from the devastation as the supreme power in Japan and then the world. In some speeches, he predicted that Armageddon would come as early as 1997 and that an omen would appear in 1995. Cult documents analyzed by Japanese police in 1995 indicate that the day for the great war may have been moved up to November of that year.[13]

The preoccupation with Armageddon influenced the very structure of the sect. To speed its takeover of the world, Aum organized itself as a shadow government, with some twenty "ministries" modeled after the Japanese executive branch. Among the offices were the Ministry of Justice, the Ministry of Science and Technology, and the Ministry of Self-Defense.[14]

The urgency of responding to this impending apocalypse helped fuel an ends-justifies-means approach by cult leaders. In 1989, Asahara's aides murdered an anti-Aum lawyer, his wife, and their one-year-old son, and also killed a cultist who questioned the guru's teachings. Asahara rationalized murder by preaching that one can kill someone who has committed evil acts, since the latter is condemned to hell regardless. By taking the life of such evildoers, one hastens their transition to a newly reincarnated life, benefitting the killer's own karma.[15]

Aum's violent attitude toward the outside world was further intensified by growing paranoia and feelings of persecution within the cult. Police say a turning point came in 1990, when a slate of Aum candidates running for the Japanese parliament, including Asahara, was largely ignored by Japanese voters. Months later, local protests against a new Aum facility led to an official investigation of the group for land fraud.

---

12. Asahara, *The Teachings of the Truth*, pp. 53–54.

13. On Asahara's predictions of doom, see Asahara, *The Teachings of the Truth*, Vol. 3, p. 119; U.S. Congress, Senate, Committee on Governmental Affairs, *Global Proliferation of Weapons of Mass Destruction: Hearings before the Permanent Subcommittee on Investigations of the Committee on Governmental Affairs*, "Testimony of Yumiko Hiraoka, Aum Shinrikyo Nun and Sect Leader," October 21, 1995, pp. 142–143; National Police Agency, *Briefing Paper on Aum*, p. 6; U.S. Senate, *Staff Statement*, pp. 6 and 15; and, more generally, Shoko Asahara, *Hiizuru kuni wazawai chikashi* [*Disaster Nears for Land of the Rising Sun*] (Shizuoka, Japan: Aum Shuppan, 1995).

14. National Police Agency, *White Paper on Police 1996*, p. 4.

15. Ibid.

Cult leaders believed both events to be conspiratorial acts of oppression by the Japanese state.[16]

It was at this point that the cult launched its weapon programs. Aum scientists considered and researched an extraordinary range of armaments. Both biological and chemical agents were manufactured, as were laser and microwave devices. Cultists traveled as far as Belgrade to study the works of inventor Nikola Tesla in the hopes of creating a seismological weapon, while others attempted to buy and to manufacture a nuclear weapon.[17] One top Aum leader, while attempting to purchase weapons in Russia, wrote in his notebook: "Nuclear warhead—how much?" followed by several prices.[18] In addition, the cult engaged in international efforts to acquire conventional weapons, including automatic rifles, pistols, and knives. The most ambitious of these efforts was a sophisticated attempt to mass-produce the Russian AK-47 assault rifle using computer-controlled machine tools.[19]

Decision-making within the cult was strictly hierarchical and enforced by punishments that could include death. Asahara, deemed the "Sacred Emperor" by his followers, held absolute power over the sect.[20] In their indictments of Aum leaders, Japanese prosecutors have made clear their belief that orders for the production of nerve gas and other weapons came directly from Asahara. Top cult members also have testified in Japanese court that only Asahara had the power to order murder, and at one hearing Asahara himself reportedly offered "to shoulder responsibility for all incidents."[21]

Aum was greatly assisted in its weapon programs by tapping the large number of young scientists and technicians who flocked to the cult. Indeed, the sect prioritized recruitment of such followers, believing that

---

16. U.S. Senate, *Staff Statement*, p. 12; and National Police Agency, *White Paper on Police 1996*, p. 5.

17. National Police Agency, *Briefing Paper on Aum*, pp. 13–14, 17; U.S. Senate, *Staff Statement*, p. 34.

18. Author's interview with a Western intelligence officer, Tokyo, November 10, 1995; See also U.S. Senate, *Staff Statement*, p. 65.

19. National Police Agency, *Briefing Paper on Aum*, p. 13.

20. Ibid., p. 3; National Police Agency, *White Paper on Police 1996*, p. 5.

21. Court statements implicating Asahara are reported in "AUM's Once No. 2 Man Says Only Guru Could Order Murder," Kyodo News Service, September 5, 1997; "Ex-Aum Member Says Only Guru Could Choose Gas," Kyodo News Service, April 10, 1998; and "Japan Cult Guru Throws Murder Trial Into Confusion," Reuters World Report, October 18, 1996.

their skills were needed to survive Armageddon. Many cultists had studied at Japan's top universities in such fields as medicine, biochemistry, biology, physics, and electrical engineering. Aum placed similar recruiting emphasis in Russia, where the cult reportedly sought out those with backgrounds in physics, chemistry, and biology.[22]

Biological and Chemical Weapons Production

The cult attempted to produce its first biological weapon—botulinum toxin—as early as 1990. The effort was led by Seichi Endo, a young microbiologist who had done research at Kyoto University's Viral Research Center. Although Endo's team encountered numerous problems, Japanese authorities believe that by 1995 the cult had produced anthrax and botulinum toxin, and was developing Q fever.[23] A large Aum "medical" mission to Zaire in 1992, purportedly to help treat Ebola victims, led investigators to suspect the cult was attempting to obtain Ebola virus for culturing in Japan.[24]

From Aum facilities, Japanese authorities seized large amounts of equipment for cultivating bacteria and viruses, electron microscopes, a huge supply of culture media, and an extensive library that discussed potential biological agents such as botulinum toxin and the microorganisms that cause cholera and dysentery. When police raided cult properties, they found a four-story concrete laboratory under construction, equipped with a clean room, a filtration system for removing contaminants, and an air lock.[25] A full accounting of Aum's biological arsenal remains unavailable, however.[26]

Investigators believe that Aum began an intensive study of chemical weapons in early 1993, with the intention of finding an agent to mass produce. Over the next few months, cult scientists produced experimental

---

22. U.S. Senate, *Staff Statement*, pp. 20–21, 59.

23. Ibid., p. 35; National Police Agency, *Briefing Paper on Aum*, pp. 14–15. Q fever is a rickettsial disease that is incapacitating but rarely fatal. Aum's anthrax was reportedly a relatively harmless vaccine strain. See "Sowing Death: How Japan Germ Terror Alerted World," *New York Times*, May 26, 1998, p. 1.

24. Author's interview with National Police Agency official, Tokyo, August 29, 1995; U.S. Senate, *Staff Statement*, p. 44. See also Associated Press, "Cult Eyed Ebola as Weapon, Visited Zaire," *Japan Times*, May 25, 1995.

25. National Police Agency, *Briefing Paper on Aum*, pp.14–15. See also "Aum Buildings Yield Evidence of Bio-Weapons," *Daily Yomiuri*, April 2, 1995.

26. Author's interview with National Police Agency official, January 30, 1998.

amounts of the nerve agents sarin, tabun, soman, and VX. They also considered hydrogen cyanide and, reportedly, phosgene and mustard gas.[27] By April 1993, Aum had selected sarin as its primary agent because of its lethality, ease of production, and the availability of raw materials. Other chemical agents continued to be of interest, however. The cult produced the nerve agent VX four times, according to Japanese police, and used it in at least three assassination attempts.[28] Although Aum's deadliest attacks employed nerve agents, cultists used hydrogen cyanide in two attempts at mass murder, and police later confiscated 8.5 kilograms of sodium cyanide from an Aum hideout.[29] Police reportedly suspect that phosgene gas was used in another murder attempt.[30]

Still, it was sarin that attracted the cult's greatest attention. In early November 1993, Aum scientists succeeded in producing about 20 grams of the substance; within months, they had produced some 30 kilograms. About this time, construction began on a plant for mass producing the agent. Plans called for the facility to produce 2 tons of sarin daily, with the intent of amassing a stockpile of 70 tons.[31] The completed plant had a computerized process-control system and was "extremely sophisticated," according to investigators. Although later stages of the production process were plagued by equipment failures, the facility produced more than 10 tons of precursor chemicals for sarin before police investigations forced the cult to abandon production.[32]

Acquisition of Materials and Equipment

The materials for Aum's various weapon programs came largely from purchases made through a series of front companies set up by the cult.

---

27. Author's interview with National Police Agency official, August 29, 1995; National Police Agency, *Briefing Paper on Aum*, p. 6; U.S. Senate, *Staff Statement*, p. 35. See also "Aum Chemist Says He Made Vast Amount of Mustard Gas," *Asahi Evening News*, July 19, 1995.

28. U.S. Senate, *Staff Statement*, p. 39; National Police Agency, *Briefing Paper on Aum*, p. 16; and *White Paper on Police 1996*, p. 12.

29. U.S. Senate, *Staff Statement*, p. 40.

30. "Aum Tried to Kill Popular Journalist," *Asahi Evening News*, June 21, 1995.

31. Tokyo District Public Prosecutor, *Opening Statement by the Prosecution in Trial of Takahashi, et al.*; National Police Agency, *White Paper on Police 1996*, pp. 9–10.

32. The three-story chemical factory was known as "Satian-7." Tokyo District Public Prosecutor, *Opening Statement by the Prosecution in Trial of Takahashi, et al.*; U.S. Senate, *Staff Statement*, p. 39.

Beginning in spring 1993, Aum operated a sophisticated international procurement network aimed at obtaining weapons, laboratory and indus- trial equipment, and precursor chemicals.[33] The cult could claim with some legitimacy that it was engaged in various industrial and medical pursuits, including health clinics, manufacturing, and scientific research. These cover activities made it remarkably easy to obtain sensitive mate- rials. For sarin production, the cult purchased through just one front company approximately 90 tons of methanol, 50 tons of diethylaniline, 180 tons of phosphorus trichloride, 550 kilograms of iodine, 950 kilo- grams of phosphorus pentachloride, 54 tons of sodium fluoride, and 51 tons of isopropyl alcohol.[34] Police also reportedly seized about 160 metal drums of peptone, a substance used for cultivating bacteria. Each drum held 18 liters; by contrast, university research classes use only about 1 liter per year.[35]

Equipment for sarin production was purchased from various manu- facturers. Among the items Aum obtained on the open market were a coil-method heat exchanger, a pump, a motor, a deaccelerator, measuring devices, vinyl chloride pipes, and Teflon tubes.[36] Although the sect pur- chased most of its chemicals within Japan, Aum buyers were also active overseas. In the United States, investigators traced cult purchases of gas masks, air filtration media, molecular modeling software, and lasers.[37] In Russia, too, the sect made repeated attempts to obtain both weapons and technology.[38] In Australia, Aum purchased a remote ranch in the western desert, where it conducted nerve agent experiments on sheep.[39]

Among the more intriguing questions left by the case is where the cult obtained its formula for sarin. Although several formulas can be used to manufacture the nerve agent, the formula employed by Aum was similar to that used by the Soviet military, according to Japanese intelli-

33. National Police Agency, *Briefing Paper on Aum*, p. 6; U.S. Senate, *Staff Statement*, p. 38.

34. Tokyo District Public Prosecutor, *Opening Statement by the Prosecution in Trial of Takahashi, et al.*

35. U.S. Senate, *Staff Statement*, pp. 42–43.

36. Tokyo District Public Prosecutor, *Opening Statement by the Prosecution in Trial of Takahashi, et al.*

37. U.S. Senate, *Staff Statement*, pp. 78–85; U.S. Senate, *Hearings Before the Permanent Subcommittee*, pp. 145–147.

38. Ibid., pp. 5, 66–68.

39. Australian Federal Police, *The Australian Investigation of the Aum Shinrikyo Sect*, October 24, 1995, p. 7.

gence officials.[40] Yoshihiro Inoue, Aum's former "intelligence chief," reportedly testified in court in May 1997 that the cult bought blueprints for a sarin production plant from Oleg Lobov, who served as Secretary of the Russian Security Council in the Yeltsin government at the height of Aum's activities in that country. Inoue claimed that the sect paid Lobov about ¥10 million (about $100,000 at the time) for the plans. Lobov, who admits to contacts with the cult, has emphatically denied any illegal dealings.[41]

Although Aum succeeded in manufacturing chemical and biological agents, it encountered repeated problems in fashioning effective delivery systems. Early in the cult's chemical weapons program, the sect planned to disperse sarin by spraying it from helicopters. As part of this plan, two followers were sent to the United States to obtain helicopter pilot licenses. The cult also purchased a large Russian military helicopter and two drone aircraft, but was unable to keep them operational.[42]

Attempted CBW Attacks

Between 1990 and 1993, Aum attempted on at least nine occasions to spread biological agents covertly in or around Tokyo and at nearby U.S. military bases, with the aim of causing great chaos and loss of life. The cult leadership evidently believed that these incidents would wake up the general populace to the imminent dangers Asahara foresaw, lending credence to his predictions of impending doom. Aum's first reported use of a biological agent was an unsuccessful attempt to spread botulinum toxin in the Tokyo region in April 1990.

In the summer of 1993, Aum members made repeated attempts to cause casualties by releasing anthrax from a hermetically sealed room, equipped with a sprayer and fan, placed atop a cult-owned eight-story building in Tokyo. Although the agent was dispersed over a four-day period, the attack had no apparent effect. Analysts believe the problem may have been with the low virulence of the agent rather than the

---

40. Author's interview with National Police Agency official, September 14, 1995. See also "Aum Made Sarin, Using Russian Method: Police," *Daily Yomiuri*, April 23, 1995.

41. "Ex-Russian Official Denies Assisting Aum," Associated Press, May 9, 1997; and "Prosecutors Investigate Lobov's Links to Religious Sect," Interfax, May 24, 1997, in FBIS-SOV-97-144 (May 28, 1997). Lobov's ties to Aum are detailed in National Police Agency, *Briefing Paper on Aum*, p. 23.

42. National Police Agency, *White Paper on Police 1996*, p. 9; Tokyo District Public Prosecutor, *Opening Statement by the Prosecution in the Trial of Takahashi, et al.*

delivery system.[43] Another failed attempt in 1995 to disseminate a bio-logical agent, believed to be botulinum toxin, used attaché cases fitted with small tanks, vinyl tubing, vents, and motorized fans powered by dry batteries. No agent was released in this incident because the Aum opera-tive reportedly had moral qualms and failed to insert the agent into the cases. Even so, investigators have found evidence suggesting that Aum planned to mass-produce these dispersal devices.[44] No casualties were reported from any of the ten known biological attacks.

The Matsumoto Attack

Having failed at its repeated efforts to inflict mass casualties with biologi-cal agents, Aum focused its attention increasingly on chemical nerve agents. In late 1993, the cult staged what was apparently its first chemical attack, in which sarin was targeted against a rival religious leader.[45] Utilizing a sprayer and heating element attached to the back of a truck, the Aum team succeeded only in nearly killing one of its own members. The cult's first successful chemical attack occurred in June 1994 in Mat-sumoto, a small city in the Japanese Alps. The primary motivation behind this attack was to block a legal decision in a civil suit by local landowners claiming that Aum had fraudulently purchased land in the community. The trial had ended and a verdict was scheduled to be announced in mid-July 1994. Fearing that the decision would go against the cult, Aum leaders planned to murder the three judges who were about to rule on the case by dispersing sarin throughout the local court building. Japanese authorities also point to a second motive for the attack: by that time, Aum had produced 30 kilograms of sarin and its leaders were anxious to test the agent's lethality on a populated target.[46]

The Matsumoto attack was carried out by chief scientist Hideo Murai

---

43. Author's interview with a U.S. government official, Washington, D.C., March 5, 1998. See also "Asahara Fingered in Anthrax Attack," Kyodo dispatch in *Asahi Evening News*, July 27, 1995; "Cultists Admit They Released Anthrax in Tokyo's Streets," *Japan Times*, July 26, 1995; "Police: Cultists Admit to Spraying Anthrax," *Mainichi Daily News*, July 27, 1995; and "Sowing Death."

44. U.S. Senate, *Staff Statement*, pp. 43–44. See also "Aum Made Devices to Spray Bacterium," *Daily Yomiuri*, June 17, 1995; and "Case Found in Member's Car Contained Humidifiers, Fans," *Mainichi Daily News*, March 25, 1995.

45. The religious figure who was targeted was Daisaku Ikeda, the head of Soka Gakkai, the largest and most successful of Japan's "new religions." Asahara saw Ikeda as a rival.

46. U.S. Senate, *Staff Statement*, pp. 49–50.

and six other senior cultists. Aum technicians had developed a sarin-vaporizing device consisting of a heating element and an electric fan, which was fitted on the back of a remodeled refrigeration truck. Accompanied by a rented station wagon, the cultists drove the truck to Matsumoto but arrived late, prompting them to switch their target from the local courthouse to the judges' living quarters.

Positioned in a nearby parking lot, the team began spraying vaporized sarin at about 11:40 P.M. and continued for about ten minutes. The cloud of toxic gas killed seven people and injured 144, many of them seriously. Among the injured were all three judges the cult had targeted, forcing the decision on Aum's land fraud case to be postponed.[47]

The Tokyo Subway Attack

Aum's deadliest and most notorious attack was its March 1995 release of sarin on the Tokyo subway, which killed twelve people and injured more than a thousand. This incident was preceded by an earlier attack on the subway system that same month—an unsuccessful attempt to release botulinum toxin. Both attacks were carried out in an effort to stop an imminent police raid on Aum's major facilities. Cult leaders hoped to disrupt the raid by attacking the closest subway station and commuter lines leading to Tokyo Police Headquarters, which was overseeing the investigation into Aum. The cult also evidently believed that the planned police raid signaled the beginning of Armageddon and felt compelled to strike a major blow against the Japanese state. Aum's main target, the Kasumigaseki transfer station, is located in close proximity to the Tokyo Police Headquarters, the National Police Agency, the Ministry of Foreign Affairs, the Ministry of Finance, and other Japanese government agencies.[48]

A solution containing 600 grams of sarin was placed in each of eleven small nylon polyethylene bags, each of which was then sealed inside a second bag. Although the delivery system was relatively simple, planning for the subway attack was complex. The bags of sarin were distributed to five cultists, who boarded different trains on three major lines of the central Tokyo subway system, all converging toward Kasumigaseki. Five other cultists served as lookouts and drivers, while cult "Intelligence Minister" Inoue was field supervisor for the overall operation. Release of the agent was timed to coincide with the height of the Monday morning

---

47. National Police Agency, *Briefing Paper on Aum*, p. 9.

48. National Police Agency, *Briefing Paper on Aum*, pp. 7–8; National Police Agency, *White Paper on Police 1996*, p. 13.

rush hour. The trains were scheduled to arrive at Kasumigaseki within four minutes of each other, between 8:00 and 8:10 A.M.[49]

The cultists wrapped the bags of sarin in newspaper and, once on board, punctured them using umbrellas with sharpened tips. The punctured bags released puddles of diluted sarin, which evaporated and exposed commuters in the subway cars and others waiting on the station platforms to the toxic fumes. The five attackers escaped and later assembled at a hideout in Tokyo, where an Aum physician gave injections of nerve-gas antidote to those who complained of reactions to the agent.[50]

The subway attack caused considerable chaos and casualties. Eleven passengers and station personnel were killed, and a twelfth later died of injuries related to the attack. Prosecutors put the official number of injuries at 3,938, although this figure may be too high.[51] Japanese authorities told a U.S. government team that of the more than 5,000 victims examined in hospitals in the first 24 hours after the incident, 73.9 percent showed no evidence of actual exposure to a nerve agent and were considered "worried well."[52] Problems with the purity of the sarin used and Aum's crude method of dissemination prevented the number of casualties from being far greater.[53]

Following the subway attack, police staged raids on Aum facilities and seized the cult's weapon production sites. Aum responded with two more sets of attacks using chemical agents. On May 5, 1995, cult members attempted to release hydrogen cyanide in one of Japan's busiest train stations. They employed a relatively simple "binary" device consisting of one plastic bag filled with sodium cyanide and another bag filled with sulfuric acid, with an incendiary device and timer. The timer set the bags on fire with the intent that the two ingredients would mix and form lethal hydrogen cyanide gas.[54] On July 4, 1995, cultists placed similar devices

---

49. Ibid. [both references]; Tokyo District Public Prosecutor, *Opening Statement by the Prosecution in Trial of Tomomasa Nakagawa*, October 1995, reprinted as "Prosecution Details Aum's Sarin Attack on Tokyo Subways," *Japan Times*, October 25, 1995; U.S. Senate, *Staff Statement*, p. 51.

50. National Police Agency, *Briefing Paper on Aum*, p. 8.

51. National Police Agency, *White Paper on Police 1995*, p. 6; Japan Times, *Terror in the Heart of Japan* (Tokyo: Japan Times, 1995), p. 7; and "Japan to Speed up Murder Trials of Cult Guru," Kyodo News Service, December 2, 1997.

52. James W. Stokes, "Psychological Aspects of Chemical Defense and Warfare," *Military Psychology*, Vol. 9, No. 4 (1997), pp. 405–406.

53. U.S. Senate, *Staff Statement*, p. 52.

54. Ibid., pp. 56–57; National Police Agency, *White Paper on Police 1996*, p. 13. See also "Source of Parts for Cyanide Device Found," *Mainichi Daily News*, July 26, 1995.

containing cyanide in four different subway stations. None of these attacks was successful. The intent, however, was clear enough—to cause mass disruption and loss of life.[55] Aum's repeated attempts to employ biological and chemical weapons between April 1990 and July 1995 are summarized in Table 12.1.

Motivations

As noted earlier, the cult's primary motivation in developing weapons of mass destruction was to defend itself and emerge victorious from the coming apocalypse, but the actual attacks were motivated by a variety of secondary factors. Aum leaders apparently believed that they needed to stage mass-casualty attacks to instigate the war between the United States and Japan that Asahara had predicted. After attempting to release botulinum toxin and anthrax bacilli in Tokyo in 1993, the cult hoped to blame the ensuing disaster on the U.S. military, providing proof of Asahara's prophecy that the United States would attack Japan.[56]

This desire to instigate a war between the two countries may also explain the cult's desire to release sarin in U.S. cities. In June 1994, one month before the Matsumoto attack, Aum considered staging attacks against New York City and Washington, D.C. According to court testimony by top cultists, Aum leaders discussed how to smuggle into the United States as much as 21 tons of sarin, which would be hidden in sculptures made of ice or concrete and transported by ship. The cult reportedly abandoned this plan when they were unable to produce enough sarin.[57]

Assassination was another important motive. Aum hit squads attempted using nerve agents—sarin or VX—at least six times against

---

55. U.S. Senate, *Staff Statement*, pp. 56–57.

56. This assessment of the cult's motivations was based on confidential briefings provided to the author by law enforcement officials in Tokyo on November 2, 1995, and February 27, 1998. Further background on the attacks can be found in National Police Agency, *Briefing Paper on Aum*, p. 16; U.S. Senate, *Staff Statement*, pp. 35–36; "Cult Plotted Germ Attack on Tokyo in April 1990," *Mainichi Daily News*, October 28, 1995; "Cultists Admit to Spraying Anthrax," *Mainichi Daily News*, July 27, 1995; "Aum Sprayed Bacteria Near Palace, Police Say," *Japan Times*, October 23, 1995; and "Sowing Death."

57. Author's interview with a U.S. government official, Washington, D.C., March 5, 1998; U.S. Senate, *Staff Statement*, pp. 15–18. See also "Aum Planned Sarin Attacks in U.S. Cities, Cultist Says," *Japan Times*, March 22, 1997; and "Japanese Cult Said to Have Planned Nerve-Gas Attacks in U.S.," *New York Times*, March 23, 1997.

Table 12.1. Attempted Aum Attacks with Biological or Chemical Weapons.

Date	Place	Agent	Casualties	Target	Apparent Motive
April 1990	Central Tokyo	Botulinum toxin	None reported	Mass civilian	Proof of prophecy
April 1990	Yokohama	Botulinum toxin	None reported	U.S. Navy base	Proof of prophecy
April 1990	Yokohama	Botulinum toxin	None reported	U.S. Navy base	Proof of prophecy
April 1990	Narita	Botulinum toxin	None reported	Tokyo airport	Proof of prophecy
June 1993	Tokyo	Botulinum toxin	None reported	Mass civilian	Proof of prophecy
Late June 1993	Tokyo	Anthrax	None reported	Mass civilian	Proof of prophecy
July 1993	Tokyo	Anthrax	None reported	Mass civilian	Proof of prophecy
July 1993	Tokyo	Anthrax	None reported	Mass civilian	Proof of prophecy
July 1993	Tokyo	Anthrax	None reported	Mass civilian	Proof of prophecy
Mid-November 1993	Tokyo	Sarin	None reported	Religious group	Eliminate rival organization
Mid-December 1993	Tokyo	Sarin	One injured	Religious group	Eliminate rival organization
Late 1993 or early 1994	Yamanashi Prefecture	Sarin	One injured	Anti-Aum attorney	Eliminate enemy
June 27, 1994	Matsumoto	Sarin	Seven dead, 144 injured	Judges	Stop adverse court decision
December 2, 1994	Tokyo	VX	One injured	Senior citizen	Eliminate enemy
December 12, 1994	Osaka	VX	One dead	Office worker	Eliminate enemy
January 1995	Tokyo	VX	One injured	Anti-Aum activist	Eliminate enemy
March 1995	Tokyo subway	Botulinum toxin	None reported	Police/mass civilian	Stop police probe, cause havoc
March 20, 1995	Tokyo subway	Sarin	Twelve dead, over a thousand injured	Police/mass civilian	Stop police probe, cause havoc
May 5, 1995	Tokyo subway	Hydrogen cyanide	Four injured	Mass civilian	Cause havoc
July 4, 1995	Tokyo subway	Hydrogen cyanide	None reported	Mass civilian	Cause havoc

SOURCES: National Police Agency (Japan), *Briefing Paper on Aum*, *White Paper on Police 1995*, and *White Paper on Police 1996*; U.S. Senate Permanent Subcommittee on Investigations, *Staff Statement: Hearings on Global Proliferation of Weapons of Mass Destruction: A Case Study of Aum Shinrikyo*; interviews. All locations listed in table are in Japan; some dates are estimates.

individuals deemed enemies of the sect. Shortly after developing its first batches of sarin in late 1993, the cult twice tried using it to murder the leader of a rival religious sect.[58] Although those attempts failed, the cult was more successful in its attacks with VX, spraying the agent in the victim's face with a hypodermic syringe. One person was killed and two others injured. Among the targets were an anti-Aum attorney and an eighty-two-year-old man who harbored an Aum defector.[59] Press accounts also report that Aum tested biological agents on dissident members of the cult, some of whom disappeared while others complained of skin rashes or losing their voices.[60]

Contributing Factors

The level of paranoia and anxiety within the cult was undoubtedly a contributing factor to Aum's propensity for violence. By 1994, paranoia among Aum members had reached a dangerously high level. Cultists believed they were under sustained chemical attack by a "state power" or "powers," and that these attacks were proof that Asahara's prophecies were coming true. *Slaughtered Lambs*, an Aum videotape released that year, claimed the sect had been repeatedly attacked by poison gas since its founding in 1988. The video reported that some 240 aircraft, including U.S. and Japanese helicopters, propeller planes, and military jets, had sprayed sarin and mustard gas over Aum facilities, causing widespread sickness among Asahara's followers. "Aum survives these attacks because it is a mystical religion that goes beyond the boundaries of life and death," explained Asahara on the tape. He also claimed, however, that the attacks were killing him, saying, "I am suffering the effects of mustard gas. I am now facing death."[61] In January 1995, an Aum journal ran an enemies list that included the imperial family, prominent politicians, and rival religious figures in Japan. Additional targets of the cult's wrath were the United States, Jews, and Freemasons.[62] Asahara and other top cultists believed the situation was so dire that they

---

58. Tokyo District Public Prosecutor, *Opening Statement by the Prosecution in the Trial of Takahashi, et al.*

59. National Police Agency, *White Paper on Police 1996*, p. 12.

60. "Aum Used Members in Microorganism Tests, Police Allege," *Japan Times*, June 19, 1995; "AUM Tested Germs on Dissidents," *Mainichi Daily News*, June 20, 1995.

61. Aum Shinrikyo, *Slaughtered Lambs* [videotape], 1994.

62. Aum Shinrikyo, *Vajrayana Sacca* [journal], January 1995.

considered staging a coup d'état to seize control of the Japanese government.[63]

Another contributing factor to Aum's behavior was the degree of impunity that the cult enjoyed. Despite an extraordinary six-year crime spree, the sect met with surprisingly little resistance from Japanese officials, who were hampered by jurisdictional problems, a reluctance to probe religious organizations, and a lack of investigative initiative. Only after the Tokyo subway attack did authorities move quickly against the cult.[64] The official reluctance to investigate Aum probably encouraged an increasing pattern of illegal conduct by the cult to further its aims. Indeed, Aum compiled such a remarkable record of criminal acts during its short history that its leaders may have felt that they could get away with almost anything.[65] Indictments and reports by Japanese authorities depict a criminal enterprise that engaged in land fraud to expand its holdings, kidnapping for ransom, drug dealing for profit, and other crimes to increase the group's wealth and power. Murder was used to eliminate opponents and to obtain financial gain.[66]

In interviews, Japanese police argue that the cult presented an unusually difficult investigative target. Aum organizers were sophisticated, college-educated criminals who engaged in high-tech crimes, and the cult was a secretive organization, tightly controlled by a handful of leaders. Given their prewar history, Japanese police were reluctant to use undercover operations and electronic surveillance, particularly against a religious organization. Moreover, Aum operations spanned a half-dozen countries and, within Japan, its weapon production facilities were centered outside the nation's major urban areas, leaving the investigation to relatively inexperienced local police. Even when more specialized detectives

---

63. National Police Agency, *Briefing Paper on Aum*, pp. 3, 31; and *White Paper on Police 1996*, p. 4.

64. Author's interview with National Police Agency official, Tokyo, January 30, 1998; National Police Agency, *White Paper on Police 1996*, pp. 21–23; and U.S. Senate, *Staff Statement*, p. 46.

65. Japanese authorities have accused the cult of the following crimes dating back to 1989: narcotics manufacture and sales, arms smuggling, firearms violations, medical fraud and malpractice, child abuse, forgery, copyright infringement, consumer fraud, land fraud, obstruction of justice, perjury, harboring fugitives, intimidation, extortion, burglary, assault, kidnapping, attempted murder, and murder. National Police Agency, *Briefing Paper on Aum*, pp. 27–28. See also "More Than 200 Cult Followers Arrested in Crackdown," *Japan Times*, May 17, 1995.

66. National Police Agency, *Briefing Paper on Aum*, p. 20; and *White Paper on Police 1996*, pp. 6–11.

were drawn into the case, none had any background in investigating terrorist cases involving weapons of mass destruction.[67]

It is worth noting that Japanese officials were not the only ones that failed to recognize the danger posed by Aum Shinrikyo. Despite the cult's virulent anti-Americanism and international procurement efforts, U.S. intelligence agencies also failed to recognize the threat at hand. As one counterintelligence official told U.S. Senate investigators, "They simply were not on anybody's radar screen."[68]

The State Responds

Japanese authorities began to take the cult seriously as a public threat in late 1994. Several weeks after the Matsumoto attack in June of that year, a toxic gas was released near Aum headquarters, prompting officials to take soil samples from around the cult's main compound. It was not until November, however, that government chemists detected a sarin residue in the samples. This finding, combined with evidence from other Aum crimes, finally gave the police "probable cause" to raid cult facilities. Before the raid could occur, however, Aum struck first with the sarin attack on the Tokyo subway.

Two days after the subway attack, on March 22, 1995, an unprecedented force of 2,500 police officers raided twenty-five facilities tied to Aum in three prefectures. Cult chemicals, laboratory equipment, and other evidence were seized. Police maintained the pressure, ultimately staging more than 500 raids on some 300 locations used by the cult. Authorities also ran a massive manhunt for fugitive cult members. Police distributed 1.6 million wanted posters and handbills, and set up checkpoints and patrols of public areas such as train stations and shopping centers. To help guard against Aum reprisal attacks, vending machines and trash cans were removed from train stations and underground malls.[69]

Police made massive arrests, detaining more than 400 Aum members for charges as minor as running red lights and operating an unlicensed

67. Author's interviews with National Police Agency officials, Tokyo, September 14, 1995 and January 30, 1998. See also National Police Agency, *White Paper on Police 1996*, pp. 21–24.

68. Author's interview with an FBI official, Washington, D.C., September 9, 1997; U.S. Senate, Hearings, pp. 273–276 and 279–280. The counterintelligence official's quote is from U.S. Senate, *Staff Statement*, p. 91.

69. National Police Agency, *Briefing Paper on Aum*, p. 5; *White Paper on Police 1996*, pp. 17–19.

massage parlor. Ultimately, criminal indictments were issued to 192 cultists for more serious crimes, including murder charges against forty-one members. Those being prosecuted include the entire hierarchy of the sect. Aum leader Asahara faces seventeen indictments, including twenty-five counts of murder.[70] Officials have also taken action against the sect itself. In October 1995, Aum Shinrikyo was stripped of its religious status. The cult's assets were later frozen and the group was declared bankrupt. Aum's assets were sold off, and the proceeds are being used to compensate its victims.[71]

The subway attack sparked investigations not only by Japanese authorities, but also by those in Australia, Germany, Russia, and the United States. In Russia, the cult was outlawed, and its top leaders were arrested. In the United States, national security wiretaps were authorized, and the cult's New York office was searched. Independent investigations of Aum activities were also conducted by the U.S. Senate and the Russian State Duma.

Aum Today: A Revival

Concern remains among analysts in both Japan and the United States that Aum continues to pose a serious terrorist threat. Japanese security agencies warn that the sect is regrouping and that current cult members have shown no repentance or remorse for their past behavior. Indeed, recent Aum preachings call for strict adherence to Asahara's word and still feature a doctrine that rationalizes killing. According to a January 1998 report by Japan's Public Security Investigation Agency, "There is no essential change in the nature of the cult, and its 'exclusive' and 'unsocial' character may further be increased."[72]

An attempt by Japanese authorities to ban Aum under a controversial, rarely used anti-subversive law failed in January 1997, and police say the cult has seized on this decision as a pretext to reorganize. Despite having lost its previous facilities, in 1997 Aum expanded from six branches to sixteen nationwide.[73] The cult has renewed its recruiting, training, and business activities. Cultists are disseminating videos, using encrypted e-mail, and operating web pages in Japanese, English, and Russian. New sources of funds are being generated from publishing and

---

70. "End to Aum Trials Still Long Way Off," *Asahi Evening News,* January 3, 1998.

71. National Police Agency, *White Paper on Police 1996,* pp. 19–22.

72. Public Security Investigation Agency, *Public Security in Japan,* January 1998, pp. 8, 12.

73. Ibid., pp. 7–8.

retail sales of computers and spiritual goods. A sign of the cult's continued strength came from its training seminars in 1998, which attracted at least 7,000 people. Aum has also worked successfully to draw back into the cult nearly a third of those arrested by authorities. Officials say the sect has targeted senior members and those with technical skills, pressuring them with warnings that "Armageddon is near."[74]

Overseas, the sect may also remain a threat. Despite being banned in Russia, Aum reportedly maintains groups of followers in that country, and Aum literature continues to circulate in Moscow. The sect is also reported active in Ukraine, Belarus, and Kazakhstan.[75] In March 1998, on the third anniversary of the Tokyo subway attack, a self-described Aum member phoned a top Russian daily newspaper, threatening to spread nerve gas through the Moscow subway system. Police are unsure whether the caller was legitimate, but they are taking seriously the possible threat posed by Aum.[76]

Although Aum is unlikely to acquire large amounts of chemical or biological weapons again, its followers have shown a worrisome ability to improvise and strike highly vulnerable targets. Moreover, it is known that Aum members hid stockpiles of various chemical agents, and police are unsure that all of them have been recovered.[77] Possible motivations for a future attack appear varied. Fears of Armageddon sparked by natural or man-made disasters, or a new crackdown on the sect by Japanese authorities, might be enough to trigger a new attack. A key factor will probably be the fate of Shoko Asahara. Should he be found guilty of murder, Aum's guru could face a sentence of death by hanging. Such a fate could make him a martyr among the Aum faithful and might again prompt violent reprisals against society. Even after the belated crackdown by Japanese authorities, the cult's continued potential for violence is troubling. Aum Shinrikyo remains a viable entity with financial resources, technical ability, and an apocalyptic ideology that still rationalizes mass murder.

---

74. Ibid., pp. 7–9.

75. "Russia Stops Aum Shinrikyo Case, Sect Still Acts," Itar-Tass, March 20, 1998.

76. "Moscow Metro Police Promise Alert on March 20," Itar-Tass, March 17, 1998; "Self-Proclaimed AUM Member Warns of Nerve-Gas Attacks," Kyodo News Service, March 17, 1998.

77. Author's interviews with National Police Agency officials, Tokyo, January 30, 1998. Among the substances recovered were VX and precursors for sarin and hydrogen cyanide. See National Police Agency, White Paper on Police 1996, p. 17; and "Japan Police Find Bottle of Cult's Deadly VX Gas," Reuters World Report, December 12, 1996.

Chapter 13

Larry Wayne Harris (1998)

Jessica Eve Stern

On February 18, 1998, federal agents arrested Larry Wayne Harris, an anti-government Christian Patriot, for violating Section 175, Title 18 of the United States Code, which prohibits the possession of a biological agent for use as a weapon. Harris had boasted to an informant that he had enough "military grade anthrax" to "wipe out" all of Las Vegas.[1] Eight flight bags marked "biological" had been found in the back of a car he and his accomplice were driving. Several days later, federal authorities learned that the "anthrax" Harris had brought to Las Vegas was a harmless vaccine strain.

Despite the false alarm, the U.S. government considers Larry Harris a dangerous man. A former neo-Nazi sympathizer, he is a trained microbiologist who earlier was caught with three vials of the bacterium that causes bubonic plague, the disease that killed nearly a quarter of Europe's population in the mid-fourteenth century. Harris has also published information that could be used by others to kill, including detailed instructions on how to obtain anthrax and disseminate it. Yet Harris claims that he is merely helping ordinary American citizens to defend themselves against a biological attack from a "rogue" state such as Iraq. Does Larry Harris fit the profile of a bioterrorist or is he merely a harmless eccentric?

The author would like to thank Darcy Bender and Melinda Lamont-Havers for extraordinary research assistance.

---

1. One informant stated that Harris had said he had "military-grade anthrax." Another claimed that Harris had referred to a vaccine or a placebo. Proceedings before the Regular Federal Grand Jury, Testimony of Robert James, February 25, 1998, United States District Court for the District of Nevada, Las Vegas, p. 17; *United States of America v Larry Wayne Harris*, Complete Transcript of Proceedings, CR-2-95-093, March 6, 1998, United States District Court for the Southern District of Ohio, p. 35.

Harris's Interest in Biological Warfare

Larry Harris is convinced that the U.S. government is deceiving the American people by not fully disclosing the danger of biological terrorism. He believes such attacks are imminent and that the government is unprepared. He is particularly concerned about inadequate stockpiles of antibiotics and vaccines. Before his arrest in February 1998, Harris was conducting independent research on biological defenses out of his home in Lancaster, Ohio. His research required biological pathogens, which he says he obtained easily from various sources. Harris's 1995 purchase of *Yersinia pestis,* the bacterium that causes plague, was the start of his troubles with the U.S. government.

Harris ordered *Yersinia pestis* from the American Type Culture Collection (ATCC), an organization that supplies microbial cultures to biomedical researchers around the world and that legally sold anthrax and other biological pathogens to Iraq in the mid- to late 1980s. No law prohibited Harris or anyone else from acquiring the agent, but he misrepresented himself in his purchase order and was later convicted of mail fraud. Although the U.S. government promulgated new regulations on transfers of microbial pathogens and toxins in 1997 largely in response to the Harris case, the regulations do not cover biological agents isolated from nature or individuals who are conducting research with biological agents they already possess. Harris emphasized in an interview that the regulations will not preclude amateur scientists, foreign powers, or terrorists from acquiring biological weapons. "The only thing the law has toughened up is the shipping requirements," he explained.[2] "You know this little run-in I had with the police [referring to his 1995 arrest]? That was just an irritation for me. I've continued my research. And I contracted with another [Biosafety] Level 3 lab to do the experiments for me on *Yersinia.*"

Harris claims that he has isolated plague bacteria from cow droppings. (In fact, cow droppings are not considered a likely source for plague bacteria.) He also says that he has isolated anthrax, brucellosis, tularemia, and cholera microorganisms from natural sources. "You know how long it took me to isolate anthrax from [soil]?" he boasted. "Ten days. It took me fourteen days to recover bubonic plague." When asked whether he was concerned about his health, Harris replied, "It's like working with Dobermans. They're not dangerous if you know what they

---

2. Author's telephone interview with Larry Wayne Harris, January 23, 1998. All Harris quotes that follow are from this interview.

are and how to deal with them. This stuff isn't dangerous if you take appropriate measures."

A former colleague of Harris's who is a molecular biologist expressed doubt about his claim to have isolated deadly pathogens. He said that Harris "loves to talk" and tends to brag. The colleague was convinced, however, that senior members of the neo-Nazi organizations with which Harris was associated have obtained biological agents, and he attributed Harris's interest in bioterrorism to his association with them.[3] Others fear that Harris may have given the right-wing movement dangerous ideas.[4]

Despite Harris's claims to the contrary, the U.S. government has been concerned about America's vulnerability to biological terrorism for a long time. The U.S. Army conducted a test in the New York subway in 1966 in which technicians surreptitiously dropped light bulbs filled with harmless simulant bacteria through ventilating grates or onto the trackbeds as trains entered or departed a station. The bulbs broke and released the simulant bacteria, which were spread by air movements through the subway tunnels. Army scientists concluded that if pathogenic agents were disseminated in several subway lines during rush hour, a large portion of the working population in downtown New York City would be exposed to the disease.[5]

According to federal prosecutors, Harris told an unidentified source that he was planning an attack on the New York subway with bubonic plague, using the same technique that the Army had employed in the 1960s to disseminate the simulant bacteria. Harris reportedly predicted that hundreds of thousands of people would die and that the government of Iraq would be blamed.[6] Harris is also familiar with other dissemination techniques, although he has not threatened to employ them personally. "You can spread this stuff with a commercial paint sprayer," he said in an interview. "You can use Venturi mounts outside older aircraft. Within forty-eight hours, over 100,000 [people] would be dead. If you have one

3. Author's interview with a former colleague of Harris's who asked not to be identified, August 11, 1998.

4. Author's interviews with public health officials involved in the 1995 case, July 29, 1998.

5. Leonard A. Cole, *Clouds of Secrecy: The Army's Germ Warfare Tests Over Populated Areas* (Totowa, N.J.: Rowman & Littlefield, 1988), p. 68; *U.S. Army Activities in the United States Biological Warfare Programs 1942–1977* (Washington: Department of the Army, 1977), Vol. I, pp. 6–3; Vol. II, p. IV-E-1-1.

6. *United States of America v Larry Wayne Harris*, William Job Leavitt, Jr., Criminal Complaint, Case No. MAG-98-2042-M-RLH, February 19, 1998, United States District Court for the District of Nevada, p. 3.

tenth of a millionth of a gram, that's enough to kill a person." Harris testified at a friend's trial that he ran "military models" of this dissemination technique. "There is [sic] no . . . symptoms till after about forty-nine hours. At that point in time, once you start showing the symptoms, you are dead. There's absolutely nothing we can do for you," he warned.[7] A relatively small biological attack, Harris believes, would make Americans more aware of the dangers they face.

Harris's Story

Harris says that he first became interested in biological warfare (BW) defense when he enlisted in the Army. He claims that he was stationed in a microbiology laboratory at Aberdeen Proving Ground, a test facility where chemical weapons were developed and stored. Harris's military record indicates that he was briefly stationed at Aberdeen for two months in 1970, where he was trained to repair trucks and tanks at the U.S. Army Ordnance Center and School. He spent the rest of his military career as a wheeled vehicle mechanic.[8] After he left the Army, he studied at Ohio State University in the early 1970s.[9] During college, Harris purportedly worked on BW defenses at the Battelle Institute, which he claims was located across the street from Ohio State. In fact, Battelle does have an office near the university but reports that Harris never worked there, although he applied for a job in January 1996.[10]

7. Author's telephone interview with Harris; Testimony of Larry Wayne Harris, *State of Ohio v Stephen Michael Wharf*, Case No. 96CR17145, August 5, 1997, State of Ohio, Warren County, Court of Common Pleas, p. 14.

8. Ibid., pp. 4–5. Unless otherwise noted, all material in this section on Harris's background is from a videotape titled *Bacteriological Warfare: A Major Threat to North America, What You and Your Family Can Do Before and After. Larry Wayne Harris, Registered Microbiologist*, distributed by Virtue International Publishing in 1997. In 1971, Aberdeen Proving Ground incorporated Edgewood Arsenal, which researched, produced, and stored chemical munitions. Larry W. Harris, Record of Assignments, U.S. Army, National Personnel Records Center; interview, Aberdeen Public Affairs officer, September 3, 1998; and interview with Ed Starrs, Aberdeen Public Affairs, October 23, 1998. The Technical Escort Unit (TEU) at Aberdeen deals with chemical and biological defenses and explosive ordnance disposal, but Harris's record indicates that he never worked there.

9. Ohio State University (OSU) keeps records of students' enrollment periods. Harris first enrolled at OSU in September 1972, and he received an Associate Degree in Biophysics in 1985. Interview with OSU Verification Office, June 19, 1998.

10. Telephone interview with Judy Meadows, personnel officer at Battelle Institute, June 19, 1998.

Harris says that in 1984 he was recruited by "the Company," slang for the Central Intelligence Agency (CIA). He claims to have worked at a "small reference lab" where the CIA trained Iraqi microbiologists in BW defense. While working at the lab, Harris says, he became friendly with one of his trainees, a woman named Mariam Arif who was a member of a prominent Iraqi family.[11] Several years later, Mariam and the other Iraqi microbiologists were purportedly fired from the CIA lab because they were considered security risks. A CIA spokesperson stated that the agency has no record of any contact with anyone by the name of Larry Harris and would not comment on its alleged involvement in training Iraqi nationals or in "reference labs" of any kind.[12]

Harris testified at a friend's trial that he had worked at many laboratories owned by secret organizations whose identity he was "not permitted to divulge." He also asserted that he had trained U.S. government officials in BW defense at Dugway Proving Ground in Utah; the Casualty and Management Team at the Pentagon; the Army's Biological Defense Research Program at Fort Detrick, Maryland; and the Michigan Biological Institute in East Lansing.[13] A Pentagon spokesperson said that she had never heard of a Department of Defense entity called the "Casualty and Management Team."[14] Moreover, although Harris named a scientist who had worked at Fort Detrick from the late 1960s until 1996, this individual

---

11. Colonel Abdul Salam Arif was involved in a military coup that ended the Hashimite monarchy in Iraq in 1958. In February 1963 he became president of Iraq, and in 1966 he was killed in a helicopter crash. His brother, General Abdul Rahman Arif, succeeded him. The Ba'athists overthrew General Arif in a July 1968 coup. (http://www.achilles.net/~sal/iraq_history.html)

12. Soon after this incident (in late 1991), Harris claims that he came to work and discovered that the small reference lab that had employed him for several years had ceased to exist. His employer handed him his personal effects in a little black bag. Fortunately, he said, he had been in the habit of throwing his (presumably classified) laboratory notes into the bottom of his closet, so he still had access to them. The CIA Public Affairs Office refused to comment on Harris's claim to have worked there or on his allegation that the agency was involved in training Iraqi nationals in biological warfare defense. The CIA wrote a letter to the District Court in Ohio, however, claiming to have no record of anyone named Larry Wayne Harris with his social security number and birth date. *United States of America v Larry Wayne Harris*, Complete Transcript of Proceedings, CR-2-95-093, March 6, 1998, pp. 29–30.

13. Testimony of Larry Wayne Harris, *State of Ohio v Stephen Michael Wharf*. An inquiry into Harris's possible employment with the U.S. government was returned with the statement that "a search of our records did not reveal a record of the claimed Federal employment." Response Letter, National Archives and Record Administration, October 20, 1998.

14. Telephone interview with a Pentagon spokesperson, August 12, 1998.

claimed that neither she nor any of her colleagues remembered having met Harris or hearing of his involvement in any Fort Detrick projects.[15]

In September 1991, Harris re-matriculated at Ohio State to take classes in preparation for an examination to become a registered microbiologist. Harris says that he encountered Mariam Arif at the university, where she was also studying microbiology. Ohio State has no record of any student named Mariam Arif, although the verification office explained that if a student changes her name after graduating, they keep a record only of the new name.[16]

In February 1993, Harris says, Mariam disclosed to him a shocking secret: Libya, Iran, Iraq, Syria, and North Korea were actively pursuing biological weapons. Nuclear weapons were too expensive, she explained, and biological weapons affect only people and not infrastructure, making them more useful for attacking the United States.[17] For several years, Mariam purportedly told Larry, the government of Iraq had sent small groups of Iraqi women to smuggle lethal biological agents into the United States. These women had already carried hundreds of vials of freeze-dried cultures into the country, concealing the vials in their private parts until they passed through customs.[18] When the time was ripe, Iraqi agents would reconstitute the microorganisms, grow them in large quantities, and disseminate them. Mariam warned Larry about the plot because she wanted him to be prepared. She purportedly told Harris that she knew that her secret was safe with him because no one would ever believe it.

A few days later, Harris called the CIA, the U.S. Centers for Disease Control and Prevention (CDC), and the Federal Bureau of Investigation (FBI) to inform them of Iraq's purported plans. Just as Mariam had allegedly foretold, no one at any government agency believed him. Harris says that a CDC employee told him that if he was so concerned, he should develop his own civil-defense manual, which he then set out to do.

Since then, it has been Harris's self-appointed mission to warn Americans about Iraq's nefarious plans and to teach citizens how to protect themselves in the event of a biological attack. He has made numerous audio and video tapes providing detailed instructions about how to prepare a simple antibiotic with colloidal silver and how to acquire large quantities of antibiotics used to treat livestock. Harris be-

---

15. Telephone interview with a U.S. government scientist, June 19, 1998.

16. Telephone interview with OSU Verification Office, June 19, 1998.

17. Larry Wayne Harris, *Bacteriological Warfare: A Major Threat to North America* (Indianapolis, Ind.: Virtue International Publishing, 1995), p. i.

18. *United States of America v Larry Wayne Harris,* Complete Transcript of Proceedings, Case No. CR-2-95-093, March 6, 1998, pp. 26–27.

lieves that people should start taking antibiotics now to prepare for imminent BW attacks. "We personally armed Saddam Hussein with enough anthrax, cholera and typhoid and plague to kill everybody in the world ten times over," Harris explains, in reference to Iraq's having purchased biological pathogens in the United States.[19] "Unfortunately, we thought the Arabs were stupid people. We had derogatory remarks we made about them. We called them towel heads and stuff of this nature. We failed to realize these people are extremely brilliant."[20]

Harris's 1995 Arrest

From November 1994 until May 1995, Larry Harris was employed by Superior Laboratories in Columbus, Ohio. His job was to test drinking water samples and to inspect septic systems. A colleague described Harris as a "very good worker" who doubled the property inspection business for the firm during the short period he was employed. At the same time, however, the colleague was troubled by Harris's racist beliefs. Harris admitted that he was on the governing board of the National Alliance, a neo-Nazi organization run by William Pierce, author of *The Turner Diaries*, the book that inspired the Oklahoma City bombing. The colleague attributed Harris's desire to acquire biological agents to his belief in the imminence of Armageddon and the need to stockpile weapons in order to survive.[21] Another Superior Laboratory employee told a reporter that Harris did good work but had "kooky ideas."[22]

In February 1995, Harris told several colleagues that he wanted to order some *Yersinia pestis* to carry out defensive research. He asked the laboratory to order the bacteria for him but his request was refused, in part because Superior had no facility equipped to handle the bacteria. Accordingly, Harris decided to order the agent on his own. On May 3, 1995, he telephoned ATCC (then based in Rockville, Maryland) to set up an account. An ATCC employee told Harris that he had to run an established laboratory to set up an account and demanded a copy of Harris's official letterhead as proof that the lab existed.[23]

---

19. Testimony of Larry Wayne Harris, *State of Ohio v Stephen Michael Wharf*, p. 13.

20. Ibid., p. 14.

21. Author's telephone interview with a Superior Laboratories employee, August 11, 1998.

22. Ann Fisher and Jill Riepenhoff, "Harris Described as Good Worker with 'Kooky Ideas,'" *Columbus Dispatch*, February 21, 1998.

23. *United States of America v Larry Wayne Harris*, Change of Plea and Sentencing, CR-2-95-93, April 22, 1998, p. 7.

Harris solved this problem by going to a local printing shop and ordering stationary with the letterhead "Small Animal Microbiology Laboratory, 266 Cleveland Avenue, Lancaster, Ohio" and "Ohio Environmental Protection Agency (EPA) approval number 890." The location was actually Harris's home address and the EPA number was the one assigned to Superior Laboratories.[24] Harris later told the police that he did not have a laboratory at his home at the time, although he intended to build one.[25] On May 4, 1995, Harris faxed ATCC a copy of his letterhead, a letter asking to set up an account, and a form on which he indicated that he had the necessary training to handle Class 3 cultures. These letters were enough to satisfy ATCC's requirements, and an account was set up in the name of Harris's imaginary company.[26]

On May 5, 1995, Harris phoned ATCC and ordered three vials of *Yersinia pestis*. On May 9, the vials were shipped. On May 10, Harris grew impatient and called ATCC to inquire why the cultures had not yet arrived. He explained to the technician that he needed the bacteria for research on rats to develop an over-the-counter antidote for bubonic plague. He also said that he was under contract with the State of California. Something about his manner made the technician suspect that Harris might not be able to handle the *Yersinia pestis* safely.[27] Since the vials of bacteria were already en route, the ATCC technician notified the CDC, which in turn contacted Harris by phone. Harris told the CDC that he was conducting biomedical research using rats to counteract an "imminent invasion from Iraq of supergerm-carrying rats."[28] He admitted that

24. *United States of America v Larry Wayne Harris*, Grand Jury charges, CR-2-95-93, p. 2.

25. Harris contradicted himself several times about whether he had a laboratory in his home or just intended to build one. When asked whether he had a home laboratory during his hearing, Harris said, "I have, by all practical purposes, a very fine laboratory, very well equipped laboratory, even backup microscopes, backup equipment, and do extensive research." Earlier he had said, however, "I've been wanting to accumulate enough laboratory equipment so that I can build my own laboratory." *United States of America v Larry Wayne Harris*, Opinion and Order, CR-2-95-93, p. 7.

26. *United States of America v Larry Wayne Harris*, Change of Plea and Sentencing, CR-2-95-93, p. 9.

27. Ibid., p. 10. Raymond Cypess, President and CEO of American Type Culture Collection (ATCC), wrote a letter to Lamont-Havers declining her interview request. He explained that ATCC was being sued in connection with the Gulf War syndrome, and that although the suit was "frivolous," ATCC was reluctant to allow interviews of any of its staff. Letter from Raymond H. Cypess to Melinda Lamont-Havers, July 9, 1998.

28. *State of Ohio v Larry Wayne Harris*, Affidavit for Search Warrant, Exhibit A in *United*

his laboratory was in his home and that he was writing a survivalist manual that would describe his research.[29]

The CDC contacted Forrest Smith of the Ohio Department of Health. At approximately 4:15 P.M. on May 11, 1995, Smith telephoned Edward Sachs of the Lancaster Health Department to inform him that a resident of Lancaster had ordered and received three vials of bubonic plague bacteria. Smith also informed Sachs that Harris was "not qualified to possess the bacteria," which had been sent to his home address in a residential neighborhood.[30] An hour later, Sachs phoned Captain Lutz of the Lancaster Police Department to discuss measures that might be taken to minimize risks to the neighborhood. They decided to try to remove the bacteria from Harris's possession, and that evening Lutz obtained a warrant to search Harris's home.[31]

Public health officials involved in the case claim that it made them realize how poorly prepared they were for a bioterrorist incident. The Lancaster Fire Department had no equipment for dealing with hazardous materials, so the Columbus Fire Department had to be called in. Yet the firefighters were trained to deal only with industrial hazards, not terrorist incidents.[32] Biological terrorism seemed so improbable at the time that one public health official had difficulty persuading a colleague that his call reporting the incident was not a joke.[33]

The *Yersinia pestis* shipped to Harris's home was freeze-dried, meaning that it was not immediately dangerous. But health officials estimated that it could be reconstituted in about a day. The police sent to search Harris's home also feared that he might spray them with some kind of poison. "We were . . . extremely concerned for our own physical well being," a Lancaster police officer recalled. "[We] were advised . . . that if Mr. Harris wanted, he could have some sort of a spray container where he could actually spray a plague type of material on us, and if he did do that, that they would have to immediately

States of America v Larry Wayne Harris, Motion to Dismiss/Suppress Evidence, CR-2-95-93.

29. *United States of America v Larry Wayne Harris,* Suppression Hearings, CR-2-95-93, April 1, 1997, pp. 7–8; *United States of America v Larry Wayne Harris,* Change of Plea and Sentencing, p. 10.

30. *United States of America v Larry Wayne Harris,* Opinion and Order, CR-2-95-93, p. 2.

31. Ibid.

32. Author's interviews with Ohio public health officials who asked not to be identified, July 29, 1998.

33. Ibid.

douse us with chlorine bleach and basically burn the top layer of skin off."[34]

A large team set out to search Harris's home, equipped with a truck full of equipment including protective masks and suits. Most of the team set up a block away. Because they did not want to alarm Harris, the police decided that only two of them would approach him and that they would wear ordinary uniforms without protective gear. The two officers would lure Harris out of the house and "take physical control of him" while officials from the Health Department, wearing protective gear, would attempt to seize the cultures.

At 1:42 A.M. on May 12, 1995, two officers knocked on Harris' door, waking him from a deep sleep. "I had taken . . . probably around seven or eight Excedrin PM's because I have some insomnia," Harris recalled. "The dog started barking. There was a ruckus. I thought someone was trying to break into the house."[35] The police told Harris that his car had been involved in a hit-and-run accident and asked him to come outside and look at the vehicle to make sure there had been no damage. Once Harris was outside, the officers handcuffed him. Harris quickly realized that they were after his vials of *Yersinia pestis* and told them the location without being asked. Officer Lutz recalled that Harris volunteered, "You don't have to do this if it's about the *pestis*. . . . The *Yersinia pestis*, it's in the car, it's in the glove box of the car."[36]

Harris's recollection is somewhat different. "I was handcuffed then and they were screaming at me, where's the germs? Where's the germs? Where's the germs? I was kind of stunned, I really didn't know what to say. . . . The yard was full of police . . . and they were literally storming in the house like a gang of stormtroopers."[37]

With some difficulty, the two police officers managed to remove Harris's car keys from his pocket. A third officer from the Hazardous Materials (HAZMAT) team, wearing full protective gear, retrieved the three vials from Harris's white Subaru. Harris realized that the police were afraid, and he told them repeatedly that the vials were safe to handle. In fact, Harris kept up an incessant banter. "Mr. Harris was told by Lieutenant Regan to please be quiet so that he could finish reading

---

34. *United States of America v Larry Wayne Harris*, Suppression Hearings, CR-2-95-93, April 1, 1997, p. 27.

35. Ibid., p. 72.

36. Ibid., p. 30.

37. Ibid., pp. 73–74.

him his rights," Officer Lutz testified. "Mr. Harris continued to talk nonstop, it seemed, during the entire time. He gave me the impression that he really wanted to tell us the story about the *pestis*. He continued to talk and talk and talk even after [we repeated] the warnings to be quiet so that he could be read his Miranda rights. . . . Lieutenant Regan did manage to get the rights in, and then he just continued to talk pretty much nonstop for several minutes."[38]

The police transported Harris to the Lancaster Police Department, where they interviewed him for an additional two hours. Harris displayed no concern about the need to secure a lawyer before his interview with the police.[39] Nor did he seem inhibited by the knowledge that he was being taped, with the tape recorder in full view. "In fact, it was quite the opposite," Lutz testified. "He wanted to talk nonstop."[40] After the interview, Harris was released.

While the police were inspecting Harris's home, they found weapons and explosives in addition to the plague bacteria. They also found a certificate stating that Harris was a lieutenant in the neo-Nazi organization Aryan Nations, based in Hayden Lake, Idaho. The group's leader, Richard Butler, initially denied that Harris belonged to his organization but later admitted that Harris had been a member from the early 1990s until 1995.[41] The Lancaster Police Department requested a second search warrant as well as an arrest warrant. They received both. In part because of Harris's apparent affiliation with the Aryan Nations, the case was considered a possible act of domestic terrorism. The police returned to Harris's house that afternoon, this time together with the FBI.[42]

The Lancaster police arrested Harris and took him into custody. An FBI agent came to the station to interview him. "I was thinking I was going to have to maybe explain a little more to get him to talk to us," FBI Special Supervisory Agent David Wilson recalled. But Harris was eager to talk. "During the entire time we talked, there was no reluctance on his

---

38. Ibid., pp. 32–33.

39. The police testified that Harris seemed nonchalant and at ease, but Harris testified that he tried "desperately" to get an attorney as soon as he was released. *United States of America v Larry Wayne Harris*, Suppression Hearings, CR-2-95-93, April 1, 1997, p. 78.

40. Ibid., p. 34.

41. A national organizer for the Aryan Nations, Tim Bishop, reportedly told an Ohio newspaper that Harris joined the Aryan Nations in 1994. Larry Henry, "Harris' Troubled Past Includes Mail Fraud, White Supremacy," *Las Vegas Sun*, February 20, 1998 (http://www.lasvegassun.com/dossier/crime/bio/harris.html).

42. *United States of America v Larry Wayne Harris*, Suppression Hearings, CR-2-95-93, April 1, 1997, p. 64.

part to talk to me. As a matter of fact, a lot of times I would have to try to stop him so I could direct questions that I wanted to ask. . . . He was providing a lot of information very willingly."[43]

On April 22, 1997, Harris pled guilty to one count of wire fraud. The maximum penalty was six months incarceration and a $25,000 fine.[44] But Judge Joseph Kinneary was lenient. He placed Harris on probation for eighteen months, ordered him to complete 200 hours of community service during the first twelve months of his probation, and assessed a $50 fee.[45] The judge told Harris that if he completed his community service in the first twelve months of his probationary period, the court might cancel the next six months of probation.[46] In addition, Harris was ordered not to misrepresent his credentials in any forum or publication and, in particular, not to claim an association with the CIA. He was also prohibited from "conducting any experiments with or obtaining any infectious diseases, bacteria, or germs, except at approved laboratories in conjunction with verified employment."[47]

After Harris's 1995 arrest, the CDC tightened up requirements for shipping twenty-four infectious agents and twelve toxins that pose a significant risk to human health, including the bacteria that cause anthrax, bubonic plague, tularemia, and brucellosis. Shippers and receivers of these infectious agents must now register with the CDC. Ironically, Harris was directly responsible for this improvement in the law.

Harris's 1998 Arrest

Larry Harris was "in many ways a model probationer," according to the District Court. He paid his $50 fine promptly, performed his 200 hours of community service within the first year, and always sought his probation officer's permission before traveling outside the state.[48] In February 1998, Harris asked permission to take a trip to Las Vegas, where he wanted to

---

43. Ibid., pp. 66–68.

44. *United States of America v Larry Wayne Harris*, Change of Plea and Sentencing, CR-2-95-93, April 22, 1997.

45. Legally, the $50.00 is not considered a fine but an assessment.

46. *United States of America v Larry Wayne Harris*, Change of Plea and Sentencing, CR-2-95-93, April 22, 1997, p. 19.

47. *United States of America v Larry Wayne Harris*, Judgment in a Criminal Case, CR-2-95-93, p. 2.

48. *United States of America v Larry Wayne Harris*, Defendant's Admission of Facts Relevant to Revocation Proceedings, CR-2-95-93, March 23, 1998, pp. 4–5.

promote his book and a video.[49] He told his probation officer, Rick Lenhart, that he would be staying at the Sam's Town Hotel and Gambling Hall in Las Vegas.[50]

The other reason Harris wanted to go to Las Vegas was that he had been hired to test a bizarre device to kill microorganisms that a friend, William Job Leavitt, Jr., was considering purchasing from a self-employed engineer named Ronald Rockwell. Leavitt was a successful manufacturer of fire extinguishers who lived in Logandale, Nevada, a small farming community fifty miles northeast of Las Vegas.[51] Like Harris, he had a penchant for independent, unorthodox research. Harris later told the FBI that Leavitt had paid him $3,000 to come to Nevada to test Rockwell's invention, called an "AZ-58 ray tube."[52] The device was purportedly capable of destroying bacteria and viruses both inside and outside the body.[53] It was based on a "rife tube," a device developed in the 1930s by a Dr. Royal Rife, who discovered that when sound waves are applied to certain noble gases in a fixed pattern, the gases emit light of specified frequencies that weaken or kill disease-causing germs.[54]

Leavitt hired Harris to test the AZ-58, believing him to be a reputable microbiologist. Despite the court's explicit order that he not make such claims, Harris told Leavitt and the latter's friend Robert James that he was working with both the CIA and the FBI on biological defense. Even during his short visit to Las Vegas, Harris told James, his "friends from the FBI and from the CIA" had come to visit him.[55] "They kind of watch out for [me] because there was an attempt on [my] life once," Harris explained.[56] If the "rife tube" proved effective in the tests in Las Vegas,

---

49. *United States of America v Larry Wayne Harris*, Complete Transcript of Proceedings, CR-2-95-93, March 6, 1998, p. 147.

50. *United States of America v Larry Wayne Harris*, Defendant's Admission of Facts Relevant to Revocation Proceedings, CR-2-95-93, March 23, 1998, p. 4.

51. Associated Press, "Agents Search Home of Man in Anthrax Case," *New York Times*, February 23, 1998, p. A14.

52. Defendant's Exhibit P, File 279A-LV-30031, Investigation in Las Vegas, Nevada, February 18, 1998.

53. Proceedings before the Regular Federal Grand Jury, Las Vegas, Nevada, Testimony of Robert James, February 25, 1998, p. 9.

54. "What Is a Rife Beam Ray Generator?" http://home.att.net/~ralph.hartwell/rifemain.htm.

55. Proceedings before the Regular Federal Grand Jury, Testimony of Robert James, February 25, 1998, p. 15.

56. Ibid., p. 24.

he promised to arrange for a more complete analysis at Dugway Proving Ground, the U.S. Army's chemical and biological testing site in Utah.[57]

Leavitt hoped to buy the rife-tube technology, if it worked, and mass-produce the devices in Germany with the idea of using them for "mass decontamination" in the event of a biological attack.[58] Rockwell was demanding $20 million for the technology and stood to make a lot of money if the AZ-58 performed as he claimed. But Rockwell—who turned out to have been convicted and imprisoned for fraud—became alarmed when Harris told him that he planned to test the device using "military-grade anthrax." Harris also purportedly informed Rockwell that he had enough anthrax on hand to "wipe out" all of Las Vegas.[59]

On the morning of February 18, 1998, Rockwell phoned the FBI and told the agent who answered the phone that he had met with two people the night before who had told him they were carrying lethal anthrax bacteria in their car. The FBI asked Rockwell to come in for an interview, and he agreed. He told the FBI that Leavitt and Harris had said that in addition to anthrax, they possessed *Bacillus licheniformis* (which Harris claimed required a Biosafety Level 3 lab) and other microbes "even worse than that."[60] After the FBI learned of Harris's earlier involvement with biological agents, they began "gearing up for what might very well [turn out to] be a catastrophe, as far as they knew."[61] They sought and received permission to monitor Rockwell's contacts with the two men, and prepared to retrieve the biological agents.

At 3:15 P.M., Rockwell phoned Leavitt with the FBI listening in. He asked Leavitt whether they really were planning to test "military-grade" anthrax, and whether Leavitt and Harris knew how to handle lethal microbes. Leavitt told Rockwell that he personally had handled the military-grade anthrax, that it was in a vial, and that he was familiar with "sterile techniques." Rockwell then asked what would happen if some-

---

57. Ibid., p. 17.

58. FBI interview of Larry Harris, File 279A-LV-30031, February 18, 1998.

59. *United States of America v Larry Wayne Harris*, Complete Transcript of Proceedings, CR-2-95-093, March 6, 1998, p. 92.

60. Ibid., p. 35. *Bacillus licheniformis* is used in industry and is considered nonpathogenic to humans, although a few cases of illness have been reported in connection with the consumption of improperly prepared food. See Anne Sietske de Boer, Fergus Priest, and Borge Diderichsen, "On the Industrial Use of *Bacillus licheniformis*: A Review," *Applied Microbiology and Biotechnology*, Vol. 40, No. 5 (1994), pp. 595–598.

61. *United States of America v Larry Wayne Harris*, Complete Transcript of Proceedings, CR-2-95-093, March 6, 1998, p. 43.

body stumbled and spilled the material. Leavitt replied that if material were to spill, "you can stand back and we'll make sure that all of the appropriate precautions are taken." They agreed to meet a local restaurant called Landry's at 7:00 P.M. Rockwell would bring the AZ-58 machine, and Leavitt and Harris would bring the biological material.[62]

At 6:30 P.M., FBI agents assigned to watch Harris and Leavitt observed the two men leave their hotel. Leavitt was carrying a white Styrofoam cooler, which he put in the trunk of the Mercedes he was driving. At the restaurant, Rockwell joined the two men in their car. The FBI had wired Rockwell with a body recorder so that they could monitor what Leavitt and Harris were saying. Rockwell again asked what would happen if they had an accident and the anthrax leaked. Harris mimicked someone playing a violin, which Rockwell interpreted to mean "run like hell."[63] The three men drove to an office complex in Henderson, Nevada, just outside Las Vegas, and were followed at a distance by a large group of federal agents, including a SWAT team, both on the ground and in the air.

Rockwell observed Harris carry the white cooler into the Green Valley Professional Office Building. Next he told the FBI that he could see Harris and Leavitt inside a doctor's office through an open venetian blind. He watched Harris pull out a red, cottage-cheese-type container and another container containing a clear substance. Soon afterwards, the Las Vegas SWAT team appeared on the scene and arrested all three men. Harris and Leavitt were transported to a local hospital to be checked for contamination.

After the arrest, a large number of federal and local agents were summoned to the scene, including members of the Las Vegas Fire Department HAZMAT team, an FBI weapons-of-mass-destruction team, the Nellis Air Force Base Explosive Ordnance Disposal Unit, and the U.S. Army biological team from Dugway Proving Ground.[64] They retrieved the white cooler from the doctor's office along with forty petri dishes sitting on a shelf, and then swathed the Mercedes in plastic "saran wrap" and transported it to Nellis Air Force Base. The Air Force shipped the

---

62. Transcript of a recorded conversation between William Leavitt and Ron Rockwell, 279A-LV-30031, February 18, 1998, pp. 3–5.

63. *United States of America v Larry Wayne Harris,* Complete Transcript of Proceedings, CR-2-95-093, March 6, 1998, p. 52.

64. Transcript of Bobby Siller, Special Agent in Charge, Nevada Division, FBI, "News Conference on the Apprehension of Two Aryan Nation Members Accused of Plotting an Attack on a City Subway System," February 19, 1998.

biological materials to the U.S. Army Medical Research Institute of Infectious Diseases (USAMRIID) at Fort Detrick, Maryland, for analysis.[65]

Until this point, the federal authorities assumed that the material they had recovered was lethal. They also believed Harris to be an extremely dangerous man. The FBI reported in its complaint that Harris had told an unidentified group "of plans to place a 'globe' of bubonic plague toxins [sic] in a New York subway station, where it would be broken by a passing subway train, causing hundreds of thousands of deaths."[66] Harris had also made vague threats in an interview with journalist David Kaplan of *U.S. News & World Report*, stating that "if they arrest a bunch of our guys, they get a test tube in the mail," and warning that white supremacists might attack U.S. cities with biological weapons if they did not get their own nation in the Pacific Northwest. "How many cities are you willing to lose before you back off?" Harris reportedly said. "At what point do you say: if these guys want to go off to the Northwest and have five states declared to be their own free and independent country, let them do it?"[67]

Several days later, government scientists told the FBI that Harris did have anthrax bacteria in his cooler but the strain was a harmless type used in veterinary vaccines.[68] They also identified a nonvirulent strain of *Escherichia coli*.[69] In the course of searching the Mercedes, officials found Harris's résumé, in which he claimed to have worked for the CIA at two locations. These statements were a violation of his probation.[70] Harris had also switched hotels without informing his probation officer, a second violation.

After Harris was arrested, federal agents went back to search his home. One of the first things they noticed was a large number of animals:

---

65. *United States of America v Larry Wayne Harris*, Complete Transcript of Proceedings, CR-2-95-093, March 6, 1998, p. 52.

66. *United States of America v Larry Wayne Harris*, William Job Leavitt, Jr., Criminal Complaint, Case No. MAG-98–2042-M-RLH, February 19, 1998, p. 3.

67. David E. Kaplan, "Terrorism's Next Wave," *U.S. News and World Report*, November 17, 1997, p. 30.

68. Vaccine strains do produce anthrax toxin components but they do not produce the poly-D-glutamic acid capsule, which is required for virulence. Letter to Supervisory Special Agent (SSA) David Wilson from John Ezzell, Chief, Department of Special Pathogens, Diagnostic Systems Division, February 24, 1998, Government Exhibit 3–5, *United States of America v Larry Wayne Harris*, CR-2-95-093.

69. Ibid.

70. *United States of America v Larry Wayne Harris*, Defendant's Admission of Facts Relevant to Revocation Proceedings, CR-2-95-93, March 23, 1998, p. 3.

approximately sixteen dogs and six cats.[71] They found a number of microscopes, a nozzle (possibly for spraying microorganisms into the air), and other assorted equipment. [72] They also found penicillin, "agricillin" (penicillin for veterinary use), anthrax vaccines, and growth media, but no virulent microorganisms.[73]

On February 22, 1998, federal authorities dropped the charges that Harris and Leavitt had acquired a lethal biological agent. Leavitt was released, but Harris remained in custody because of his probation violations. On March 6, a federal magistrate found "probable cause" that Harris had threatened to possess a biological agent (anthrax) but not to use it as a weapon. The judge also found probable cause to believe that Harris had misrepresented his credentials (by claiming an affiliation with the CIA) and that he had changed his address in Nevada without informing his probationary officer.[74] The court released Harris from jail pending a final decision.

The sentencing guidelines allowed the court to send Harris to jail for nine months, but Judge Kinneary was lenient once again. On March 25, he allowed Harris to remain free, extending his probation by five months and ordering him to perform fifty additional hours of community service. He also ordered Harris to appear before a probation officer once a week for two months. After the trial, Harris told reporters he felt "fantastic" about the judge's decision. He repeated that his only purpose, in both the 1995 and 1998 cases, had been to protect America against the threat of biological terrorism.[75]

Is Larry Harris a Terrorist?

Harris is an adherent of the Christian Identity Church, which teaches that blacks are subhuman and that Jews are the offspring of Satan. Harris's religious views are peculiarly intertwined with his belief in an imminent Iraqi BW attack. When Iraq strikes the United States with biological weapons, he claims, plagues will ravage the North American continent

---

71. *United States of America v Larry Wayne Harris,* Complete Transcript of Proceedings, CR-2-95-093, March 6, 1998, p. 106.

72. FBI Evidence of Recovery Log from Search of Harris's Home, February 20, 1998, *United States of America v Larry Wayne Harris,* CR-2-95-093.

73. Letter to SSA David Wilson from John Ezzell, March 2, 1998.

74. Courtroom Minute Sheet, *United States of America v Larry Wayne Harris,* CR-2-95-93, March 6, 1998.

75. Robert Ruth, "Harris Pleads Guilty, Is Free," *Columbus Dispatch,* March 25, 1998, p. 1A.

as predicted in the Book of Revelation.[76] Harris says he became convinced of the truth of Biblical prophecy when he "accidentally" proved the existence of God in a series of experiments. These experiments also demonstrated that "evolution is a total impossibility" and that the "Endtime" predicted in the Book of Revelation will occur "within a reasonable period of time."[77]

Immediately after his trial in March 1998, Harris told a journalist he had given up his neo-Nazi beliefs and was now a born-again Christian.[78] The Aryan Nations reportedly expelled him after his 1995 arrest, which may have influenced his claimed decision to repudiate his racist views. Right-wing groups do not like their members going to prison because it is bad for their image, a government official explained.[79]

In some ways, Harris fits the profile of a CBW terrorist. He displays typical symptoms of political paranoia.[80] He has a grandiose view of his own capabilities and importance, claiming to have worked at or advised numerous government organizations—most of which had never heard of him until Harris was arrested for acquiring plague bacteria. He professes to have an "advanced" knowledge of biology and to have proven the existence of God in scientific experiments, a feat presumably worthy of a Nobel Prize, if not sainthood.[81] He also sees himself as a savior of the American people.

At the same time, Harris feels victimized. He claims that an unnamed person made an attempt on his life and that his "friends" at CIA and FBI now watch out for him. He has paranoid ideas about his own government and that of Iraq. (Even if a few of his beliefs about Iraq are probably true, that does not make him less paranoid.[82]) To some extent, his belief that

---

76. Testimony of Larry Wayne Harris, *State of Ohio v Stephen Michael Wharf*, pp. 12–13.

77. Ibid., p. 12.

78. Ruth, "Harris Pleads Guilty, Is Free."

79. Henry, "Harris' Troubled Past Includes Mail Fraud, White Supremacy."

80. Robert S. Robins and Jerrold M. Post, *Political Paranoia: The Psychopolitics of Hatred* (New Haven: Yale University Press, 1997), p. 104.

81. There is no evidence that Harris earned any advanced degrees in biology. Ohio State University awarded him an Associate Degree in Biophysics in 1985. Harris was a member of the American Society for Microbiology (ASM), which requires a minimum of a bachelor's degree or equivalent in microbiology for membership. In 1998 Harris was expelled from ASM by their Committee on Ethical Practices in response to his 1997 conviction for wire fraud, which violated their code of ethics. Interview with Barbara Hyde, ASM Press Office, October 30, 1998.

82. For more on how people can be simultaneously paranoid and correct about the negative intentions of others, see Robins and Post, *Political Paranoia*.

the U.S. government is out to get him has become a self-fulfilling prophecy now that he has shown himself to be dangerous. He believes in the imminence of Armageddon and formerly subscribed to the racist beliefs of Christian Identity, although he claims to have repudiated them.

Harris holds many of these beliefs and fears in common with a number of extremely violent groups that have used, or tried to use, CBW agents. For example, Aum Shinrikyo leader Shoko Asahara believed a foreign power was about to attack his country, that his own government was out to get him, and that the apocalypse was imminent. He had grandiose views of his own importance and capabilities, claiming to be capable of passing through walls and envisaging himself as the leader of a new race. Asahara also denigrated Jews in his writings, although few Jews live in Japan. Likewise, The Covenant, the Sword, and the Arm of the Lord (CSA) leader James Ellison was simultaneously suspicious, megalomanical, grandiose, and racist. He feared imminent strikes by foreign powers and had paranoid views about his own government, believing that the offspring of Satan (Jews) had taken control. Like many religious terrorists, Ellison told his followers that he personally had direct contact with God through visions and dreams, and that the group's violent activities were divinely inspired.

Unlike Asahara and Ellison, Harris is not the leader of an activist organization. As a technically trained individual, however, he could disseminate CBW agents on his own—particularly if his main objective were to panic the public or frighten the government. Nevertheless, many aspects of Harris's behavior and views are not those generally associated with individuals or groups that have sought to carry out CBW attacks. He does not live on an armed compound or isolated from society, and it is not clear that he has violent objectives. He is not secretive—indeed, he was so talkative during police investigations that it was difficult for officers to read him his Miranda rights. There is no evidence that Harris is alienated from society, and he seems to have been liked by his colleagues, who describe him as an able, energetic worker.

Harris makes dramatic statements that appear to indicate violent intentions. For example, in defending the dissemination of BW information, Harris claimed, "It's deterrence. . . . If you know that everyone in the neighborhood has an atomic bomb, civility returns to the neighborhood very quickly."[83] Yet these statements seem calculated to fascinate

---

83. Interview with Harris by David E. Kaplan, *U.S. News & World Report* web site, September 2, 1997 (http://www.usnews.com/usnews/news/chemhigh.htm). During the interview, Harris also said: "the people I'm talking to . . . they're going to post step-by-step instructions how to obtain anthrax, how to disperse it."

and frighten. In the end, Harris seems far more interested in drawing attention to himself than in carrying out mass murder.

Before the Las Vegas incident, Harris hired a publicity agent. He claims to be working on a mysterious deal in Hollywood and has actively sought out television and radio interviews. After his February 1998 arrest, Harris founded a consulting firm that specializes in training individuals, groups, and communities about how to survive BW attacks. He told a reporter, "I guess there is no such thing as negative publicity," referring to the notoriety he earned after his arrest and how it led to his starting a company.[84] These are not behaviors one would expect to find in a terrorist. If Harris were actually planning to disseminate anthrax in the New York subway system in the expectation that the U.S. government would blame the attack on Iraq, it seems unlikely he would go out of his way to draw so much attention to himself in advance.

Although Harris has not killed anyone and probably has no immediate plans to do so, he is still dangerous for two reasons. First, he has made statements that have been interpreted as threatening. The citizens of Las Vegas were deeply alarmed when they learned that Harris had claimed to have military-grade anthrax and that in the summer of 1997 he had allegedly earlier threatened to attack New York City with plague bacteria.[85] The mere threat of a biological attack on a city could cause casualties if citizens panicked and tried to evacuate *en masse*, even if no biological agents were actually released.

The second reason Harris is dangerous is that he is spreading ideas that might be taken up by other right-wing activists who are less flamboyant, more hateful, and more discrete. Harris is a frequent guest at survivalist fairs and on right-wing and anti-abortion talk-radio and television. He may have given ideas to dedicated terrorists who would otherwise have stuck with less lethal weapons, and he may have persuaded amateurs to attempt the kind of attacks that he repeatedly describes. Shortly after the February 1998 incident, which received a great deal of press coverage, a wave of hoaxes and threats involving anthrax began. Some of these hoaxes were probably inspired by the attention that Harris generated.

---

84. Michael Sangiacomo, "Man's Chemical Arrest Used to Promote Firm," *Cleveland Plain Dealer*, May 16, 1998, p. 4B.

85. Tamala M. Edwards, "Catching a 48-Hour Bug," *Time*, Vol. 151, No. 8 (March 2, 1998), p. 56.

Part II
Findings and Conclusions

Chapter 14

Lessons from the Case Studies

Jonathan B. Tucker

The twelve historical case studies in this volume—three of which appear to be apocryphal—indicate that terrorism involving the use of chemical or biological weapons (CBW) is an extremely diverse phenomenon. Not only do the motivations and patterns of behavior of the individuals and groups depicted in the case studies vary widely, but the attempted attacks also range from assassination to mass murder and involve the use of incapacitating as well as lethal agents (see Table 14.1.). Although one cannot draw firm conclusions from twelve rather idiosyncratic cases, this chapter attempts to identify some broad trends and characteristics that appear to predispose terrorists to acquire or use CBW agents.

Apocryphal Cases

The first observation is that the three cases in this volume involving the alleged acquisition of chemical or biological weapons by traditional so-cial-revolutionary terrorist organizations—the Weather Underground, the Baader-Meinhof Gang, and the Red Army Faction—appear to be apocry-phal. Despite the fact that all three alleged incidents have been widely cited in the terrorism literature, little solid evidence exists (at least in the public domain) that the groups in question actually acquired, or even sought to acquire, CBW agents. In the case of the Weather Underground, the story originated with a newspaper column that was never corrobo-rated, was denied by a former member of the group, and was inconsistent with the group's typical *modus operandi* of attacking symbolic targets and avoiding casualties.

Similarly, the allegation that the Baader-Meinhof Gang stole chemical weapons from a U.S. storage bunker in West Germany in 1975 appears to have arisen when supporters of the group seized on media reports of missing British mustard-gas canisters in an apparent attempt to blackmail

Table 14.1. Comparison of Various Parameters Across the Case Studies.

Case	Motivation/Objective	Ideology	Target(s)	Agent(s)	Delivery	Outcome
Avenging Israel's Blood (1946)	Mass killing of German civilians to avenge the Holocaust	A heavily brutalized community seeking revenge	Initially German cities, scaled back to Nazi POW camps	Arsenic-containing mixture	Poisoning of water supply, then food (bread in a POW camp)	Thousands sickened, number of fatalities unknown
Weather Underground (1970)	Temporarily incapacitate populations to demonstrate impotence of the U.S. government	Revolutionary movement opposed to U.S. imperialism and the Vietnam War	Temporarily incapacitate urban populations in the United States	Reportedly sought to obtain BW agents from Fort Detrick by blackmail of gay soldier	Reportedly planned to put CW/BW incapacitating agents in urban water supplies	Informant reported planned attempt to blackmail soldier
R.I.S.E. (1972)	Kill off most of humanity to prevent destruction of nature, then start human race over with a select few	Radical and ecoterrorist ideology influenced by 1960s drug culture	Initially the entire world population, then narrowed to residents of five states around Chicago	Microbial pathogens	Planned BW aerosol attacks (dispersed by aircraft) and poisoning of urban water supplies	Attack aborted when Pera's cultures were discovered; Schwandner and Pera then fled to Cuba
Alphabet Bomber (1974)	Revenge against city of Los Angeles and the U.S. legal system for denying him a permit to open a dancehall	Opposed to religion, communism, nationalism, discrimination against foreigners, and sex laws	Residents of Los Angeles, then senior government officials in the Supreme Court, Congress, White House, and Pentagon	High-explosive bombs, followed by effort to produce nerve agents	Planned to use a cannon to deliver nerve-gas shells against the U.S. Capitol	Nerve agent was not actually produced or the threatened attack carried out; perpetrator was arrested
Baader-Meinhof Gang (1975)	Release of imprisoned leaders of group	Marxist-revolutionary ideology	Stuttgart and other West German cities	Missing canisters containing mustard gas	Unknown	Probably a hoax based on reports of missing CW
Red Army Faction (1980)	Alleged biological attacks against West German officials or business leaders	Marxist-revolutionary ideology	Specific targets unknown	A group member allegedly cultivated botulinum toxin in a Paris safe house	Unknown	Probably an erroneous report, later denied by German government authorities

Group	Ideology	Goal	Target	Agent	Method	Outcome
Rajneeshees (1984)	Indian religious cult headed by a charismatic guru	Scheme to incapacitate voters to win local election, seize political control of county	Residents of the town of The Dalles and Wasco County, Oregon	*Salmonella* Typhimurium, a type of food-poisoning bacterium	Multiple methods, mainly contamination of restaurant salad bars	Plot was revealed when members turned informant
The Covenant, the Sword, and the Arm of the Lord (1986)	Belief that whites are God's chosen people, Jews are offspring of Satan, and blacks are subhuman	Carry out God's judgments, overthrow U.S. federal government, hasten return of Messiah	Nonbelievers and targeted minorities living in major U.S. cities	Potassium cyanide	Poisoning of urban water supplies; CSA assumed God would direct poison to targeted individuals	Group was penetrated by FBI and leaders were arrested
Minnesota Patriots Council (1991)	Anti-government tax protesters; right-wing "Patriot" movement	Cause damage to the federal government, obtain personal revenge	IRS officials, U.S. deputy marshal, local law enforcement officials	Ricin extracted from castor beans obtained by mail order	Planned to deliver ricin through skin with DMSO and aloe vera, or as dry aerosol	Group was penetrated by FBI informants; four key members arrested
World Trade Center Bombers (1993)	Anti-American and anti-Israeli sentiment	Personal and political revenge for Arabs killed by the United States and Israel	Indiscriminate attack designed to kill a large number of American citizens	Terrorists allegedly included cyanide in their urea nitrate bomb	Allegedly, they hoped the explosion would vaporize the cyanide into a toxic gas	Members of group were arrested; the cyanide allegation is probably false
Aum Shinrikyo (1995)	New Age apocalyptic religion and associated political ideology; cult of personality	Proof of prophecy, eliminate enemies and rivals, halt adverse court ruling, cause havoc, seize control of Japanese government	Mass civilian populations, individual opponents of cult, judges ruling against the cult, Japanese police investigating cult	Biological agents (anthrax, botulinum toxin, Q-fever, Ebola virus) and chemical agents (sarin, VX, hydrogen cyanide)	Plastic bags containing sarin solution punctured with sharpened umbrellas to release agent. BW agents dispersed as an aerosol	Multiple chemical attacks (in Matsumoto, Tokyo, and assassination campaign) killed at least 20 people and injured more than a thousand
Larry Wayne Harris (1995, 1998)	Member of Identity Christian movement, links to white supremacist groups (Aryan Nations and National Alliance)	Produce BW vaccines and antidotes for defensive purposes; alert Americans to the Iraqi BW threat	Made vague threats against U.S. federal government officials on behalf of right-wing "Patriot" groups	Obtained plague and anthrax (vaccine strain), and reportedly isolated several other bacteria	Discussed disseminating BW agents with crop-duster aircraft and other methods	Arrested because he talked openly about BW terrorism and made threatening remarks to U.S. officials

the West German authorities into releasing Baader, Meinhof, and the other imprisoned leaders of the group. Finally, the allegation that the Red Army Faction (a later incarnation of the Baader-Meinhof Gang) produced botulinum toxin in a Paris safe house in 1980 also appears to be erroneous, since many elements of the story—notably, Silke Maier-Witt's purported training in microbiology—are factually incorrect. Further, the Public Prosecutor's Office in Karlsruhe denied categorically that the incident had occurred.

In the interest of caution, it may be premature to dismiss these frequently cited cases of CBW acquisition by political terrorists out of hand. Classified documents or other evidence may exist that the case-writers have not uncovered, and the U.S. and German authorities may have had political reasons to cover up or suppress such incidents. For decades, no U.S. government officials released information about CBW terrorism or even discussed it openly for fear of giving terrorists "ideas." Thus, it is conceivable that there may be more substance to the allegations than currently appears to be the case. Until more definitive information becomes available, however, the evidence currently in the public domain is so weak that these three alleged incidents should be treated as apocryphal. This apparent lack of interest in CBW on the part of traditional left-wing terrorists such as the Weather Underground and the Red Army Faction is consistent with the conventional wisdom that politically motivated groups view indiscriminate attacks as counterproductive.

A fourth case study of the alleged use of chemical weapons in the 1993 bombing of the World Trade Center also appears to be apocryphal, but for different reasons. No forensic evidence supports the judge's statement from the bench during the 1994 trial that the terrorists had packed their bomb with cyanide so that the explosion would vaporize and disperse the poison throughout the building, claiming thousands of additional lives. Even so, Ramzi Yousef, the mastermind behind the bombing, admitted after his arrest that he had seriously considered using CW agents for terrorist purposes. The only reason he did not do so in the World Trade Center bombing, he said, was because the group did not have enough money to purchase a large enough amount of cyanide. Since Yousef apparently intended to stage a chemical attack but failed to do so, this case was included in the analysis.

Preliminary Observations

Having excluded the three apocryphal incidents, the conclusions presented in this chapter are drawn from the nine validated case studies involving the intent to acquire or use chemical or biological agents. What broad lessons can be drawn from the cases about the motivations and patterns of behavior associated with CBW terrorism?

First, the use of CBW agents is not unknown in the history of terrorism, but it is strikingly infrequent. The historical record also includes few such incidents in which mass casualties were intended, and none in which they occurred. One explanation is that this form of terrorism requires not only the motivation to employ toxic weapons but also the ability to produce and disseminate them. As noted in Chapter 1, acquiring a deliverable CBW capability requires terrorists to overcome a series of major hurdles: gaining access to specialized chemical ingredients or virulent microbial strains; acquiring equipment and know-how for agent production and dispersal; and creating an organizational structure capable of resisting infiltration or early detection by law enforcement. Although some terrorist groups may be able to acquire small amounts of chemical or biological agents, very few are likely to have the technology and expertise needed to deliver such agents efficiently over large areas.

Of the nine validated case studies, only three describe the successful use of chemical or biological agents (Avenging Israel's Blood, the Rajneeshees, and Aum Shinrikyo). Significantly, all three of these attacks involved "low-tech" delivery systems. In the first two incidents, a chemical or biological agent was delivered by the contamination of food; in the third case, dilute nerve agent was released as a liquid in an enclosed space and exposed the victims by evaporation. These crude delivery methods are likely to remain the most common forms of CBW terrorism. They are potentially capable of inflicting at most tens to hundreds of fatalities—within the destructive range of high-explosive bombs, but not the mass death predicted by the most alarmist scenarios. Although the devastating potential of a "catastrophic" event of CBW use warrants examination, history suggests that the most probable terrorist use of CBW agents will be tactical and relatively small-scale.

A second important lesson of the case studies is that a lone terrorist such as Muharem Kurbegovic (the "Alphabet Bomber") or a small group such as R.I.S.E. or the Minnesota Patriots Council may acquire CBW agents. Although such entities may not be able to match larger terrorist organizations with respect to the quantity of agent they can produce or the sophistication of their delivery systems, their use of CBW could have a psychological impact greater than that achievable by conventional means.[1]

A third observation is that elaborate and plausible CBW hoaxes, such

---

1. There is a negative correlation, however, between the desire of schizophrenics and sociopaths to commit extremely violent acts and their actual ability to do so. Such

as Kurbegovic's postcards to the members of the U.S. Supreme Court, should not be dismissed as irrelevant to CBW terrorism.[2] Even if the threatened attack turns out to be a hoax, it still means that the terrorist was thinking seriously enough about chemical or biological weapons to develop credible scenarios for their use. In contrast, the hundreds of anthrax hoaxes involving envelopes filled with harmless powders lack a plausible delivery system and hence are more of a nuisance than a serious danger. These hoaxes do indicate, however, that extremists believe that the mere threat of CBW terrorism provides a powerful source of leverage because it is an area where society is clearly vulnerable and where public anxieties have been aroused and reinforced by government officials and the media. Most extremists who stage hoax attacks presumably aim to harass and intimidate government agencies or other hated targets, such as abortion clinics. Even so, the strong public reaction evoked by a wave of BW hoaxes could potentially inspire a technically capable terrorist organization to carry out a real attack.

Fourth, it is important to distinguish between discrete and indiscriminate attacks involving CBW. Just because chemical and biological agents are often described as "weapons of mass destruction" does not mean that the ability to inflict mass casualties is an inherent property. The use of VX nerve agent or the biological toxin ricin for assassination purposes is fundamentally different from releasing an aerosol of anthrax over a city. Whereas some of the groups in the case studies sought to kill thousands or even millions of people (Avenging Israel's Blood, R.I.S.E., CSA), others planned to use CBW agents in a tactical, discriminating way to assassinate or punish specific individuals such as police officers or senior government officials (Alphabet Bomber, Minnesota Patriots Council). The Rajneeshee cult employed an incapacitating but nonlethal biological agent not to elicit terror but to achieve a tactical objective—throwing the outcome of a local election in their favor. Aum Shinrikyo had a wide range of targets, from discrete to indiscriminate. Although the fulfillment of Asahara's apocalyptic prophecies was the primary motivation behind the cult's production and use of CBW agents, Aum also had a number of secondary objectives such as silencing critics and enemies, blocking a legal judgment against the cult, and interfering with police operations. Indeed, the immediate target of the March 1995 sarin attack was Tokyo

---

individuals have difficulty working with others, yet a group effort would be required for the large-scale dissemination of chemical or biological agents.

2. Todd S. Purdum, "In a Mysterious Germ Case, 2 Worlds Collide," *New York Times*, February 21, 1998, p. A1.

police headquarters, with the aim of disrupting an imminent police raid on the cult.

Fifth, the choice of agent and method of delivery vary considerably among the validated cases. Among the chemical agents employed or considered for terrorist use were arsenic, cyanide, and various nerve agents; biological agents included ricin, botulinum toxin, and a variety of lethal and incapacitating microbes. Delivery methods ranged from contamination of food and water (Avenging Israel's Blood, R.I.S.E., the Rajneeshees, CSA), to planned aerosol attacks (R.I.S.E., Alphabet Bomber, Aum Shinrikyo), to the application of a toxin through the victims' skin (Minnesota Patriots Council). A general lesson is that terrorists may seek to employ CBW agents for a variety of purposes and to deliver them in various ways, with the aim of inflicting either discrete or indiscriminate casualties.

Characteristics of Likely CBW Terrorists

The individuals and terrorist groups in the validated case studies frequently exhibit certain characteristics and patterns of behavior, which appear to contribute to their propensity to employ CBW agents for either discrete or indiscriminate attacks. Eight such attributes are described in the following sections.

ESCALATORY PATTERN OF VIOLENCE

One characteristic of groups that acquire or use CBW agents is a tendency to employ ever greater levels of violence over time. Such groups may perceive that conventional terrorist tactics are no longer effective and that a more lethal and dramatic form of violence is needed. Kurbegovic, for example, escalated his threats and violence in a relatively short period of time. His terrorist career began with setting fires and progressed rapidly to placing a homemade incendiary device in a victim's car, detonating a large bomb at an airport, and finally threatening the use of nerve agents to inflict mass casualties in Washington, D.C. "You can notice the absence of explosives from our hardware," Kurbegovic said in one of his tapes. "We have them all right, but we consider explosives inferior tools of war."[3] In his troubled mind, he probably believed that only by escalating his threats to include chemical agents would he be able to force the U.S.

---

3. Transcript of Kurbegovic tape recovered by the FBI on August 12, 1974. (Citation provided by Jeffrey D. Simon.)

government to meet his demands to repeal all immigration, naturalization, and sex laws.

INNOVATION IN WEAPONS AND TACTICS, WILLINGNESS TO TAKE RISKS
Another characteristic of terrorists who are likely to resort to CBW agents is a certain degree of innovation in designing weapons and carrying out attacks. Since the use of poison and disease represents a departure from traditional terrorist activity, groups that are considering such weapons are likely to be more creative in their thinking about violence. Kurbegovic, for example, impressed Los Angeles police and fire officials with his ability to build unique homemade incendiary and explosive devices. His ingenious use of the alphabet to spell out the name of his fictitious group in bombings also indicates that he was continually devising new ways to commit violence and to instill fear among the public. Similarly, the Rajneeshees were inventive in their use of *Salmonella* cultures to contaminate restaurant salad bars, the town's water supply, a nursing home, a grocery store, a men's room, and specific individuals. Ramzi Yousef was also driven to carry out ever more daring and destructive attacks to fulfill his self-perception as a "genius," a "professional terrorist," and an "explosives expert."

Another characteristic of individuals or groups that may be likely to employ toxic terror is a willingness to take risks by experimenting with unfamiliar and dangerous weapons. Kurbegovic, the R.I.S.E. plotters, and Aum Shinrikyo's scientists all showed a keen interest in experimenting with CBW agents despite the fact that such research was extremely hazardous.

PARANOIA AND GRANDIOSITY
Although comparative psychological studies of terrorists have not revealed the existence of a single "terrorist mind," psychiatrist Jerrold Post contends that people with paranoid personality traits are drawn disproportionately to terrorist careers (see Appendix). Such individuals generally have a fragmented sense of self, have often experienced major setbacks in their personal or professional lives, and combine a sense of grandiosity with delusions of persecution. They disavow their intense feelings of inadequacy, self-hatred, and rage and project them onto others by blaming their misfortune on individual enemies, a despised minority group, or society as a whole.[4] Terrorists also disengage themselves from the moral consequences of their actions. They have a strong tendency to

4. Jerrold M. Post, "Terrorist Psycho-Logic: Terrorist Behavior as a Product of Psychological Forces," in Walter Reich, ed., *Origins of Terrorism: Psychologies, Ideologies,*

devalue and dehumanize their potential victims, who are no longer perceived as people with feelings, hopes, and dreams, but as subhuman objects.[5]

Such psychological factors appear to be most significant with respect to individual terrorists who act alone or with the support of a few followers.[6] The cases of Kurbegovic, Schwandner, Puja, and Yousef suggest that lone terrorists who are technically trained (or who have access to an accomplice with technical know-how) may pose a real threat of CBW use. Such individuals often obtain psychological gratification from committing violent acts. As Walter Laqueur has argued, "The causes and the ideologies are a matter of secondary importance; the urge to destroy is the primary urge."[7] Within the Rajneeshee cult, for example, Puja, a suspected serial poisoner, was the driving force behind the restaurant contaminations and clearly obtained personal gratification from them. In contrast, several other cult members who participated in the *Salmonella* attacks did so reluctantly and were later stricken with a guilty conscience.

Kurbegovic used his terrorist career to seek revenge against the officials who had thwarted him and to compensate for the feelings of powerlessness and rage arising from his arrest on lewd conduct charges and subsequent failure to obtain approval from the city government to open a taxi dance hall. His successful terrorist acts appear to have provided an intoxicating sense of power and superiority over the system that had rejected him. The most important audience for his terrorist activities was himself—to prove how brilliant and clever he was. Consumed by grandiosity, he sought public notoriety and believed he could outsmart the FBI.

Similarly, Larry Wayne Harris appears to live in a fantasy world in which instead of an obscure small-town laboratory technician he is a

---

Theologies, States of Mind (Washington, D.C.: Woodrow Wilson Center Press, 1990), pp. 25–40.

5. Albert Bandura, "Mechanisms of Moral Disengagement," in Reich, ed., *Origins of Terrorism*, pp. 161–191.

6. Interestingly, lone terrorists with paranoid personality traits often pretend to be members of a larger organization. Kurbegovic acted in the name of a fictitious entity called "Aliens of America," Yousef assigned responsibility for the World Trade Center bombing to a "Liberation Army" with followers throughout the United States, and Unabomber Theodore Kaczynski claimed to represent an unnamed anti-technology group.

7. Walter Laqueur, "The New Face of Terrorism," *Washington Quarterly*, Vol. 21, No. 4 (Autumn 1998), p. 177.

valued technical consultant to the CIA, FBI, and other top-secret government agencies. Harris claims to possess privileged information about a nefarious Iraqi plot to smuggle biological weapons into the United States and has undertaken a lonely crusade to warn the American public. At the same time, Harris has connections to right-wing anti-government groups and has made threatening remarks about the possible use of biological weapons to blackmail the federal government into giving white supremacists their own homeland. Although Harris appears to be more of a self-promoter than a true terrorist, under certain conditions he might become more dangerous.

Paranoid belief systems also appear to play a key role in motivating far-right militia groups and terrorist organizations. Elaborate conspiracy theories are attractive to farmers and blue-collar workers who have fallen on economic hard times and need someone to blame for their problems. Once people have bought into a conspiratorial worldview, they generally become convinced of the reality of the postulated external threat, making them prone to engage in defensive aggression. According to psychologist Glen Wallace, "The same community psychosis that pulls people into the anti-government movement in the first place can eventually lead to cult mentality."[8] For example, the decision by the Minnesota Patriots Council to obtain and conspire to use ricin to assassinate government officials originated in a complex interplay of ideology, group dynamics, and individual psychology. Conspiracy theories circulating within the militia movement resonated with the individual members' personal insecurities and fears, which were then validated and reinforced by other members of the group.

SMALL GROUPS OF MILITANTS

Five of the validated cases of CBW terrorism involved either a small group of two to five people or a militant subgroup within a larger organization. There are a number of possible explanations for this observation. First, normative constraints that may be present within a larger organization may not apply to small groups. Second, radical splinter groups are often more prone to take violent action.[9] When a terrorist organization that is ambivalent about the best path to its goals breaks up, one faction—which constitutes a newly emergent group—may contain all

---

8. Quoted in Joel Dyer, *Harvest of Rage: Why Oklahoma City is Only the Beginning* (Boulder, Colo.: Westview Press, 1997), pp. 212–213.

9. Ehud Sprinzak, *From Theory to Practice: Developing Early Warning Indicators for Terrorism* (Washington, D.C.: United States Institute of Peace, 1998).

of the propensity to violence previously present in the larger organization. Radical splinter groups can be quite dangerous and are capable of
rationalizing extreme acts in the service of their cause. During the Vietnam War era in the United States, for example, a militant faction calling
itself the Weather Underground split off from the nonviolent anti-war
group Students for a Democratic Society and began a terrorist bombing
campaign in pursuit of its revolutionary goals. Similarly, after the Irish
Republican Army committed itself to the Good Friday Agreement in
Northern Ireland, a splinter group named the Real IRA sought to derail
the peace process by perpetrating an indiscriminate bombing in August
1998 that killed twenty-nine people and wounded more than two hundred.

In the cases of R.I.S.E., the Rajneeshees, and the Minnesota Patriots
Council, a small core of radical activists within a larger organization was
involved in the acquisition and use of toxic weapons. The four members
of the Minnesota Patriots Council who obtained the ricin did not trust
the less radical members of the group and were careful to keep their
discussions about the poison to themselves. Although R.I.S.E. had approximately a dozen members, Schwandner and Pera were the only ones
directly involved in cultivating biological pathogens. Both young men
were deeply involved in the drug culture, had difficulty fitting into
society, and viewed themselves as revolutionaries. Pera may also have
been addicted to amphetamines, which tend to induce paranoia and
grandiosity. The plan laid out in Schwandner's manifesto was to halt the
destruction of the environment by exterminating the rest of humanity
with BW agents, after which a small group of "enlightened" individuals
(led by himself) would repopulate the Earth. This dark adolescent fantasy
reflected Schwandner's intense rage against society and his desire to play
god. The plot can therefore be thought of as a joint delusion, or *folie à
deux*, in which the stronger personality (Schwandner) imposed its will on
the weaker (Pera).

ISOLATION, NO OUTSIDE CONSTITUENCY

The case studies suggest that terrorists with a vague, undefined constituency are among the most likely candidates for acquiring and using CBW
agents. Lone criminals such as Kurbegovic, religiously motivated groups
such as CSA, fantasy-based groups such as R.I.S.E., and "closed" cults
such as the Rajneeshees and Aum Shinrikyo do not depend on a segment
of the population for financial, logistical, or political support and hence
are unconcerned about alienating supporters by engaging in indiscriminate attacks. As Kurbegovic stated in one of his tapes, "We do not ask

American people to support us; in fact, we don't give a damn whether they like what we have to offer or not."[10]

The extent to which a terrorist group or cult is isolated from the rest of society rather than continuing to interact with the outside world is also an important factor with respect to the predisposition to extreme violence. The distorting psychological effects of "groupthink" are most evident in closed cults and underground terrorist cells in which the members believe they are surrounded by hostile forces and the leadership circle enforces conformity and punishes deviation (see Appendix). Such groups tend to view themselves as separate from society and not subject to its norms, making them more capable of the moral disengagement needed to inflict mass-casualty attacks. In contrast, groups whose members continue to function actively in society are less prone to distorted extremist thinking without reality checks.

CHARISMATIC LEADERSHIP

A charismatic leader who enjoys unquestioned respect and authority and is psychologically inclined to extreme violence can influence the members of a terrorist group to engage in behaviors that they would not normally consider. For example, the plan developed by Avenging Israel's Blood for the mass poisoning of German cities would not have come to fruition without the leadership of Abba Kovner, whose heroism and suffering during the anti-Nazi resistance gave him a powerful moral authority within the group.

Charismatic cult leaders, such as Shoko Asahara or the Bhagwan Shree Rajneesh, often assume a god-like status—a self-perception reinforced by the reverence with which they are treated by their followers— and can become obsessed with power. Especially in closed religious cults, the leader often determines what is moral and required, even who will live or die. Asahara, for example, was a "malignant narcissist" who had a totalitarian mindset and exerted complete control over his followers.

DEFENSIVE AGGRESSION

Terrorists may be more likely to employ extreme violence if they believe that they are locked in a struggle for survival against a demonized enemy that must be destroyed. Among militant right-wing and religiously inspired groups, the perception that the group is under siege by hostile

---

10. Transcript of Kurbegovic tape recovered August 20, 1974, at Sunset and Western (scene of arrest), Los Angeles Police Department Item No. 1338, Files, Los Angeles County District Attorney's Office. (Citation provided by Jeffrey D. Simon.)

forces may trigger extreme violence by causing the group to respond with "defensive aggression." Among far-right "survivalist" groups, the members' pervasive sense of paranoia combined with external pressure from the FBI often leads them to stockpile weapons in preparation for a showdown with the federal government, with the ironic result of provoking the very confrontation that they fear. In the case of the Rajneeshees, the cult's escalating legal battles with the county and state governments caused it to adopt increasingly aggressive tactics as a means of "defense," from importing homeless people, to contaminating food and water supplies, to cold-blooded murder.

APOCALYPTIC IDEOLOGY

Several of the groups in the case studies envisioned an apocalyptic battle with the forces of darkness, Satan, the Anti-Christ, or some other absolute evil that had to be destroyed so that God's will or justice would prevail. Adherents of a religious group whose ethos is compassionate and loving of mankind can still inflict violence if they distinguish between themselves and the members of a dehumanized "outgroup" who are viewed as a separate and evil species deserving of extermination.[11] Religious terrorists, convinced of their moral superiority and the sanction of a higher power, may engage in terrorism for no audience but themselves and God.

Survivalist groups, with their stockpiles of ammunition, dried beans, and other gear, are receptive to the Christian Identity movement's message that a coming race war against Jews and blacks will signal the apocalypse for which they have waited so long.[12] CSA, for example, believed that the "Tribulation" predicted in the New Testament Book of Revelation had already begun and that foreign governments were about to invade the United States, triggering the "final battle" of Armageddon. Group leaders planned the large-scale murder of nonbelievers, blacks, and Jews—whom they considered subhuman or the "children of Satan"—through the cyanide poisoning of municipal water supplies. In a perverse example of blind faith, cult members said they would leave it to God to separate out the intended victims from the rest of the population. Other groups may seek a glorious death in an apocalyptic battle with the "forces of evil." This deadly

11. Robert S. Robins and Jerrold M. Post, *Political Paranoia* (New Haven: Yale University Press, 1997), p. 104.

12. James Coates, *Armed and Dangerous: The Rise of the Survivalist Right* (New York: Hill and Wang, 1987), p. 90.

logic applies to the confrontation between federal officials and David Koresh and the Branch Davidian cult near Waco, Texas, on April 19, 1993. R.I.S.E. also had an apocalyptic vision, although its ideology was secular rather than religious. Schwandner and Pera dreamed of eradicating human society, which they viewed as fundamentally corrupt and evil in its systematic destruction of the natural world, and of beginning a new human race that would be in harmony with nature.

Aum Shinrikyo's millenarian ideology was woven from an eclectic mix of Eastern and Western traditions, including Shiva (the Hindu god of destruction), the concept of Armageddon from the Book of Revelation, the prophecies of Nostradamus, yogic practices, pseudo-scientific beliefs, and science-fiction writer Isaac Azimov's *Foundation* trilogy. Cult members became obsessed with the imminence of an apocalyptic war between Japan and the United States, a conflict that Aum members believed they would survive to dominate a future Japanese society. This growing sense of urgency fueled an ends-justifies-the-means approach. Cult leaders believed that a series of CBW attacks would persuade the Japanese public that Asahara's predictions of Armageddon were coming true, inspiring new recruits to flock to the cult.

Millenarian cults operating at a time when apocalyptic fears are widespread are more likely to engage in violence. With the arrival of the year 2000, such groups can be expected to experience a heightened sense of urgency, perhaps leading some to contemplate indiscriminate CBW attacks in an effort to precipitate Armageddon. Possible indicators of a millenarian group's potential for extreme violence are its level of paranoia and the extent to which it delegitimizes and dehumanizes its "out-group" targets in manifestos or statements of intent. Jessica Stern has speculated that millenarian groups modeling themselves on an avenging angel or a vindictive god, such as Christ with a sword, Kali, or Phineas, may be more likely to engage in mass-casualty attacks than those whose core belief is the suffering Messiah.[13]

In an effort to profile the individuals and groups of greatest concern, some of the predisposing characteristics found to be associated with CBW terrorism in the nine validated case studies are summarized in Table 14.2. Note that the three apocryphal cases involving politically motivated groups serve to some extent as "controls," since most of the characteristics identified in the validated cases are absent.

---

13. Jessica Stern, *The Ultimate Terrorists* (Cambridge, Mass.: Harvard University Press, 1999), p. 72.

Table 14.2. Selected Motivational Factors Associated with CBW Terrorism.

CASES	Charismatic leadership	No outside constituency	Apocalyptic ideology	Loner or small militant subgroup	Sense of paranoia and grandiosity	Defensive aggression
Avenging Israel's Blood	X	X			X	
R.I.S.E.	X	X	X		X	
Alphabet Bomber		X		X	X	
Rajneeshee Cult	X	X		X	X	X
CSA	X	X	X	X	X	X
Minnesota Patriots Council	X	X		X	X	X
World Trade Center bombers	X			X	X	
Aum Shinrikyo	X	X	X		X	
Larry Wayne Harris		X	X	X	X	X
Apparently Apocryphal Cases						
Weather Underground	X				X	
Baader-Meinhof Gang	X				X	
Red Army Faction	X				X	

Motivational Factors for the Use of CBW

What specific factors might motivate terrorists to employ CBW agents, as opposed to conventional guns and explosives? Although the desire to inflict mass casualties is one factor, there may be others. Conventional bombings are attractive to terrorists because of the shock, drama, and cathartic effect of the explosion. Chemical and biological weapons, in contrast, are invisible, odorless, tasteless, silent, and insidious. Despite their lack of cathartic power, these weapons evoke deep human anxieties and instill a qualitatively different type of terror. Nerve agents attack the central nervous system, resulting in seizures, loss of voluntary control, and a gruesome death by respiratory paralysis; biological agents such as anthrax and smallpox elicit horrific symptoms of disease such as disfiguring skin eruptions. These symptoms, and the pervasive threat of contamination with an invisible yet deadly agent, may be even more frightening than the sudden trauma of an explosion.

From an operational standpoint, CBW agents have both advantages and disadvantages compared with conventional weapons. Chemical nerve agents can kill in minutes, and their invisible, insidious nature gives them a powerful psychological impact. Further, the ability of persistent CW agents to contaminate buildings and people creates the potential for sowing disruption and chaos in an affected urban area. On the down side, chemical weapons are hazardous to handle, unpredictable to disperse in open areas, and can be countered with timely medical intervention such as administration of antidotes.

With respect to BW agents, terrorists might wish to exploit the ability of certain microorganisms to incapacitate temporarily rather than kill, as in the Rajneeshee cult's use of *Salmonella* bacteria to contaminate food. Conversely, apocalyptic terrorists seeking to inflict a catastrophic blow against society might employ a highly contagious and lethal agent such as the Ebola virus, which Aum Shinrikyo reportedly sought to acquire in Zaire. The time lag associated with biological weapons effects also makes them well suited to covert delivery. In recent years, a new pattern of terrorist activity has emerged in which the most lethal attacks have often gone unclaimed, in part because countries are pursuing terrorists more aggressively.[14] Perpetrators seeking to conceal their responsibility and avoid arrest or repression might therefore have a greater incentive to employ biological agents.

---

14. Bruce Hoffman, "A New Kind of Terrorism: Silence Is Deadlier," *Los Angeles Times*, August 18, 1996, Section M (Opinion), p. 1.

For other terrorists, however, the very ambiguity of a BW attack might be perceived as a disadvantage. A sudden epidemic of illness resulting from the deliberate release of a microbial agent—particularly an indigenous strain—might be misinterpreted as a natural outbreak of disease, reducing or negating its ability to terrorize. Indeed, the major outbreak of *Salmonella* food poisoning in Oregon in 1984, caused by the deliberate contamination of restaurant salad bars by the Rajneeshee cult, was assessed by public health officials to be of natural origin until a member of the cult confessed what had really happened.

Beyond operational considerations, the choice of toxic weapons may be related to deep psychological needs or motivations on the part of individual terrorists. From a psychoanalytical perspective, poisons may be attractive to angry, paranoid personality types by enabling them to project symbolically their "poisoned" thoughts and feelings onto out-group targets. This subconscious motivation may apply to Kurbegovic, Schwandner, Puja, Henderson, and Yousef. On the other hand, the de-layed effects of biological agents may reduce the psychological gratifica-tion associated with a terrorist attack by creating intense anxiety and tension until the outcome is known. The Rajneeshees, for example, had to remain in suspense for two weeks before they learned that the restau-rant contaminations in The Dalles had been successful.

Terrorists may occasionally have strong ideological motivations for employing toxic weapons. In the case of Avenging Israel's Blood, a des-perate group of Holocaust survivors sought to avenge the deaths of relatives, friends, and millions of other Jews murdered with Zyklon-B (hydrogen cyanide) in the Nazi gas chambers by using another poison—arsenic—to retaliate against the German population, creating a symmetry of horror. In contrast, Shoko Asahara was attracted to sarin because he was an admirer of Nazi Germany, the first country to develop and manufacture nerve agents during World War II.

Some quasi-religious terrorist organizations also appear to have a mystical fascination with poisons and disease. Christian Identity extrem-ists, for example, might seek to employ BW agents against their desig-nated enemies in imitation of God's use of plagues to punish Pharaoh for preventing the Israelites' exodus from Egypt. Indeed, an ominous 1996 declaration by an Identity-inspired terrorist group called the Phineas Priesthood included the following passage:

And after these things I saw another angel come down from heaven, having great power. And he cried mightily with a strong voice, saying Babylon the great is fallen, is fallen, and is become the habitation of devils, and the hold of every foul spirit, and a cage of every unclean and hateful bird. Shall her plagues come in one day, death and mourning, and famine, and she shall be utterly burned with fire.[15]

Finally, the right-wing Patriot movement is fascinated with the protein toxin ricin because it has the glamorous aura of a powerful, KGB-type "spy weapon" and is mistakenly believed to be an untraceable poison that will enable perpetrators to evade arrest and prosecution. Members of the Minnesota Patriots Council were also attracted to ricin because it was sold by Maynard Campbell, a far-right activist whom they admired. Indeed, the plotters gave their supply of toxin the code name "Maynard" in his honor.

Summary and Conclusions

The case studies suggest that diverse motivations—operational, psychological, ideological, and quasi-mystical—may be involved in the decision to engage in CBW terrorism, although the process by which terrorists select their weapons is poorly understood. In the past, politically motivated terrorists have not sought to acquire or use CBW agents for several reasons, including unfamiliarity with the relevant technologies, the hazards and unpredictability of toxic agents, moral constraints, concern that indiscriminate casualties could alienate current or future supporters, and fear that a mass-casualty attack could bring down on the terrorists' heads the full repressive power of the affected government.

The validated case studies suggest that lone terrorists and terrorist organizations that have acquired CBW agents share a number of characteristics not seen in politically motivated terrorists. Individuals or groups motivated by religious fanaticism, supremacist ideology, or apocalyptic prophecy may seek to employ CBW agents if they possess the necessary technical expertise. Such attacks may be motivated by a variety of perceived goals, such as destroying a corrupt social structure, fighting a tyrannical government, fulfilling an apocalyptic prophecy, exacting revenge on evil-doers or oppressors, or as a form of "defensive aggression" against outsiders believed to be seeking the destruction of the group.

The case studies further suggest that CBW terrorists manifest personality traits of paranoia and grandiosity, are innovative in their use of violence, tend to escalate over time, typically have no clearly defined base

---

15. Quoted in Michael Reynolds, "Toxic Terror: Use of Chemical and Biological Weapons by Terrorists," *Playboy*, Vol. 43, No. 11 (November 1996), p. 62.

of political support and hence are unconcerned about adverse public opinion, and are often convinced that they are fulfilling a divine command or prophecy that legitimates murder. The "hothouse" atmosphere present in underground terrorist groups being pursued by law enforcement agents, or in closed millenarian cults led by a charismatic but authoritarian leader, is most likely to create the psychological conditions conducive to extreme violence. Lone psychopaths may also be motivated to engage in CBW use, although technical and resource limitations make them unlikely to carry out acts of mass-casualty terrorism.

It is also important to stress that terrorists may be attracted to CBW agents not to inflict indiscriminate casualties but rather for tactical or discrete attacks. Indeed, despite the fact that CBW agents are often termed "weapons of mass destruction," agents such as ricin and VX have also been employed for assassination purposes. Conversely, although some groups may be motivated to inflict mass casualties, the technical hurdles associated with the efficient dissemination of CBW agents over large areas make catastrophic attacks unlikely.

Terrorist organizations are generally conservative, relying on traditional weapons and tactics and innovating only when necessary. Like late industrializers, however, terrorists have been known to leapfrog to new-generation technologies when required to circumvent novel security measures or when conventional weapons no longer arouse the level of shock and fear needed to accomplish their perceived goals.[16] Terrorists are also highly prone to imitation, so that an innovation such as airplane hijacking typically spawns a string of "copycat" incidents. For this reason, the well-publicized acquisition of CBW agents by outlaw states, doomsday cults, and lone sociopaths may inspire other groups and individuals to follow suit, albeit in pursuit of different objectives. Based on the historical trends identified in this study, however, only a tiny minority of terrorists will seek to inflict indiscriminate fatalities, and few if any of them will succeed.

Of course, governments cannot afford to be complacent about the potential for high-casualty CBW attacks by terrorists who gain access to military-grade chemical or biological agents and delivery systems, particularly if they receive assistance from a state sponsor. To date, there are no known cases of state-sponsored CBW terrorism (at least in the public domain), probably because of the likelihood of severe retaliation against the sponsoring government if its involvement were to become known.

---

16. Bruce Hoffman, *Inside Terrorism* (New York: Columbia University Press, 1998), p. 182.

Still, a state sponsor that believed it could shield its identity through proxies or intermediaries might take the risk, particularly in a crisis situation or wartime. In addition, an ad hoc or "transnational" terrorist organization, such as the group that bombed the World Trade Center, may be only loosely affiliated with a state sponsor and hence less constrained to act on its behalf. Terrorists with sufficient financial resources might also seek to acquire technical expertise from freelance weapon scientists formerly employed by countries with advanced CBW programs, such as the Soviet Union, South Africa, or Iraq.

Although the small number of case studies included in this volume means that the findings presented here must be seen as preliminary, they nonetheless provide a basis for further research. Empirical analysis of additional case studies should help to refine the profile of terrorist groups most likely to acquire and use CBW agents. It is important to assess the extent to which the predisposing factors identified in the case studies are not only indicators but also discriminators—that is, whether other terrorist groups or individuals that have *not* acquired or used CBW agents might be similarly described. Dissecting out the unique characteristics of those actors most likely to engage in CBW attacks will require the investigation and analysis of a broader array of cases, including several "control" examples of terrorist groups that have sought to inflict mass casualties with conventional bombs. Ideally, a large number of cases might be classified into a matrix such as that in the Appendix, which uses the following three categories: (1) attempts to inflict mass casualties with conventional weapons; (2) tactical or discrete use of CBW agents (e.g., for assassination purposes); and (3) strategic or catastrophic use of CBW agents to inflict mass casualties. This analytical approach suggests that society should be less concerned with the terrorist use of CBW agents *per se*, and more concerned with mass-casualty terrorism from any source.

Identifying the indicators and motivations associated with CBW terrorism would eventually make it possible for intelligence and law enforcement agencies to narrow the "bandwidth" of organizations or individuals considered of greatest concern, permitting the most efficient application of limited intelligence resources that might otherwise be dissipated unproductively on too broad a field of suspects. Such an approach offers a realistic possibility of enhancing the ability to prevent terrorist attacks before they occur. Even so, the potential CBW threat posed by lone terrorists and small splinter groups, which can easily slip through the surveillance net, suggests that the feasibility of preemptive action may be limited.

Since policymakers cannot count on prevention alone, they must deploy a multilayered approach to counterterrorism in which efforts to profile and monitor those terrorists deemed most likely to acquire and use CBW agents are backed up with mitigation measures in the event of an unexpected attack. At the same time, the historical analysis of patterns of behavior of CBW terrorists, such as the choice of agent and delivery system, can help to inform public health and consequence-management activities.

Appendix

Psychological and Motivational Factors in Terrorist Decision-Making: Implications for CBW Terrorism

Jerrold M. Post

The era of modern terrorism burst upon the world scene in 1972 when, during the Munich Olympic Games, Palestinian terrorists from the Black September Organization took Israeli athletes hostage and transfixed an international television audience. Since then, social scientists have attempted to decipher the psychological factors involved in terrorist decision-making. This appendix examines terrorist motivations from the diverse perspectives of individual psychology, group dynamics, and ideological belief systems.

Individual Psychology

Initial efforts to comprehend terrorist psychology concentrated on elucidating the psychology of individual terrorists. These studies were seriously compromised by the lack of a research population available for systematic study, including clinical interviewing and psychological testing. As a result, the study of terrorist psychology has tended to be inductive rather than deductive, generalizing from individual anecdotes, memoirs, or biographical accounts.

The most comprehensive effort to understand the "mind of the terrorist" was undertaken in the early 1980s by an interdisciplinary group of West German social scientists under the auspices of the Ministry of the Interior, in response to an epidemic of political terrorism then ravaging that country.[1] Although the results of this research effort were applicable only to the German terrorists studied, many have extrapolated from these findings to the broader range of terrorists. An interesting effort to understand the psychology of terrorists through their own words was that of

---

1. Ministry of the Interior, Federal Republic of Germany, *Analysen Zum Terrorismus* 1–4, (Darmstadt: Deutscher Verlag, 1981, 1982, 1983, 1984).

Bonnie Cordes, who systematically analyzed the content of terrorist statements and writings.[2] Her work did not illuminate individual psychology, however, but rather the degree to which individuals became captive to group rhetoric and group psychology.

Indeed, the most notable result of these efforts to decode "the mind of the terrorist" was that they did *not* identify a unique terrorist psychology. A wide range of psychologies—from entirely normal to severe personality disorders—have been observed in individual terrorists. For the most part, extremely disturbed people are not involved in carrying out terrorist acts. Just as mentally unstable individuals pose a security threat to military units, they also pose a security threat to terrorist organizations and tend to be excluded from membership. Thus, whereas the most irrational individuals may be the most prone to using mass-casualty weapons, they are also the least likely to master the complex technical skills needed to do so, or to function well in an organizational context.

Although these studies did not identify a *single* personality pattern or trait associated with terrorism, an impression emerged that two personality types were disproportionately represented among terrorists, especially among group leaders. Such individuals had features of narcissistic and sociopathic personality disorders, as well as angry paranoia.[3] Narcissistic/sociopathic individuals tend to be self-absorbed, restless, and action-oriented, with a low frustration tolerance. They suffer from an impaired conscience and a reduced capacity to empathize with the pain and suffering of others. Angry paranoids tend to externalize their problems, idealizing the "in-group" and demonizing the "out-group." Such individuals, who often suffer from a lack of personal, educational, and professional success, seek an outside enemy to blame for their problems. The statement "It's not us, it's them; they are responsible" provides a psychologically satisfying explanation for what has gone wrong in their lives. Individuals with this personality structure may feel an imperative to strike out at the external objects they perceive as the source of their misfortune.[4]

---

2. Bonnie Cordes, "Terrorists in Their Own Words," in Paul Wilkinson and Alasdair M. Stewart, eds., *Contemporary Research on Terrorism* (Aberdeen, Scotland: Aberdeen University Press, 1987), pp. 318–336.

3. Jerrold M. Post, "Terrorist Psycho-Logic: Terrorist Behavior as a Product of Psychological Forces," in Walter Reich, ed., *Origins of Terrorism: Psychologies, Ideologies, Theologies, States of Mind* (Washington, D.C.: Woodrow Wilson Center Press, 1990), pp. 25–40.

4. Ibid.

These psychological defense mechanisms contribute to the striking uniformity of terrorists' rhetorical style and psycho-logic. Polarizing and absolutist, it is a rhetoric of freedom-fighters against an evil establishment, of the "brothers of light" against the "brothers of darkness." Psychologically vulnerable personalities find such rhetoric extremely attractive. This analysis suggests that individuals become terrorists not to achieve instrumental (e.g., political, economic) goals but rather to rationalize violent acts that they are compelled to commit.[5] For these individuals, the act of joining a terrorist group represents an attempt to consolidate a fragmented psychological identity and, most importantly, to belong.

Group Dynamics

Increasingly, the focus of attention of scholars trying to understand terrorist psychology has shifted from individual to group psychology. It may not be overstated to assert that the principal reason for becoming a terrorist is to belong to a terrorist group.[6] Psychological studies suggest that alienated, disaffected, and lonely individuals seek entry to a terrorist group and, once having joined, tend to subordinate their personal interests to those of the organization, which becomes a kind of surrogate family. For people with a fragmented sense of self and a history of professional and personal failure, becoming a member of a terrorist group may be the first time they feel that they truly belong and what they do is significant. When such individuals function in a group setting, the influence of the powerful forces of group dynamics on their judgment and behavior is particularly strong.

For this reason, group psychology rather than individual psychology appears to be the primary determinant of terrorist behavior. A study of resistance group decision-making during World War II found that it was the psychological climate within the group, rather than the external security environment, that determined group decision-making. A resistance-group leader who advocated prudence and moderation nearly lost

---

5. Ibid., p. 25.

6. Jerrold M. Post, "Group and Organizational Dynamics of International Terrorism: Implications for Counterterrorist Policy," in Wilkinson and Stewart, eds., *Contemporary Research on Terrorism*, pp. 307–317; J.M. Post, "Hostilité, Conformité, Fraternité: The Group Dynamics of Terrorist Behavior," *International Journal of Group Psychotherapy*, Vol. 36, No. 2 (April 1986), pp. 211–224; J.M. Post, "It's Us Against Them: The Group Dynamics of Terrorist Behavior," *Terrorism: An International Journal*, Vol. 10, No. 1 (1987), pp. 23–36.

his position to a bolder rival, and thus felt compelled to lead the group into a dangerous course of action.[7] A terrorist group may also be driven to commit acts of terrorism simply to justify its existence. Once a group has tasted the joys of righteous struggle in its fantasy war against society, its members may feel impelled to continue the struggle, regardless of what "objectives" have been achieved.

If group dynamics influence terrorist decision-making in general, this factor is particularly intense in illegal underground groups. Several characteristics of group dynamics contribute to the tendency of terrorist organizations to engage in violent action. These factors include distorted psychological assumptions, the phenomenon of "groupthink," and the tendency of groups to make riskier decisions than their members would individually.

DISTORTED PSYCHOLOGICAL ASSUMPTIONS

The British psychiatrist Wilfred Bion discovered that even in the healthiest organizations, groups of people regularly demonstrate self-defeating tendencies by acting as if they were operating under the influence of psychological "basic assumptions." These underlying psychological states seriously interfere with the group's ability to fulfill its assigned task or mission.[8] Bion identified three basic assumption states:

- The "fight-flight group," wherein members behave as if they have come together to do battle with or flee from outside enemies;
- The "dependency group," wherein members behave as if their primary goal is to obtain security and protection from an all-knowing and all-powerful leader, with no independent judgment or knowledge of their own; and
- The "pairing group," wherein members act as if they are working for the arrival of the Messiah, who will rescue them and create a better tomorrow.

Whereas these basic assumption states are in direct opposition to the mission of most groups, they are congruent with the activities of terrorists. Terrorist groups *do* create a situation in which they are fighting with or fleeing from an enemy; they regularly yield to an authoritarian leader,

---

7. J.K. Zawodny, "Internal Organizational Problems and the Sources of Tension of Terrorist Movements as Catalysts of Violence," *Terrorism: An International Journal*, Vol. 1, Nos. 3/4 (1978), pp. 277–285.

8. Wilfred Bion, *Experiences in Groups and Other Papers* (London: Tavistock, 1961).

particularly in extremist religious cults; and they behave as if their acts of destruction are the prelude to a brave new world.[9]

"GROUPTHINK"

Although many scholars have observed the positive consequences of high group cohesion, such cohesion can also have negative consequences because differences will be obscured in the service of maintaining group solidarity. In *Groupthink*, a classic study of the effects of group processes on decision-making, Irving Janis identified the conditions under which consensus-seeking groups interfere with optimal decision processes.[10] The basic conditions for groupthink include (1) high group cohesiveness and an accompanying tendency to seek consensus that overrides an objective appraisal of alternative courses of action; (2) insulation of the group from outside influences; (3) lack of methodological procedures for search and appraisal; (4) directive rather than impartial leadership; and (5) high levels of stress with little hope of finding a better solution than the one favored by the leader or other influential persons. These in-group pressures lead to a deterioration of mental efficiency, reality testing, and normal judgment. In such a group, the members' striving for unanimity overrides their motivation to appraise the situation realistically.

A cohesive group of decision-makers is likely to engage in concurrence-seeking behavior when confronted with a provocative situational context, including high stress from external threats, fear of differing with the leader, low self-esteem temporarily induced by recent failure, and the presence of moral dilemmas stemming from a lack of feasible alternatives except ones that violate ethical standards. This description fits many terrorist groups.

The symptoms of groupthink fall into three clusters: overestimation of the group, close-mindedness, and pressures to conform.

- *Overestimation of the group* refers to an illusion of invulnerability, shared by most or all group members, that creates excessive optimism and encourages taking extreme risks. At the same time, an unquestioned belief in the group's inherent moral superiority inclines members to ignore the ethical and moral consequences of their actions.

9. Jerrold M. Post, "The Basic Assumptions of Political Terrorists" in J.Z. Kranz, ed., *Irrationality in Social and Organizational Life: Proceedings of the Eighth A.K. Rice Institute Scientific Meeting* (Washington, D.C.: A.K. Rice Institute, 1987), pp. 68–75.

10. Irving Janis, *Groupthink*, 2nd ed. (Boston: Houghton-Mifflin, 1982).

- *Close-mindedness* refers to collective efforts by the group to rationalize its behavior and to discount warnings that might lead members to reconsider their assumptions. The group creates stereotyped images of rivals and enemies as too evil to warrant genuine attempts at negotiation, or too weak or stupid to counter whatever risky attempts are made to defeat their purposes.
- *Pressures to conform* include self-censorship of deviations from the apparent group consensus, reflecting each member's inclination to minimize the importance of personal doubts and counterarguments; a shared illusion of unanimity partly resulting from this self-censorship and augmented by the false assumption that silence implies consent; direct pressure on any member who expresses strong arguments against any of the group's stereotypes, illusions, or commitments, making clear that such dissent is contrary to what is expected of all loyal members; and the emergence of self-appointed "mindguards"—members who protect the group from adverse information that might shatter their shared complacency about the effectiveness and morality of their decisions.

With reference to terrorism, groupthink is particularly apt to occur in groups or organizations that are isolated, in contrast to those in which the members continue to function actively in society. The former conditions would seem to be most applicable to social-revolutionary groups operating underground and closed charismatic religious cults in which the leadership circle around the cult leader enforces conformity and punishes deviation from the leader's directions. When members of terrorist organizations continue to interact with the outside world, they are less prone to distorted extremist thinking without reality checks.

Group dynamics in West German social-revolutionary groups were particularly intense because they operated underground, seeking to avoid arrest by law enforcement agencies.[11] As one West German terrorist observed, "Our only common destiny was that of pursuit."[12] Once social-revolutionary terrorists make the irrevocable decision to enter the underground, the group becomes the only source of information, confirmation, and security. Danger and stress tend to increase the cohesiveness of the group by unifying members against the external enemy. These pressures contribute to a "hothouse" atmosphere within the group in which the

---

11. Wanda von Baeyer-Kätte, Dieter Classens, Hubert Feger, and Friedhelm Neihardt, eds., *Analysen zum Terrorismus 3: Gruppenprozesse* (Darmstadt: Deutscher Verlag, 1982).

12. West German terrorist Beate Sturm, quoted in "In die Bank und durchgeladen," *Der Spiegel*, No. 7 (1972), p. 50.

expression of doubt can be fatal. Ironically, although left-wing terrorists subscribe to the principle of "democratic centralism" derived from Leninist doctrine, these nominally anti-authoritarian groups are extremely authoritarian, tolerating no dissent and demanding unquestioning obedience.

RISK-TAKING BEHAVIOR

Groups are generally more prone to take risks than their constituent members. In a study of group dynamics and risk taking, social psychologists Andrew Semmel and Dean Minix observed that when the ethos of a group is one of courage and boldness, the individual members will often suppress personal doubts during decision-making sessions, lest they be seen as cowards who are not living up to the group's ideals.[13] This dynamic may lead the group to make a risky collective decision that none of the members would have made individually, each one suppressing his or her doubts.

Terrorist groups can also be pushed to make increasingly dangerous decisions when their survival is threatened or when they perceive themselves as ineffective. A terrorist group that does not commit acts of terrorism or gain recognition as a feared opponent of the establishment has lost its reason for existence. Thus, a group that is failing to capture headlines or to recruit new members may be moved to consider a particularly sensational course of action. It is as if they conclude that they have nothing to lose.

In considering the psychologies, group dynamics, and incentives and disincentives to employ chemical or biological weapons (CBW) by various types of sub-state terrorist groups and organizations, it is useful to consider the following dimensions: (1) the willingness to inflict mass casualties by conventional means, as in the bombings of Pan Am Flight 103, the Murrah Federal Building in Oklahoma City, and the World Trade Center in New York; (2) an interest in using chemical or biological weapons tactically to inflict a limited numbers of casualties; and (3) the motivation to employ CBW agents for catastrophic "superterrorist" attacks with tens of thousands of casualties.

A Spectrum of Terrorist Group Psychologies

Just as there is no one individual terrorist psychology, so, too, is there no one group psychology of terrorism. In considering the variegated land-

---

13. Andrew Semmel and Dean Minix, "Group Dynamics and Risk Taking," in Lawrence S. Falkowski, ed., *Psychological Models in International Politics* (Boulder, Colo.: Westview Press, 1979), pp. 251–281.

scape of sub-state terrorism, it quickly becomes apparent that instead of seeking a single unified model, it is necessary to examine a spectrum of terrorist group psychologies in relation to the different types of groups and organizations: social-revolutionary terrorism, nationalist-separatist terrorism, religious-extremist terrorism (both fundamentalist and new religions), transnational terrorism, right-wing terrorism, and the "community of belief." These categories cover a spectrum of ideological belief systems and each have differing incentives and disincentives with respect to the use of chemical and biological weapons (CBW).

SOCIAL-REVOLUTIONARY (LEFTIST) TERRORISM

Social-revolutionary terrorism includes those acts perpetrated by groups seeking to overthrow the capitalist economic and social order. Such groups are typified by the "fighting communist organizations" active in Europe during the 1970s and 1980s, such as the Red Army Faction in Germany and the Red Brigades in Italy. Over the past two decades, social-revolutionary terrorist groups have experienced a significant decline, paralleling the collapse of communism in Europe and the end of the Cold War. Nevertheless, such groups still exist and include the Japanese Red Army (JRA), Sendero Luminoso (Shining Path) and the Movimiento Revolutionario Tupac Amaru (MRTA) in Peru, and Ejército Zapatista de Liberación Nacional (EZLN) of Chiapas, Mexico.

Although seeking to undermine the capitalist state system and its leadership, social-revolutionary terrorist organizations generally act in the name of the "people" and seek the support of the population at large. For this reason, such groups target government officials or leading industrialists who represent the state or the capitalist system and destroy symbolic targets such as buildings, but they almost never engage in indiscriminate attacks. An act of mass-casualty terrorism would assuredly alienate the populace and would thus be counterproductive. Nevertheless, the tactical use of CBW against a government installation or a gathering of senior political or industrial leaders might be rationalized as serving the organization's revolutionary goals.

It is also true that the constraints militating against mass-casualty attacks for terrorist groups operating within national borders may diminish significantly when they operate abroad. For example, members of the Japanese Red Army have often served as mercenaries for other terrorist organizations or state sponsors with intense anti-American feelings. A planned JRA terrorist operation in the United States in 1988 involving a conventional bomb attack against a U.S. Navy recruiting station in lower Manhattan's Wall Street financial district at the crowded noon-time lunch hour was foiled serendipitously when police stopped the terrorists' car on the New Jersey turnpike while en route to New York.[14] This particular JRA mission was funded by Libya, and its timing was designed to coincide with the second anniversary of the U.S. air strike against Tripoli in 1986. Tactical use of CBW for such operations, designed not only to serve the goals of the sponsors but also to destabilize the leading capitalist nation, seems plausible.[15]

NATIONALIST-SEPARATIST TERRORISM

Nationalist-separatist terrorism, also known as "ethno-nationalist terrorism," includes groups fighting to establish a new political order or state based on ethnic dominance or homogeneity. Prominent examples include the Provisional Irish Republican Army (IRA), the Liberation Tigers of Tamil Eelam (LTTE) of Sri Lanka, ETA (*Euzkadi Ta Askatasuna* or Basque Fatherland and Liberty) in Spain, and radical Palestinian groups such as the Abu Nidal Organization and the Palestinian Front for the Liberation of Palestine-General Command (PFLP-GC). Unlike social-revolutionary terrorists, nationalist-separatist terrorists are often known within their communities and tend to maintain relationships with friends and family outside the group, enabling them to move in and out of the larger society with relative ease.

Nationalist-separatist terrorists usually attempt both to garner international sympathy for their cause and to coerce the dominant group to make concessions. ETA, for example, is attempting to pressure the government of Spain to yield to its demands for an independent Basque state. The causes of nationalist-separatist terrorist groups and organizations are particularly intractable, for bitterness and resentment against the domi-

---

14. Bruce Hoffman, *Inside Terrorism* (New York: Columbia University Press, 1998), p. 188.

15. The issue of state-sponsored terrorism is not considered here in terms of psychological analysis, but the example of the Japanese Red Army makes clear the danger posed by terrorist groups sponsored by regimes hostile to the United States. In addition to the JRA, groups supported by Iraq, such as the Abu Nidal Organization, have been and would be of particular concern when Iraq has suffered a major reversal at the hands of the United States. After Operation Desert Storm, there was good reason for concern about covert retaliation through acts of terrorism. Given the attraction of Mu'ammar Qadhafi and Saddam Hussein to weapons of mass destruction, it is conceivable that they might strike out covertly by providing terrorist proxies with chemical or biological agents. In this case, however, decision-making is with the state, not the terrorist group, and the likelihood of massive (possibly nuclear) retaliation against the state should its sponsorship of the act be revealed would be a constraint against such decisions.

nant ethnic group have been passed down from generation to generation.[16]

Given the nature of national-separatist terrorists' motivation and
goals, acts designed to produce mass casualties would seem to be counterproductive. Such groups are attempting to call attention to their cause
in the court of world opinion, and they have a constituency in the society
at large to which they speak and from which they draw support and new
members. Accordingly, they cannot afford to engage in acts of dispropor-
tionate violence that could alienate their supporters.

Even escalation with conventional weapons may be counterproductive if the terrorist group misjudges the likely public reaction. Consider
the Real IRA, the radical offshoot of the IRA that continued to pursue
violence after the main body of the IRA had committed itself to the Good
Friday peace agreement. In August 1998, the Real IRA perpetrated a
particularly bloody bombing in Omagh, Northern Ireland, that led to
twenty-nine deaths, mostly of women and children.[17] This attack inspired
such public outrage that the group's leadership was forced to apologize.
In this case, an act of indiscriminate terrorism resulted in a serious setback
for the organization by alienating its main constituency and audience.

As in the case of the Real IRA, nationalist-separatist groups may still
resort to indiscriminate violence even if it is not in their rational interest
to do so. In general, however, such groups will be constrained from
committing acts that could imperil other members of their ethnic group
or lose them Western support. Members of nationalist-separatist terrorist
organizations are in close contact with their social group, reducing the
likelihood of the kind of distorted extremist thinking without reality
checks that may occur in a closed, underground group. Although the
tactical use of CBW by radical Palestinian terrorists against Israeli targets
is possible for symbolic reasons, mass-casualty attacks would again seem
to be counterproductive.

RELIGIOUS-EXTREMIST TERRORISM

Religious-extremist terrorism is characterized by groups seeking to maintain or create a religious social and political order. This category includes
two types of groups and organizations: those adhering to a radical fundamentalist interpretation of mainstream religious doctrines, including
Islam, Judaism, Christianity, and Sikhism, and those representing "new

16. Post, "Terrorist Psycho-Logic," pp. 25–40.

17. James Clarity, "I.R.A. Splinter Group Says It Carried Out Bombing," *New York
Times*, August 19, 1998, p. A3.

religions" such as Aum Shinrikyo, the Japanese cult responsible for the March 1995 nerve gas attack on the Tokyo subway.

For religious-extremist groups, in contrast to social-revolutionary and nationalist-separatist terrorists, the decision-making role of the preeminent leader is of central importance. For these true believers, the radical cleric is seen as the authentic interpreter of God's word, not only eliminating any ambivalence about killing but endowing the destruction of the defined enemy with sacred significance. The radical cleric, whether ayatollah, rabbi, or priest, may draw on sacred text to justify killing in the name of God.

The Ayatollah Khomeini, for example, used a radical interpretation of the Koran to provide the ideological foundation for Iran's Islamic revolution and to justify terrorist extremism. For Khomeini, the world was divided into good and evil—devout Muslims and followers of Satan, respectively. He regularly employed the metaphor of the clean spring and the stagnant pond. However much sweet water the spring pours into the pond, it will remain stagnant; to restore its purity, the pond must be drained. Khomeini and his clerical followers found justification for acts of violence in the Koranic *suras* calling for the shedding of blood.[18] In inciting his followers during the Iran-Iraq War, he rhetorically asked, "Why don't you recite the sura of killing? Why should you always recite the sura of mercy? Don't forget that killing is also a form of mercy."[19] To those who died fighting for Islam's holy cause, Khomeini assured a higher place in paradise.

The activities of religious-extremist groups have been associated with attacks resulting in some of the largest numbers of casualties of any terrorist activities. In contrast to nationalist-separatist terrorists, who are attempting to influence contemporary society, religious-fundamentalist terrorists, such as the radical Islamist group Hezbollah, are threatened by secular modernism and seek to defend their faith by attacking those groups or nations they perceive as threats. Thus, they are not constrained by the counterproductive effects of indiscriminate violence.[20] Religious-extremist terrorism probably accounts for many of the 40 percent of

---

18. Robert S. Robins and Jerrold M. Post, *Political Paranoia: The Psychopolitics of Hatred* (New Haven: Yale University Press, 1997), pp. 153–154.

19. "Khomeini, the Ultimate Theocrat," *The Independent* (London), August 8, 1987, p. 8.

20. Jerrold M. Post, "Prospects for Nuclear Terrorism: Psychological Inventives and Constraints," in Paul Leventhal and Yonah Alexander, eds., *Preventing Nuclear Terrorism: The Report and Papers of the International Task Force on the Prevention of Nuclear Terrorism* (Lexington, Mass.: Lexington Press, 1987), pp. 91–103.

terrorist acts for which no responsibility is claimed. The religious-extremist group does not need headlines in the newspaper or the lead story on the television news, for its primary audience is God.[21]

Insofar as the United States is seen as the leading secular modernizing nation and a close ally of Israel, it represents a major threat to radical fundamentalist Islam. Should the Israeli-Palestinian peace process move forward, these groups will probably be moved to increasingly extreme acts, and they are not deterred by the prospect of retaliation. Indeed, acts of mass-casualty terrorism have already been perpetrated by radical Islamic groups against U.S. military installations in Arab lands, such as the conventional bombing of the Air Force's Khobar Towers living facility in Saudi Arabia on June 25, 1996. The tactical use of CBW agents against such a target would not seem to represent a major escalation.

TRANSNATIONAL TERRORISM

Ramzi Yousef, the mastermind behind the 1993 World Trade Center bombing, and Sheikh Abdul Rahman, the spiritual mentor of the radical Islamists involved in the attack, are leading figures in a phenomenon called "transnational terrorism," which is not as bounded and well defined as traditional terrorist organizations. The origins of transnational terrorism can be traced to the Islamist insurgency against the Soviet occupation of Afghanistan, where many of the guerrilla fighters were trained and indoctrinated.

Yousef, educated as an electrical engineer, planned the 1993 bombing of the World Trade Center in New York City to inflict mass casualties in a target with high symbolic value, thereby avenging U.S. attacks on Arab countries and capturing international attention. The following year, he planned to detonate sophisticated time bombs on twelve U.S. airliners departing from Asia for the United States. For Yousef, a high-tech specialist, the motivation of inflicting mass casualties would be consistent with the use of CBW. Indeed, he considered carrying out a chemical attack shortly before his arrest (see Chapter 11).

Osama bin Laden, the Saudi-born terrorist believed responsible for the August 1998 bombings of the U.S. embassies in Kenya and Tanzania, also traces his revolutionary credentials to Afghanistan. Bin Laden has defined the United States as the enemy of Islam, and he asserts that his mission is to drive U.S. military forces out of Saudi Arabia and the Middle

---

21. David C. Rapoport, "Messianic Sanctions for Terror," *Comparative Politics*, Vol. 20, No. 2 (1988), pp. 195–213.

East by targeting U.S. civilians, potentially with mass-casualty weapons. In a press interview, he explained:

If the Israelis are killing the small children in Palestine and the Americans are killing the innocent people in Iraq, and if the majority of the American people support their dissolute president, this means the American people are fighting us and we have the right to target them. . . . We don't consider it a crime if we tried to have nuclear, chemical, biological weapons. Our holy land is occupied by Israeli and American forces. We have the right to defend ourselves and to liberate our holy land.[22]

Bin Laden has consistently justified terrorist violence against the United States as a legitimate response to U.S. aggression against Arab states. Washington's declaration of war against terrorism in the wake of the embassy bombings will not deter bin Laden but will be seen as recognition of his stature as an Islamic warrior, and may provoke him to more dramatic acts of terrorist extremity. His original goal of expelling the U.S. presence from Saudi Arabia has expanded so that his arena of operations is now international. Strategic mass-casualty attacks against the homeland of the United States, possibly involving CBW, would be a natural step in this escalating spiral of violence.

NEW RELIGIONS TERRORISM

New religions extremist groups, such as Aum Shinrikyo, are generally closed cults that perceive themselves in a struggle for survival against a demonized enemy that must be destroyed. The followers yield their individual judgment to the leader and become "de-skilled," acting as if they have no independent critical faculties. Ruthless social controls within the cult reinforce this tendency. No doubters were permitted in Aum Shinrikyo's powerful, hermetically sealed organization, and the price of defection was death.

Unlike many millenarian cults, which characteristically withdraw from the world to passively await the apocalypse, some religious belligerents are seeking to force the end. Asahara's fascination with potent weaponry led him to recruit highly trained scientists and engineers to develop nuclear, biological, and chemical arms. In carrying out a series of (failed) biological attacks in downtown Tokyo, Asahara was attempting to precipitate a final apocalyptic conflict between Japan and the United States (see Chapter 12).

---

22. Jamal Ismail, "I Am Not Afraid of Death" [interview with Osama bin Laden], *Newsweek*, January 11, 1999, p. 37.

Convinced of their own moral superiority and their relationship with a higher power, new religious terrorists care little for the beliefs and opinions of society and tend to execute their terrorist acts for no audience but themselves and God. As a result, they may experience fewer constraints with respect to the use of mass-casualty weapons.

RIGHT-WING TERRORISM

Right-wing terrorism includes those groups seeking to preserve the status and privileges of a "dominant" race or ethnicity. These groups generally espouse racist and anti-Semitic beliefs. In the United States, many right-wing groups fear the federal government, which they see as illegitimate and dominated by Jews—hence their term "Zionist Occupational Government (ZOG)."

An ideology that identifies an enemy and provides an external locus for aggression is attractive to the discontented.[23] While no overarching organization exists for the racist, anti-Semitic, and anti-government "survivalist" groups of the radical right, increasingly a pseudo-religion called Christian Identity has drawn these previously disparate movements together under a common paranoid banner.

Christian Identity combines traditional elements of fundamentalist Protestantism with a persecutory ideology.[24] Apocalyptic in their rhetoric, Identity Christians call on their fellows to prepare for the "final battle" foretold in the Book of Revelation between the forces of good led by the true chosen people, the Aryans, and the forces of evil under the direction of the Jews, the spawn of the devil. The dehumanization of Jews and racial minorities justifies acts of violence that can be freely committed without violating biblical injunctions. The militant arm of the leading Christian Identity church—the Church of Jesus Christ, Christian—is the Aryan Nations.

Christian Identity has so distorted its traditional Protestant elements as to make the relationship almost unrecognizable, converting a religion of love into one of hate. Its appeal rests in large part on the fact that it is preached from the pulpit with religious authority and has a lineal connection to Christian doctrine. A key goal of the movement is to "biblicize" U.S. law, initially by bringing it into conformity with Christian Identity's interpretation of the Bible and ultimately by replacing it with "divine" law. Given the paranoid nature of Christian Identity ideology, it is not

---

23. Robins and Post, *Political Paranoia*, pp. 179–180.

24. Michael Barkun, *Religion and the Racist Right: The Origins of the Christian Identity Movement* (Chapel Hill: University of North Carolina Press, 1996).

surprising that its members have developed a political agenda that justifies defensive aggression against Jews, non-whites, and the federal government, which they believe is out to deprive them of basic rights such as gun ownership. Tactical use of CBW agents by Christian Identity groups against racial, Jewish, or government targets would be consistent with their extremist ideology.

THE COMMUNITY OF BELIEF

Ideologies of right-wing hatred and religious extremism extend beyond the scope of formal organizations, resulting in a phenomenon that carries particular danger for mass-casualty terrorism—the "community of belief." One can be exposed to and influenced by a poisonous ideology or doctrine without ever belonging to an extremist group or a religious cult. A hate-filled ideology that identifies an enemy and provides an external locus for aggression may be highly attractive to alienated and discontented individuals, potentially motivating them to commit acts of violence.[25]

Timothy McVeigh was outside the formal structure of the militia movement but clearly subscribed to its extremist agenda. He sold *The Turner Diaries*, a hate-filled diatribe that is the "bible" of the radical right, below cost at gun shows. In the novel, written by far-right activist William Pierce, the federal government seizes guns from the people under the "Cohen Act," after which an underground group of Aryan patriots retaliates by blowing up FBI Headquarters in Washington, D.C. with a fertilizer bomb.[26]

McVeigh was a true believer in anti-government ideology and showed a complete indifference to public opinion. Nor was he concerned with loss of life, apparently seeking to inflict maximal casualties on the men, women, and children in the Alfred E. Murrah Federal Building in Oklahoma City by detonating a massive fertilizer bomb—similar to that described in *The Turner Diaries*—during working hours. The date of the attack, April 19, 1995, was one of mythic significance to the right wing because April 19, 1993 was the date of the assault by federal agents on Ranch Apocalypse, the compound of Branch Davidian leader David Koresh and his followers near Waco, Texas.

Communities of belief can be greatly expanded through the Internet, enabling the lonely paranoid to find validation for his anger and frustra-

---

25. Robins and Post, *Political Paranoia*, pp. 207–214.

26. Kenneth S. Stern, *A Force Upon the Plain: The American Militia Movement and the Politics of Hate* (Norman: University of Oklahoma Press, 1996), pp. 187–194.

tion. More than 300 web sites of right-wing groups have been identified, propagating their messages of hate throughout the world and creating a sense of virtual community. The U.S. militia movement has numerous web sites providing a right-wing spin on news and current events, selling survivalist gear, and providing information on techniques for harassing local government officials and avoiding the tax collector. Because censoring the Internet is a practical impossibility, neo-Nazi groups use the web to propagate hate material in places where such publications are banned.

Organizations that monitor hate crimes, such as the Southern Poverty Law Center, the Simon Wiesenthal Center, and the Anti-Defamation League, have expressed concern that the prevalence of ideas related to mass-casualty weapons on the Internet could move psychologically vulnerable individuals from belief to action. This possibility suggests the importance of monitoring far-right web sites, since an escalation in extremist rhetoric could incite a member of the community of belief to undertake a violent attack. Indeed, in the weeks preceding the Oklahoma City bombing, neo-Nazi and extremist militia web sites exhorted sympathizers to commemorate April 19 with acts of violence. Some sites even listed vulnerable federal buildings without adequate security, including the one in Oklahoma City.

The phenomenon of the community of belief is particularly prevalent in right-wing circles, but it is also manifest in religious extremism. For example, Yigal Amir, the twenty-seven-year-old assassin of Israeli Prime Minister Yitzhak Rabin, was an orthodox Jew, an ardent Zionist, and a member of Israel's extreme religious right, but he did not belong to a terrorist organization. After his arrest, Amir claimed that religious law had obligated him to kill Rabin because his leadership of the peace process was placing Israel in mortal danger by creating a haven for Palestinian terrorists. During the hearings that followed the Rabin assassination, it emerged that radical religious circles in Israel, including a number of extremist rabbis, had argued that the biblical "judgment of the pursuer" should be invoked against Rabin for his role in negotiating the Oslo peace accords. The reference was to the biblical injunction that a righteous man is obligated to kill to prevent innocent blood from being spilled. After his arrest, Amir declared, "I acted alone, on God's orders. I have no regrets."[27]

---

27. Serge Schmemann, "An Assassination in Israel," *New York Times*, November 10, 1995, p. A8. See also Schmemann, "Rabin Slain After Peace Rally," *New York Times*, November 5, 1995, p. A1.

To the degree that individual members of an ideological or religious-extremist community of belief could overcome the technological barriers, the tactical use of CBW against a hated target is quite conceivable.

Summary and Conclusions

To assess the psychological incentives and constraints for terrorists to employ chemical and biological weapons, the individual, group, and organizational psychology of terrorism has been reviewed. Especially for closed underground groups, the capacity for groupthink and the tendency of groups to make riskier decisions than any individual member tend to magnify the potential for violence. Groups and organizations that have been ineffective may be inspired to create a "terrorist spectacular" to regain their sense of efficacy and to restore their reputation.

In analytically differentiating the motivations of the spectrum of terrorist groups, the incentives and disincentives to employ CBW vary widely. Insofar as terrorist groups pursue political goals and seek to call public attention to their cause or to influence a political audience, they have significant disincentives for inflicting mass casualties. The disincentives are particularly strong with reference to strategic "catastrophic" use of CBW agents.

Table A.1. summarizes the groups and individuals judged to pose the greatest risk of CBW use. Three dimensions of terrorist motivation are represented: the willingness to inflict mass casualties using conventional weapons; the desire to employ CBW for tactical ends such as assassination; and the motivation for "catastrophic" CBW attacks involving tens of thousands of casualties.

Several types of terrorists, indicated by an asterisk in the table, will be reluctant to carry out terrorist acts that could imperil their own constituency or ethnic group, but may be less constrained under other circumstances. For example, a radical Palestinian organization might be prepared to carry out a mass-casualty attack in Tel Aviv but would be constrained from doing so in Jerusalem, which has a large Arab population and is the site of two of Islam's holiest shrines. Similarly, Basque terrorists might stage a large-scale bombing in Madrid but not in San Sebastian. The table also identifies nonaffiliated individuals who pose a risk of CBW terrorism: those belonging to the right-wing and religious-fundamentalist communities of belief.

This analysis suggests that the greatest danger of CBW terrorism lies with two groups: religious extremists (both religious-fundamentalist terrorists and millenarian cults) and right-wing extremists. Transnational

Table A.1. Risk of CBW Use by Various Types of Terrorist Organizations.

Group Type	Mass-Casualty Attack with Conventional Weapons	Tactical Use of CBW (e.g., Assassination or Targeted Attacks)	Catastrophic, Mass-Casualty Use of CBW
Social-Revolutionary Organization			
Nationalist-Separatist Organization	X*	X*	
Right-Wing Organization	X	X	
Individuals in the Right-Wing Community of Belief	X	X	
Religious-Fundamentalist Organization	X*	X*	X*
Individuals in the Religious-Fundamentalist Community of Belief	X*	X*	
Religious Cult	X	X	X

*Acts that do not endanger their constituents, usually outside the home region.

radical Islamists, as exemplified by Osama bin Laden, are of particular concern. Moderation is the enemy of extremism, and as progress is made in the Middle East peace process, U.S. military bases and embassies abroad and symbolic targets in the United States will be at particular risk. Even the strategic catastrophic use of CBW on American soil, with the goal of destabilization and revenge, cannot be ruled out. Although most religious cults are passive and nonviolent, exceptions such as Aum Shinrikyo are worrisome, for cult members are true believers carrying out a sacred mission as defined by their holy leader.

Right-wing extremist groups in the United States also pose a significant danger. The right wing is by no means a unified movement, but its radical extreme sees itself at war with the federal government. Such groups could rationalize the tactical use of CBW against government targets such as a federal building. The federal city of Washington, D.C., would also seem to be a prime target.

Of particular concern, with reference to both right-wing and religious extremism, is the community of belief. Extremist ideology extends beyond formal membership in an organization, and unstable individuals may take hate-filled rhetoric as a call to individual action. The Oklahoma

City bombing and the assassination of Rabin by a Jewish fundamentalist are examples of this phenomenon. Some technologically sophisticated individuals who subscribe to extremist ideologies may be impelled to employ CBW, although resource limitations will probably rule out catastrophic mass-casualty attacks.

Contributors

W. Seth Carus is a senior research professor at the Center for Counterproliferation Research of the National Defense University in Washington, D.C.

David Claridge is the geopolitical intelligence analyst for Rubicon International Services, a London-based security and crisis-management company. He was formerly a terrorism specialist at the University of St. Andrews in Scotland.

David E. Kaplan is a senior writer at *U.S. News & World Report* and co-author of *The Cult at the End of the World* (New York: Crown, 1996), a book on the Aum Shinrikyo cult.

John Parachini is a senior research associate with the Center for Nonproliferation Studies at the Monterey Institute of International Studies' branch office in Washington, D.C.

Jason Pate is a research associate in the CBW Nonproliferation Project at the Monterey Institute's Center for Nonproliferation Studies in Monterey, Calif.

Jerrold M. Post is professor of psychiatry, political psychology and international affairs and director of the Political Psychology Program at The George Washington University in Washington, D.C.

Jeffrey D. Simon is president of Political Risk Assessment Company, Inc., a consulting firm in Santa Monica, Calif., specializing in security and terrorism research. He is author of the book, *The Terrorist Trap: America's Experience With Terrorism* (Bloomington: Indiana University Press, 1994) and was formerly a terrorism analyst with the RAND Corporation.

Ehud Sprinzak is professor of political science at the Hebrew University of Jerusalem. His latest book is *Brother Against Brother: Violence and Extremism in Israeli Politics from Altalena to the Rabin Assassination* (New York: Free Press, 1999).

Jessica Eve Stern is a senior fellow at the Belfer Center for Science and International Affairs at Harvard University, and the author of *The Ultimate Terrorists* (Cambridge, Mass.: Harvard University Press, 1999).

Terence Taylor is assistant director of the International Institute of Strategic Studies in London.

Tim Trevan, a freelance consultant and author, was formerly the special assistant to the Executive Chairman of the United Nations Special Commission on Iraq (UNSCOM).

Jonathan B. Tucker directs the Chemical and Biological Weapons Nonproliferation Project at the Center for Nonproliferation Studies in Monterey, California. In 1999–2000, he is the Robert Wesson Fellow in Scientific Philosophy and Public Policy at the Hoover Institution, Stanford University.

Idith Zertal teaches Israeli Studies at the Hebrew University of Jerusalem and in the Interdisciplinary Center in Herzelia. Her latest book is *From Catastrophe to Power: Holocaust Survivors and the Emergence of Israel* (Berkeley: University of California Press, 1998).

Index

The Robert and Renée Belfer Center for Science and International Affairs

Graham T. Allison, Director
John F. Kennedy School of Government
Harvard University
79 JFK Street, Cambridge MA 02138
Tel: (617) 495-1400; Fax: (617) 495-8963
http://www.ksg.harvard.edu/bcsia   bcsia_ksg@harvard.edu

The Belfer Center for Science and International Affairs (BCSIA) is the hub of research, teaching and training in international security affairs, environmental and resource issues, science and technology policy, human rights, and conflict studies at Harvard's John F. Kennedy School of Government. The Center's mission is to provide leadership in advancing policy-relevant knowledge about the most important challenges of international security and other critical issues where science, technology and international affairs intersect.

BCSIA's leadership begins with the recognition of science and technology as driving forces transforming international affairs. The Center integrates insights of social scientists, natural scientists, technologists, and practitioners with experience in government, diplomacy, the military, and business to address these challenges. The Center pursues its mission in five complementary research programs:

- The **International Security Program** (ISP) addresses the most pressing threats to U.S. national interests and international security.

- The **Environment and Natural Resources Program** (ENRP) is the locus of Harvard's interdisciplinary research on resource and environmental problems and policy responses.

- The **Science, Technology and Public Policy Program** (STPP) analyzes ways in which science and technology policy influence international security, resources, environment, and development, and such cross-cutting issues as technological innovation and information infrastructure.

- The **Strengthening Democratic Institutions Project** (SDI) catalyzes support for three great transformations in Russia, Ukraine and the other republics of the former Soviet Union—to sustainable democracies, free market economies, and cooperative international relations.

- The **WPF Program on Intrastate Conflict, Conflict Prevention and Conflict Resolution** analyzes the causes of ethnic, religious, and other conflicts, and seeks to identify practical ways to prevent and limit such conflicts.

The heart of the Center is its resident research community of more than 140 scholars: Harvard faculty, analysts, practitioners, and each year a new, interdisciplinary group of research fellows. BCSIA sponsors frequent seminars, workshops and conferences, maintains a substantial specialized library, and publishes books, monographs and discussion papers.

The Center's International Security Program, directed by Steven E. Miller, publishes the BCSIA Studies in International Security, and sponsors and edits the quarterly journal *International Security*.

The Center is supported by an endowment established with funds from Robert and Renée Belfer, the Ford Foundation and Harvard University, by foundation grants, by individual gifts, and by occasional government contracts.